Surviving to 3000

An Introduction to the Study of Lethal Conflict

Surviving to 3000

An Introduction to the Study of Lethal Conflict

Roy L. Prosterman

AUTHOR AND EDITOR

DUXBURY PRESS,
A DIVISION OF WADSWORTH PUBLISHING COMPANY, INC.
BELMONT, CALIFORNIA 1972

DUXBURY PRESS
A DIVISION OF WADSWORTH PUBLISHING COMPANY, INC.

L. C. CAT. CARD NO.: 72-187395
ISBN 0-87872-021-9
PRINTED IN THE UNITED STATES OF AMERICA

To

My Mother and Father

Preface

There are many people whose work contributed to this volume. First and foremost, thanks must go to Charles A. Taylor, my research assistant at the University of Washington, who did invaluable supporting research and who helped immeasurably in the editing of the text. Professor J. G. Dash of the Physics Department introduced me to Conflict Studies at the University and twice co-taught with me the course in which the precursors of the present materials were first drawn together and used with students. Over a period of several years, Frank Herbert contributed his enormous insight and, together with Anne Stadler and James Leonard, worked with me on the World Without War Council to help apply and develop the materials in a variety of seminars, retreats, and "bull sessions"; they were aided by Tom Alkire, Reggie Wilson, and other internes at the Council, and by Dr. Irving Berlin, of the Division of Child Psychiatry at the University.

Robert Gilmore of the Center for War/Peace Studies, Mary Temple of the National Committee for a Political Settlement in Vietnam, and Robert Pickus and Robert Woito of the national office of the World Without War Council, all helped to show that these ideas can be applied responsibly and effectively in practice to a variety of educational, media, and citizen-action contexts, and that violent activism and despair are not our only alternatives; while Jack Doughty, Svein Gilje, Elizabeth Pond and others demonstrated that the press does indeed care about these issues.

Dean Joseph McCarthy of the Graduate School, and Dean Aldon Bell of the Division of General and Interdisciplinary Studies, helped sustain the Conflict Studies program. Richard Roddis, Robert Hunt, Lehan Tunks, and others at the University of Washington Law School helped encourage and facilitate my work on this new frontier. Alex Kugushev had the perception to see immediately what was needed and the courage to see that perception through. Beatrice Gormley helped greatly with the final editing, and Chris Rhinehart and Vera Marsh bore, successively, the burden of typing and retyping. There were many more at the University and around the country whose contributions were significant. But in the end, of course, it is I alone who must accept responsibility for the selections and for the views expressed in the text.

Table of Contents

Introduction

The last millennium?

Early in his term of office, John F. Kennedy told historian Arthur Schlesinger he thought the chances of nuclear war with the Russians between then and 1970 were fifty-fifty. One group of experts polled in 1964 were more "optimistic": they believed there was a twenty-five percent chance that World War III would occur before 1990. Little wonder, then, that when I asked fifty students at the beginning of my Introduction to Conflict Studies course at the University of Washington, "Do you think all or most of humanity will be destroyed by war before another millennium has passed?" only *one* student thought we would make it to 3000.

It is a hard fact that lethal conflict—murder, riot, war, and revolution—has been with us a long time, and that the newest nuclear "playthings" for carrying on such conflict add up to an explosive power of more than 50 billion tons of TNT, enough to kill us all, with a great deal left over. And as many as forty nations could possess nuclear weapons by 1980, not to mention biological weapons or other monstrosities that might now be in the test-tube. By the twenty-first century, the successors of the Mafia or Papadopoulos, the Palestinian Liberation Organization or the Quebec Liberation Front, the Weatherpeople or the White Knights of the Ku Klux Klan, may well have the capacity to destroy all life on earth.

One can imagine the announcer's terse voice, like a replay of yesterday's science fiction: "The source of the attack is unknown, but the authorities have confirmed that anthrax and plague bacteria were released off the coast west of Los Angeles one week ago. Fifty thousand are now dead . . ."

Or perhaps: "The President has declared that victory is near. Some nuclear weapons continue to explode, however, in the remaining East Coast cities. Final tolls are expected to exceed forty million dead in the United States. Worldwide, over one billion have died in the past two weeks. Radioactive fallout continues, and round-the-clock curfews remain in effect in the following areas . . ."

Or then, again: "It was confirmed that the water supply of the exclusive suburb had been contaminated by a powerful toxic chemical. Four hundred are dead, including many children. The terrorist group which has claimed credit warned that unless all designated persons were released, worse would follow. Meanwhile, national police were carrying out mass arrests of suspects . . ."

In the past, one might say that it was desirable or convenient to end lethal group conflict (or to put it in what some would regard as the most precise way, to end the use of lethal aggression as a mode of resolving conflict between groups), but not necessary. Today the message has changed and is absolutely clear: _we must end the system of resolving conflicts by large-scale lethal aggression_.

These are unsettling facts to face. Indeed, they are overwhelming, and for many of us, almost paralyzing. Even pollution and overpopulation are comparatively pleasant to think about, after spending five minutes contemplating nuclear or biological warfare disaster.

But is it possible to end such conflict? It is psychologically easy to assume that a holocaust is inevitable, for during the late years of the nineteenth century and the first four decades of the present century, it was widely believed that lethal aggression was innate in man. Even after the accumulating evidence had put to rest Freud's "death instinct," which was a supposed innate human drive toward destruction and death, and the bastardized Darwinism that spoke of the "law of the jungle," the culture in which all of us grew up was still filled with shadows of old Hollywood film clips: two wolves destroying each other in a battle over the steaming carcass of prey, a gorilla locked in a death grip with a boa constrictor, or Og braining Gog with his club and dragging Oona away by her hair.

This is all nonsense, however. In recent years, scientists have *studied* the "jungle," for the first time carefully observing and noting what they see. And they have studied the detailed traces left behind by early man.

What we now know is this: In the natural habitat, instances in which one animal inflicts deadly wounds on another animal of the same species are virtually unknown. This holds universally, regardless of how formidable the "armament" of the particular animal may be — wolves, hawks, boa constrictors, bear, geese, gorillas, baboons, whatever. Instances in which one animal inflicts deadly wounds on another of a *different* species are almost exclusively limited to the act of killing prey. Thus, gorillas don't fight boa constrictors, for example (gorillas are chiefly vegetarians, incidentally, as are most of the higher apes).

Early human society, from all of the recent evidence unearthed by paleontology and archeology, was also generally pacific. Occasional lethal conflict may have occurred, but there is no certainty that it did; almost assuredly, it was not common, widespread, or systematic.

Freud, like Hollywood, has come a-cropper of the facts. The evidence discredits the existence of a biologically rooted "death instinct" such as he describes. On the contrary, there is considerable evidence that nearly all lethal aggression derives from a number of mechanisms—frustration, boredom, imitation, and obedience, among others—that reflect the individual's detailed interaction with the family and social settings. On extremely rare occasions, violent behavior is traceable to specific brain damage, but never to self-contained features of the physically normal brain. Man does not have an innate urge toward lethal aggression; the overwhelming preponderance of violent behavior is culturally conditioned, or learned behavior.

The modern evidence also discredits a group of views that were never conceived as empirically based or "scientific" in the contemporary sense, but that have played an important role in the development of Western thought, and to which the ideas of "social Darwinism" and the "death instinct" were highly congenial. At the root of these points of view have been some of the harsher expressions of the doctrine of "original sin," particularly ones which gained currency in the early years of the Reformation. Thomas Hobbes' political theories and John Calvin's theology were different expressions of this point of view, one which itself may be regarded as a significant contributing factor in past conflict. For if violence is inevitable, efforts to prevent it are doomed; and human "responsibility" for acts of violence exists in only an attenuated sense, if at all.

Yet, if past explanations have proven inadequate, *why* does one man murder another? *Why* does a leader resort to war? *Why* does a population follow? *Why* do individual soldiers follow commands to commit lethal acts against the bodies of other human beings? (How frequently, by the way, *do* they obey such commands? Always? Not by any means, as it turns out from actual studies.) As with any gravely threatening phenomenon, there is a tendency to grasp at *some* "explanation" so that we can soothe ourselves that we understand and can deal with the threat. But in such a case, the deliberate putting aside of primitive or simplistic explanations is the only true beginning of wisdom. Not until we steel ourselves to look at the threatening phenomenon in all of its complexity, to weigh and study all its aspects, can we have any real hope for understanding and control. Not until

xiii

men decided to look elsewhere than the "hand of Zeus" for the explanation of lightning could they move away from propitiating the gods with goats' blood and towards setting up lightning rods as a means of control.

Lethal aggression is a complex phenomenon, and we should not be surprised if the motives or factors leading to it cannot be defined in some simple and unified way. To begin with, it should be made clear that what is meant here by "lethal aggression" is the outward, objective act by which one human being deliberately kills another, not some inward state of rage, hatred, or "aggressiveness." The outward act may or may not be accompanied by hate. In this sense, we may find that there is something of the same relation between "lethal aggression" and "hate," as there is between "copulation" and "love." The external, physical act of love, like lethal aggression, is a complex phenomenon. It may grow out of many different motivations: it may be done for deep affection or "love"; it may also be done for monetary gain or other material benefits; it may be done to produce a child; it may be done for immediate pleasure or satisfaction; it may be done out of a sense of duty; it may even be done in hatred or vengeance; or it may be done out of a combination of some of these, or other, factors. It may be done for one reason by one partner and another reason by the other. Surely we should not be surprised if the external act of lethal aggression—an act, fortunately, which is much less frequent—arises out of human motivations at least as complex as those for the external act of love.

Yet, precisely because the great preponderance of lethal aggression originates in culturally conditioned behavior—no matter how complex the strands of causality—there is hope for its control and eventual elimination. The complexity of the phenomenon, as well as the evident failure of single-track explanations that have had their vogue within particular disciplines, points toward the need for a systematic study of the causes and means of resolution of lethal human conflict that utilizes the insights and materials developed in many different disciplines. The central concern of this volume is to place the understanding of lethal conflict, chiefly lethal group conflict, in the most modern interdisciplinary setting. This includes not only the disciplines that offer insights into when and where such conflict has arisen, and into the causal mechanisms underlying such conflict, but also those that suggest how such conflict may be resolved or prevented.

Of course, conflict, in its wider sense, will always be with us: in sibling rivalry, in "gamesmanship" or heated words between husband and wife, in striving for promotion or recognition against one's fellows, in playing to win. It provides much of the variety and stimulation in many people's lives, and much of it is socially constructive and psychologically fulfilling.

But conflict in which human beings may be seriously injured or killed is conflict gone awry, conflict far from the course of biological necessity, in which any constructive results are far over-balanced by the harm. In this volume, the focus is chiefly upon lethal conflict in groups (such as riots, revolutions, and wars) because this is where the greatest dangers lie for the human race, and also because this is probably where there is the best chance of taking specific steps to resolve or reduce the conflict. But individual lethal conflict (murder) will also be considered, especially to the extent that it may throw light on some of the mechanisms involved in the lethal conflict of groups. And at times, non-lethal conflict will also be considered, where it assists us in understanding the mechanisms underlying the lethal kind. To obtain the materials on which to develop our understanding of lethal conflict, excerpts from regular academic studies in a wide range of disciplines are used, as well as reports by Presidential commissions, United Nations agencies, periodicals, newspapers, and other non-academic sources. These materials are accompanied by an extensive textual commentary to supply critical perspective, questions, and final integration.

It should be emphasized that *the final section of the book, on measures of conflict resolution or prevention, is of central importance, and should on no account be left out of a course using these materials simply because its logical position is last.* If it is omitted, the reader or student may be left with a sense of profound pessimism which is not warranted. Summarily stated, my conclusion is that, while the problems of lethal conflict are complex and enormous, they are not overwhelming. They *can* be analyzed and understood, and practical ameliorative measures drawn from the complementary insights of many disciplines — almost certainly measures that will be of mid-term effectiveness, and probably also ones that will be of long-term effectiveness — *can* be proposed.

The threshold problem, of course, and my reason for writing this book, is that there are so few people *trained* to think systematically, constructively, and concretely about the prevention or resolution of lethal conflict situations, or to consider these problems in a context broad enough to foreswear pigeonholes before we even understand what we are pigeonholing. What is needed is a context broad enough to consider a spectrum of lethal conflict, ranging from murder and riot to revolution and world war, and likewise broad enough to recognize that psychology and political science, anthropology and law, the "hard sciences" and engineering, all may have something to contribute, if we are not to emerge with an understanding that arbitrarily reflects only the habitual preoccupations of the building in which we have our classes. In the effort to supply this broader context, and to deal with the real complexities of the phenomenon being studied, the discipline of "conflict studies" has grown up.

"Conflict studies" is, clearly, a new discipline, yet one drawing upon materials from a vast range of sources in the traditional fields of study. Academically, it is perfectly capable of being taught within any of several existing departments, as long as the clear interdisciplinary perspective is maintained; or it can be established as a separate "conflict studies" or "peace studies" program.

Conflict studies is probably best considered a profession, in the sense that it is oriented towards problem-solving, with a specifically defined function. Medicine aims to prepare its students to cure—and, increasingly, to prevent—disease. Conflict studies aims to prepare its students to prevent—or at least to limit—wars, revolutions, and other forms of lethal conflict. Like the medical student, the student of conflict must spend a great deal of time learning about the causes and symptoms of the phenomenon he is attempting to prevent or cure.

The medical professional will practice his profession in hospitals and in his office. The conflict studies professional will practice his profession as an official in the State Department or the Arms Control and Disarmament Agency, as a senatorial assistant; on the staff of the White House, or of a United Nations specialized agency, or of the World Bank; with the World Without War Council or the New York Friend's Group or Common Cause or the international affairs office of the AFL-CIO, or with any of a hundred other public or private agencies. He will advise how specific policies can best be developed to avoid war or revolution and to achieve lasting peace. Or, like some doctors, he may spend much of his time teaching others what he knows about conflict at a university. Or, while not a full-fledged professional, the student may become a well-informed amateur who knows enough to exert himself constructively and creatively within his community and in his political life. He will be able to perceive concrete alternatives to despair and violent activism—neither of which is likely to bring closer a world without lethal group conflict.

The time is short. Within the next few years, major support must develop internationally—from universities, foundations, faculty, and students—for the creation of curricula of study and professional training in the conflict studies field. By the 1980's, unless our society and others have many more people in positions of influence who are capable of thinking about these problems systematically and from a perspective that embodies the knowledge of many fields, the prognosis for mankind is grim indeed.

Surviving to 3000

An Introduction to the Study of Lethal Conflict

1

Lethal Conflict:

The body count

This chapter is a particularly disheartening one, but it unfortunately seems the logical place to begin. Before we move on to analyze the causes and search for the cures, we must take the basic measurements of the malady of lethal conflict. Therefore, this first chapter discusses the abstract, statistical data on what we know of man's inhumanity to man — the death toll from murder, war, and riot over the years. In addition, this chapter begins the complex process of relating these raw statistical measurements to some of the possible causes — at least to some of the causes that can be expressed numerically — of man's inhumanity to man.

Murder and Suicide

While the chief concern of this book is with lethal *group* violence—wars, revolutions, guerrilla warfare, riots, and so on—it is relevant to consider at the beginning some data bearing on individual violence. The following material on homicide and other major crimes comes from "The Challenge of Crime in a Free Society," a report of the President's Commission on Law Enforcement and Administration of Justice. This was one of the earliest presidential commissions, and the report was issued in 1967, before the catch-phrase "law and order" came into widespread political use. It is considered by both liberals and conservatives in the legal profession to be a work of perspective and solid scholarship, rather than a polemic document of any kind.

As you read this excerpt, notice especially the extent, and the possible significance, of the *differing* proportions of violent behavior—or other criminal behavior—in the populations of various countries, and the further distinctions in such behavior, within the United States, for rich and poor, black and white, young and old. The rates in the table are per 100,000 population.[1]

OTHER COUNTRIES

Crime is a worldwide problem. For most offenses it is difficult to compare directly the rates between countries because of great differences in the definitions of crime and in reporting practices. It is clear, however, that there are great differences in the rates of crime among the various countries, and in the crime problems that they face. These differences are illustrated to some extent by the homicide rates for a number of countries shown in Table 1. The comparisons show only the general range of difference, as definitions and reporting even of homicide vary to some extent. In the years covered by the table, Colombia had the highest rate for all countries and Ireland the lowest.

* * *

Commission and other studies of crime trends indicate that in most other countries officially reported rates for property offenses are rising rapidly, as they are in the United States; but that there is no definite pattern in the trend of crimes of violence in other countries. . . .

Crimes of violence could be studied in only a few countries. Rates declined in Belgium, Denmark, Norway, and Switzerland, but rose more than 150 percent in England and Wales between 1955 and 1964. Sexual offenses, which are usually kept as a separate statistic in Europe, also showed a mixed trend.

2

TABLE 1. HOMICIDE RATES FOR SELECTED COUNTRIES

COUNTRY	RATE	YEAR REPORTED
Colombia	35.5	1962
Mexico	31.9	1960
South Africa	21.8	1960
United States	4.8	1962
Japan	1.5	1962
France	1.5	1962
Canada	1.4	1962
Federal Republic of Germany	1.2	1961
England/Wales	.7	1962
Ireland	.4	1962

ARREST DATA ON OFFENDERS

National arrest statistics, based on unpublished estimates for the total population, show that when all offenses are considered together the majority of offenders arrested are white, male, and over 24 years of age. Offenders over 24 make up the great majority of persons arrested for fraud, embezzlement, gambling, drunkenness, offenses against the family, and vagrancy. For many other crimes the peak age of criminality occurs below 24.

. . . For crimes of violence the peak years are those from 18 to 20, followed closely by the 21 to 24 group. Rates for these groups are 300 and 297 [arrests per 100,000 in that age group, for murder, robbery, rape and other crimes of violence] as compared with 24 for the 50-year-old and over group.

One of the sharpest contrasts of all in the arrest statistics on offenders is that between males and females. Males are arrested nearly seven times as frequently as females for Index offenses plus larceny under $50. The rate for males is 1,097 per 100,000 population and the corresponding rate for females is 164. The difference is even greater when all offenses are considered.

The differences in the risks of arrest for males and females seem to be diminishing, however. Since 1960 the rate of arrest for females has been increasing faster than the rate for males. . . . Most of the increase was due to the greatly increased rate of arrest of women for larcenies . . . .

The factor of race is almost as important as that of sex in determining whether a person is likely to be arrested and imprisoned for an offense. Many more whites than Negroes are arrested every year but Negroes have a significantly higher rate of arrest in every offense category except certain offenses against public order and morals. For Index offenses plus larceny under $50 the rate per 100,000 Negroes in 1965 was four times as great as that for whites (1,696 to 419).

In general, the disparity of rates for offenses of violence is much greater

3

than comparable differences between the races for offenses against property. For instance, the Negro arrest rate for murder is 24.1 [per 100,000] compared to 2.5 for whites, or almost 10 times as high. [In 1967, the respective figures reached 50.4 and 3.7.] This is in contrast to the difference between Negroes and whites for crimes against property. For example, the rate of Negro arrest (378) for burglary is only about 3½ times as high as that for whites (107). (By 1967, it was 756 versus 170.) The statistics also show that the difference between the white and Negro arrest rates is generally greater for those over 18 years of age than for those under 18. Negroes over 18 are arrested about 5 times as often as whites (1,684 to 325). In contrast, the ratio for those under 18 is approximately three to one (1,689 to 591).

The differences between the Negro and white arrest rates for certain crimes of violence have been growing smaller between 1960 and 1965. During that period, considering together the crimes of murder, rape, and aggravated assault, the rate for Negroes increased 5 percent while the rate for whites increased 27 percent.

Many studies have been made seeking to account for these differences in arrest rates for Negroes and whites. They have found that the differences become very small when comparisons are made between the rates for whites and Negroes living under similar conditions. However, it has proved difficult to make such comparisons, since Negroes generally encounter more barriers to economic and social advancement than whites do. Even when Negroes and whites live in the same area the Negroes are likely to have poorer housing, lower incomes, and fewer job prospects. The Commission is of the view that if conditions of equal opportunity prevailed, the large differences now found between the Negro and white arrest rates would disappear.

PROBATION DATA ON OFFENDERS

Arrest statistics supply only a limited amount of information about offenders. More detailed descriptions can be obtained from the probation records maintained by the courts. An illustration of what such records reveal is provided in a report by the Stanford Research Institute to the President's Commission on Crime in the District of Columbia. The study examined the background characteristics contained in the probation records of a sample of 932 felons convicted during the years 1964 and 1965 in Washington, D.C.

Among those offenders for whom income information was available, 90 percent had incomes of less than $5,000. At the time of the 1960 census, 56 percent of the adult population in Washington earned less than $5,000. The highest median incomes were found among those who had been convicted of forgery, fraud, and embezzlement. Of the sample, 78 percent were Negro, as contrasted with an estimated 61 percent of Negroes in the population of Washington. The median age of arrest was 29.2 years, and approximately three-fourths of the sample was between 18 and 34 years, a proportion very much higher than that for the same age group in the general population of the District. Adult criminal records were found in 80 percent of the cases. More than half, 52 percent, had six or more prior arrests and 65 percent had previously been confined in some type of juvenile or adult institution.

The picture that emerges from this data is of a group of young adult males who come from disorganized families, who have had limited access to educational and occupational opportunities, and who have been frequently involved in difficulties with the police and the courts, both as juveniles and adults.

PRISON DATA ON OFFENDERS

An even more disadvantaged population can be identified from the characteristics of prisoners tabulated in the 1960 U.S. Census of Population. Every 10 years, the census lists the characteristics of persons in custodial institutions, including Federal and State prisons and local jails and workhouses. These tabulations show the median years of school completed for the State and Federal prison and reformatory population is 8.6 years, in contrast to 10.6 years for the general population in the country. It also shows that 23.9 percent of the offenders were laborers, compared to 5.1 percent in the total population. Only 5.8 percent of the offender population engaged in high status occupations, such as professional, technical work, manager, official, proprietor, and similar groupings, compared to 20.6 percent of the general population. Prisoners are also much more likely to be unmarried than other males 14 or over in the general population. Only 31.1 percent of the prisoners are married compared to 69.1 percent of males generally. The comparable rates for single status are 43.7 percent and 25.1 percent, and for separated, widowed and divorced, 24.6 and 7.2.

Homicide and group violence. The above excerpt shows large differences in homicide rates in the early 1960s (and these differences generally continue today). If you picked someone at random within the population of Colombia, that person's risk of being murdered during the next year was roughly ten times the risk of a randomly selected American, and the American's risk was over ten times greater than that of an Irishman. The chances of being murdered were approximately 100 times as great in the highest-risk country (Colombia) as they were in the lowest (Ireland). Do these figures, by themselves, permit any broad generalizations—or at least "guesses"—about the "violent" or "non-violent" nature of these societies that would be true for wars, revolutions, and other forms of *group* violence as well as murder? Or would the "guesses" be wrong as often as they were right?

Germany has a relatively low homicide rate, but during this century

5

this nation has launched a major war, deliberately slaughtered millions of Jewish and Eastern European civilians, and has probably been responsible for more deaths by group violence in the twentieth century than any other country on the list. Japan, also comparatively low on the homicide list, also started a major war (or really a series of major wars, beginning with her attack on Manchuria in 1931). Colombia, Mexico, and South Africa, on the other hand, where the homicide ratings are high, have done hardly any fighting outside their borders in this century.

Or can one readily find, then, an *inverse* correlation between homicide and group violence? Perhaps there is a certain quantity of "aggression" in any society, and if it doesn't "come out" in murder, it must come out in war or revolution. Unfortunately, this explanation doesn't seem to fit the facts very well either. England and the United States, for example, appear to have had slightly higher homicide rates during World War II than in the 1950s and early 1960s. Spain seems to have had a steady decline in the homicide rate since its bloody civil war of 1936–39. The Irish Republic was involved in neither war nor civil strife in the 1940s and 1950s, but maintained one of the world's lowest homicide rates.

No ready touchstone then, in numbers: yet it may prove cause for optimism *that no easy, universal correlation exists between individual acts of lethal violence and group acts of lethal violence, either positive (that is, the more murders, the more wars and revolutions) or inverse (that is, the more murders, the fewer wars and revolutions).* Having said this, are we saying, for example, that there *never* could be a "blood-thirsty" or "violent" society having both a high homicide rate and a high incidence of wars and revolutions? Or are we simply saying that it is not a generally applicable model that describes all or most countries?

Problems in categorization. How adequate is the data that we are using? Are there, for example, problems of deciding what to categorize as "homicide?" There are some people in this country who argue that we are murdering Vietnamese, and perhaps would add the weekly "body count" to the homicide toll to arrive at a much higher total figure. Are there, however, likely to be differences in the individual events reflected in the present homicide figure and the events reflected in the "body count" that might make it confusing and unwise simply to add the figures together, even if one didn't like the war? The differences between murders and killing in war is a matter that will concern us, one way and another, through much of the material in subsequent chapters.

But are there other ambiguous situations that might be included in the homicide statistics? What, for example, does one do with the shootings at Kent State? Or the killing of policemen by snipers? What about the deaths caused by a gang of bandits roaming the back country in some Latin American republic? What if the regime calls them "bandits," but they say they are "revolutionaries" who occasionally rob the well-to-do to support their political movement? A few examples of such groups are Pancho Villa, the Tupamaros in Uruguay, some of the "Huks" still operating in Central Luzon in the Philippines, or the group that robbed a Boston bank and shot a guard in September 1970. What of the deaths caused by the activities of the Palestinian guerrillas?

Given this ambiguity, is it nonetheless useful to maintain a separate category for deaths caused by revolutionary, or proto-revolutionary, or pre-revolutionary activity? Is it easier simply to keep a separate count of deaths caused by any organized group that maintains its activities over a period of time? But what about Al Capone, or the Mafia, or Bonnie and Clyde—do we want to include *their* activities with the statistics for revolution and civil war? On the other hand, what about Watts and Newark and Detroit, or Kent State and Jackson State? Do we want to exclude these figures because the group may not have been "organized" or may not have carried on activities over a period of time? What if, instead, we had a separate count of deaths caused by a group (even of rioters who weren't organized) whose aims are basically political? This would exclude Al Capone and Bonnie and Clyde, although we might still have problems with Robin Hood or Pancho Villa, and even with the Mafia, whose aims in some cases may include limited political control over a whole city or a major part of the city's government.

Certainly we will still have some questionable cases for applying the word "political." Nevertheless, "political aims" provides one working basis on which to categorize group violence figures. These figures may in many contexts have a meaning and explanation quite different from the homicide figures (or may not, in which case we can then add them together and get a single figure). Some of these problems appear in the data on domestic group violence in the next major excerpt. You should consider whether, or how well, the authors of that excerpt have dealt with these definitional problems.

Factors other than nationality. The previous excerpt also suggests some possible correlations between high rates of homicide and other crimes of violence, and other factors, such as being black, or being young, or being male, and (with perhaps somewhat less specific data on the particular correlation with a particular category of crime) being poor or unskilled or uneducated. (Some of these correlations are extremely high: approximately two-thirds of *all* homicides, for example, are killings *of* blacks *by* blacks — if this category of homicides were excluded, the homicide rate for the rest of the United States population would be reasonably close to that of Japan, France, or Canada.) Homicide rates are also higher, for *both* whites and blacks, in the cities than in the rural areas, and higher in certain regions (such as the South) than in others (such as New England). To what extent may some or all of these same factors be correlated with group violence, or with particular categories of group violence? Are these correlations necessarily the same for all societies?

For example, if you are poor in a society where 80 percent of the people are poor, or black where 80 percent are black — as in South Africa — rather than black where 10 percent are black? To carry the idea to its logical extreme, would "discrimination" be resented as strongly in a country where one white man ruled over 10,000 blacks or Indians as it is in the United States? Would "poverty" seem as unjust to the poor in a country where one rich man ruled over 10,000 poor? Is it possible that some of the correlations increase with greater numbers of people fitting the description, while others decrease, depending on the connection between the personal feature and the engagement in group violence? Of course, in many real-life situations the factors tend to combine; to be black and uneducated is often to be poor. Such combination makes it even harder to base immediate answers on available data or experience. These are, in any case, highly complex questions, whose implications thread their way through much of this material. We shall be doing well to venture answers by the end of this volume.

Homicide and suicide. If group violence and homicide do not show any significant correlations, either positive or inverse, is it possible that the picture will change if we add suicide? Some, after Freud, have argued that suicide is simply "a desire to murder, directed against the self." For comparative data, we can look to the following table of murder and suicide rates, per 100,000 population, in 1965–66, com-

piled from Interpol, United Nations, and World Health Organization
data:[2]

**MURDERS AND SUICIDES, PER 100,000 POPULATION, FOR
THIRTY SELECTED COUNTRIES**

COUNTRY	TOTAL	MURDER	SUICIDE
West Berlin	44.5	3.2*	41.3
Hungary	31.5	1.9*	29.6
Taiwan	29.2	12.4	16.8
Ceylon	29.1	12.2	16.9*
Colombia	27.6	21.5*	6.1
Austria	25.1	2.0	23.1
West Germany	23.0	3.0	23.0
Sweden	21.9	0.3	21.6*
Finland	21.5	1.7	19.8
Luxembourg	20.2	6.8	13.4*
Denmark	19.5	0.2	19.3
Switzerland	19.2	0.8*	18.4
United States	17.7	6.8*	10.9
France	17.6	2.6	15.0
Australia	16.9	2.0	14.9
Japan	16.4	2.3	14.1
Venezuela	15.0	8.0*	7.0
England and Wales	13.7	0.3	10.4
Hong Kong	11.3	1.1	10.1*
New Zealand	11.0	1.0	10.0*
Canada	10.5	1.9	8.6
Poland	10.0	1.0*	9.0
Israel	9.4	2.9	6.5
Scotland	9.4	1.9	7.5*
Netherlands	9.2	3.0	6.2*
Italy	9.0	3.6	5.4
Norway	7.1	0.1	7.0*
Spain	5.3	0.5	4.8
Greece	3.8	0.7	3.1
Ireland	2.0	0.2	1.8

*Indicates 1967 data.

Does the above data improve our correlations? Apparently not. Some
countries have high murder rates and low suicide rates (for example,
Colombia), while others have high suicide and rather low murder

9

rates (for example, Denmark and Finland). But others are rather high on *both* counts (for example, Taiwan), while others are rather low both for murder and suicide (for example, Ireland, Greece, Spain).

Adding the two figures, the comparative rates go from 2.0 per 100,000 for the Republic of Ireland (which had very little lethal group conflict, either, through the late 1960s); to 23.0 for West Germany; to 29.1 for Ceylon; and finally to 44.5 for West Berlin, a city unique both geographically and politically. Doing a similar addition of homicide and suicide figures for the year 1946 in *The Sane Society*, Erich Fromm found a range from 4.24 to 35.76. He remarks, "This contradicts Freud's assumption of the comparative constancy of destructiveness which underlies his theory of the death instinct. It disproves the implication that destructiveness maintains an invariable rate, differing only in directions toward the self or the outside world."[3]

Considering additional data and looking at those countries with fewer than one murder per 100,000* inhabitants, one finds an enormous diversity: the very poor, rural, and undeveloped (Indonesia, Malaysia, Ghana) and the very rich, urban, and industrialized (Sweden, England); all varieties of religious and secular leanings; an enormous range in geography, culture, and racial background (blacks in the United States commit murder nearly one hundred times as frequently as blacks in Ghana). Some of the countries with a low murder rate have been involved in major domestic group struggles or international wars, while others have gone through a long period of neutrality and domestic tranquillity.

Among the few regularities that *can* be noted, perhaps the most salient is that none of the wealthy, urban, and industrialized societies of Western Europe, North America, or Japan is found in the highest ranges of the murder list; while none of the poorer, less developed countries, with the possible exceptions of Taiwan and Ceylon, are found in the highest ranges of the suicide list.

Changes in homicide rate. Have homicide rates changed over time? World-wide data collected by Lewis Richardson (discussed in the last section of this chapter, together with his data on war) indicates the occurrence of roughly 250 homicides during the entire *lifetime* of a population of 100,000, as a rate averaged over the period 1820–1945. Taking a lifetime of around 40 to 50 years as an average for

*Indonesia, 0.79	Malaysia, 0.50	Denmark, 0.20
Greece, 0.70	Ghana, 0.48	Ireland, 0.20
Iran, 0.70	England and Wales, 0.34	Norway, 0.13
Spain, 0.54	Sweden, 0.30	

that population, the rate—again an *average*—would be between 5 and 6 homicides per year over the 126-year period. This would appear to be slightly higher than current rates, but not markedly so. The average may, of course, conceal substantial fluctuations over time.

Despite talk of "crime in the streets," the *United States* homicide rate has certainly not shown a long-term increase. While there has been an increase over the past decade, a longer perspective shows the following statistics (derived from United States Public Health Service figures):[4]

YEAR	HOMICIDES PER 100,000 POPULATION
1900	1.2
1910	4.7
1920	6.7
1930	8.5
1940	6.3
1950	5.3
1960	4.7
1969	7.2

Around 1933–34, the rate peaked close to 10 per 100,000, and while complete data are lacking, there appears to have been an earlier peak in the 1870s, perhaps even higher.

On the other hand, it has been suggested that "many persons who formerly might have died from crimes of violence are now saved on operating tables, and their assailants are charged with assault with intent to kill rather than with murder or manslaughter."[5] Thus, there may not in fact have been a decline in homicidal violence relative to the 1870 and 1930 peaks, but rather an improvement in medical care for the victim. Without further detailed research, the impact of the medical variable cannot be estimated.

Character of homicides. One study in Chicago of United States homicides showed 82 percent to be unplanned and impulsive, rather than premeditated or associated with crime. Only 12 percent of the murders occurred in association with a robbery, and 3 percent in association with teen-age gang disputes. "Typically, homicides occurred during arguments over domestic matters, alcohol, money, or children. A majority of the murder victims were relatives, lovers, or friends of the murderer."[6] The use of guns as weapons was significant;

11

2.4 victims died for ever 100 reported knife attacks, "while for every 100 reported gun attacks, an average of 12.2 victims died." Thus, even "though more persons were attacked with knives than guns, more people died from gun attacks." In the United States as a whole, about 60 percent of homicides are commited with guns, about 20 percent with knives, and most of the rest with blunt objects, beatings, and strangulation (beating, strangulation, and other homicides involving the direct laying-on-of-hands account for under 10 percent of all homicides). It has been suggested that the ready availability of guns in the United States may turn many assaults into lethal ones. In some other countries with much lower homicide rates, where there is little use of guns, the proportion of violent assaults may be closer to that of the United States than homicide rates suggest.

Are the real reasons for these "impulsive" homicides likely to lie just in the particular personal relationship and the immediate precipitating events? Consider again the significance of the fact that two thirds of *all* United States homicides are committed against blacks, by blacks.

Indirect homicide. There is potentially still another major *caveat* lurking in our definition of "homicide" or "murder," although it is virtually impossible to quantify. Events described as "homicides" have a rather short "time-line," an immediate sequence of cause and effect, and a clearcut conscious intention on the part of the actor. There are, however, those who would argue that societies may kill large numbers of people through studied ignorance or apathy, without a conscious intent to kill or injure. The facts that, in the United States, the black infant-mortality rate is nearly twice as high as that of white infants, and that the non-white life expectancy is six to seven years shorter than that of whites, tend to support this position. It could be argued that the failure to provide health care facilities and adequate nutrition, which the society is fully capable of providing, has a clear, although subtle, causal relationship to a large proportion of these additional deaths. Therefore, it might be said, the public and politicians who fail to provide these things are actually guilty of murder. Others might argue that the years-long failure to develop safe cars or to control pollution makes automobile manufacturers, the public, and politicians guilty of deaths caused by car accidents and air pollution. Still others would say that the responsibility for many deaths from lung cancer, emphysema, and so on, belongs to those who failed to control cigarette advertising, and perhaps cigarette sales, earlier and more rigidly. However, the cigarette smoker certainly has more choice in the matter than the person who has a baby, drives a car, or breathes the air of a city.

It is certainly legitimate to view these facts as grave social wrongs, and we shall see that, historically, wrongs of similar kinds have frequently evoked a violent response, perhaps a lethally violent response, from those affected. But there are a number of difficulties in lumping these phenomena with the accepted categories of lethal violence. First of all, it is impossible to develop even approximate statistics to reflect such causes. In itself, this would not be an adequate objection. Second, many, *but not all,* of the psychological mechanisms operating in those who may bear responsibility for these deaths are markedly different from those in situations where one man directly kills another. When we study these mechanisms, we shall certainly point out any parallels. Even the "studied ignorance" or "apathy" of which we have spoken may, in most cases, only extend to saying, "I don't care if such-and-such a social, economic, or racial group doesn't eat well or doesn't have good medical care," in the sense that the general public visualizes them as "slightly hungry" or "slightly sick," and *not* in the sense that the public recognizes the very real possibility that members of the disadvantaged group may die as a result. One striking illustration of this attitude was the reaction of certain politicians—such as Senator Hollings of South Carolina, or more recently the mayor of Jackson, Mississippi—who for the first time actually *saw* the hunger and misery of ghetto residents, and became champions of foodstamp programs and other measures. However, someone who was *fully aware* of the problem and yet remained in opposition to remedial measures might well be regarded as closer in mental state to a premeditating murderer.

Third, no specific individual is the target of the action, although this fact may simply analogize such a situation more to war than to murder—that is, there may be a *group* "target," in the sense that an individual taxpayer or politician may be unconcerned about starving blacks, or about the poor regardless of race. Furthermore, it is the more conventionally defined lethal aggression which soon threatens to get wholly out of hand. "Long-time-line" oppression is of enormous concern, but it does not threaten imminent destruction of the species. Finally, if we make it our central task to understand lethal aggression

structural violence

13

as it is more commonly and manageably defined, we may be able to formulate notions of cause and prevention that will also help us understand and eliminate many of the forms of "long-time-line" oppression.

Domestic Group Violence

Contemporary data on domestic group violence (that is, the kind of violence that involves not conflict between nations, but rather conflict between *groups* within nations, hence excluding murder) can be found in the following excerpt from Bruce M. Russett, et al., *World Handbook of Political and Social Indicators* (1964), a product of the Yale Political Data Program, which was established in 1962. Russett also suggests certain alternative ways of measuring group violence, as well as giving the basic sources of his data.[7]

**DEATHS FROM DOMESTIC
GROUP VIOLENCE PER
1,000,000 POPULATION,
1950–62**

One of the most widely used concepts in political analysis is stability. It is, however, often used imprecisely or is used by different authors to mean different things. To some "stability" means maintenance of a particular system of government, a particular constitutional order. To others "stability" may mean the continuance of a particular leader, or party, or coalition in power. By the first definition the French Third Republic was "stable" over a long period of time; by the second it most certainly was not. Yet another definition might be concerned with the frequency of political violence; an unstable system would be one marked by frequent riots, coups, assassinations, or rebellions. Another might be concerned with the basic economic relationships of the country; an unstable state would be one in which ownership of the means of production changed sharply. Still other definitions have appeared in the literature.

Faced with a conceptual problem of this nature there is little point in trying to isolate a single meaning of "stability" so as to use it exclusively. We have used here two quite distinct indices to measure different aspects of stability. Neither is by itself adequate as a means to tap the complex of events often covered by this broad term, but they do to some extent tap particular aspects of the concept. They are best used together, or even with still other measures the reader may devise. We emphasize that each is a *partial* measure, and furthermore that the two indices are not highly correlated. We do

14

not imply that because a country is high on one of these indices it is necessarily high on another. On the contrary, overemphasis on either of the indices will produce some striking anomalies.

One index measures, for the period 1950 through 1962, "the number of people killed in all forms of domestic violence: any deaths resulting directly from violence of an intergroup nature, thus excluding deaths by murder and execution." The forerunner of this series was compiled, for the 1955–57 period only, by Rudolph J. Rummel. To reduce the effect of unique events, such as the Hungarian revolution of 1956, we have extended Rummel's series both backward and forward to a total of 13 years. We have limited ourselves to independent states so as to avoid the distorting effects of violence directed against a colonial power; in the interests of retaining a substantial number of Asian states in the series we have therefore not been able to extend it back before 1950. To control for country size we have transformed the absolute data on deaths into deaths per 1,000,000 population.

The basic sources used include *The New York Times Index, New International Yearbook, Facts on File,* and *Britannica Book of the Year.* Occasionally we have resorted to specialized works to remove ambiguities. The most likely source of error is systematic under-reporting of deaths in some countries, due either to press censorship or to lack of world interest. In his original study Rummel attempted to control for these factors, using a "censorship scale" and an index of world interest based on the number of resident embassies and legations in a country. Neither showed a significant correlation with the violence data, indicating that censorship and world interest, *as tapped by these measures,* had little effect on the results. Nevertheless we have found quite a number of instances where, though violence was reported, the number of deaths was not known with any precision. We were forced in these cases to make very rough estimates. The most approximate figures are footnoted, and must be assigned a very wide error range, usually not less than ±50%. The coder's judgment might also be thought to bias the results, but an independent check of our data by a second coder showed less than .1% disagreement on the number of deaths. The chief source of error remains inadequate information.

Several other imaginative efforts have been made to measure violent change, and should be mentioned. Ivo Feierabend and associates have compiled a seven-point index of political stability. Various possible events are assigned scores of from zero to seven, with an orderly general election scored zero and civil war scored six. The time period is 1955 to 1961. This would appear to be a fruitful approach, but at the moment the time span employed is fairly short, and, more serious, the stability score has not been thoroughly validated. There is some question as to whether the kinds of events in any one scoring group are not too heterogeneous, and even as to the relative degree of violence attributed to events assigned different scores.

Another attempt to grapple with this difficult problem is represented by Harry Eckstein's data on internal war. Eckstein has recorded, from the *New York Times Index,* the number of violent events occurring in the period 1946–59. All recorded events, from rioting to civil and guerilla warfare, are counted. He gives for each country both the overall total number of events and the sub-

15

totals for each of seven categories such as "turmoil," "terrorism," and "mutiny." The overall number of events probably does not make a good index, as it weights equally events of very different magnitude. Probably a scale like Feierabend's could be constructed, but that would not be entirely satisfactory. Furthermore, Eckstein mentions some significant omissions which diminish the data's usefulness. And finally, the dependence on a single source, the *Times Index,* also introduces some distortions.

While these two approaches are valuable, and while we are aware of deficiencies in our own index, it nevertheless seems to us that the violent deaths index is the most satisfactory.

Possible inaccuracy of figures. The Yale figures (facing) certainly are meant to include all deaths from civil wars, guerrilla conflicts, riots, strikes, lynchings, and other kinds of internal group violence. But have the Yale researchers solved all the definitional problems previously raised in discussion of the homicide data? In the case of the Philippines or Colombia, for example, there was extensive civil conflict during the 1950–62 period (the "violencia" in Colombia, the struggle with Hukbalahap guerrillas in the Philippines). But there was also an extensive breakdown of civil order in these two societies, and thus an increased amount of killing in the course of robbery, revenge-taking, and similar activities. Is there a danger of overstating the figures because of confusion of these individual killings with group violence, and their unintended inclusion in the reporting of a civil war? (Or, there may be some situations where individual killings are deliberately characterized by a regime as rebellious violence, if it is trying to gain sympathy or material support from another country.)

Or is the danger, perhaps, of understating such group violence? Consider the position of a regime that wishes to play down the serious-ness of its civil conflict and emphasize its stability (perhaps to attract foreign business investments or tourists, or to appear more completely in control in its external political relations or even in the eyes of its own populace). Such a regime might be tempted to characterize and report as murders some deaths from politically motivated group activ-ities. And if the "murderer" were caught and executed, both groups of deaths might escape the Yale index, even though the rebels, who did not get their side of the story into the *New York Times* or the other source materials, might characterize what had really happened as a "guerrilla raid followed by armed reprisals against the guerrillas." In fact, it appears that there may have been considerable understate-ment of the figures for both Colombia and the Philippines for this reason.

16

DEATHS FROM DOMESTIC GROUP VIOLENCE PER 1,000,000 POPULATION, 1950–1962
[Specialized statistical-analysis data has been omitted; data for Cuba, Indonesia, Iraq, Burma, Afghanistan, China and India are rough approximations only.]

COUNTRY	DEATHS FROM DOMESTIC GROUP VIOLENCE PER 1,000,000 POPULATION 1950–62
Cuba	2,900 [22.3]*
Hungary	1,335 [10.3]
Indonesia	860 [6.6]
Bolivia	663 [5.1]
Iraq	344 [2.7]
Colombia	316 [2.4]
Philippines	292 [2.2]
Argentina	217 [1.7]
Burma	152 [1.2]
Honduras	111 [0.9]
Venezuela	111 [0.9]
Paraguay	60**
Guatemala	57
South Korea	49
Syria	44
Ceylon	42
Iran	36
South Africa	33
Dominican Republic	31
Peru	26
Panama	25
Costa Rica	24
Afghanistan	21
China (Mainland)	20
Ecuador	18
Haiti	16
Lebanon	16
Nicaragua	16
India	14
Ethiopia	10
Pakistan	9
Yemen	8
Jordan	7
Nepal	7
Poland	5

* To facilitate comparison with the previous homicide figures, which are stated in terms of deaths per 100,000 persons per year, I have added the bracketed figures, which convert this data (deaths per 1,000,000 over a 13-year period) into an equivalent *annual* rate per *100,000*.
** All figures beyond this point represent a rate of less than 0.5 per 100,000 per year, during 1950–62.

COUNTRY	DEATHS FROM DOMESTIC GROUP VIOLENCE PER 1,000,000 POPULATION 1950–62
Mexico	4
Bulgaria	3
East Germany	3
Israel	3
Thailand	3
Chile	2
El Salvador	2
Greece	2
Egypt	1.6
Brazil	1.0
Portugal	1.0
Belgium	.9
Turkey	.9
Czechoslovakia	.7
U.S.S.R.	.7
France	.3
Uruguay	.3
Italy	.2
Saudi Arabia	.2
Spain	.2
Japan	.1
West Germany	.02
United States	.01
Australia	.0
Austria	.0
Canada	.0
Denmark	.0
Finland	.0
Ireland	.0
Liberia	.0
Netherlands	.0
New Zealand	.0
Norway	.0
Romania	.0
Sweden	.0
Switzerland	.0
Taiwan	.0
United Kingdom	.0
Yugoslavia	.0

Problems of categorization. Looking at the figures themselves, what exactly do they stand for? In the case of Cuba, for example, an island with a population of about 7,000,000 suffered 2,900 deaths per million during the period 1950–62. This means that roughly 20,000 people died, over that period of time, from domestic group violence. Most of this violence occurred in the late 1950s, when Fidel Castro was leading a guerrilla army against the dictator Fulgencio Batista. It is not clear how the index has treated the deaths of several thousand Batista supporters who were killed, generally after brief "trials," in 1959 and 1960, after Castro came to power. At some point these killings may gain legitimacy and, as "executions," may be excluded from the index, especially if there is no active, continuing resistance from the opposing group. But, as we shall see below, there have been several cases in this century in which such eliminations of opposition have been extensive, and unless some count of these deaths is kept so that we can at least choose to add them to the index figures if we wish, the total figure and comparative position for a particular country may be heavily distorted.

Such questions might, for example, be of considerable significance for a country like Indonesia in the more recent period. In 1965, after a brief unsuccessful coup attempt by the Communist PKI party, a wave of terror swept the countryside. An estimated 200,000 people died — most of them after all active or organized opposition had ended — because they were suspected in their village of being Communists or Communist sympathizers. These figures are equivalent to over 2,000 deaths per million population for *one* year alone. If these figures were included in an updated index, Indonesia would rank much higher, even, than it does now; if they were excluded as "executions," they would not affect the rank. Should figures no longer be included once organized opposition has ceased? Or should their exclusion depend on whether or not there is a formal and legal process of execution? Or should they be included, even though opposition has ceased and the executions are legal, if they are still part of the "mopping up" or reprisal after a clear-cut civil conflict? Perhaps the best answer that can presently be given is that these latter figures at least should be available for possible addition to the index, until we have a better idea of the analytical or investigative uses of this kind of index.

Are there other kinds of very major definitional problems? What if South Vietnam were included on a current version of the index? It would make a great deal of difference whether one characterized the conflict as "an invasion from the North" or as a "civil war chiefly supported by the unhappy peasants of the South." What if it were, in part, *both*? What would be the effect of the participation of American forces on the attempt to classify the deaths from the conflict in Vietnam as either domestic group violence or an international war? Note that the authors state, "We have limited ourselves to independent states so as to avoid the distorting effects of violence directed against a colonial power." Thus, the chart does not include the civil wars in Indochina and Algeria against the French, or in Kenya and Malaya against the British. Presumably, the Hungarian figure does not include the effects of the Russian intervention during the 1956 Hungarian uprising. Do the authors exclude these conflicts because they resemble international wars in some respects, rather than domestic conflicts? Again, should not such data at least be available?

Examination of increases in lethal group conflict. Look at the index figure for the United States during 1950–62. Roughly how many deaths does the .01 figure represent? Amazingly, it represents only about *two* deaths during the entire period (with a population of 200,000,000, an index figure of 1 per million would mean 200 deaths over 1950–62. The figure of one one-hundredth per million means two deaths.) Perhaps this figure is not very amazing, when one sees that many developed countries like Canada, Sweden, and the United Kingdom had *zero,* as did Liberia. On the other hand, it does suggest some contrasts between the United States 10–20 years ago and today. During that earlier era, as the figure indicates, there were virtually no deadly riots, lethal strikes, or lynchings. In recent years, ghetto riots such as those in Watts, Newark, Detroit, Washington, and Chicago have taken over 200 lives. Six lives were lost at Jackson State and Kent State, and 40 died in the prisoner rebellion at Attica.

Beyond those events, other widely publicized occurrences present important questions of categorization. Do lethal exchanges of fire between police and black militants belong on the index? The 1970 bank robbery in Boston, and bombing of the Math Center at Wisconsin, both the work of radical groups of young whites? What of killing of individual policemen by individual radicals? There is little doubt that the Yale index would include a single sniper's killing of a soldier, even though only one man is immediately involved, if the sniper were acting as part of an established insurrectionary movement like the Huk guerrillas. If one included all of the deaths currently attributable to one or more individuals who form part of politically motivated United States groups, it appears that a figure in the range of 50–100 deaths per year might now be accurate. Continued over thirteen years, this rate would come to 650–1,300 deaths, making the index figure between 3.5 and 7. Translated into annual deaths per 100,000, comparable to the homicide figures, this comes out to between .025 and .05, less than one one-hundredth of the homicide rate. If one included killings by groups without any clear-cut political motivation in the usual sense — such as teenage gang wars — the figure would be higher, but such "wars" appear to have been excluded during the 1950–62 period.

While still far from the highest or medium-high index figures, and comparable to figures from some of the developed states, such as Israel (whose very small population, however, means that a figure of 3 only encompasses about 6 deaths over a 13-year period, so that small changes in absolute figures mean substantial changes in rate), Poland, or East Germany, an index of 3.5–7 is substantially higher than the 1950–62 figures for the Western European countries or Canada. But the domestic situation of some of these countries has changed, and their rates at least are no longer zero. The rebellion in Northern Ireland and the Separatist movement in Quebec, for example, have raised both Canada and the United Kingdom from zero. Indeed, if the present 200 deaths per year in Ulster continued for a number of years, the United Kingdom index figure might rise to 40 or more, though this still represents a number of deaths less than two-thirds the British homicide figure. Some countries have, in the years since 1962, quite clearly experienced an increase in levels of lethal group violence; equally clearly, others have experienced a marked decline, including Cuba, Hungary, Bolivia, and Colombia, each of which underwent a major civil struggle during the 1950–62 period, but not subsequently.

If the index were redone today, there is no reason to believe it would show a sharp overall rise in *world* deaths from domestic group violence, at least apart from the figures from the very destructive struggles in Nigeria during the Biafran secession and in Bangladesh. Many of these deaths, moreover, are due to starvation and disease among non-combatants, which is a category of deaths that might be excluded from the index, or at least separately tabulated. (If Vietnam were included in both the 1950–62 list and a subsequent list, it would also make a heavier contribution to the recent index.) But there were earlier civil struggles of vast proportions in China (the 1940s), Spain (the 1930s), Russia (1917–22), and Mexico (the teens), which would also have a disproportionate weight. 1950–62 was, as it happens, a period in which there were major civil conflicts, but none that came even close to the million-death category. Even if there has not been a significant rise in these figures on a world basis, does this mean such a rise is unlikely? Is the index, perhaps, fairly constant over many decades or even centuries? Or is group violence increasing? Are there other measures we might look at?

Group violence and individual violence. Again, although there are many questions as to the definition of domestic group violence and as to the adequacy of the data, it appears that there is no ready correlation between the Yale figures and the data on individual lethal violence. Many societies with low homicide rates are also low on the 1950–62 scale of group violence. Indonesia, however, is low on the homicide scale but high on that for group violence. Colombia is high in homicides and relatively high in group violence as well (although this apparent fact may reflect some difficulties in categorizing particular results of the *violencia*). Mexico has a high homicide rate,* but is low in group violence, while Spain is low in both homicides and group violence. Earlier in the century, however, both Mexico and Spain went through a decade when they would have gone off the scale at the high end of the group violence ratings, with figures more than ten times the highest shown in the 1950–62 period (roughly 30,000 to 50,000 dead per 1,000,000 population, or between 231 and 385 per 100,000 per year, if averaged over a comparable 13-year period).

Another index of domestic violence. The Yale extract refers to the work of Ivo Feierabend to develop another index of domestic violence. Consider the following newspaper report, which appeared in September 1968.[8]

The United States has been a politically violent nation, stable but with No. 1 ranking in assassinations, according to a study prepared for a national commission on violence.

Preliminary study findings were presented to the National Commission on the Causes and Prevention of Violence in Washington, D.C., by Dr. Ivo K. Feierabend of San Diego State College.

Feierabend, a political scientist, said there were eight assassinations and attempted assassinations in the U.S. from 1948 through 1965. Venezuela was next highest with seven.

*31.9 per 100,000, in 1960.

22

Feierabend said there were more than 120 assassination events during those 18 years in 84 countries.

Some 8000 of the world's violent incidents, ranging from strikes to assassinations, have been cataloged in the study.

Feierabend said the study covers the 84 independent nations existing in 1948. Excluded are 40 countries established since then.

The researchers ranked violence by severity of incidents from zero to six, basing assessments on news reports and encyclopedia records.

PROFILES

Results were violence profiles for each country, ranging from the highest, 699 for Indonesia and Cuba, to the lowest, zero for New Zealand.

The U.S. profile was 316, below average and indicating political stability. Russia's score was 430, considered unstable, he said.

But Feierabend said the U.S. profile would have been above 400 if domestic violence between 1961 and 1966 was considered.

He said the chief world-wide causes of violence are oppressive governments and high frustration among the populace.

The following is a further description of Feierabend's seven-point scale of incidents, from a summary of the statement presented to the National Commission on Causes and Prevention of Violence:[9]

For this measurement a 7-point rating system was developed that ranges from 0 to 6, from extreme stability to extreme political instability. Each point on the scale represents some specific event. For example, a general election is rated 0; resignation or dismissal of a cabinet official or dissolution of a legislature, 1; peaceful demonstrations and strikes, 2; riots or assassinations of significant political figures (but not of heads of state), 3; large-scale arrests, plots or terrorism, 4; revolts or coups d'état, 5; revolution or civil war, 6.

Consider the Yale group's criticism of this scale, on the ground that there is some question as to whether "the kinds of events in any one scoring group" may be "too heterogeneous" and also "as to the relative degree of violence attributed to events assigned different scores." Does this criticism appear valid? Consider the range of occurrences that might underlie the events given a "1" rating: a British cabinet official may resign for reasons of health, or a strong man in charge of police and defense may be forced to resign against his will in Bolivia or Syria; a constitutional call for a new election may be made, or legislators may be ordered out of the capital in a decree suspending constitutional government. Under "2," even a peaceful demonstration or strike may range from thirty elderly anti-vivisectionists parading in front of the state legislature, to a general strike in Italy mobilizing millions of workers to stop everything from auto manufacturing to the municipal power and garbage services. Northwest Airline clerks may strike for higher pay, or several hundred thousand postmen may leave their government jobs in an illegal work stoppage. Demonstrators may be two hundred or two hundred thousand, demonstrating for abortion laws or against Vietnam. But each event gets a "2" rating.

Or consider some of the events in different categories: In a "coup d'état" (rated 5), the opposition may drive to the Presidential palace at dawn, confront the President verbally, and force him to resign and move out without a shot being fired. "Large-scale arrests" (rated only 3) may put every member of the recognized political opposition in jail, and leave terrorists or fanatics as the only alternative to the existing regime. A single "riot" (rated only 2) may cause the deaths of ten thousand people, as in India after independence, or Bogata in a 1948 flare-up of political rivalries, and leave a heritage of national bitterness.

If Feierabend's scale is still not sufficiently refined, does it mean that we should discard it entirely? Or is the range of data he seeks, while theoretically capable of thorough comparison, too extensive and complex to make his approach a really promising one? Are there other kinds of comparative measures, scales, or indices of violence that might be more simplified, but still helpful? What may be the advantages of an index based on a category or categories of *lethal* violence — violence from which human deaths result?

Group violence and economic backwardness. Another approach, concerned chiefly with protracted or politically significant civil conflict, does not focus initially so much on deaths as on other types of measurable data. Consider the following extracts from what has become known as "the Montreal speech," delivered in May 1966 by Robert S. McNamara, then Secretary of Defense, and now the head of the World Bank:[10]

Roughly 100 countries today are caught up in the difficult transition from traditional to modern societies.

There is no uniform rate of progress among them, and they range from primitive mosaic societies — fractured by tribalism and held feebly together by the slenderest of political sinews — to relatively sophisticated countries, well on the road to agricultural sufficiency and industrial competence.

This sweeping surge of development, particularly across the whole southern half of the globe, has no parallel in history.

It has turned traditionally listless areas of the world into seething cauldrons of change.

On the whole, it has not been a very peaceful process.

In the last eight years alone there have been no less than 164 internationally significant outbreaks of violence — each of them specifically designed as a serious challenge to the authority, or the very existence, of the government in question.

82 different governments have been directly involved.

What is striking is that only 15 of these 164 significant resorts to violence have been military conflicts between two states.

And not a single one of the 164 conflicts has been a formally-declared war.

Indeed, there has not been a formal declaration of war — anywhere in the world — since World War II.

The planet is becoming a more dangerous place to live on — not merely because of a potential nuclear holocaust — but also because of the large number of *de facto* conflicts and because the trend of such conflicts is growing rather than diminishing.

At the beginning of 1958, there were 23 prolonged insurgencies going on about the world. As of February 1, 1966, there were 40.

Further, the total number of outbreaks of violence has increased each year: in 1958, there were 34; in 1965, there were 58.

But what is most significant of all is that there is a direct and constant relationship between the incidence of violence and the economic status of the countries afflicted.

The World Bank divides nations on the basis of per capita income, into four categories: rich, middle-income, poor, and very poor.

The rich nations are those with a per capita income of $750 per year or more. The current U.S. level is more than $2700. There are 27 of these rich nations. They possess 75% of the world's wealth, though roughly only 25% of the world's population.

Since 1958, only *one* of these 27 nations has suffered a major internal upheaval on its own territory.

But observe what happens at the other end of the economic scale. Among the 38 very poor nations — those with a per capita income of under $100 a year — no less than 32 have suffered significant conflicts. Indeed, they have suffered an average of two major outbreaks of violence per country in the eight year period. That is a great deal of conflict.

What is worse, it has been, predominantly, conflict of a prolonged nature.

The trend holds predictably constant in the case of the two other categories: the poor, and the middle-income nations. Since 1958, 87% of the very poor nations, 69% of the poor nations, and 48% of the middle-income nations have suffered serious violence.

(injustice)?

There can, then, be no question but that there is an *irrefutable relationship between violence and economic backwardness.* And the trend of such violence is up, not down.

Now, it would perhaps be somewhat reassuring if the gap between the rich nations and the poor nations were closing, and economic backwardness were significantly receding.

But it is not. The economic gap is widening.

By the year 1970, over one half of the world's total population will live in the independent nations sweeping across the southern half of the planet. But this hungering half of the human race will by then command only one-sixth of the world's total of goods and services.

By the year 1975, the dependent children of these nations alone—children under 15 years of age—will equal the *total* population of the developed nations to the north.

Even in our own abundant societies, we have reason enough to worry over the tensions that coil and tighten among underprivileged young people, and finally flail out in delinquency and crime. What are we to·expect from a whole hemisphere of youth where mounting frustrations are likely to fester into eruptions of violence and extremism?

Annual per capita income in roughly half of the 80 underdeveloped nations that are members of the World Bank is rising by a paltry one per cent a year or less. By the end of the century, these nations—at their present rates of growth—will reach a per capita income of barely $170 a year. The United States, by the same criteria, will attain a per capita income of $4,500.

The conclusion to all of this is blunt and inescapable: given the certain connection between economic stagnation and the incidence of violence, the years that lie ahead for the nations in the southern half of the globe are pregnant with violence.

This would be true even if no threat of Communist subversion existed—as it clearly does.

Both Moscow and Peking—however harsh their internal differences—regard the whole modernization process as an ideal environment for the growth of communism. Their experience with subversive internal war is extensive; and they have developed a considerable array of both doctrine and practical measures in the art of political violence.

What is often misunderstood is that communists are capable of subverting, manipulating, and finally directing for their own ends the wholly legitimate grievances of a developing society.

But it would be a gross oversimplification to regard communism as the central factor in every conflict throughout the underdeveloped world. Of the 149 serious internal insurgencies in the past eight years, communists have been involved in only 58 of them—38% of the total—and this includes seven instances in which a Communist regime itself was the target of the uprising.

* * *

But—though all the *caveats* are clear enough—the irreducible fact remains that our security is related directly to the security of the newly developing world.

26

And our role must be precisely this: to help provide security to those developing nations which genuinely need and request our help, and which demonstrably are willing and able to help themselves.

The rub comes in this: we do not always grasp the meaning of the word *security* in this context.

In a modernizing society, *security means development.*

Security is *not* military hardware—though it may include it. Security is *not* military force—though it may involve it. Security is *not* traditional military activity—though it may encompass it.

Security *is* development.

Without development, there can be no security.

A developing nation that does not in fact develop simply cannot remain "secure."

It cannot remain secure for the intractable reason that its own citizenry cannot shed its human nature.

If security implies anything, it implies a minimal measure of order and stability.

Without internal development of at least a minimal degree, order and stability are simply not possible. They are not possible because human nature cannot be frustrated beyond intrinsic limits. It reacts—because it *must.*

Now, that is what we do not always understand; and that is also what governments of modernizing nations do not always understand.

What does McNamara see as the chief cause or causes of protracted group violence within a society? Is "poverty," without further differentiation, the key factor? Take the case of two peasants, one of whom grows two tons of rice on two acres of land that he *owns,* and thus is measured as having an annual family personal income of, say, $200 (with a per capita personal income of $40 for each of five persons). The second peasant grows four tons of rice on four acres of land which he *rents* from a landowner on a year-to-year basis, paying half the crop as rent, and thus is left with two tons for himself, and the same $200 personal income for the year (and $40 per capita personal income) as the first peasant. Which peasant is more likely to become a revolutionary? If the second peasant's children go to school, are they less likely than their father to become revolutionaries, or more likely? Might this depend on other factors, such as the availability of jobs? What if the peasant is black or brown or yellow, and the landowner is white?

Are there close parallels between the factors that McNamara believes causative, and those discussed in the report of the President's Commission on Crime in the first extract of this chapter? If so, should there be a close positive correlation between the figures for homicide and the figures for serious internal group conflict? (But then see Ethiopia and Mexico, both very high on murder, but rather low on domestic group conflict; or Indonesia, very low on murder, but high on domestic group conflict.) Or might McNamara be right, without this conclusion necessarily following? For example, if the translation of poverty or other factors into violent *group* action required the presence of additional catalytic or expediting factors, such as a revolutionary ideology, or adequate communication, or the concentration of population in a single village rather than spread out in individual farms? In McNamara's view, is it likely that, over the long term, deaths from serious or protracted internal conflict (he does not consider *all* group conflict deaths, does he?) would remain about constant on a worldwide basis, would rise, or would fall? Is whatever happens an inexorable process, or does his view carry the necessary conclusion that something can be done to change the acceleration of domestic conflict? Certainly, McNamara's speech opens fascinating vistas as to the factors that might be considered in predicting, and perhaps in preventing, the occurrence of large-scale internal group conflict.

International Group Violence

The preceding selections have dealt with internal conflicts. The major category of lethal conflict not yet covered is, of course, war. Basically, war is a conflict in which the resources and manpower of two or more different societies are engaged in violent opposition.

Discussing the casualty figures from wars, in his book *A Study of War*, Quincy Wright notes the following:[11]

. . . A fifth trend has been toward an increased human and economic cost of war, both absolutely and relative to the population. The human cost of war is a difficult problem to get data upon. The proportion of persons engaged in a battle who are killed has probably tended to decline. During the Middle Ages 30–50 percent of those engaged in a battle were often killed or wounded. In the sixteenth century 40 percent of the defeated side might be killed or wounded and about 10 percent of the victors. The latter cut down the members of the defeated army as they ran away. Thus at the beginning of the modern period the average casualties in battle were probably about 25 percent of those engaged. In the three succeeding centuries the proportion has been estimated as 20, 15, and 10 percent, respectively, and in the twentieth century about 6 percent. Prior to 1900 about a quarter of the battle casualties died, and in World War I about a third; thus the proportion of those engaged in a battle who die as a direct consequence of the battle seems to have declined from about 6 percent to about 2 percent in the last three centuries.

The proportion of the population engaged in the armies, however, has tended to become larger, and the number of battles has tended to increase. As a result, the proportion of the population dying as a direct consequence of battle has tended to increase. The losses from disease in armies has declined. Dumas gives figures of the Napoleonic period suggesting that 80 or 90 percent of the total army losses were from disease. Bloch states that in the nineteenth century this proportion averaged 65 percent. In World War I, while disease accounted for 30 percent of the losses in the Russian army and 26 percent in the American army, in the German army only 10 percent of deaths were from this cause. It has been estimated that, of 1,000 deaths in the French population in the seventeenth century, about 11 died in active military service. The corresponding figure for the eighteenth century is 27; for the nineteenth, 30; and for the twentieth, 63. For England the corresponding figures for these four centuries are 15, 14, 6, and 48.

Now consider the following Department of Defense data on United States casualties in major wars.

WAR	NUMBERS ENGAGED	BATTLE DEATHS	OTHER DEATHS	WOUNDS NOT MORTAL	TOTAL CASUALTIES
Revolutionary War 1775–83	–	4,435	–	6,188	–
War of 1812 1812–15	286,730	2,260	–	4,505	–
Mexican War 1846–48	78,718	1,733	11,550	4,152	17,385
Civil War (Union forces) 1861–65	2,213,363	140,414	224,097	281,881	646,392
Spanish American War – 1898	306,760	385	2,061	1,662	4,108
World War I 1917–18	4,734,991	53,402	63,114	204,002	302,518
World War II 1941–45	16,112,566	291,557	113,842	670,846	1,076,245
Korean War 1950–53	5,720,000	33,629	20,617	103,284	157,530
Vietnam War 1961–		43,737		289,134	

Inaccuracy of figures. The foregoing table raises a variety of questions. Note that this country did not keep reasonably complete records until the Mexican War. What may this suggest about the accuracy of such figures for wars, on a regional or global basis, for the eighteenth and preceding centuries? In fact, the work that has been done by scholars using such figures suggests that room exists for considerable disagreement.

Problems of categorization. The United States data includes both "Battle Deaths" and "Other Deaths" in the "Total Casualties" figure. The "Other Deaths" category comes fairly close to equalling, in number, "Battle Deaths," and may include the effects of such diverse factors as the breakdown of sanitation, bad drinking water, or influenza. Should these deaths be regarded as part of "casualties"? Is it, for some purposes of analysis, significant that "Other Deaths" may not measure the ferocity or effectiveness of the enemy? Are these data adequate to spot trends over time in, for instance, the ratio of mortal to non-mortal wounds? Recall the discussion, on page 11, of the possible impact of improved medical care on apparent homicide rates. Would it be relevant to know what proportion of the wounds that are now non-mortal leave behind lifetime incapacities?

Note in passing that the historical importance attached to a war may not always be reflected in the size of casualty figures. The Revolutionary War, for example, was quite a small conflict, by the standards of both that time and the present. Do all of these United States figures belong on a war-deaths list as distinct from a list of the Yale type on *internal* group violence, assuming that we wished, at least to begin with, to keep two separate lists? What about the Revolution? The Civil War? How would one classify the recent Nigeria-Biafra conflict? If there is a clear geographical division between the contending parties, would it be useful to call the conflict a "war," even though both contenders started as parts of a single political entity? This criterion would categorize the Civil War and the Nigeria-Biafra conflict as "wars" for data-keeping purposes, but wouldn't the American Revolution still belong on the Yale list?

Another index of lethal international conflict. Keeping in mind that there may be serious problems with both the adequacy of definitions ("battle," "casualties") and with the accuracy of the data, consider the following two charts from Wright,[12] *A Study of War:*

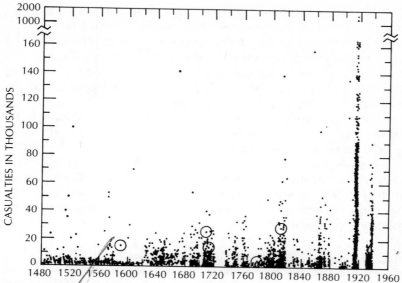

FIG. 8—Dates and casualties of battles of modern civilization, 1480—1940. The circles indicate the battles listed by Creasy.

SOROKIN'S ESTIMATE OF WAR CASUALTIES IN EUROPE, BY CENTURIES, 1000–1925
(000's omitted)

COUNTRY	11th	12th	13th	14th	15th	16th	17th	18th	19th	20th	AVER-AGE SINCE 1600
France		4	11	59	61	107	658	1,055	1,769	3,682	1,791
Austria		8	11	7	100	257	1,560	1,505	226	3,000	1,573
Great Britain	1	7	17	64	86	91	160	310	141	3,095	901
Russia	5	12	29	37	38	118	119	752	777	6,371	2,005
Germany								360	459	6,060	2,293
Spain						160	559	94	166	44	216
Netherlands						64	290	170	34		124
Italy							17	41	54	1,783	474
Poland and Lithu-ania						66	91	348	219		219
Total	7	31	68	167	285	863	3,454	4,635	3,845	24,035	
Per 1,000 popula-lation		2	5	8	10	15	37	33	15	54	

31

It should be mentioned that "casualties" in the preceding tables include both dead and wounded. Also, the figure "per 1,000 population" is compared to the *average* population for the century, not to the *total* number of persons who were born or who died in the century. Sorokin's figure for the twentieth century, of course, includes World War I but stops short of World War II, which would have made his figure per 1,000 population significantly higher.

Conclusions from data on wars. Even though the data may be far from satisfactory, these tables, together with Wright's previously quoted remarks about the proportions of total deaths in the French and English populations attributable to active military service, suggest certain very tentative conclusions. The frequency of battles may have slightly decreased from 1460 to 1960, but the magnitude of battles has generally increased. In this connection, what do you think of the following statement?[13]

Basically, this suggests that modern wars are more likely to be fought in clusters of battles involving multiple national participants, with more time needed to prepare for the next war. But modern technology is likely to make casualties in any given battle higher as that technology develops.

Do Wright's materials also indicate that the relative proportion of populations dying in battles is increasing, as well as the absolute number — that is, that the rate of increase in battle deaths is more than keeping up with the rate of population growth?

Wars and internal group violence. What is the comparative incidence of deaths from clearly international wars, and deaths from internal group violence of the kind measured by the Yale data? It is very difficult to make overall comparisons, although certain general conclusions can be drawn. Does the McNamara speech extract suggest some of these conclusions? Would he expect more large-scale internal conflict as growing, poverty-ridden populations pressed on limited resources of food or farmland?

The more severe internal conflicts (measured at least by deaths intentionally inflicted) have, indeed, occurred in less developed countries in this century. Each of the four internal struggles that has taken an estimated million lives or more in this century has occurred in a society that was chiefly agrarian, underdeveloped, and unindustrialized at the time of the conflict: Mexico (1912–20), Russia (1917–20), Spain (1936–39), and China (1927–49). Another modern

32

conflict, involving such an underdeveloped society, that has taken more than a million lives is, of course, Vietnam (1960–   ). (It is not clear, however, whether this conflict should be classified as internal.) Nigeria and Pakistan might also be included in this category of largest-scale conflicts, if deaths from starvation and disease among non-combatants are counted. If one includes the figures for elimination of the kulaks in Russia in 1927–35 and the gentry in China in 1947–50, the deaths from each of these events would register in the above-one-million range. Similarly, if the Stalinist purges of the late 1930s and the Nazi extermination of Germany's own Jewish population are included within this category of data, several million more deaths must be added. Of all the events just mentioned, only the Nazi acts occurred in an urban and industrialized society.

Data on deaths related to internal group conflict in preceding centuries is very unsatisfactory, but it seems that large-scale conflicts have never been as prevalent as in the twentieth century. Numerous such conflicts in which many thousands of persons died, however, sprinkled the nineteenth and preceding centuries, as well as the present one. (If, however, one takes into account indirect results of fighting, such as deaths from starvation and disease, the most costly internal struggle of the past two centuries is clearly the T'ai P'ing rebellion in China. This struggle is estimated to have cost as many as thirty million lives between 1850 and 1864, mostly from starvation or disease.)

The two largest wars between nations have taken larger overall tolls than even the largest civil conflicts, unless one compares the indirect casualties of the T'ai P'ing rebellion. The mind recoils from the figures in sheer horror. In World War II, there were at least 15,000,000 battle deaths (but this figure includes deaths in military service from all causes for Germany and Russia, the most totally committed combatants). In World War I, there were over 8,500,000 casualties, including deaths in military service from all causes for all countries. Civilian casualties were also enormous in World War II, especially in Russia, which suffered over 6,000,000 dead just among the military. Total deaths have been estimated as high as 20,000,000, including several million deaths from starvation. The Nazis systematically slaughtered millions in Eastern Europe as well as in Russia, and Germany itself may have suffered over a million civilian deaths from bombing and other acts of war.

Against these enormous figures, it is perhaps possible to gain some perspective on various categories of deaths suffered in the United States:

CAUSE	ESTIMATED DEATHS IN 1970
Homicides	15,000
Internal group violence	50–100
External war (Indochina)	5,000
Automobile accidents	55,000

Index of lethal violence in general. Another effort to examine and classify violent deaths was made by Lewis F. Richardson, a mathematical physicist and meteorologist, who devoted many years to the careful collection and analysis of statistics on violent deaths from all causes. Quincy Wright and C. C. Lienan prepared the manuscript of Richardson's *Statistics of Deadly Quarrels,* published after Richardson's death in 1953. Before he died, Richardson had collected exhaustive statistics on violent conflicts from 1820 to 1929 and supplemental statistics on those from 1930 to 1949. Richardson was unhappy with the definitional problems of categorizing various kinds of data on lethal violence, and chose a broader approach. By "wars," Richardson meant both international and civil conflicts,[14] as is seen in the following excerpt; by "deadly quarrel" he meant still more.

It is proposed to count wars of different kinds in order to examine their causes. Before the counting can begin, we need to form a collection or list of wars of all kinds. The less conspicuous incidents are the more numerous — as among the stars — so that it is impossible to make a list of them all. Some rule is therefore necessary for excluding the smaller incidents. The conclusions derived from the subsequent counts are likely to depend on what principle of exclusion has been adopted. The chief obstacles in the way of any objective study of the causes of war are national sentiment and personal prejudice. It is important therefore that the rules for selecting and excluding fightings should be stiff against modification by such influences. Fightings selected for their romance and glory, such as those in *Battles of the Nineteenth Century* by Forbes, Henty, and Griffiths, are quite unsuited to statistical investigation, because one nation's glory is usually another nation's shame. An impressively long list of 278 wars between A. D. 1482 and 1939 has been published by Quincy Wright. Of his selection-rule he says (1942, p. 36): "The legal recognition of the warlike action, the scale of such action, and the importance of its legal and political consequences have, therefore, all been taken into consideration in deciding whether a given incident was sufficiently important to include in a list of wars."

Wright's selection-rule, though probably more objective than glory, is however hardly satisfactory for statistical purposes; because the importance of results is surely a matter of opinion; because opposing belligerents have often differed about what was legal; and because important legal and political effects, such as the separation of Norway from Sweden, have been arranged without war.

An essential characteristic of a war may be said to be casualties. In Sorokin's list of wars, that goes back even further than Wright's to A. D. 1100 (1937, Vol. III), there is for each war a number representing casualties. For the Boer War of 1899–1902 Sorokin's number agrees with statements of the total killed. For some other wars the wounded are added (p. 283). Where more definite evidence is lacking, Sorokin's number is an appraisal depending on the product of the following three factors: (a) the typical size of the army; (b) the number of years of war; (c) an estimate of the intensity of the struggle. In commentary on this plan it may be said that wounds are not suitable for enumeration, because they vary so much from slight to severe. Deaths are more alike, and therefore more reliable as statistical evidence.

Sorokin states the casualties for the greater nations only. If we were to do that, it would introduce a great bias between mechanized and unmechanized peoples. Without going so far as to assert that all men are exactly equal, we can easily forsee what unfair deductions might ensue if we were to record the casualties at the battle of Omdurman as under 500, that being the number for the British and Egyptians, and were to ignore the 10,000 deaths of dervishes.

The list of wars is, I believe, the only one selected and subdivided simply by the total number of deaths. Reasons have been given for thinking that to be the most reliable method for statistical purposes.

From the psychological point of view a war, a riot, and a murder, though differing in many important aspects, social, legal, and ethical, have at least this in common, that they are all manifestations of the instinct of aggressiveness. This Freudian thesis has been developed by Glover, by Durbin and Bowlby, and by Harding. There is thus a psychological justification for looking to see whether there is any statistical connection between war, riot, and murder. By a deadly quarrel is meant any quarrel which caused death to humans. The term thus includes murders, banditries, mutinies, insurrections, and wars small and large; but it excludes accidents, and calamities such as earthquakes and tornadoes. Deaths by famine and disease are included if they were immediate results of the quarrel, but not otherwise. In puzzling cases the legal criterion of "malice aforethought" was taken as a guide.

The record of the number killed in a particular war is often uncertain by a factor of two. The meaningful part of the record can be separated from its uncertainty by taking the logarithm to the base ten and rounding the logarithm off to a whole number, or to the first decimal, according to the quality of the information. For simplicity I have lumped together the deaths on the opposing sides of the quarrel. *The magnitude of a fatal quarrel is defined to be the logarithm to the base ten of the number of people who died because of that quarrel.* The magnitude will be denoted by μ. The range of magnitude extends from 0 for a murder involving only one death, to 7.4 for World War II.

Other well-known wars had magnitudes as follows: 1899–1902 British versus Boers 4.4; 1939–40 Russians versus Finns 4.83; 1861–65 North American Civil War 5.8. The magnitude of a war is usually known to within ±0.2; so that a classification by unit ranges of magnitude is meaningful. These ranges have been marked off at 7.5, 6.5, 5.5, 4.5, 3.5, 2.5, 1.5 and perhaps at 0.5 and −0.5.

This abstract framework becomes of interest when the facts are sorted into it. As far as I have been able to ascertain, the historians have never sorted their facts by the scale of magnitude. The chief obstacle to any scientific study of wars-and-how-to-avoid-them is each nation's habit of blaming other nations. National prejudice can, however, be avoided by taking the whole world as the field of study; and by taking a time-interval longer than personal memory. For this reason I have made a search for the records of fatal quarrels in the whole world since the beginning of A. D. 1820. The task has been long; and the results are here presented in brief summary. For magnitudes greater than 2.5, the facts were mostly obtained from works on history. For magnitudes less than 0.5 they were taken from criminal statistics. For magnitudes between 0.5 and 2.5 the information is scrappy and unorganized; what there is of it suggests that such small fatal quarrels were too numerous and too insignificant to be systematically recorded as history, and yet too large and too political to be recorded as crime.

* * *

An advantage of the logarithmic scale is that it is well adapted to the imperfect state of knowledge, and that it automatically keeps us away from the ridiculous pretense of unjustifiable accuracy, which another notation fosters. For example, three sources quoted by Dumas (1923, p. 23) state the number of dead in the Union army in the American Civil War as 359,528 or 279,376 or 166,623; each, if seen alone, apparently accurate to a man. The corresponding logarithms may be rounded off to 5.6, 5.4, 5.2; a notation which brings out their substantial agreement and indicates their uncertainty by the setting of the last digits below the line.

To get an idea of the significance of Richardson's magnitude figures in the higher ranges, a "quarrel" of the magnitude $7 \pm \frac{1}{2}$, that is, in the range 6.5 to 7.5, involves between 3,162,278 deaths and 31,622,777 deaths. Magnitude 5.5 to 6.5 ranges from 316,228 to 3,162,277 deaths, magnitude 4.5 to 5.5 from 31,623 to 316,227 deaths, magnitude 3.5 to 4.5 from 3,163 to 31,622 deaths, and magnitude 2.5 to 3.5 from 317 to 3,162 deaths.

Further problems of categorization. A number of definitional problems still persisted in Richardson's work, however. In determining what deaths were to be attributed to a given "quarrel," Richardson included deaths of armed personnel, whether the deaths occurred in the fighting, from wounds, or from disease or exposure.

36

He also included civilians who died from wounds, starvation, or "other malicious acts of their enemies." He excluded civilian deaths from exposure or infectious disease growing out of general wartime conditions, "as they appear to have been caused by negligence, or by unforeseen accident, rather than by intention." Most of the deaths in the T'ai P'ing rebellion, for example, appear to be excluded. An equally difficult problem lay in the definition of a "quarrel." Richardson was not satisfied with Wright's "battle" as the unit of statistical investigation, but still recognized problems in seeking an alternative unit of study:[15]

Various actions, scattered both in time and place, are commonly regarded as parts of one war, because they are all expressions of one quarrel, a psychological whole. We recognize in a war a purposive completeness, which a battle has not. That is a good psychological reason for counting wars rather than battles.

The various histories are usually agreed as to what parts make up any war. But occasionally the histories differ; and an awkward choice has to be made between them. For example, all the European revolutions of 1848–49 are lumped together in the following list after the manner of Karl Marx, who regarded them as one class-quarrel; whereas Quincy Wright (1942, p. 645) has selected two portions and called them "Austria-Sardinia" and "Hungarian Insurrection." On the contrary Wright shows a single long war called the "Conquest of Turkestan," 1852–64; whereas, from the descriptions by Curzon, Hellwald, and Milioukov, it would seem proper to regard the conquest as resulting from the Russians' separate quarrels with the Kirghiz, the Khokandians, and the people of Bukhara; each of which incidents was too small to be named in the following list of wars. Some people may object to that omission, saying that the separate quarrels were merely temporary manifestations of a *persistent purpose of expansion*, which was the important psychological unity. There is much to be said for that view. British wars in India before 1857 would form another bunch of the same type. Metcalfe, writing to the Governor-General of India in the early part of last century, expressed the imperialistic secret purpose thus: "There is no doubt that opportunities will arise for effecting such conquests, for with the utmost moderation and justice upon our part, misunderstandings and wars in the course of time will be occasionally unavoidable" (Thompson and Garratt, 1934, p. 267). But if wars are to be lumped together under persistent purposes we should need to do it in all cases: the North American Whites against the Indians would form one bunch, the French wars in Africa another, Bismarck's three wars another, the Japanese wars in Asia another, and so on. There are two reasons why it is more convenient to classify by quarrels than by more persistent purposes: (i) The cause of quarrel has usually been published, whereas the more persistent purpose has been concealed and denied. (ii) Statistical significance, in the technical sense, is more likely to be attained by counting many small pieces than by counting few large lumps. So in the present book the unit is, rightly or wrongly, the quarrel, not the more persistent purpose.

Lethal effects of different size conflicts. The 80 pages of data on specific "quarrels" of magnitude 2.5 to 7.5 (conflicts in the range of 317 to 31,622,777 deaths), in the period 1820 to 1949, reflects a monumental effort of data-gathering. It is by far the best thing of its kind, and constitutes perhaps the most permanently useful part of the volume. In these 130 years, there were just two "quarrels"— World War I and World War II—in the highest range, 6.5 to 7.5. In other magnitude ranges, Richardson made the following count.

5.5 to 6.5	7 conflicts
4.5 to 5.5	26 conflicts
3.5 to 4.5	70 conflicts
2.5 to 3.5	209 conflicts (1820 to 1952, list not fully complete)

Richardson also supplies some data on "quarrels" of smaller magnitudes, particularly on murder (a quarrel of magnitude zero) for which the data since 1820 are at least somewhat complete. For smaller quarrels, especially those in the magnitude range of 0.5 to 2.5 (2 deaths to 316 deaths), complete data is virtually impossible to accumulate. With some interpolation, therefore, Richardson summarizes as follows for the data from 1820 to the end of World War II.[16]

THE TOTAL NUMBER OF PERSONS WHO DIED BECAUSE OF QUARRELS DURING THE 126 YEARS FROM A. D. 1820 TO 1945

ENDS OF RANGE OF MAGNITUDE	TOTAL NUMBER OF DEATHS IN MILLIONS	
$7 \pm \frac{1}{2}$	36	
$6 \pm \frac{1}{2}$	6.7	46.8
$5 \pm \frac{1}{2}$	3.4	
$4 \pm \frac{1}{2}$	0.75	
$3 \pm \frac{1}{2}$	0.30	
$2 \pm \frac{1}{2}$	0.40	2.9
$1 \pm \frac{1}{2}$	2.2	
$0 \pm \frac{1}{2}$	9.7	

Total   59

A remarkable feature of the above table is that the heavy loss of life occurred at the two ends of the sequence of magnitudes, namely the world wars and the murders. The small wars contributed much less to the total. The total deaths because of quarrels should be compared with the *total deaths from all causes*. There are particulars given by de Jastrzebski (E, Death Rate), and in the Statistical Year Books of the League of Nations, which allow the total to be estimated. A mean world population of 1.5×10^9 and a mean death rate of 20 per thousand per year would give during 126 years 3.8×10^9 deaths from all causes. Of these the part caused by quarrels was 1.6 percent. This is less than one might have guessed from the large amount of attention which quarrels attract. Those who enjoy wars can excuse their taste by saying that wars after all are much less deadly than disease.

Thus, during that 126-year period, less than two out of every hundred deaths appear to have been due to lethal violence. This is an extremely striking conclusion. In many ways, however, it is like saying "up until 1945 only ten people died of air pollution." For, as one of the editors subsequently notes with respect to Richardson's comment at the end of the excerpt,[17]

The U.S. Joint Congressional Atomic Energy Sub-Committee in June 1959 invited testimony from the ablest government experts, concerning the *virtual casualties* (to be expected) in the U.S.A. as a result of what it called a "moderate sized" nuclear war.

This was defined as an attack on 70 key U.S.A. cities and 154 military bases with 263 nuclear bombs, at 1,446 equivalent megatons of T.N.T. It was estimated by the experts that the attack would kill 23.0 millions outright, fatally injure 25.9 millions, inflict non-fatal burn injuries on 7.3 million, and harmful radiation dosages on 12.7 million. Estimated deaths for New York City 6.10 million or 47%; Boston 2.14 million or 75%; Baltimore 1.06 million or 79%. The crude virtual death rate would therefore be one in four U.S. persons for the duration (hours). If every U.S. family were to construct a $175 basement shelter, deaths might be cut by 12 million and the injured by 12 million. The Office of Civil and Defense Mobilization was at the moment distributing 50 million books of instructions to further this end (*Time*, July 6, 1959).

This is the most recent of a series of estimates of the virtual magnitude of U.S.A. deaths in a nuclear war. If there are added to 40 or 50 million virtual deaths in the U.S.A., an equal number of deaths in the population staging the attack, the virtual magnitude of quarrel dead equals 8.

The population of the earth is represented, on Richardson's scale, by a magnitude slightly over 9. As we shall see subsequently in discussing modern weapons technology (Chapter 7), it is unfortunately true today that man has it in his capacity, *in a single quarrel*, to extinguish virtually the whole population of the planet. Putting it in Richardson's terms, a 9-magnitude quarrel is technologically possible today. It is no longer necessarily true that "wars after all are much less deadly than disease."

Still, if the pre-atomic age data can give us any clues as to when or where future wars are likely to break out, it can be extremely useful. And Richardson's figure, indicating that less than two out of every hundred deaths over the 1820–1945 period are attributable to lethal violence, at least shows that man is not universally and inexorably bloodthirsty, a broad conclusion to keep in mind when we later study the psychology of human violence (even if one includes suicides, plus unintended deaths from starvation and disease, the deaths traceable to lethal violence appear to be fewer than three out of every hundred). Indeed, one striking fact that Richardson's data underlines is that the greatest risk from even this degree of lethal violence over the 126-year period was from very large-scale wars. World Wars I and II together account for 36 million out of the entire 59 million deaths in his table. Apart from these two conflicts, a person's chance of dying from the direct results of any form of lethal conflict was far less than one in one hundred. The chance of eventually dying as a murder victim was a little over one in four hundred.

Factors related to occurrence of wars. At various points in the text, Richardson attempts to relate the occurrence of wars to observed characteristics of the opposing groups, whether the groups are entire states or groups within states in civil conflict. His tentative conclusions are summarized by the editors in their Introduction.[18]

States have varied from one another in the frequency of their participation in wars during this period, but each has varied so much during its history that none can be properly characterized as inherently belligerent or inherently pacific. The problem of war does not arise from the diabolism of one or a few states.

States have tended to become involved in wars in proportion to the number of states with which they have common frontiers. Contiguity has been an important factor in war during this period.

Common citizenship has not assured peace, nationalism has both induced and prevented wars, but there appear to have been pacifying influences such as common government, intermarriage, common fears, and common culture tending to prevent civil and local wars. The actual occurrence of war has been far less than would be expected from the opportunities for war presented by geographical contiguity. Such occurrences have been even less, proportionately, as the opportunities for war have increased through the advance of sea and air power.

The longer groups have been united by common government, the less has been the probability of war between them.

Allies in one war may become enemies in the next, but alliances seem to have had some influence in preventing war between former allies. That influence, however, declines with the passage of time since the war alliance.

Desire for revenge seems to have been an important cause of war during this period, declining as the inciting war recedes in history but rising slightly after a generation.

Economic causes seem to have figured directly in less than 29 percent of the wars since 1820 and have been more important in small than in large wars. Among such causes taxation of colonials and minorities; economic assistance to an enemy; restrictions on movements of capital, trade and migration; and dissatisfaction of soldiers have had an influence, the importance of which has been approximately in this order. The influence of all these factors together has been less than that of quarrels over territory which may be more political than economic. Relative wealth and poverty of people seem to have had very little influence during this period, contrary to the Marxian assumption that wars arise from class conflict.

Similarity and difference of language seem to have had little influence on the occurrence of wars during this period, contrary to the belief of some advocates of universal languages, except that the Chinese language has been correlated with peacefulness and Spanish with warlikeness.

Similarity of religion seems not to have made for peace, except in the case of Confucianism, but differences of religion have apparently caused war, especially the differences of Christianity and Islam. The statistics suggest, but do not prove, that "Christianity incited war between its adherents."

The larger the number of belligerents in a war, the more neutrals have tended to be drawn in. Wars with many participants have tended to be longer and less frequent.

A trend for war to become indivisible, that is, for every war to become universal, has not been proved. Most wars have been localized. Neutrals have tended to become belligerents only if two or more world powers have been fighting each other.

In proportion to their possible contacts for war-making, sea powers seem to have been less belligerent than land powers.

International relations cannot be considered a chaotic field with all nations equally likely to be infected by war. Geographical relations have exerted great influence.

Several of the findings are based on factors that are reasonably and objectively identifiable, such as the presence of common frontiers. The conclusions in the seventh paragraph about economic causes, however, are based on classifications of data which are extremely complex and very difficult to measure. The tentative conclusions that Richardson reached on this point appear open to grave question, most pointedly in the case of civil conflict.

41

High incidence of lethal conflict.   Finally, we may wish to consider particular countries with high incidences of the various kinds of contemporary lethal violence considered in this chapter. On a basis relative to population, we find the following:

DEATHS PER 100,000 POPULATION, PER *YEAR* DURING THE PERIOD SHOWN, FROM	MEXICO (TYPICAL RECENT YEAR)	SPAIN (1936–39)*	RUSSIA (1941–45)**
Homicide	31.9		
Group violence		1,500+	
War			3,000+

By way of comparison, the death rate within the South Vietnamese population, during the height of the conflict in the late 1960's, was probably on the order of 1,000 per 100,000 population. These statistics create a kind of "Richter scale" of the impact of a particular conflict on a population. Such a scale has many limitations, but at least it allows us one form of comparison that cuts across a variety of kinds of lethal violence.

Concluding note

The data in this chapter is somewhat harder to grasp and apply than much of the other data in this book. What is the gist of the chapter? Perhaps four basic things:

1. There are enormous problems of data classification and selection in the conflict studies area, even with regard to such presumably objective facts as the number of human beings killed by other human beings, at various times and in various places.

2. The available data allows a number of tentative conclusions. Lethal conflict (even including homicide as well as group conflict) has not been a major worldwide cause of death, at least in recent cen-

*This uses the actual period of the conflict, instead of averaging over a longer time span.
**About one third of this figure represents deaths in battle.

turies. Even in terms of existing levels of violence, one must beware of simplistic assertions such as "the United States is a violent society." (If one means to include non-lethal conflict in "violence," or to include "long-time-line" oppression, there is, of course, wide room for judgments which are complex and not easily verifiable.) Lethal conflict as actually practiced still remains a disease chronic and wasting, but not yet in the actual process of destroying the whole human organism. Certain very tentative correlations can be made, such as those between homicide and deprivation (Crime Commission report), internal group conflict and poverty (McNamara), and international war and existence of common boundaries (Richardson). Of the three categories—war, internal group conflict, and homicide—the least meaningful correlations, so far, seem to be for war between nations.

3. Despite an absence of any sweeping or systematic correlations, the various statistics display a number of interesting features that may be significant in relation to other data, or that may lead to a search for other kinds of data. Homicides in a wide variety of cultures, including the Scandinavian states, the Republic of Ireland, England, Malaysia, and Ghana, appear to be very infrequent. By contrast, homicides among black Americans, Colombians, Mexicans, and Ethiopians occur 50 to 100 times as often as in these low-frequency societies. However, while the study of homicide may give us clues to the causation of at least certain other kinds of lethal conflict, it must be kept in mind that roughly five out of six deaths from *all* lethal conflict in the 1820–1945 period came from lethal *group* conflict, and that the two great wars alone accounted for 60 percent of all deaths by lethal violence during that period. At least six primarily internal conflicts, each claiming more than a million lives, have also erupted since 1910. The twentieth century so far appears to have been markedly more violent than the nineteenth in terms of group conflict and in the proportion of all deaths caused by conflict. Even allowing for very wide margins of error in the older data, the twentieth is probably the most violent century of the past millennium (in terms of proportion of population killed), at least for the Western societies, although the seventeenth and eighteenth centuries may not be far behind.

4. Simple statistical data, however, holds out no readily apparent hope for shortcutting further analysis. It certainly does not tell us that war or lethal conflict are inevitable. But neither does it tell us that, pending our discovery of what causes lethal conflict, we can predict when it will occur or prevent it. On the contrary, it leaves fully open

the horrendous possibility that, having now developed the means with which to destroy all life on earth, man will someday exercise them.

Must we add that he will do so "for reasons unknown and causes unpreventable"? We now set down the long path of determining whether this fatalistic statement can be altered.

FOOTNOTES, CHAPTER 1

[1] "The Challenge of Crime in a Free Society," *Report of the President's Commission on Law Enforcement and Administration of Justice* (Washington: 1967), pp. 30–45.

[2] Data are taken from the *New York Times Encyclopedic Almanac, 1970* (New York: 1969), p. 494; and World Health Organization, *World Health Statistics Annual, 1968* (New York: 1968).

[3] Erich Fromm, *The Sane Society* (New York: Rinehart, 1955), pp. 16–17.

[4] Data are taken from Fred P. Graham, "A Contemporary History of American Crime," in *Violence in America, Report of the National Commission on the Causes and Prevention of Violence* (New York: Bantam Books, 1969), p. 491; and the *Statistical Abstract of the United States, 1965* (New York: Pocket Books, Inc., 1965), Table 226.

[5] H. A. Block and G. Gleis, *Man, Crime and Society: the Forms of Criminal Behavior* (New York: Random House, Inc., 1962), p. 261.

[6] J. C. Gillin and F. M. Ochberg, "Firearms Control and Violence," in *Violence and the Struggle for Existence,* ed. Daniels, Gilula, and Ochberg (Boston: Little, Brown & Co., 1970), pp. 241–257. The study was made by Frank Zimring of the University of Chicago Law School.

[7] Bruce M. Russett, Haywood R. Alker, Jr., Karl W. Deutsch, Harold D. Lasswell, *World Handbook of Political and Social Indicators* (New Haven: Yale University Press, 1964), pp. 97–100.

[8] Associated Press Dispatch, September 1968.

[9] Ivo K. Feierabend, undated mimeograph (San Diego State College).

[10] From a speech by Robert S. McNamara, delivered in Montreal, Canada, on May 18, 1966.

[11] Quincy Wright, A Study of War (Chicago: University of Chicago Press, 1965), pp. 242–43.

[12] Wright, *A Study of War,* p. 656.

[13] Wright, *A Study of War,* p. 242.

[14] Lewis F. Richardson, *Statistics of Deadly Quarrels,* ed. Quincy Wright and C. C. Lienau (Pittsburgh: Boxwood Press, 1960), pp. 4–7.

[15] Richardson, *Statistics of Deadly Quarrels,* p. 4.

[16] Richardson, *Statistics of Deadly Quarrels,* p. 153.

[17] Richardson, *Statistics of Deadly Quarrels,* p. 161.

[18] Richardson, *Statistics of Deadly Quarrels,* p. x–xiii.

2

Views on Causation:

Biology and psychology

Is man the only species that deliberately kills his own kind? If so, why is this deplorable characteristic found only in *Homo sapiens?* And is it an inherited trait that cannot be altered, or is lethal aggression induced by environmental circumstances? These are some of the questions that this chapter attempts to answer.

Aggression in Other Species

Consider the following passage from Konrad Lorenz' *On Aggression*, a contemporary study of the role of aggression in certain other species, and of the relevance of this animal behavior to the understanding of human aggression. This excerpt is from a chapter entitled "What Aggression is Good For":[1]

Darwin had already raised the question of the survival value of fighting, and he has given us an enlightening answer: It is always favorable to the future of a species if the stronger of two rivals takes possession either of the territory or of the desired female. As so often, this truth of yesterday is not the untruth of today but only a special case; ecologists have recently demonstrated a much more essential function of aggression. Ecology — derived from the Greek *oikos*, the house — is the branch of biology that deals with the manifold reciprocal relations of the organism to its natural surroundings — its "household" — which of course includes all other animals and plants native to the environment. Unless the special interests of a social organization demand close aggregation of its members, it is obviously most expedient to spread the individuals of an animal species as evenly as possible over the available habitat. To use a human analogy: if, in a certain area, a larger number of doctors, builders, and mechanics want to exist, the representatives of these professions will do well to settle as far away from each other as possible.

The danger of too dense a population of an animal species settling in one part of the available biotope and exhausting all its sources of nutrition and so starving can be obviated by a mutual repulsion acting on the animals of the same species, effecting their regular spacing out, in much the same manner as electrical charges are regularly distributed all over the surface of a spherical conductor. This, in plain terms, is the most important survival value of intraspecific aggression.

Now we can understand why the sedentary coral fish in particular are so crazily colored. There are few biotopes on earth that provide so much and such varied nutrition as a coral reef. Here fish species can, in an evolutionary sense, take up very different professions: one can support itself as an "unskilled laborer," doing what any average fish can do, hunting creatures that are neither poisonous nor armor-plated nor prickly, in other words hunting all the defenseless organisms approaching the reef from the open sea, some as "plankton," others as active swimmers "intending" to settle on the reef, as millions of free-swimming larvae of all coral-dwelling organisms do. On the other hand, another fish species may specialize in eating forms of life that live on the reef itself and are therefore equipped with some sort of protective mechanism which the hunting fish must render harmless.

* * *

It is essential to consider the fact that all these opportunities for special careers, known as ecological niches, are often provided by the same cubic

46

yard of ocean water. Because of the enormous nutritional possibilities, every fish, whatever its specialty, requires only a few square yards of sea bottom for its support, so in this small area there can be as many fish as there are ecological niches, and anyone who has watched with amazement the thronging traffic on a coral reef knows that these are legion. However, every one of this crowd is determined that no other fish of his species should settle in his territory. Specialists of other "professions" harm his livelihood as little as, to use our analogy again, the practice of a doctor harms the trade of a mechanic living in the same village.

In less densely populated biotopes where the same unit of space can support three or four species only, a resident fish or bird can "afford" to drive away all living beings, even members of species that are no real threat to his existence; but if a sedentary coral fish tried to do the same thing, it would be utterly exhausted and, moreover, would never manage to keep its territory free from the swarms of noncompetitors of different "professions." It is in the occupational interests of all sedentary species that each should determine the spatial distribution that will benefit its own individuals, entirely without consideration for other species. The colorful "poster" patterns, described in Chapter One, and the fighting reactions elicited by them, have the effect that the fish of each species keep a measured distance only from nutritional competitors of the same species. This is the very simple answer to the much discussed question of the function of the colors of coral fish.

As I have already mentioned, the species-typical song of birds has a very similar survival value to that of the visual signals of fishes. From the song of a certain bird, other birds not yet in possession of a territory recognize that in this particular place a male is proclaiming territorial rights. It is remarkable that in many species the song indicates how strong and possibly how old the singer is, in other words, how much the listener has to fear him. . . .

Among mammals, which mostly "think through their noses," it is not surprising that marking of the territory by scent plays a big role. Many methods have been tried; various scent glands have been evolved, and the most remarkable ceremonies developed around the depositing of urine and feces; of these the leg-lifting of the domestic dog is the most familiar. . . .

Even in the case of animals whose territory is governed by space only, the hunting ground must not be imagined as a property determined by geographical confines; it is determined by the fact that in every individual the readiness to fight is greatest in the most familiar place, that is, in the middle of its territory. In other words, the threshold value of fight-eliciting stimuli is at its lowest where the animal feels safest, that is, where its readiness to fight is least diminished by its readiness to escape. As the distance from this "headquarters" increases, the readiness to fight decreases proportionately as the surroundings become stranger and more intimidating to the animal. If one plotted the graph of this decrease the curve would not be equally steep for all directions in space. In fish, the center of whose territory is nearly always on the bottom, the decline in readiness to fight is most marked in the vertical direction because the fish is threatened by special dangers from above.

The territory which an animal apparently possesses is thus only a matter of variations in readiness to fight, depending on the place and on various local factors inhibiting the fighting urge. In nearing the center of the territory the aggressive urge increases in geometrical ratio to the decrease in distance from this center. This increase in aggression is so great that it compensates for all differences ever to be found in adult, sexually mature animals of a species. If we know the territorial centers of two conflicting animals, such as two garden redstarts or two aquarium sticklebacks, all other things being equal, we can predict, from the place of encounter, which one will win: the one that is nearer home.

When the loser flees, the inertia of reaction of both animals leads to that phenomenon which always occurs when a time lag enters into a self-regulating process — to an oscillation. The courage of the fugitive returns as he nears his own headquarters, while that of the pursuer sinks in proportion to the distance covered in enemy territory. Finally the fugitive turns and attacks the former pursuer vigorously and unexpectedly and, as was predictable, he in his turn is beaten and driven away. The whole performance is repeated several times till both fighters come to a standstill at a certain point of balance where they threaten each other without fighting.

The position, the territorial "border," is in no way marked on the ground but is determined exclusively by a balance of power and may, if this alters in the least, for instance if one fish is replete and lazy, come to lie in a new position somewhat nearer the headquarters of the lazy one. An old record of our observations on the territorial behavior of two pairs of cichlids demonstrates this oscillation of the territorial borders. Four fish of this species were put into a large tank and at once the strongest male, A, occupied the left, back, lower corner and chased the other three mercilessly around the whole tank; in other words, he claimed the whole tank as his territory. After a few days, male B took possession of a tiny space immediately below the surface in the diagonally opposite right, front, upper corner. There he bravely resisted the attacks of the first male. This occupation of an area near the surface is in a way an act of desperation for one of these fish, because it is risking great danger from aerial predators in order to hold its own against an enemy of its own species, which, as already explained, will attack less resolutely in such a locality. In other words, the owner of such a dangerous area has, as an ally, the fear which the surface inspires in its bad neighbor. During succeeding days, the space defended by B grew visibly, expanding downward until he finally took his station in the right, front, lower corner, so gaining a much more satisfactory headquarters. Now at last he had the same chances as A, whom he quickly pressed so far back that their territories divided the tank into two almost equal parts. It was interesting to see how both fishes patrolled the border continuously, maintaining a threatening attitude. Then one morning they were doing this on the extreme right of the tank, again around the original headquarters of B, who could now scarcely call a few square inches his own. I knew at once what had happened: A had paired, and since it is characteristic of all large cichlids that both partners take part in territorial defense, B was subjected to double pressure and his territory had decreased accordingly. Next day the fish were again in the middle of the tank, threatening each other across the "border," but now there were four, because B had also taken a mate, and thus the balance of power with the A family was restored. A week later I found the border far toward the left lower area, and encroaching on A's former territory. The reason for this was that the A couple had spawned and since one of the partners was busy looking after the eggs, only one at a time was able to attend to frontier defense. As soon as the B couple had also spawned, the previous equal division of space was re-established. Julian Huxley once used a good metaphor to describe this behavior: he compared the territories to air-balloons in a closed container, pressing against each other and expanding or contracting with the slightest change of pressure in each individual one. This territorial aggression, really a very simple mechanism of behavior-physiology, gives an ideal solution to the problem of the distribution of animals of any one species over the available area in such a way that it is favorable to the species as a whole. Even the weaker specimens can exist and reproduce, if only in a very small space. This has special significance in creatures which reach sexual maturity long before they are fully grown.

* * *

We can safely assume that the most important function of intra-specific aggression is the even distribution of the animals of a particular species over an inhabitable area, but it is certainly not its only one. Charles Darwin had already observed that sexual selection, the selection of the best and strongest animals for reproduction, was furthered by the fighting of rival animals, particularly males. The strength of the father directly affects the welfare of the children in those species in which he plays an active part in their care and defense. The correlation between male parental care and rival fighting is clear, particularly in those animals which are not territorial in the sense which the Cichlids demonstrate but which wander more or less nomadically, as, for example, large ungulates, ground apes, and many others. In such animals, intra-specific aggression plays no essential part in the "spacing out" of the species. Bisons, antelopes, horses, etc., form large herds, and territorial borders and territorial jealousy are unknown to them since there is enough food for all. Nevertheless the males of these species fight each other violently and dramatically, and there is no doubt that the selection resulting from this aggressive behavior leads to the evolution of particularly strong and courageous defenders of family and herd; conversely, there is just as little doubt that the survival value of herd defense has resulted in selective breeding for hard rival fights. This interaction has produced impressive fighters such as bull bison or the males of the large baboon species; at every threat to the community, these valiantly surround and protect the weaker members of the herd.

The survival value of fighting. Although Lorenz offers many other examples of the survival value of fighting, the chief example in the above text is one about cichlids, a species of fish. Is this example likely to be more or less persuasive, in drawing analogies from the animal behavior to human behavior, than an example taken from the behavior of baboons or chimpanzees? Of ants or bees?

Is it also of possible significance that the quoted example concerned captive cichlids? What of the fact that they were put in a large tank? How might the conditions of captivity affect the outcome of the experiment? What are some comparable problems that might arise in experiments constructed to find out why humans fight other humans?

Consider Lorenz' discussion of sound, color, and odor and how they mark territorial claims for various species. Can you think of possible human analogies?

In the excerpt, Lorenz talks about the "survival value of fighting." Does he mean to suggest that *all* fighting has such survival value? What fighting might *not* have survival value, in Lorenz' terms?

Mechanisms inhibiting aggressions. Consider, in connection with the last question, the following compilation of the observations of naturalists and others concerning intra-specific aggression in mammals. L. Harrison Matthews is the author of the report, "Overt Fighting in Mammals," which comes out of a 1964 British symposium on *The Natural History of Aggression*.[2]

Intraspecific fighting has been divided into two kinds, ritual and overt, the first a formalized sparring match with strict rules, the second a fight to the death with the gloves off and nothing barred. In preparing this paper the more I have sought examples of such intraspecific overt fighting in mammals the less I have succeeded, and I doubt that it normally occurs in nature.

Fighting needs weapons, and most mammals use their teeth and claws, structures that originally had other functions. Both teeth, primarily used for seizing food and reducing it to fragments, and claws, primarily a protection for the ends of the digits, are easily adapted as efficient weapons of aggression through a little emphasis on their size, shape, and sharpness. In many orders of mammals they are variously adapted as weapons, tools with many different uses, and, at least the teeth, even as sexual and status symbols.

Aggressive weapons that are neither teeth nor claws have been evolved in only a very few orders of mammals. Because one of these orders, the artiodactyles, is widely distributed and numerous in species we are inclined to think that special aggressive weapons are of widespread occurrence among the mammals. But are they? They are present in only three orders, the monotremes, the perissodactyles, and the artiodactyles. (Stink glands are so only interspecifically; intraspecifically they are scent glands. Spines and armour are defensive, not aggressive adaptations.) The male platypus and echidna have on the inner side of the ankle a spur connected with a "poison" gland. Among the perissodactyles the rhinoceroses have nasal horns, and among the artiodactyles the deer have antlers, and the cattle, sheep, goats, and antelopes have horns. These three orders have two characters in common — they have reduced dentition and, except the echidna, no effective claws.

The function of the monotreme spur, whether as weapon or sexual stimulant is unknown, so we cannot discuss it here. The feet of rhinoceroses, adapted for carrying great weight and protected by hoof-like nails, are not weapons. The African rhinoceroses, which have the largest nasal horns, have no incisor teeth whereas the Asiatic species, which have comparatively small horns, have incisors modified as tusks. In all species, however, the horn or horns seem to be used less as intraspecific weapons than as sexual stimulants in the rough horse-play of courtship behaviour. In all the artiodactyles except the pigs and hippopotamus the upper incisors are reduced or absent; in many the upper canines are small and the lower ones incisiform. The limbs, with digits reduced in number and highly specialized for running, are provided with hooves. It is the artiodactyles with deficient anterior dentition that possess antlers or horns; in those without special weapons such as the musk and water deer, the chevrotain and some others the upper canines are tusks large enough to project between the lips when the mouth is shut. The weapons of the camelids are the canines reinforced by the retained caniniform outer incisor of the upper jaw.

Weapons, other than teeth and claws, are thus uncommon among the mammals although the accident of the artiodactyles containing a great diversity of species gives the contrary impression at first sight. It might be suggested that the diversity is the result of efficient arming with special weapons, but that argument seems invalid in view of the much greater number of species among orders such as the bats or rodents which are armed with nothing more than teeth and claws.

The use of weapons in interspecific fighting is primarily for protection against predators or for the capture of prey, functions that are readily understandable as biologically advantageous to the species. But it is not easy to see how intraspecific strife can have any value; it might eliminate the weaker individuals but the hazards of the environment will do that without action within the species.

Indeed on examining intraspecific fighting more than superficially it is at once apparent that an important part of animal behaviour, at least in the mammals, is directed towards avoiding intraspecific fighting. The weapons are potentially so dangerous that fighting is ritualized into display, threat, and submission or appeasement, so that fights are generally no more than trials of strength followed by disengagement and rapid withdrawal by the weaker. This does not mean that fights never end fatally, for a threat that is never carried out loses its meaning, but fighting to the death rarely happens in the normal environment.

It is, indeed, very difficult to find any examples of true overt fighting resulting in the death of the loser among mammals under normal conditions in the wild. It occurs only when population numbers have overtaken the resources of the environment so that serious overcrowding is brought about. This produces a situation similar to that of animals in captivity where the environment is artificially restricted so that aggression is increased and any chance of escape from the aggressor is denied. In both situations the animals are living in a biologically unsound environment which inevitably distorts the normal patterns of social behaviour. Even in overcrowded conditions, as

51

for example during a vole plague, when the crash comes the animals do not necessarily die as a consequence of intraspecific fighting but rather from a general condition of stress.

The hippopotamus provides an example of overcrowding leading to fatal fighting. Verheyen found that in the Upper Semliki between Lake Edward and the River Karurume, a distance of 32 kilometres, there was a minimum of 2,087 hippopotamuses, or an average of one hippo to every 15 metres, with a greatest concentration of one hippo to every 5 metres in the upper $5\frac{1}{2}$ kilometres. In these conditions each group of females and young is attended by up to six adult males of approximately equal social rank in the hierarchy, each dominant only in the neighborhood of his own wallow in the river. The males maintain their territories and their social rank by threat and fighting, most commonly by threat alone followed by withdrawal of the weaker. Fighting in different degrees of severity occurs, and wounds that appear to be very severe are inflicted, but as Verheyen points out hippos are well adapted to fighting and its consequences by their very thick skin on the back, flanks, rump, and tail, and by the astonishing speed with which the wounds heal. Nevertheless, when overcrowded, fighting sometimes ends with the death of one combatant: Verheyen examined the bodies of five hippos thus killed during the period when he made his observations.

Among the ungulates, fighting between stags of the red deer has been studied by Fraser Darling (1937) who shows that the antlers are used for threat and for fierce sparring but that the death of the vanquished is uncommon. For instance he watched an old switch stag take possession of a group of twelve hinds; among them there were six young stags which the old one chased out of the group one by one. Not one of them stopped to contest the point. The stag herded the hinds to join with two other groups of nine and six near which two eight pointer stags were standing. "These two stags, which were fairly fresh and in fine fettle, took good care to keep out of the way of the old switch, and he took no notice of them." The two stags roared at each other and approached with heads lowered; "the stags took slow steps forward, then a quick run, and their antlers were together. . . . And now one of them side-stepped and lunged, but the other wheeled his hind end and met his opponent's antlers with his own. The point in all these fights is to lunge a broadside in the opponent's ribs, and to prevent this happening to oneself. Much of the fight therefore, consists of a shoving match, antlers to antlers. The stag which can shove the harder is usually the winner, his opponent retiring before he gets a broadside." Darling further states, "Their hurts in fight seem to be of small account and a fatality is rare. The incidence of fighting is much exaggerated in popular literature describing deer. There is more noise and show than real fight . . . only stags of equal merit fight each other. No stag will face another better than himself."

Darling makes a very interesting remark about deer confined in parks where their numbers reach a high artificial density. "There stags fight in season and out, and stags will kill calves and strange hinds under such conditions. In short, overcrowding results in anti-social behaviour which in itself is one type of check to the further increase of a cramped population."

52

Pedersen (1962) found that in Greenland in areas with large populations of musk ox many skirmishes could be seen in the spring but rarely decisive fights. Often the solitary bulls try their luck against the superior herd leaders, and generally they are chased off at the first encounter. If a bull in full vigour is separated from his herd he becomes very restless at the rutting season and tramps around looking for another. As soon as he scents one he approaches and challenges the owner who will not be chased away so that a more serious fight occurs, the animals charging each other head on and crashing their frontal shields together. Pedersen watched such a fight for half an hour until one of the bulls seemed to be weakening: "The last shock pushed it over on to its hindquarters, and while its adversary prepared for a new assault it got up, turned round, and fled. The other bull made a show of pursuing it, and then returned to the herd." Pedersen adds that sometimes one of the bulls is killed and that he had seen the skeleton of a musk ox that had died from a fracture of the frontal part of the skull, and says he had been told of two others. He concludes, "It is, however, only rarely that fights finish in this way."

These examples are typical of the fighting behaviour in all the horned ungulates, where the weapons may be used in real earnest interspecifically, particularly against predators, but intraspecifically only to maintain territory or social rank or both, and not usually for killing rivals.

Barnett includes some interesting observations on intraspecific fighting in his studies on social behaviour in wild rats. He was able to establish caged colonies of wild *Rattus norvegicus* in which there was little or no fighting unless a strange rat was introduced. Fighting is essentially territorial and depends upon one rat, especially an adult male, being in a familiar place and encountering a stranger. Combat consists of tooth-chattering, threat posturing, leaping over the stranger and biting him. Barnett states that the biting is a pain-causing action likely to evoke flight in the rat attacked, and that it did attempt to escape by climbing up the side of the cage. In the experiments, however, there was little opportunity for flight and invariably the attacked rat soon died. The cause of death was not, as might be expected, the wounds caused by biting for they were always superficial and slight; the animals died from internal stress produced by the impossibility of completing their normal pattern of behaviour by escaping from the aggressor.

Among the carnivora the pinnipedes are generally highly social and polygamous animals during the breeding season in which the bulls defend territories and maintain harems of cows. In a polygamous species in which the sex ratio at birth is approximately even there must be a large number of males superfluous to the breeding needs of the species. Among the pinnipedes the master bulls keep their places by fighting their rivals. In a rookery of elephant seals numerous bachelor bulls loiter on the outskirts of the harems and try to poach the outlying.cows while the master bull's attention is engaged elsewhere, but they generally quickly retreat without waiting to fight if he makes a rush at them. A serious fight takes place only when a strange bull seriously challenges the master. The method of fighting is stereotyped; the bulls approach each other closely, rear up on the hinder part of the body to a height of eight or nine feet, inflate their trunks and open their mouths widely giving vent to loud belching roars. They then throw themselves forward upon each other trying to tear the opponent with the large upper canine teeth. The blows are generally taken on the sides of the neck which are much lacerated so that the old bulls are covered with a mass of wrinkled scars. Sometimes the damage is more serious, as when eyes are burst or knocked out or trunks are torn open, but the elephant seal, like the hippopotamus, is well adapted to fighting and can take a lot of punishment without serious results. I have never seen or heard of well matched elephant seals killing each other; the fights though apparently furious do not last long and as soon as the vanquished breaks away the victor chases him only to the territory boundary before returning to his cows. Fighting on a much less intense level often occurs between younger bulls without harems, and although many scars result the contestants, which are not defending territories, do not appear to be in great earnest.

The grey seal has a similar social structure of territories and harems, but its fighting is much less spectacular. If a master bull can catch an interloper a fight follows in which the bulls bite and tear each others' necks, but an intruder seldom waits to fight and retreats when the bull in possession of territory hastens towards him.

In the walrus the canine teeth are enlarged as long external tusks which are used for helping to hoist the heavy animals on to floating ice or over rocks ashore, and for fighting. Lamont (1876) says that "walruses use their tusks against one another very much in the method that game cocks use their beaks. From the animal's unwieldy appearance and the position of his tusks one is apt to fancy that the latter can only be used in a stroke downwards but on the contrary they can turn their necks with great facility and quickness and can strike either upwards, downwards, or sideways with equal dexterity. I frequently observed them fighting with great ferocity on the ice and the skins of the old bulls which are light coloured and nearly devoid of hair, are often covered with scars and wounds received from these encounters." He does not, however, suggest that fighting results in more than superficial damage — the walrus, like other large animals, is pretty tough and ignores anything but a mortal wound.

The sea lions and fur seals also are tough hard-fighting pinnipedes, which defend territories and harems during the breeding season. Bull fur seals of the Pribilof Islands are large animals weighing three or four times as much as the cows. They come ashore on to the breeding beaches a week or more before the cows arrive, and while waiting for them they take up their territories. The best territories are near the water's edge, and the first comers are quickly challenged by latter arrivals which try to drive them from their positions to the lower grade territories further up the shore. They are immensely strong animals and fight ferociously but, although they appear to inflict grievous wounds, the damage is generally superficial and it is the exception for one of the contestants to be killed. When the cows arrive the bulls with territories nearest the water get the first pick so that it is not until their harems become too large for effective supervision that the bulls holding the less valuable territories further inland receive the overflow. The heavily pregnant cows get very rough treatment from the bulls but they too are tough and can take it. In a few days they give birth to their pups and quickly become receptive to the bulls at their post partum oestrus.

Among the fissipede carnivores that are gregarious and have a highly evolved social structure, such as the wolf, fighting is so ritualized that it lies beyond the scope of this paper. Wolves are potentially so dangerous to each other that an elaborate chain of submissive reactions of increasing intensity culminating in the weaker contestant throwing itself on its back to expose all the vulnerable parts of the body defenceless to the superior who refrains from taking the advantage presented, ensures that intraspecific fighting does not end fatally.

Crowcroft (1957) found that the common shrew fully lives up to its reputation of being very quarrelsome. A shrew holds only a small territory consisting of little more than its nest, and forages over an extensive home range which overlaps those of its neighbours. When two foraging shrews blunder into each other through their limited powers of sight—they rely chiefly on their sense of touch—they scream shrilly, bite each other's tail and feet, and appear to be locked in mortal combat. Suddenly one breaks away, rears up, and throws itself on its back, showing the lighter colouring of the belly. Does the victor at this signal rush in and tear out the throat of his helpless rival? On the contrary it immediately turns tail and runs silently away. This pattern of aggressive behaviour is independent of sex and individual recognition, and ceases only during oestrus and copulation. Crowcroft points out that "the food of shrews is scattered about in tiny parcels" each of which must supply sufficient energy to keep the animal going long enough to find another. "The road to survival lies, not in hunting intensively through a patch of litter or soil for something which may not be there, but in rapidly and superficially inspecting many such patches. In a familiar area an animal learns the best places to find food and makes its way from one to another quickly and by safe routes." He concludes that the fighting of shrews is a mechanism which helps to separate animals whose feeding areas overlap, and which does so with the minimum expenditure of time and energy. It does not result in injury or death.

Work on the social structure of groups of several species of primates such as the pioneer studies of Zuckerman, has mostly been carried out on colonies in captivity. Similar work in the field, such as that of Goodall (1963) on chimpanzees and of Hall (1963) on baboons has shown that the social hierarchies in the natural environment are much less rigid than in the artificial one of captivity. In captivity the animals of lower social rank cannot avoid infringing the territories of their superiors so that there is much emotional arousal, continual displays of threat or submission, and frequent fights from which the weaker cannot escape. In the wild the animals do not live in this state of emotional tension, and although the dominant animal takes the first place he is not forced to be constantly holding his position by aggressive behaviour.

Goodall found that among groups of chimpanzees the dominant male tolerated the presence of other adult males, and that there is no fighting for food or females provided he is given precedence. The baboons studied in South Africa by Hall, on the other hand, lived in troops with only one dominant adult male, a number of females and young of both sexes. The subadult males when approaching maturity leave the troop. The baboon resembles the

55

seals in being polygamous and in having an approximately even sex ratio at birth; a high proportion of the males must therefore be superfluous to the reproductive needs of the species. There is no evidence, however, that the dominant males fight with or kill these superfluous potential rivals, and at present nothing is known of what happens to them. In polygamous mammals nature seems to be as lavishly wasteful of male somatic cells as she is universally of male gametes.

Wood Jones describes fighting in some of the marsupials of South Australia when confined in captivity and he says: "Bandicoots are desperately pugnacious . . . their methods of fighting are peculiar. The aggressor will tirelessly follow his victim until he wears him down . . . when one animal overtakes the other and presses it to an engagement the assault is made by a jump and an endeavour to strike with the claws of the hind feet. Each stroke carried home removes some hair from the victim's back and scratches the thin skin. . . . They seem never to fight face to face for when the chase leads to such a meeting, one instantly jumps over the other inflicting a blow with the hind foot in passing and renews the attack from the rear. Only as a last resort, although the whole encounter has been conducted with open mouths, do they start to bite each other." . . . "Barred bandicoots (*Perameles*) become very tame and familiar in captivity but although they are extremely gentle when kept as pets, they are desperately pugnacious among themselves. On one occasion when eight live specimens were sent from Ooldea, all eight were dead and almost devoid of hair when they arrived in Adelaide. They had fought each other to the death on the railway journey . . . the fighting is done largely with the long feet."

Of the Nuyt's Islands bandicoot, *Isoodon nauticus,* Wood Jones says: "In captivity the island bandicoot displays habits exactly similar to those of its larger mainland relatives. . . . Owing to the density of the bandicoot population on the island, fights must be very frequent and only one specimen with a whole tail was captured; all other examples possessed nothing but mere stubs of varying length; ragged ears are also the rule." These injuries, however, do not tally with the method of fighting he describes, which is also found in the rat-kangaroo (*Bettongia*). "Even if kept in large runs when in captivity the males will fight to the death . . . one animal pursuing and scratching the fur from the other as it jumps over it. In this way the victim is worn out; and plucked of its fur and scored by deep furrows produced by its rival's strong claws, it dies of exhaustion."

By no means are all the marsupials so aggressive intraspecifically for in describing the habits of *Chaetocercus,* the crest-tailed pouched mouse, he tells how it kills mice and birds for food and adds: "Although such bloodthirsty little animals they do not quarrel among themselves and they may be placed together in a cage regardless of sex or acquaintance; in this respect they differ remarkably from several less carnivorous marsupials."

These Australian fighters are evidently strongly territorial so that they cannot tolerate the presence of an intruder. The fighting to the death described by Wood Jones took place when the animals were held in captivity in quarters too narrow to provide space for more than one territory. He does not suggest that fighting among these creatures when free has a similar result, and he tacitly admits as much in pointing out that the high density of the population of bandicoots on Nuyt's Island was the cause of fighting and mutilation.

All the examples of intraspecific fighting described in this brief survey show the impossibility of sharply separating overt from ritual fighting, for the two form a cline with very different ends joined by an unbroken line. Even in overt fighting the technique of the ring follows a stereotyped pattern with the result that a fight seldom ends with the death of the weaker, which is generally able to break away and escape. Observations on animals in the restricted environment of captivity, where the victor kills the vanquished because it cannot escape, give no reliable conclusions about what happens in the wild.

Overt fighting usually ends with the submission of one of the contestants. The action of fleeing is equally as submissive as the action of the wolf or shrew that throws itself on its back before the victor. Just as the dominant wolf does not go in for the kill when he could so the winning stag, rat, or seal is content with a token pursuit which he quickly abandons to return to his territory or females. Perhaps the pattern of submission in the wolf is correlated with the fact that the wolves of a pack do not hold individual territories so that fleeing would only invite pursuit and could not express submission because there is no territory to vacate in favour of the stronger.

Both overt and ritual fighting show a conflict between the interests of the individual and those of the species. The interest of the individual is to have no rivals for the possession of his territory or females. Carried to its extreme this interest would result in the survival of so few males that the gene pool might become so restricted that the species could not survive. The interest of the species is to keep the gene pool well mixed, and it is therefore probable that natural selection has preserved patterns of behaviour that do not result in widespread slaughter. It may be that species which did not possess such a pattern have by its very absence become extinct.

The suggestion is sometimes made that intraspecific fighting is of survival value to a species because it ensures that the strongest males breed. But there is no proof that these animals will beget better offspring, for it is the genotype not the phenotype that matters — although the strongest phenotype is no doubt the best vehicle for the genotype. In South Georgia during the last forty years the effect of the sealing industry in killing the largest bull elephant seals has been the extinction of the huge "beachmasters" that formerly dominated the harems of cows. The bulls now have a much shorter expectation of life, but were sealing abandoned there is no doubt that in the course of time they would grow into monsters similar to their great grandfathers.

There must be an extremely strong inhibition restraining the victor in a fight from giving the death blow when the rival submits. In man the forebearance might be termed mercy, but ascribing the quality of mercy to animals would be straining things too far. Further work is needed to determine whether the inhibition is innate or learnt, but whatever its origin its effect prevents violent aggressive behaviour within a species from bringing about the death of large numbers of animals. Only one species of mammal habitually disregards it — and he is at present in a very insecure state, in spite of the fact that he is the world's dominant species.

Fatal fighting in man may be associated with the use of tools; it is not easy to kill a rival with the bare hands, though it can be done. But when tools are used weapons can become so dangerous that a rival can be quickly killed before he has a chance to break away or submit. . . .

Do the facts cited by Matthews generally tally well with Lorenz' views? If so, is this information about mammal behavior more persuasive than Lorenz' cichlid example?

Matthews, at several points in his paper, refers to the fact that certain observed animals were in captivity. How does he appear to regard the possible effect of captivity on the usefulness of these observations? Might such observations be more valid or less valid as analogies for understanding human behavior? Consider, in this connection, the following exchange, which took place between Matthews and another participant at the symposium:[3]

Bourne: I would like to ask Dr. Harrison Matthews whether he has any evidence of overt killing in the Killer Whale (*Orcinus orca*). I saw members of this species attacking each other off Iceland a few years ago. The Killers had been troublesome to the fishing fleet at the time and depth charges had been used to scare them away; there was no evidence of injury to the animals, but soon after the bombing fighting broke out and continued to break out frequently over the two subsequent days, during which time two animals were seen to be badly damaged and one actually devoured.

Harrison Matthews: I have not hitherto heard of Killer Whales attacking one another. I think the example quoted can hardly be regarded as normal behaviour if the animals had been bombed with depth charges by fishermen.

What does Matthews mean by "normal behavior"? In what setting or environment might one look to find normal behavior patterns for humans? What features of a species' environment does the Matthews paper suggest might be regarded as abnormal? What is the result of such abnormality?

Matthews finds that intra-specific aggression in animals is usually non-lethal. He suggests various inhibitory mechanisms that prevent animals from actually killing each other. Can you think of possible analogies in human behavior? (Consider the last two or three Westerns in which you saw a character get down on his knees and beg for mercy. What happened to him? In most of those *I* can remember, he was promptly shot. Why did the script writer choose this result, do you suppose? Was his message, "Those who beg for mercy are cowards and weaklings, and deserve to die"? But is such a scene from a Western a fair example of human behavior?)

Man's lack of natural inhibitions. Matthews suggests that "Only one species of mammal habitually disregards" the strong inhibition that keeps the victor, in intra-specific fights, "from giving the death blow when the rival submits." This species is man. If intra-specific aggression does not have lethal consequences in other species, except in very rare instances, why does it frequently have such consequences in man? Or is it correct to say "frequently"? After all—see page 3—even the highest national homicide rate, in Colombia, is 35.5 (in 1962, 21.5 in 1967) per 100,000, which means that any given person in Colombia's population has less than one chance in 2,500 of being murdered in any given year. In the United States, the risk of murder is currently around one chance in 14,000. Have we made enough observations of animal populations to be sure that "murder" is not as frequent, statistically, among other animal species?

Whether further observation might cast doubt on the conclusion is not known, but at present most naturalists, ethologists, zoologists, and others who have observed animals in their natural habitat believe that intra-specific killing is *extremely* rare. We shall have more to say about this in Chapter 4. But for the moment, assuming for purposes of further investigation that intra-specific killing is markedly more frequent among humans, one articulate theory of why this is so can be found in a later chapter of Lorenz' *On Aggression*.[4]

In the chapter on behavior mechanisms functionally analogous to morality, I have spoken of the inhibitions controlling aggression in various social animals, preventing it from injuring or killing fellow members of the species. As I explained, these inhibitions are most important and consequently most highly differentiated in those animals which are capable of killing living creatures of about their own size. A raven can peck out the eye of another with one thrust of its beak, a wolf can rip the jugular vein of another with a single bite. There would be no more ravens and no more wolves if reliable inhibitions did not prevent such actions. Neither a dove nor a hare nor even a chimpanzee is able to kill its own kind with a single peck or bite; in addition, animals with relatively-poor defense weapons have a correspondingly great ability to escape quickly, even from specially armed predators which are more efficient in chasing, catching, and killing than even the strongest of their own species. Since there rarely is, in nature, the possibility of such an animal's seriously injuring one of its own kind, there is no selection pressure at work here to breed in killing inhibitions. The absence of such inhibitions is apparent to the animal keeper, to his own and to his animals' disadvantage, if he does not take seriously the intra-specific fights of completely "harmless" animals. Under the unnatural conditions of captivity, where a defeated animal cannot escape from its victor, it may be killed slowly and cruelly. In my book *King Solomon's Ring,* I have described in the chapter "Morals and Weapons" how the symbol of peace, the dove, can torture one of its own kind to death, without the arousal of any inhibition.

Anthropologists concerned with the habits of Australopithecus have repeatedly stressed that these hunting progenitors of man have left humanity with the dangerous heritage of what they term "carnivorous mentality." This statement confuses the concepts of the carnivore and the cannibal, which are, to a large extent, mutually exclusive. One can only deplore the fact that man has definitely not got a carnivorous mentality! All his trouble arises from his being a basically harmless, omnivorous creature, lacking in natural weapons with which to kill big prey, and, therefore, also devoid of the built-in safety devices which prevent "professional" carnivores from abusing their killing power to destroy fellow members of their own species. A lion or a wolf may, on extremely rare occasions, kill another by one angry stroke, but, as I have already explained in the chapter on behavior mechanisms functionally analogous to morality, all heavily armed carnivores possess sufficiently reliable inhibitions which prevent the self-destruction of the species.

In human evolution, no inhibitory mechanisms preventing sudden man-slaughter were necessary, because quick killing was impossible anyhow; the potential victim had plenty of opportunity to elicit the pity of the aggressor by submissive gestures and appeasing attitudes. No selection pressure arose in the prehistory of mankind to breed inhibitory mechanisms preventing the killing of conspecifics until, all of a sudden, the invention of artificial weapons upset the equilibrium of killing potential and social inhibitions. When it did, man's position was very nearly that of a dove which, by some unnatural trick of nature, has suddenly acquired the beak of a raven. One shudders at the thought of a creature as irascible as all prehuman primates are, swinging a well-sharpened hand-ax. Humanity would indeed have destroyed itself by its first inventions, were it not for the very wonderful fact that inventions and responsibility are both the achievements of the same specifically human faculty of asking questions.

Not that our prehuman ancestor, even at a stage as yet devoid of moral responsibility, was a fiend incarnate; he was by no means poorer in social instincts and inhibitions than a chimpanzee, which, after all, is—his irascibility not withstanding—a social and friendly creature. But whatever his innate norms of social behavior may have been, they were bound to be thrown out of gear by the invention of weapons. If humanity survived, as, after all, it did, it never achieved security from the danger of self-destruction. If moral responsibility and unwillingness to kill have indubitably increased, the ease and emotional impunity of killing have increased at the same rate. The distance at which all shooting weapons take effect screens the killer against the stimulus situation which would otherwise activate his killing inhibitions. The deep, emotional layers of our personality simply do not register the fact that the crooking of the forefinger to release a shot tears the entrails of another man. No sane man would even go rabbit hunting for pleasure if the necessity of killing his prey with his natural weapons brought home to him the full, emotional realization of what he is actually doing.

60

The same principle applies, to an even greater degree, to the use of modern remote-control weapons. The man who presses the releasing button is so completely screened against seeing, hearing, or otherwise emotionally realizing the consequences of his action, that he can commit it with impunity —even if he is burdened with the power of imagination. Only thus can it be explained that perfectly good-natured men, who would not even smack a naughty child, proved to be perfectly able to release rockets or to lay carpets of incendiary bombs on sleeping cities, thereby committing hundreds and thousands of children to a horrible death in the flames. The fact that it is good, normal men who did this, is as eerie as any fiendish atrocity of war!

Does Lorenz appear to regard the inhibitions against killing members of the same species as innate or as learned? As innate in certain species, but not in man? Do these views foreclose a possibility that Matthews would still hold open, and thereby make Lorenz appear— at least on the basis of these two excerpts alone—as the more pessimistic of the two authors?

Do Lorenz and Matthews put similar weight on the importance of technology in making man more lethal towards other members of his species? Matthews, at the end of his paper, talks of the development of "tools," and Lorenz' well-sharpened hand-ax seems to fall in this category. But is Lorenz still talking about "tools" when he refers to "modern remote-control weapons"?

What possible differences can you see? Does it matter if a weapon can only be operated by a group? If it can only be used with the authorization of the President? Is the process by which the President might order the use of an H-bomb, and a B-52 crew might receive and carry out that order, simply "murder writ large"? Is it a process to which observations of fighting wolves, fighting deer, fighting fish, or even men fighting in a barroom brawl, have any relevance? Is it possible to argue that the B-52 crew's actions are not even "aggression"? How might such an argument go?

The effect of crowding on aggression. To the extent that the observations of animal behavior described by Matthews and Lorenz help us to understand particular instances of lethal behavior by man towards his fellow men, does their data suggest any *other* possible explanations for man's lethal activities, apart from the introduction of deadly tools or technologies? What is the possible relevance of Matthew's data on captive animals? Consider the following extract from *The Human Zoo,* by Desmond Morris, a zoologist who for many years was curator of mammals at the London Zoo.[5]

Under normal conditions, in their natural habitats, wild animals do not mutilate themselves, masturbate, attack their offspring, develop stomach ulcers, become fetishists, suffer from obesity, form homosexual pair-bonds, or commit murder. Among human city-dwellers, needless to say, all of these things occur. Does this, then, reveal a basic difference between the human species and other animals? At first glance it seems to do so. But this is deceptive. Other animals do behave in these ways under certain circumstances, namely when they are confined in the unnatural conditions of captivity. The zoo animal in a cage exhibits all these abnormalities that we know so well from our human companions. Clearly, then, the city is not a concrete jungle, it is a human zoo.

* * *

Imagine a piece of land twenty miles long and twenty miles wide. Picture it wild, inhabited by animals small and large. Now visualize a compact group of sixty human beings camping in the middle of this territory. Try to see yourself sitting there, as a member of this tiny tribe, with the landscape, your landscape, spreading out around you farther than you can see. No one apart from your tribe uses this vast space. It is your exclusive home-range, your tribal hunting ground. Every so often the men in your group set off in pursuit of prey. The women gather fruits and berries. The children play noisily around the camp site, imitating the hunting techniques of their fathers. If the tribe is successful and swells in size, a splinter group will set off to colonize a new territory. Little by little the species will spread.

Imagine a piece of land twenty miles long and twenty miles wide. Picture it civilized, inhabited by machines and buildings. Now visualize a compact group of six million human beings camping in the middle of this territory. See yourself sitting there, with the compexity of the huge city spreading out all around you, farther than you can see.

Now compare these two pictures. In the second scene there are a hundred thousand individuals for every one in the first scene. The space has remained the same. Speaking in evolutionary terms, this dramatic change has been almost instantaneous; it has taken a mere few thousand years to convert scene one into scene two. The human animal appears to have adapted brilliantly to his extraordinary new condition, but he has not had time to change biologically, to evolve into a new, genetically civilized species. This civilizing process has been accomplished entirely by learning and conditioning. Biologically he is still the simple tribal animal depicted in scene one. He lived like that, not for a few centuries, but for a million hard years. During that period he did change biologically. He evolved spectacularly. The pressures of survival were great and they moulded him.

So much has happened in the past few thousand years, the urban years, the crowded years of civilized man, that we find it hard to grasp the idea that this is no more than a minute part of the human story.

* * *

As I said at the outset, only in the cramped quarters of zoo cages do we

62

find anything approaching the human state. If, in captivity, a group of animals is assembled which is too numerous for the species concerned, and they are packed too tightly together, then, with an inadequate cage environment, serious trouble will certainly develop. Persecutions, mutilations and killings will occur. Neuroses will appear. But even the least experienced zoo director would never contemplate crowding and cramping a group of animals to the extent that man has crowded and cramped himself in his modern cities and towns. *That* level of abnormal grouping, the director would predict with confidence, would cause a complete fragmentation and collapse of the normal social pattern of the animal species concerned. He would be astonished at the folly of suggesting that he should attempt such an arrangement with, say, his monkeys, his carnivores, or his rodents. Yet mankind does this willingly to himself; he struggles under just these conditions and somehow manages to survive. . . . Remarkably few of the struggling super-tribesmen succumb to the extreme forms of action I have discussed.

Still, we must beware of over-generalizing on the crowding factor and its applicability to man. Recall the earlier data on homicides and deaths from domestic group violence in various societies. Immensely crowded India (homicides 2.7 per 100,000 in 1965) has only a middle position on both scales. Spacious Libya has four times India's murder rate (11.2 in 1965), and roomy countries such as Argentina and Afghanistan have higher rates of deaths from group violence than India. Crowded Japan is even lower on the murder scale, far down on the group-violence list, and only slightly above average in its suicide rate. Some recent United States studies have suggested that population density as such has no relationship to overall crime rates, although other factors such as income level, racial mix, or migration into the neighborhood may have such a relationship. When these other factors are present *with* crowding, the latter may incorrectly get the blame. On all present data, crowding may be a factor in interpersonal violence, but there is clearly no satisfactory evidence that it is the overriding one.

Evaluation of Morris, Lorenz, and Matthews. Are you satisfied that the readings thus far have gone a long way towards explaining lethal aggression in *humans?* Is Morris in some ways the most useful? How about the usefulness of these readings in explaining the *group* activity of modern warfare?

What do you think of the following evaluation?

"Lorenz and Matthews are both pretty useless in understanding human aggressive behavior. They have good evidence for the idea that aggression furnishes real advantages to the survival of the lower species—by insuring they spread over the whole feeding area, and

63

by selecting the strongest and bravest males as parents. But they rashly conclude from this evidence that a propensity for aggressive behavior of the kind that they describe is built into the genes, that it is present in these animals from birth, and doesn't have to be learned at all. (Lorenz also suggests that the inhibition against killing the loser is built into the genes of animals with natural weapons, but Matthews is a little more cautious, and says that *this* behavior could be either innate or learned.) Now, even if you assumed that aggressive behavior was a genetic trait and was present in man, what would it prove? Disputes among animals are mostly of the kinds that we have all sorts of elaborate social conventions to take care of. We go to a law court with property disputes, and if you poke some guy in the eye because he took out a girl you've been dating, five will get you fifty she'll never go out with you again.

"Now this doesn't mean that *no* occasions very similar to those in which animals, birds, or fish will do battle ever arise. Someone may actually threaten to take over your home or your land, or menace your wife or family, and perhaps the only alternative will be to fight.

"But these occasions are rare. And if Lorenz and Matthews are saying that some sort of 'gene for aggressiveness' is the motivating force in situations—drunken brawls or political assassinations, for example—that don't remotely resemble the "triggering" situation in nature, they are taking a very long leap into the dark. Their leap is even darker and longer if they are suggesting that this biologically inherited aggressiveness has anything to do with lethal *group* violence like riots, insurrections, or wars. Human situations are quite unlike anything in nature for which the behavior that Lorenz and Matthews call "aggression" was developed; calling the human conduct the same thing, "aggression," simply papers over the fact that we may well be talking about two entirely different things. Even in behavior where there is clearly a strong innate pattern, such as eating in response to hunger, the human behavior is often outwardly similar to animal behavior, but has little kinship with it in motivation or feeling. Tasting wine, eating caviar, drinking Diet Pepsi, overeating grandma's cooking because it makes her feel good, or drinking a double martini all may look, on very superficial inspection, like the same activity as a hungry rabbit nibbling lettuce, but all are in fact vastly different and more complex in their motivation, and reflect a great many cultural values and pressures that have nothing to do with hunger.

"In the same way, the guy who gets slugged or knifed at a bar, let alone the soldier who gets mowed down by a machine gun, may be the victim of actions whose motivation is light-years removed from that of the rhesus monkey defending its territory. Individual human acts of lethal behavior take place in a complex cultural, material, and communicational setting for which there is no parallel anywhere in nature. Group acts of lethal behavior, like war, are so far away from anything found in nature that there is not even the slightest reason to believe that they reflect any kind of genetic programming. To understand human violence, we have to deal with it, first and foremost, in a specifically human setting. We don't, after all, think we gain any significant degree of understanding of human sexual behavior by looking at rats and cichlids."

Non-hereditary aspects of aggression. Even in animals, there have been serious questions raised as to the extent to which pro-survival aggressive behavior (aimed at specific functions, like territorial dispersion of the species) has been irreversibly programmed into the genetic material. In experiments performed by Victor H. Denenberg and M. X. Zarrow of the Biobehavioral Sciences Department at the University of Connecticut, groups of newborn mice were reared by rat mothers. While control groups of ordinary male mice, reared by mice mothers, would fight each other 46 percent of the time, when they had been left on two sides of a divided box and the divider was subsequently removed, the rat-reared mice fought each other only four percent of the time. When the experiment was repeated with one rat-reared mouse on one side and one mouse-reared mouse on the other, the fight was *always* initiated by the latter. The experimenters concluded that "aggressive behavior was relatively low" in the "hierarchy of responses" of rat-reared mice. Experiments were also performed which showed that the difference in mothers' milk was not responsible for the difference in fighting behavior. One paper on these experiments concludes:[6]

From the experiments we may definitely conclude that species-specific behavior patterns as well as fundamental physiological processes, both of which have a strong underlying genetic basis, can be modified dramatically by appropriate social experiences in early life. How genes express themselves is a function of the environment in which the organism grows and develops. The fact that an organism has genes that may ultimately contribute to aggressive behavior does not mean that those genes will necessarily have to express themselves in that manner. We feel that appropriate rearing con-

65

ditions can have a marked effect in modifying presumably inborn aggressive tendencies, and that they may even keep the tendencies from being expressed.

Conclusions. Before we go on to consider additional materials bearing on human aggression, it seems worthwhile to underline three potentially significant points from the preceding readings.

First, naturalists seem generally agreed that it is extremely rare for one member of a species to kill another member of that same species, in "natural" or wild conditions.

Second, men have, through their weapons technology, achieved in a very short span of time the ability to kill instantaneously and at a distance; they have moved rapidly from a very weak "armament" to one that far exceeds that of the wolf or the lion. Even if there are biological mechanisms for inhibiting lethal aggression that typically evolve where the need is strong, man has not had the need sufficiently long to have developed such mechanisms.

Third, lethal conflict, and other varieties of destructive or anomalous behavior, occurs among animals in very crowded or caged conditions. Contemporary human society may bear some important analogies, but from present evidence it is not possible to say with assurance that, all other things being equal, crowding increases the likelihood of lethal violence among human beings.

Thus, technology and crowding are two *possibly* significant factors that lead man to commit what, under wild conditions, would be considered a wholly "unnatural" act. This is not earth-shaking news, but it at least suggests that, given the best scientific data we can currently muster, measures such as gun-control legislation, the limitation of population growth, or the development of less densely packed patterns of residence can have an effect on the frequency of lethal violence.

Aggression in Man

But have we yet focused on material that will directly explain human aggression? Particularly lethal human aggression, which outsteps the bounds of functionality known in the animal kingdom, and especially the lethal aggression of humans in *groups*, which we know as war in revolution? To what materials or experiments may we look to understand *this* aggression? (Concerning the immediate occasions for homicide, recall the Chicago study discussed on page 11.)

Freud on aggression. The early psychoanalytic movement represents one of the first efforts to come to grips directly with the problem of human aggression. Sigmund Freud had, by the beginning of this century, developed a theory emphasizing the importance of unconscious impulses and of the earliest period of life in shaping personality development. In Freud's early work, a broadly defined sexuality was considered the most important innate drive. Sexual energy, or libido, was continuously being generated and flowing through the psyche and had to be continuously dissipated by some relevant activity. Sometimes Freud compared the libido to a river which, if dammed up, will find some other channel.

In later work, Freud developed the further concept of a "death instinct," an innate impulse towards destruction. Like sexuality, this energy was constantly generated, and had to be diverted to the destruction of external objects unless it was to destroy the person himself.

Freud's view has sometimes been analogized to the idea of original sin. It is a view unlikely to encourage strong efforts to end human destructiveness and war, for it implies that such behavior is inevitable. It also may tend to excuse our conduct, for if we are instinctually programmed to be destructive, who can blame us for following the dictates of our nature?

In a famous exchange of letters with Albert Einstein in 1932 on the causes of war, Freud offered the following deeply pessimistic view:[7] Among the motives with which a populace responded to a summons to war was the "lust for aggression and destruction," and

. . . With the least of speculative efforts we are led to conclude that this instinct functions in every living being, striving to work its ruin and reduce life to its primal state of inert matter. . . . The death instinct becomes an impulse to destruction when, with the aid of certain organs, it directs its action outward, against external objects. The living being, that is to say, defends its own existence by destroying foreign bodies. But, in one of its activities, the death instinct is operative *within* the living being, and we have sought to trace back a number of normal and pathological phenomena to this *introversion* of the destructive instinct. We have even committed the heresy of explaining the origin of human conscience by some such "turning inward" of the aggressive impulse. Obviously when this internal tendency operates on too large a scale, it is no trivial matter, rather a positively morbid state of things; whereas the diversion of the destructive impulse toward the external world

67

must have beneficial effects. Here is then the biological justification for all those vile, pernicious propensities which we now are combating. We can but own that they are really more akin to nature than this our stand against them, which, in fact, remains to be accounted for.

Is Freud saying the same thing as Lorenz? While both of them regard aggression as innate, or "something in the genes," there is an important difference in what each means by "aggression." What do you think of the following:

"Freud equates innate 'aggression' with the 'death instinct' and destruction. Lorenz, however, regards 'aggression' as an innate impulse that has many positive and healthy functions, and does not regard it as primarily, or even significantly, aimed at causing destruction or death. Thus, while there is a certain superficial similarity in their views, Freud's are much more extreme and much more pessimistic."

What sort of evidence do you suppose Freud offered for his theory? Is Freud's explanation of aggression supported by the previous materials on animal behavior?

Frustration and aggression. Currently, there is believed to be very little evidence that there is some human "instinct" specifically directed at causing death or destruction. Some of the more contemporary psychoanalytic views of human destructive behavior are found in Anthony Storr's *Human Aggression*,[8] a book highly praised by Konrad Lorenz.

We all know that the hungry child from which bottle or breast is prematurely removed will cry and thrash about in frustrated rage. Psychologists anxious to establish the relation between frustration and aggression on a firm statistical basis have measured the time-interval between the removal of the bottle from a baby and the appearance of crying, and have related this numerically to the child's supposed degree of hunger. It is easy to construct experiments which measure frustration, but difficult to demonstrate that, in early infancy, aggression may serve other functions than that of protest.

As soon as the infant becomes capable of crawling, however, it is clearly demonstrating the beginning of an effort to explore and master the external world. As Dr. Winnicott has put it: 'At origin, aggressiveness is almost synonymous with activity.' If Freud had been right in supposing that our chief aim is blissful satiation, it would be hard to explain this exploratory behaviour; but if we assume an Adlerian 'striving for superiority,' or else an equivalent to the appetitive behaviour of animals seeking for stimulation, the difficulty disappears.

One of the unfortunate features of the human condition is that the natural exploratory behaviour of human infants has to be curtailed, especially in conditions of civilization, where the hazards of traffic, electricity, gas, stairs and many other complex dangers have been added to those which are found in primitive, rural circumstances. We are forced to overprotect our children psychologically, because we live in an artificial environment; and, because small children are ill-equipped to look after themselves when surrounded by the dangerous trappings of civilization, we tend to guard them too carefully in situations where this is not necessary.

* * *

. . . The American analyst Clara Thompson writes:

Aggression is not necessarily destructive at all. It springs from an innate tendency to grow and master life which seems to be characteristic of all living matter. Only when this life force is obstructed in its development do ingredients of anger, rage, or hate become connected with it.

It is a pity that our culture makes such obstruction inevitable: and one reason why aggressiveness is a problem to modern man is that the natural exploratory urge to grasp and master the environment has perforce to be limited in a way which is bound to cause frustration. There are far too many things which children must not do or must not touch; so that within all of us who have been brought up in Western civilization, especially in urban civilization, there must be reserves of repressed, and therefore dangerous, aggression which originate from the restrictions of early childhood.

The motility of the infant can be looked upon as a germinal assertion of the individual as something separate from the mother, and it is likely that this spontaneous motility is the earliest manifestation of a positive aggressive drive. From the moment of birth, each infant is a separate entity, with an individual life of its own. Although helpless and dependent, the baby has within itself, and soon starts to express, its individuality, and the rest of its life will be an increasing affirmation of its uniqueness. As the child becomes more able to fend for itself, so its individual characteristics are more confidently asserted. Every child, if it is to become an adult in its own right, has to escape from dependency: and it does so by a gradually increasing demonstration, both to others and to itself, of its power to master the environment sufficiently to obtain satisfaction for its needs.

* * *

It is not really surprising that psycho-analysts have disclosed an infant world of phantasy in which aggression plays so large a part, for dependency and aggression are intimately and reciprocally connected. As we shall see when later discussing depression, the more a person remains dependent on others the more aggression will be latent within him. To be dependent on another person is to be in the power of that person; and therefore to feel

69

their power as a restrictive influence which must be overcome. If there were no aggressive drive towards independence, children would grow up into and remain helpless adults so long as anyone could be persuaded to care for them, a fate which actually does befall some individuals who either lack the normal quota of assertiveness or else who have been subjected to regimes of childhood training which makes any kind of self-assertion seem a crime. The infant's world is peopled with giants to be mastered and witches to be overcome just because it is dependent; and so, the further back into the mists of infancy the analyst probes, the more aggression does he discover.

The reciprocal relation between dependency and aggression is one factor which accounts for the particular aggressiveness of the human species. For man, compared with most other animals, is peculiar in the length of time which he takes to develop from birth to maturity, and therefore in the length of time during which he remains dependent. Physical development in man is not complete until the age of twenty-five—that is, until about a third of the total lifespan has passed—whilst psychological development is never finished, and psychological maturity remains an ever-receding goal which, in some sphere or other, continues to elude each one of us. One important function of the aggressive drive is to ensure that the individual members of a species can become sufficiently independent to fend for themselves, and thus, in their time, to become capable of protecting and supporting the young which they beget. It is to be expected, therefore, that the aggressive drive will be particularly marked in a species in which the young are dependent for an unusually protracted period.

The ideal that aggression is *only* a response to frustration has given rise to faulty methods of rearing children; for it has been assumed by kindly and liberal persons that, if only children were given enough love and frustrated as little as possible, they would not show any aggression at all. To the surprise of parents who have attempted regimes of maximum indulgence and liberty, the children become emotionally disturbed and often more aggressive than if they had been exposed to firmer discipline. For, if the parents never assert their own rights as individuals, but invariably submit to the wishes of the child, the latter comes to believe either that he is omnipotent, and that his every passing whim must immediately be gratified, or else that all self-assertion is wrong, and that he has no justification at all in seeking satisfaction for himself. . . .

The normal disposal of aggression requires opposition. The parent who is too yielding gives the child nothing to come up against, no authority against which to rebel, no justification for the innate urge towards independence. No child can test out his developing strength by swimming in treacle. If there is no one to oppose, the child's aggression tends to become turned inwards against the self so that he pulls his own hair, bites his nails, or becomes depressed and self-reproachful. Often this reaction may alternate with outbursts of senseless rage directed at no one in particular. Normal disposal of aggression is also made more difficult if a child has no brothers and sisters, or little opportunity of playing with contemporaries. As the Harlows have demonstrated with monkeys, relations with contemporaries can to a large degree compensate for inadequate relations with parents. When both

70

are absent, the internal accumulation of aggressive tension becomes extremely difficult to deal with; and the most isolated animal is likely to show both self-destructive behaviour and also rage if anyone approaches it.

*   *   *

It is impossible to refrain from the conclusion that, in human beings, a show of weakness on the part of the defeated is as likely to increase hatred as to restrain it. Perhaps our most unpleasant characteristic as a species is our proclivity for bullying the helpless.

The use of the word 'hatred' rather than 'aggression' in the last paragraph is deliberate. Throughout most of this book emphasis has been laid upon the positive aspects of the aggressive drive, since these have been largely ignored by contemporary psychology. But the relation of aggression to hate was briefly touched upon in the chapter on aggression in the relation between the sexes, in the chapter on depression, and again in the chapter on schizoid defences. Aggression turns to hatred when it comes to contain an admixture of revenge; and the tendency to persecute those who are already defeated, or who are obviously weaker than the aggressor, can only be explained by the latter's need to revenge himself for past humiliations.

It is the failure to distinguish between aggression and hatred which has led naïve, liberal humanists to label all aggression as 'bad,' and which has also led them to hold the ridiculous belief that, if human beings were never frustrated, they would not be aggressive at all.

It is, of course, obvious that frustration increases aggression. Indeed, even frustration has its positive aspects. When our drive to master the environment, or take from it what we need, is obstructed, we become angry; and our anger increases our power to overcome the obstacle. The tree which blocks our path, and which is just too heavy for us to lift when we are placid, evokes our anger and puts us into the best physiological condition for making our strongest muscular efforts. The woman who resists a man's sexual advances arouses more aggression within him; and this increase in male dominance may enable him to overcome her resistance and obtain satisfaction for his desire. But, as our study of the positive functions of aggression has amply demonstrated, the hypothesis that all aggression can be explained as a response to frustration cannot possibly be true. When, however, we turn to examine hatred, frustration, past or present, plays a much more important part.

In ordinary day-to-day existence a modicum of introspection will often reveal the point at which aggression becomes hate. We all have, and need, opponents; and, even within our own families, there are bound to be perpetual struggles for dominance. Sometimes our will prevails, and sometimes that of the other who is opposing us: and we accept this interchange as a normal part of life. There can be few parents, however, who have not sometimes punished a child in a way inappropriately severe for a particular offence; and who have not later realized with some shame that they were 'taking it out on' the child, either because of the latter's past misdeeds, or else as a result of other, personal frustrations which may have nothing to do with the child at all. It is at the point at which 'taking it out on' someone supervenes that aggression is liable to turn into hatred. Indeed, the colloquial phrase 'taking it out on' implies that there is an 'it' within the person — perhaps a chronic state of irritability — which causes an angry response inappropriate to the actual situation. It may seem absurd to choose such an inconsiderable and homely example to illustrate the relation between aggression and hate; and many parents will probably deny that they ever hate their children, even if they admit that they have sometimes 'taken it out on' them. Nevertheless, this illustration depicts two facts about human nature which go far to explain why men, unlike animals, are likely to behave with cruelty towards the defeated and the weak.

The first is man's liability to react to present situations in terms of the past. . . .

[I]n man the capacity of memory is fantastically developed. It is not only man's prolonged infancy which distinguishes him from other animals; it is also the size and complexity of his brain. Although it is justifiable to question the accuracy of the earliest memories which are disinterred by psychoanalysts, there can be no doubt that we are shaped by the experience of our infancy. As the anthropologist, Professor Washburn, said at a recent symposium:

> We can now say that there is no question that the earliest events in life, in the first year or two, are profoundly important, whether for a young rhesus monkey or a human being. This is not something which is generally recognized around the world; infants are frequently treated with the greatest casualness.

The 'it' which we are likely to 'take out' on others may be our frustrated anger following a bad day at work; or it may be something less easily purged, echoes of humiliation and disappointment from our earliest, most helpless days . . . there can be little doubt that, because of our prolonged dependency as infants and children, and our consequent vulnerability to humiliation and disregard, we all contain within us, in varying degree, impulses of hate and revenge which have a vindictive quality that is absent from 'normal' aggression.

. . . Many of man's peculiarities are as much related to his lengthened childhood as to the prolongation of his dependency in infancy. Not all these peculiarities are as distasteful as his tendency towards cruelty. The development of conceptual thought, symbolization, the power to create, and man's astounding adaptability and flexibility, are all consequences of his delayed maturation.

A second feature in which we appear to be different from other animals is in our capacity for projection. By projection is meant the tendency to attribute to other persons emotions, ideas, or attitudes which they do not in fact possess, but which take origin within ourselves. Almost any characteristic can be projected upon another. Persons in love habitually project an ideal of the opposite sex upon one another; political leaders often receive projections of authoritative wisdom which they seldom deserve; analysts are commonly regarded as infinitely understanding parents, priests as spiritual beings superior to the desires of the flesh. In this context, however, we are chiefly concerned with what is generally known as paranoid projection: that is, with the attribution to others of malignant hostility.

In clear-cut form, this is best seen in the mental illness known as paranoid schizophrenia. Those who have succumbed to this condition have been unable, like schizoid persons, to deal with their own hostility by withdrawal. Instead they attribute it to other people, and believe themselves to be the subject of unwarranted persecution. In some instances, the imagined persecutors are a comparatively small group; freemasons, Jews, Negroes or merely the subject's own family. In others, the whole world seems to be set against him, so that he cannot go out into the street without feeling that people are talking about him, that casual passers-by are regarding him with contempt, and that he is the object of malicious attention from total strangers.

* * *

Although most obvious in the insane, the capacity for paranoid projection is, regrettably, not confined to them. . . . The tendency towards paranoid projection, though more deeply buried in 'normal' people, is far less intermittent and even more ubiquitous than the tendency towards depression.

In primitive cultures, for example, physical illness is seldom attributed to the internal malfunction of the subject's own body. Instead, he believes that he has been poisoned or bewitched, and conceives that his disorder is the result of deliberate malice on the part of another person . . .

* * *

It might be expected that, when men finally capture the individuals upon whom they have projected images of evil, they would discard their illusions and see their imagined persecutors as no more powerful nor more wicked than themselves. Yet, as we know both from the medieval witch-trials and from the concentration camps, this is far from being the case. The abominable cruelties which have been inflicted upon many thousands of men, women and children attest the relish with which the human victor torments the vanquished, even when the latter is totally in his power. It is at this point that a third human peculiarity comes into operation.

We have already said that a cat cannot be supposed to identify with a mouse, and is therefore not being cruel to the mouse with which it plays, since it cannot imaginatively enter into the mouse's sufferings. Men, however, possess the capacity of identification as well as that of projection. They are able to enter into the pain of another, and to imagine what the sufferer feels. Upon this basis of identification with the insulted and injured rests man's charity and altruism: for no one would have been concerned to free slaves or to prevent child-labour unless, imaginatively, he could put himself into the shoes of a slave or an ill-treated child. But upon this basis also rests man's capacity for cruelty. His wish to torture and humiliate someone over whom he has already proved his superiority is clearly related to his ability to enter imaginatively into his enemy's agony.

There can be no doubt that we wish to behave to persecutors as we believe or fear that they would behave to us. There can be few people who, reading of Auschwitz or Belsen, have not had phantasies of submitting the

73

torturers to the same punishments as they inflicted upon others. Humane, liberal people realize intellectually that such retaliation is useless. There is no point in adding to the sum of human barbarity by talion retribution. But even the most tender-hearted, often especially the most tender-hearted, generally react to the description of cruelty by feeling such hatred towards those who inflict it that their immediate emotional response is to wish them to suffer the same punishment.

It is because, in varying degree, we have all, as infants, had the experience of total helplessness combined with frustration and humiliation, that we can identify with the enemy we have rendered powerless, and wish him to experience still further pain and humiliation. The cruelty with which man treats his defeated enemy can only be understood in terms of retaliation and revenge. Scapegoats personify both power and weakness at the same time. We project the former attribute upon them and identify with the latter characteristic. Victor and vanquished thus become linked by a bond of mutual hatred which goes far beyond the aggressive struggle for dominance which we see in other animals; and our potential for cruelty is one price we pay for the singular prolongation of our dependency in childhood.

* * *

. . . We have to face the fact that man's proclivity for cruelty is rooted in his biological peculiarities, in common with his capacity for conceptual thought, for speech, and for creative achievement.

What kind of data is Storr's analysis based on? Psychoanalytic sessions? Observations of children? Clinical experience with severely disturbed or psychotic persons? Historical events? Surmise from the author's own experience? Does it matter?

Destructiveness and aggressiveness. Note that Storr distinguishes various kinds of aggression, beginning with a very broad definition that, "[a]t origin, aggressiveness is almost synonymous with activity." He then identifies various subcategories of aggression, particularly one involving constructive, self-assertive growth of the individual, and a second — arising especially out of deep frustration — that is identified with hatred and violence. Do Storr's explanations seem adequate to describe all lethally violent human behavior? Does he offer enough different categories to describe the phenomena? Dr. Erich Fromm, one of the most prominent of contemporary psychoanalysts, has written:[9]

The discussion about destructiveness and aggressiveness suffers in general from the lack of discrimination between various kinds of destructiveness. Such a discrimination is possible only from a dynamic viewpoint, and it is very difficult from a merely behavioristic viewpoint. The quality of various types of destructiveness is related to the causes for it. And in order to under-

74

stand these different causes, one has to have a picture of the whole system Man as one of structured energy, a system that we usually call character if the concept of character is used in a dynamic sense. Clinical observation of various types of destructiveness in relation to the specific causes that act as stimuli can help in recognizing that the phenomena that usually are subsumed under the category of aggression, aggressiveness and destructiveness are among themselves qualitatively entirely different, even if they are sometimes overlapping.

Can you think of some major phenomena of lethal human violence that are not even touched by Storr's explanation?

What does Storr mean when, at the end of the excerpt, he says "man's proclivity for cruelty is rooted in his biological peculiarities"? He does not mean, as it might seem, that cruelty is "innate," genetically programmed, but rather that it is caused by the inevitable length of child development, with its attendant feeling of helplessness and the probability of frustration. At first glance it may seem that Storr is inconsistent, having said previously that "aggressive expression may be as necessary a part of being a human being as sexual expression." But any apparent inconsistency disappears when you remember his very broad definition of "aggression," in contrast to the much more specific subcategory of "cruelty."

Displaced aggression. A possible basic mechanism of human aggressive behavior is suggested by the following passage from Berelson and Steiner, *Human Behavior, an Inventory of Scientific Findings:*[10]

When an external barrier stands between a motivated subject and his goal, he normally tries to circumvent, remove, or otherwise master it. (The rat may learn to run the maze or push the bar; the man, to solve the problem.) But when the barrier is not mastered and/or the motivation increases in intensity, the resulting frustration of the goal-directed behavior produces a number of less adaptive results: The barrier itself may be attacked, physically or symbolically. The man kicks or curses the broken lawnmower; the child strikes the table corner that has caused him pain, at the cost of incurring some more; and the speeding motorist has appropriate feelings and comments about the policeman who stops him.

In part, this transformation of frustration into aggression probably stems from the state of nature where physical attack was often necessary and successful in removing the barrier. Within the human context, however, where direct physical assault is not normally required or adaptive, this mechanism rarely helps attain the initial goal. Further, and still less realistically adaptive:

When the actual barrier is physically, psychologically, or socially invulnerable to attack, aggression may be displaced to an innocent but more vulnerable bystander ("displaced aggression").

So, for example, boys at camp showed significantly increased hostility toward minority groups (Mexicans, Japanese) after they had been subjected

**THE EFFECT OF A FRUSTRATION IMPOSED BY THE IN-GROUP
UPON ATTITUDES EXPRESSED TOWARD OUT-GROUPS[11]**

	TRAITS ATTRIBUTED TO MINORITY			
	FAVORABLE		UNFAVORABLE	
	BEFORE	AFTER	BEFORE	AFTER
Mean	5.71	4.11	2.93	3.26
After minus before		−1.60		+.33

to a long and frustrating testing session that deprived them of their weekly night at the movies. The frustrating agent — the tester — was neither Mexican nor Japanese.

"To the extent that the less favorable attitude toward the foreigners may be termed aggression, the results suggest that the frustrations imposed on the young men by the experimenters elicited aggression which was generalized somewhat to the far away foreigners who could not possibly have been to blame for the situation [*ibid.,* p. 441]."

Similarly, historical data reveal that lynchings used to increase when economic indices, and especially the farm value of cotton, went down. The chart shows the historical pattern; the following table, the correlation coefficients:[12]

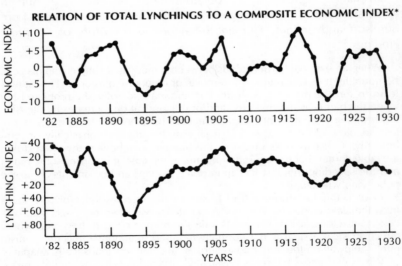

RELATION OF TOTAL LYNCHINGS TO A COMPOSITE ECONOMIC INDEX*

*Both curves represent deviations from a trend line.

(Hovland and Sears, 1940, p. 307)

CORRELATIONS BETWEEN ECONOMIC INDICES AND LYNCHING DATA*

VARIABLES

Economic index — Total lynchings	.65
Per-acre value of cotton — Negro lynchings	.63
Farm value of cotton — Negro lynchings	.72

*Data based on deviations from trend lines.

A later study reduced these correlations somewhat, but they still remained in effect.

"In the present instance the frustrating agent is not an object; one cannot be aggressive against a condition represented by index numbers. It is true, however, that certain individuals probably *represent* the condition symbolically, e.g., merchants, landlords, wealthy persons. These are individuals in a preferred and protected situation in society, however, and aggression directed toward them would elicit a relatively great amount of retribution (punishment). Hence, following the principle that anticipation of punishment inhibits acts of direct aggression (Dollard et al., 1939), the aggression is directed toward persons in a less favorable and protected position who are unable to mobilize adequate retribution [*ibid.*, p. 308]."

Although the "frustration" theory outlined by Berelson and Steiner also reflects Storr's concerns about features of the human environment, is the aggressive behavior they describe likely to be as uniform or generalized in occurrence as the mechanism that Storr postulates? Is it possible that, in a given case, Storr's postulate, Berelson and Steiner's "frustration," and other models might all apply simultaneously to explain a particular occurrence of extreme aggressive behavior? For example, were the men who carried out the lynchings described by Berelson and Steiner not in fact subjected, each and every one, to the regime of infantile dependency that Storr describes?

Note that the second example in the above excerpt involves *lethal* violence. Are there special features of that situation that might have lent themselves to such an extreme result? How might you describe those special features, if you wished to be able to identify other situations where frustration might have a lethal result? Do you suppose that persons in the position of "merchants, landlords, [and] wealthy persons" would *always* be protected from the venting of such frustrations? What factors might change that would cause the frustration to be vented directly on them? Are there even more notable examples of

77

frustration being vented on "persons in a less favorable and protected position"? Consider the killing of 200,000 "communists" in the Indonesian villages after the communist PKIs attempted putsch was prevented in 1965. Should "merchants, landlords, [and] wealthy persons" breathe easily because, as some might argue, "the peasants have now worked off their frustrations"?

The physiology of aggression. We have not yet discussed violence in relation to the most tangible sort of "biological peculiarities." The actual physiological changes accompanying anger and other emotions have been studied by a number of researchers since W. B. Cannon wrote his classic, *Bodily Changes in Pain, Hunger, Fear and Rage,* in 1929. Still, not much is yet known, partly because it is difficult to set up experiments with humans in which it is ethically permissible to stimulate strong, clearly identifiable emotional reactions. In a chapter entitled "The Physiology of Anger" in *The Psychology of Aggression,* J. P. Buss notes that Cannon introduced the view that the physiological counterparts of anger and fear were identical. Cannon, he states,[13]

emphasized the bodily preparations for "flight or fight" — the twin responses to danger. In the face of danger the organism must prepare itself for sustained, violent activity: to run long enough to outdistance a pursuer or to attack with sufficient force to overcome the source of the danger. Cannon listed the following changes that occur in anger or rage:

Slowing or stopping of processes in the digestive tract
Shift of blood from the abdominal organs to skeletal muscles
More vigorous contraction of the heart
Deeper respiration
Dilatation of the bronchioles
Mobilization of sugar in the circulation.

These physiological reactions, which prepare the organism for violent, sustained activity, are ostensibly set in motion by discharges of the sympathetic nervous system.

Subsequent experiments, Buss points out, are full of difficulties of interpretation and yield highly tentative results. Still, they seem to suggest that cardiovascular measurements (that is, systolic and diastolic blood pressure, heart rate, cardiac output) are somewhat different in situations where the subject is angered than in those where he is fearful, and that these are differences that might correspond to differences in the proportions of adrenalin and noradrenalin secreted by the glands. These physiological changes, however, are detected long before the fifteen or twenty seconds that must pass before these chemical substances could be operative, and "Changes occurring within, say, 10 seconds must be mediated by neural action."[14] Recent experimental data as to the possible mechanism of this neural action in animals indicates that the source of aggressive responses in both fear and anger is in a small almond-shaped portion of the brain called the *amygdala,* which lies within the ancient, limbic region of the brain. K. E. Mayer, in "Kinds of Aggression and their Physiological Basis" (*Communications in Behavioral Biology* (1968)) states very tentatively the results of experimental work involving surgery and "mapping," through selective electrical stimulation, of this small portion of the brains of various animals.[15]

Interpretation of the above findings must remain tentative until further research is done which recognizes the different types of aggression and tests for them specifically while manipulating the particular amygdaloid nuclei. It does not appear possible to reconcile the results of all of the studies done on the amygdala, but several points seem to stand out. Fear-induced, irritable, and predatory aggression are probably controlled by separate but overlapping anatomical areas. Fear-induced is, in general, located more dorsal, lateral and rostral, whereas irritable is more ventral, medial and caudal. Predatory aggression control is located in the more dorsal portion of the amygdala.

Thus, at least a very preliminary physiological basis is laid for distinguishing anger ("irritable aggression") and fear responses, and for confirming the differentiation of predatory behavior directed towards other species from intraspecific aggression. Man, of course, may lack such "predatory aggression;" moreover, the applicability of the results from these animal experiments to differentiate fear and anger in man has not been proven.

A Boston group, working out of Massachusetts General Hospital, has studied and treated some 200 men and women who exhibit special episodic patterns of great violence. This special kind of behavior has often been traced to specific brain damage, and there has been some successful treatment with brain surgery (following electrical "mapping" of the implicated areas) or chemicals. The Boston group has suggested that brain damage may be underestimated as a cause of violent behavior, pointing out also that conditions of poverty and social deprivation are more likely to lead to brain damage than middle-class conditions, and that there may be a correlation between violent crime and a poverty background that involves more than simply the social and economic deprivation of the poor.

Some studies have suggested that a substantial proportion of convicted murderers are persons who, as children, were subjected to severe physical punishment. Would this information tend to confirm the broader suggestions of the Boston researchers? Or are there other reasons why beatings might make a man more likely than others to commit murder? For one thing, a beaten child would certainly feel intense frustration and pent-up rage. For another thing, a parent who beats his child displays for the child a model of physical violence as acceptable behavior. Are there other possibilities as well? Do animals in the wild seem as likely as slum children to suffer brain damage? Do they kill within their species? Does the Boston group's work seem likely, even if their views were fully confirmed, to be of as much significance for group violence as for individual violence?

Presumably, if specific physiological correlatives of anger for human beings in general can be identified, two possible uses can be made of this information. First, we may be able to gain a greater insight into the psychological stimuli that trigger the anger response; secondly, there will be at least a theoretical opportunity to deal with the problem symptomatically by developing and administering some chemical that would keep people from getting angry, even if the psychological stimuli were present. Furthermore, if anger is physiologically different from fear, one might be able to develop a pill sufficiently selective so that potentially useful or even life-saving fear responses would not be likewise blanked out. In late 1971 one biochemist pointed out that urine samples from 3,000 Texans had shown that there were heavy lithium concentrations in El Paso's water, drawn from deep wells. Lithium is a tranquilizing chemical, often used to treat manic depression and other disorders, and it was suggested that this might help explain El Paso's relatively low homicide rate (4 per 100,000 population in 1970) as against, for example, Dallas' rate of 28 per 100,000. Dallas also had a far greater rate of admission to state mental hospitals. One national magazine, while noting that there was some dispute over the effects of lithium, asked, "If lithium does have anything to do with the relative peace in El Paso, what would it do for other cities like New York and Chicago?"

Altruistic violence. Such chemical tampering with the personality raises, of course, the most profound ethical questions. And even if the physiology of anger were known, and if chemical interference

80

with violent behavior were regarded as desirable, it is questionable whether such control could have any effect on major group violence. Consider the following excerpt from a paper by Arthur Koestler, best known as an essayist and novelist:[16]

We know that among social animals fighting is a ritualized affair that stops short of serious injury. The prey that the predator kills always belongs to a different species. Murder *within* the species on an individual or collective scale is a phenomenon unknown in the whole animal kingdom, except for man and a few varieties of ants and rats.

Evidently something must have gone wrong at some point in the evolution of *Homo sapiens*. But when we ask what it is that has gone wrong, we usually get the dusty answer that all evil stems from the selfish, greedy, aggressive tendencies in human nature. That is the explanation that has been offered to us for the last three thousand years by Hebrew prophets, Indian sages, Christian moralists and contemporary psychoanalysts; but speaking in all humility, I find this answer unconvincing and unsupported by the historical record. What the record indicates is that in the major disasters in our history, individual aggressiveness for selfish motives played an almost negligible part compared to unselfish loyalty and devotion to tribe, nation, religion or political ideology. Tribal wars, national wars, civil wars, religious wars, world wars, are waged in the purported interest of the community, not of the individual, to decide issues that are far removed from the personal self-interest of the combatants. No doubt the lust for rape and plunder provided occasional incentives for a minority, but for the great majority the primary motive was fanatical loyalty, to the point of self-sacrifice, to king and country, leader or group. In other words, the main trouble with man appears to be not that he is an excessively aggressive creature, but an excessively loyal one. He seems to have stronger biological needs than any other species to belong, to attach himself to a person, a group or idea, to transcend the claustrophobic confines of self. He cannot live alone, and he cannot leave alone.

One possible reason for this tendency may be the protracted helplessness and dependence of the human infant. Another reason may be the increased dependence on solidarity and cooperation of our primate ancestors when they turned into carnivorous hunters of prey bigger and faster than themselves. Primate societies living in the wild are also held together by strong bonds, and groups of the same primate species living in different localities may also develop different traditions and customs. But the cohesive bonds within primate families do not grow into neurotic attachments, the cohesive forces within primate groups do not attain the intensity and fervor of tribal feeling, and the differences between primate groups of the same species do not lead to violent conflicts. Only in *Homo sapiens* did the cohesive forces within the group develop into fanatical loyalty to tribe, totem and its later symbolic equivalents; and only in our species did the repellent forces between groups develop into intra-specific warfare.

81

What I am trying to suggest is that the aggressive, self-assertive tendencies in the emotional life of the human individual are less dangerous to the species than his self-transcending or integrative tendencies. Most civilizations throughout our history have been quite successful in taming individual aggressiveness and teaching the young how to sublimate their self-assertive impulses. But we have tragically failed to achieve a similar sublimation and canalization of the self-transcending emotions. The number of victims of individual crimes committed in any period of history is insignificant compared to the masses cheerfully sacrificed *ad majorem gloriam,* in blind devotion to the true religion, dynasty or political system. When we speak of "blind devotion" we implicitly recognize the uncritical nature of the self-transcending urge in forming attachments to a person, group, race, flag or system of beliefs.

. . . (T)he emotion displayed by a crowd of demonstrators is an unselfish type of emotion derived from the identification of the individual with the group. When alone, man is inclined to act in his own interest; when identified with a group, the situation is reversed. The egotism of the group feeds on the altruism of its members.

Human history is pockmarked with the scars of this infernal dialectic. As to its origins, some clues are perhaps provided by . . . biological factors . . . : the long infantile dependence and strong social interdependence characteristic of our species; and the peculiarity of the human brain to sustain affect-based belief-systems that are incompatible with its reasoning faculties but nevertheless coexist with them. [By the latter, the author later indicates he refers to the possible lack of coordination between archaic brain structures which dominate affective, or emotional, behavior and the recently developed portion of the human neocortex which carries on our intellectual functions.]

Does Koestler offer an explanation for group violence markedly different from Storr's explanation of aggressive behavior? Perhaps the main reason for the difference is that Storr's theory explains individual aggression, while Koestler explains group aggression. Would both writers mean quite different things in characterizing a destructive act as "aggression?" Would Koestler be more or less likely than Storr to expect a subjective feeling of anger or hatred in each individual in a situation of group violence or warfare? Would you expect Koestler's explanation to have the same degree of validity for a riot, a guerrilla insurrection, and a classic war between two nations? Might both Koestler's and Storr's explanations be partially accurate in assessing the causes of each kind of violence? How might this be so?

What kind of "cure for our collective ailments" might Koestler have in mind? Obviously an "anti-aggression pill," or "lithium," or some equivalent, would not end war, in Koestler's view; would an

82

"assertive individuality pill," really a kind of "pro-aggression pill," do the job? Even if Koestler may be right, or partially right, in explaining group violence, do you agree with his statement that "The number of victims of individual crimes committed in any period of history is insignificant compared to the masses cheerfully sacrificed . . . in blind devotion to the true religion, dynasty, or political system?" Consider the statistics on murder, group violence, and warfare in Chapter 1.

FOOTNOTES, CHAPTER 2

[1] Konrad Lorenz, *On Aggression* (New York: Harcourt Brace, & World, Inc., 1963), pp. 30–31, 33–9.

[2] L. Harrison Matthews, "Overt Fighting in Mammals," *The Natural History of Aggression*, ed. J. D. Carthy and F. J. Ebling (New York: Academic Press, 1964), pp. 23–32.

[3] J. D. Carthy and F. J. Ebling, eds., *The Natural History of Aggression*, p. 33.

[4] Lorenz, *On Aggression*, pp. 240–43.

[5] Desmond Morris, *The Human Zoo* (New York: Dell Publishing Co., Inc., 1969), pp. 8, 11–12, 77–78.

[6] Victor H. Denenberg and M. X. Zarrow, "Rat Pax," *Psychology Today*, May 1970, Vol. 1, No. 12, p. 67.

[7] Sigmund Freud, "Why War?," *Collected Papers*, Vol. 5 (New York: Basic Books, 1959).

[8] Anthony Storr, *Human Aggression* (New York: Atheneum Publishers, 1968), pp. 41–46, 91–99.

[9] Erich Fromm, "On Sources of Human Destructiveness," in *Alternatives to Violence*, ed. Larry Ng (New York: Time-Life Books, 1968), p. 12.

[10] Bernard Berelson and Gary A. Steiner, *Human Behavior, An Inventory of Scientific Findings* (New York: Harcourt Brace Jovanovich, Inc., 1964) pp. 267–69.

[11] From Neal E. Miller and Richard Bugelski, "Minor Studies of Aggression: II. The influence of frustrations imposed by the in-group on attitudes expressed toward out-groups," *Journal of Psychology* (1948, 25), p. 440.

[12] From Carl Iver Hovland and Richard R. Sears, "Minor Studies of Aggression: VI. Correlation of lynching with economic indices," *Journal of Psychology* (1940, 9), p. 307.

[13] J. P. Buss, *The Psychology of Aggression* (New York: John Wiley & Sons, Inc., 1961), p. 91.

[14] Buss, *The Psychology of Aggression*, p. 100.

[15] K. E. Mayer, "Kinds of Aggression and Their Physiological Basis," in *Communications in Behavioral Biology* (New York: Academic Press, 1968), p. 76.

[16] Arthur Koestler, "The Predicament of Man," in *Alternatives to Violence*, pp. 18–20.

3   Views on Causation:

Lethal followers and deadly leaders

As Arthur Koestler suggests in his excerpt in the preceding section, the understanding of destructive behavior committed by *individual* humans, such as murder, has very little to do with understanding much of the destructive behavior of *groups* of humans, such as war or revolution. And it is the large-scale conflicts, recalling Richardson's data on page 38, that have claimed over three quarters of the victims of *all* lethal human violence in modern times (quarrels above "magnitude 4.5," or 31,000 deaths, claimed 78 percent of all victims from 1820 to 1945). In Koestler's view, societies organize for war or groups organize for violent conflict much more because of the internal dynamics of the society or group than because of "destructive aggression" felt by the individual members towards their opponents. A man may kill an "enemy," in other words, generally without feeling any rancor or hostility towards that enemy.

But what kind of internal dynamic may a society or group require to sustain such activity? Must there be some kind of strong internal ideology to bind the group together? Does the individual who fires the gun or drops the bomb do so saying, "I believe"? Or is he saying, "I'm just doing my job, like any other job"? Could the distinction be significant, if we wish to predict the likelihood of lethal conflicts and to control them?

Command and Obedience in
the Laboratory

At Yale University, in the 1960s, Stanley Milgram performed certain experiments that may be among the most frightening, in their implications, of any psychological experiments yet performed. Here is the account of some of his central work, "Some Conditions of Obedience and Disobedience to Authority."[1]

The situation in which one agent commands another to hurt a third turns up time and again as a significant theme in human relations. It is powerfully expressed in the story of Abraham, who is commanded by God to kill his son. It is no accident that Kierkegaard, seeking to orient his thought to the central themes of human experience, chose Abraham's conflict as the springboard to his philosophy.

War too moves forward on the triad of an authority which commands a person to destroy the enemy, and perhaps all organized hostility may be viewed as a theme and variation on the three elements of authority, executant, and victim.[2] We describe an experimental program, recently concluded at Yale University, in which a particular expression of this conflict is studied by experimental means.

In its most general form the problem may be defined thus: if X tells Y to hurt Z, under what conditions will Y carry out the command of X and under what conditions will he refuse. In the more limited form possible in laboratory research, the question becomes: if an experimenter tells a subject to hurt another person, under what conditions will the subject go along with this instruction, and under what conditions will he refuse to obey. The laboratory problem is not so much a dilution of the general statement as one concrete expression of the many particular forms this question may assume.

One aim of the research was to study behavior in a strong situation of deep consequence to the participants, for the psychological forces operative in powerful and lifelike forms of the conflict may not be brought into play under diluted conditions.

* * *

[2]Consider, for example, J. P. Scott's analysis of war in his monograph on aggression:

". . . while the actions of key individuals in a war may be explained in terms of direct stimulation to aggression, vast numbers of other people are involved simply by being part of an organized society.

". . . For example, at the beginning of World War I an Austrian archduke was assassinated in Sarajevo. A few days later soldiers from all over Europe were marching toward each other, not because they were stimulated by the archduke's misfortune, but because they had been trained to obey orders." (Slightly rearranged from Scott (1958), Aggression, p. 103.)

[Footnotes are Milgram's; some have been omitted.]

TERMINOLOGY

If *Y* follows the command of *X* we shall say that he has obeyed *X;* if he fails to carry out the command of *X*, we shall say that he has disobeyed *X*. The terms to *obey* and to *disobey*, as used here, refer to the subject's overt action only, and carry no implication for the motive or experiential states accompanying the action.[4]

To be sure, the everyday use of the word *obedience* is not entirely free from complexities. It refers to action within widely varying situations, and connotes diverse motives within those situations: a child's obedience differs from a soldier's obedience, or the love, honor, and *obey* of the marriage vow. However, a consistent behavioral relationship is indicated in most uses of the term: in the act of obeying, a person does what another person tells him to do. *Y* obeys *X* if he carries out the prescription for action which *X* has addressed to him; the term suggests, moreover, that some form of dominance-subordination, or hierarchical element, is part of the situation in which the transaction between *X* and *Y* occurs.

A subject who complies with the entire series of experimental commands will be termed an *obedient* subject; one who at any point in the command series defies the experimenter will be called a *disobedient* or *defiant* subject. As used in this report, the terms refer only to the subject's performance in the experiment, and do not necessarily imply a general personality disposition to submit to or reject authority.

SUBJECT POPULATION

The subjects used in all experimental conditions were male adults, residing in the greater New Haven and Bridgeport areas, aged 20 to 50 years, and

---

[4]*To obey* and *to disobey* are not the only terms one could use in describing the critical action of *Y*. One could say that *Y* is cooperating with *X*, or displays conformity with regard to *X*'s commands. However, *cooperation* suggests that *X* agrees with *Y*'s ends, and understands the relationship between his own behavior and the attainment of those ends. (But the experimental procedure, and, in particular, the experimenter's command that the subject shock the victim even in the absence of a response from the victim, preclude such understanding.) Moreover, cooperation implies status parity for the co-acting agents, and neglects the asymmetrical, dominance-subordination element prominent in the laboratory relationship between experimenter and subject. *Conformity* has been used in other important contexts in social psychology, and most frequently refers to imitating the judgements or actions of others when no explicit requirement for imitation has been made. Furthermore, in the present study there are two sources of social pressure: pressure from the experimenter issuing the commands, and pressure from the victim to stop the punishment. It is the pitting of a common man (the victim) against an authority (the experimenter) that is the distinctive feature of the conflict. At a point in the experiment the victim demands that he be let free. The experimenter insists that the subject continue to administer shocks. Which act of the subject can be interpreted as conformity? The subject may conform to the wishes of his peer or to the wishes of the experimenter, and conformity in one direction means the absence of conformity in the other. Thus the word has no useful reference in this setting, for the dual and conflicting social pressures cancel out its meaning.

In the final analysis, the linguistic symbol representing the subject's action must take its meaning from the concrete context in which that action occurs; and there is probably no word in everyday language that covers the experimental situation exactly, without omissions or irrelevant connotations. It is partly for convenience, therefore, that the terms *obey* and *disobey* are used to describe the subject's actions. At the same time, our use of the words is highly congruent with dictionary meaning.

engaged in a wide variety of occupations. Each experimental condition described in this report employed 40 fresh subjects and was carefully balanced for age and occupational types. The occupational composition for each experiment was: workers, skilled and unskilled: 40 percent; white collar, sales, business: 40 percent; professionals: 20 percent. The occupations were intersected with three age categories (subjects in 20s, 30s, and 40s, assigned to each condition in the proportions of 20, 40, and 40 percent respectively).

THE GENERAL LABORATORY PROCEDURE

The focus of the study concerns the amount of electric shock a subject is willing to administer to another person when ordered by an experimenter to give the "victim" increasingly more severe punishment. The act of administering shock is set in the context of a learning experiment, ostensibly designed to study the effect of punishment on memory. Aside from the experimenter, one naïve subject and one accomplice perform in each session. On arrival each subject is paid $4.50. After a general talk by the experimenter, telling how little scientists know about the effect of punishment on memory, subjects are informed that one member of the pair will serve as teacher and one as learner. A rigged drawing is held so that the naïve subject is always the teacher, and the accomplice becomes the learner. The learner is taken to an adjacent room and strapped into an "electric chair."

The naïve subject is told that it is his task to teach the learner a list of paired associates, to test him on the list, and to administer punishment whenever the learner errs in the test. Punishment takes the form of electric shock, delivered to the learner by means of a shock generator controlled by the naïve subject. The teacher is instructed to increase the intensity of electric shock one step on the generator on each error. The learner, according to plan, provides many wrong answers, so that before long the naïve subject must give him the strongest shock on the generator. Increases in shock level are met by increasingly insistent demands from the learner that the experiment be stopped because of the growing discomfort to him. However, in clear terms the experimenter orders the teacher to continue with the procedure in disregard of the learner's protests. *Thus, the naïve subject must resolve a conflict between two mutually incompatible demands from the social field. He may continue to follow the orders of the experimenter and shock the learner with increasing severity, or he may refuse to follow the orders of the experimenter and heed the learner's pleas. The experimenter's authority operates not in a free field, but against ever-mounting countervailing pressures from the person being punished.*

A few technical points need to be considered before the findings of the study are described. For the purpose of delivering shock, a simulated shock generator is used, with 30 clearly marked voltage levels that range from 15 to 450 volts (and each activated by one of 30 individual lever switches set in a horizontal line). The naïve subject is given a sample shock of 45 volts to con-

87

vince him of the authenticity of the instrument. The generator bears verbal designations that range from "Slight Shock" to "Danger: Severe Shock."

The responses of the victim are standardized on tape, and each protest is co-ordinated to a particular voltage level on the shock generator. Starting with 75 volts the learner begins to grunt and moan. At 150 volts he demands to be let out of the experiment. At 180 volts he cries out that he can no longer stand the pain. At 300 volts he refuses to provide any more answers to the memory test, insisting that he is no longer a participant in the experiment and must be freed. In response to this last tactic, the experimenter instructs the naïve subject to treat the absence of an answer as equivalent to a wrong answer, and to follow the usual shock procedure. The experimenter reinforces his demand with the statement: "You have no other choice, you must go on!" (This imperative is used whenever the naïve subject tries to break off the experiment.) If the subject refuses to give the next higher level of shock, the experiment is considered at an end. A quantitative value is assigned to the subject's performance based on the maximum intensity shock he administered before breaking off. Thus any subject's score may range from zero (for a subject unwilling to administer the first shock level) to 30 (for a subject who proceeds to the highest voltage level on the board). For any particular subject and for any particular experimental condition the degree to which participants have followed the experimenter's orders may be specified with a numerical value, corresponding to the metric on the shock generator.

This laboratory situation gives us a framework in which to study the subject's reactions to the principal conflict of the experiment. Again, this conflict is between the experimenter's demands that he continue to administer the electric shock, and the learner's demands, which become increasingly more insistent, that the experiment be stopped. The crux of the study is to vary systematically the factors believed to alter the degree of obedience to the experimental commands, to learn under what conditions submission to authority is most probable, and under what conditions defiance is brought to the fore.

* * *

IMMEDIACY OF THE VICTIM

This series consisted of four experimental conditions. In each condition the victim was brought "psychologically" closer to the subject giving him shocks.

In the first condition (Remote Feedback) the victim was placed in another room and could not be heard or seen by the subject, except that, at 300 volts, he pounded on the wall in protest. After 315 volts he no longer answered or was heard from.

The second condition (Voice Feedback) was identical to the first except that voice protests were introduced. As in the first condition the victim was placed in an adjacent room, but his complaints could be heard clearly through a door left slightly ajar, and through the walls of the laboratory.[6]

The third experimental condition (Proximity) was similar to the second, except that the victim was now placed in the same room as the subject, and $1\frac{1}{2}$ feet from him. Thus he was visible as well as audible, and voice cues were provided.

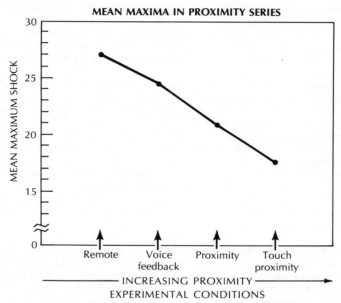

MEAN MAXIMA IN PROXIMITY SERIES

INCREASING PROXIMITY
EXPERIMENTAL CONDITIONS

[6] It is difficult to convey on the printed page the full tenor of the victim's responses, for we have no adequate notation for vocal intensity, timing, and general qualities of delivery. Yet these features are crucial to producing the effect of an increasingly severe reaction to mounting voltage levels. (They can be communicated fully only by sending interested parties the recorded tapes.) In general terms, however, the victim indicates no discomfort until the 75-volt shock is administered, at which time there is a light grunt in response to the punishment. Similar reactions follow the 90- and 105-volt shocks, and at 120 volts the victim shouts to the experimenter that the shocks are becoming painful. Painful groans are heard on administration of the 135-volt shock, and at 150 volts the victim cries out, "Experimenter, get me out of here! I won't be in the experiment any more! I refuse to go on!" Cries of this type continue with generally rising intensity, so that at 180 volts the victim cries out, "I can't stand the pain," and by 270 volts his response to the shock is definitely an agonized scream. Throughout, he insists that he be let out of the experiment. At 300 volts the victim shouts in desperation that he will no longer provide answers to the memory test; and at 315 volts, after a violent scream, he reaffirms with vehemence that he is no longer a participant. From this point on, he provides no answers, but shrieks in agony whenever a shock is administered; this continues through 450 volts. Of course, many subjects will have broken off before this point.

A revised and stronger set of protests was used in all experiments outside the Proximity series. Naturally, new baseline measures were established for all comparisons using the new set of protests.

There is overwhelming evidence that the great majority of subjects, both obedient and defiant, accepted the victims' reactions as genuine. The evidence takes the form of: (a) tension created in the subjects (see discussion of tension); (b) scores on "estimated pain" scales filled out by subjects immediately after the experiment; (c) subjects' accounts of their feelings in post-experimental interviews; and (d) quantifiable responses to questionnaires distributed to subjects several months after their participation in the experiments. This matter will be treated fully in a forthcoming monograph.

(The procedure in all experimental conditions was to have the naïve subject announce the voltage level before administering each shock, so that—independently of the victim's responses—he was continually reminded of delivering punishment of ever-increasing severity.)

The fourth, and final, condition of this series (Touch-Proximity) was identical to the third, with this exception: the victim received a shock only when his hand rested on a shockplate. At the 150-volt level the victim again demanded to be let free and, in this condition, refused to place his hand on the shockplate. The experimenter ordered the naive subject to force the victim's hand onto the plate. Thus obedience in this condition required that the subject have physical contact with the victim in order to give him punishment beyond the 150-volt level.

Forty adult subjects were studied in each condition. The data revealed that obedience was significantly reduced as the victim was rendered more immediate to the subject. The mean maximum shock for the conditions is shown in *Figure 1*.

Expressed in terms of the proportion of obedient to defiant subjects, the findings are that 34 percent of the subjects defied the experimenter in the Remote condition, 37.5 percent in Voice Feedback, 60 percent in Proximity, and 70 percent in Touch-Proximity.

How are we to account for this effect? A first conjecture might be that as the victim was brought closer the subject became more aware of the intensity of his suffering and regulated his behavior accordingly. This makes sense, but our evidence does not support the interpretation. There are no consistent differences in the attributed level of pain across the four conditions (i.e. the amount of pain experienced by the victim as estimated by the subject and expressed on a 14-point scale). But it is easy to speculate about alternative mechanisms:

Empathic cues. In the Remote and to a lesser extent the Voice Feedback condition, the victim's suffering possesses an abstract, remote quality for the subject. He is aware, but only in a conceptual sense, that his actions cause pain to another person; the fact is apprehended, but not felt. The phenomenon is common enough. The bombardier can reasonably suppose that his weapons will inflict suffering and death, yet this knowledge is divested of affect, and does not move him to a felt, emotional response to the suffering resulting from his actions. Similar observations have been made in wartime. It is possible that the visual cues associated with the victim's suffering trigger empathic responses in the subject and provide him with a more complete grasp of the victim's experience. Or it is possible that the empathic responses are themselves unpleasant, possessing drive properties which cause the subject to terminate the arousal situation. Diminishing obedience, then, would be explained by the enrichment of empathic cues in the successive experimental conditions.

Denial and narrowing of the cognitive field. The Remote condition allows a narrowing of the cognitive field so that the victim is put out of mind. The subject no longer considers the act of depressing a lever relevant to moral judgement, for it is no longer associated with the victim's suffering. When the victim is close it is more difficult to exclude him phenomenologically. He necessarily intrudes on the subject's awareness since he is continuously visible. In the Remote conditions his existence and reactions are made known only after the shock has been administered. The auditory feedback is sporadic and

90

discontinuous. In the Proximity conditions his inclusion in the immediate visual field renders him a continuously salient element for the subject. The mechanism of denial can no longer be brought into play. One subject in the Remote condition said: "It's funny how you really begin to forget that there's a guy out there, even though you can hear him. For a long time I just concentrated on pressing the switches and reading the words."

Reciprocal fields. If in the Proximity condition the subject is in an improved position to observe the victim, the reverse is also true. The actions of the subject now come under proximal scrutiny by the victim. Possibly, it is easier to harm a person when he is unable to observe our actions than when he can see what we are doing. His surveillance of the action directed against him may give rise to shame, or guilt, which may then serve to curtail the action. Many expressions of language refer to the discomfort or inhibitions that arise in face-to-face confrontation. It is often said that it is easier to criticize a man "behind his back" than to "attack him to his face." If we are in the process of lying to a person it is reputedly difficult to "stare him in the eye." We "turn away from others in shame" or in "embarrassment" and this action serves to reduce our discomfort. The manifest function of allowing the victim of a firing squad to be blindfolded is to make the occasion less stressful to him, but it may also serve a latent function of reducing the stress of the executioner. In short, in the Proximity conditions, the subject may sense that he has become more salient in the victim's field of awareness. Possibly he becomes more self-conscious, embarrassed, and inhibited in his punishment of the victim.

Phenomenal unity of act. In the Remote conditions it is more difficult for the subject to gain a sense of *relatedness* between his own actions and the consequences of these actions for the victim. There is a physical and spatial separation of the act and its consequences. The subject depresses a lever in one room, and protests and cries are heard from another. The two events are in correlation, yet they lack a compelling phenomenological unity. The structure of a meaningful act—*I am hurting a man*—breaks down because of the spatial arrangements, in a manner somewhat analogous to the disappearance of phi phenomena when the blinking lights are spaced too far apart. The unity is more fully achieved in the Proximity conditions as the victim is brought closer to the action that causes him pain. It is rendered complete in Touch-Proximity.

Incipient group formation. Placing the victim in another room not only takes him further from the subject, but the subject and the experimenter are drawn relatively closer. There is incipient group formation between the experimenter and the subject, from which the victim is excluded. The wall between the victim and the others deprives him of an intimacy which the experimenter and subject feel. In the Remote condition, the victim is truly an outsider, who stands alone, physically and psychologically.

When the victim is placed close to the subject, it becomes easier to form an alliance with him against the experimenter. Subjects no longer have to face the experimenter alone. They have an ally who is close at hand and eager to collaborate in a revolt against the experimenter. Thus, the changing set of spatial relations leads to a potentially shifting set of alliances over the several experimental conditions.

Acquired behavior dispositions.   It is commonly observed that laboratory mice will rarely fight with their litter mates. Scott (1958) explains this in terms of passive inhibition. He writes: "By doing nothing under . . . circumstances [the animal] learns to do nothing, and this may be spoken of as passive inhibition . . . this principle has great importance in teaching an individual to be peaceful, for it means that he can learn not to fight simply by not fighting." Similarly, we may learn not to harm others simply by not harming them in everyday life. Yet this learning occurs in a context of proximal relations with others, and may not be generalized to that situation in which the person is physically removed from us. Or possibly, in the past, aggressive actions against others who were physically close resulted in retaliatory punishment which extinguished the original form of response. In contrast, aggression against others at a distance may have only sporadically led to retaliation. Thus the organism learns that it is safer to be aggressive toward others at a distance, and precarious to be so when the parties are within arm's reach. Through a pattern of rewards and punishments, he acquires a disposition to avoid aggression at close quarters, a disposition which does not extend to harming others at a distance. And this may account for experimental findings in the remote and proximal experiments.

Proximity as a variable in psychological research has received far less attention than it deserves. If men were sessile it would be easy to understand this neglect. But we move about; our spatial relations shift from one situation to the next, and the fact that we are near or remote may have a powerful effect on the psychological processes that mediate our behavior toward others. In the present situation, as the victim is brought closer to the man ordered to give him shocks, increasing numbers of subjects break off the experiment, refusing to obey. The concrete, visible, and proximal presence of the victim acts in an important way to counteract the experimenter's power and to generate disobedience.[7]

CLOSENESS OF AUTHORITY

If the spatial relationship of the subject and victim is relevant to the degree of obedience, would not the relationship of subject to experimenter also play a part?

There are reasons to feel that, on arrival, the subject is oriented primarily to the experimenter rather than to the victim. He has come to the laboratory to fit into the structure that the experimenter—not the victim—would provide. He has come less to understand his behavior than to *reveal* that be-

---

[7]Admittedly, the terms *proximity, immediacy, closeness,* and *salience-of-the-victim* are used in a loose sense, and the experiments themselves represent a very coarse treatment of the variable. Further experiments are needed to refine the notion and tease out such diverse factors as spatial distance, visibility, audibility, barrier interposition, etc.

The Proximity and Touch-Proximity experiments were the only conditions where we were unable to use taped feedback from the victim. Instead, the victim was trained to respond in these conditions as he had in Experiment 2 (which employed taped feedback). Some improvement is possible here, for it should be technically feasible to do a proximity series using taped feedback.

havior to a competent scientist, and he is willing to display himself as the scientist's purposes require. Most subjects seem quite concerned about the appearance they are making before the experimenter, and one could argue that this preoccupation in a relatively new and strange setting makes the subject somewhat insensitive to the triadic nature of the social situation. In other words, the subject is so concerned about the show he is putting on for the experimenter that influences from other parts of the social field do not receive as much weight as they ordinarily would. This overdetermined orientation to the experimenter would account for the relative insensitivity of the subject to the victim, and would also lead us to believe that alterations in the relationship between subject and experimenter would have important consequences for obedience.

In a series of experiments we varied the physical closeness and degree of surveillance of the experimenter. In one condition the experimenter sat just a few feet away from the subject. In a second condition, after giving initial instructions, the experimenter left the laboratory and gave his orders by telephone; in still a third condition the experimenter was never seen, providing instructions by means of a tape recording activated when the subjects entered the laboratory.

Obedience dropped sharply as the experimenter was physically removed from the laboratory. The number of obedient subjects in the first condition (Experimenter Present) was almost three times as great as in the second, where the experimenter gave his orders by telephone. Twenty-six subjects were fully obedient in the first condition, and only 9 in the second (Chi square obedient vs. defiant in the two conditions, 1 d.f. $= 14.7$; $p < .001$). Subjects seemed able to take a far stronger stand against the experimenter when they did not have to encounter him face to face, and the experimenter's power over the subject was severely curtailed.

Moreover, when the experimenter was absent, subjects displayed an interesting form of behavior that had not occurred under his surveillance. Though continuing with the experiment, several subjects administered lower shocks than were required and never informed the experimenter of their deviation from the correct procedure. (Unknown to the subjects, shock levels were automatically recorded by an Esterline-Angus event recorder wired directly into the shock generator; the instrument provided us with an objective record of the subjects' performance.) Indeed, in telephone conversations some subjects specifically assured the experimenter that they were raising the shock level according to instruction, whereas in fact they were repeatedly using the lowest shock on the board. This form of behavior is particularly interesting: although these subjects acted in a way that clearly undermined the avowed purposes of the experiment, they found it easier to handle the conflict in this manner than to precipitate an open break with authority.

Other conditions were completed in which the experimenter was absent during the first segment of the experiment, but reappeared at the point that the subject definitely refused to give higher shocks when commanded by telephone. Although he had exhausted his power via telephone, the experimenter could frequently force further obedience when he reappeared in the laboratory.

Experiments in this series show that the physical *presence* of an authority is an important force contributing to the subject's obedience or defiance. Taken together with the first experimental series on the proximity of the victim, it would appear that something akin to fields of force, diminishing in effectiveness with increasing psychological distance from their source, have a controlling effect on the subject's performance. As the victim is brought closer, the subject finds it harder to administer shocks to him. When the victim's position is held constant relative to the subject, and the authority is made more remote, the subject finds it easier to break off the experiment. This effect is substantial in both cases, but manipulation of the experimenter's position yielded the more powerful results. Obedience to destructive commands is highly dependent on the proximal relations between authority and subject.

TENSIONS

The description of final scores does not fully convey the character of the subjects' performance, and it would be useful to interrupt our reporting of quantitative relationships to remark on the subjects' general reaction to the situation.

One might suppose that a subject would simply break off or continue as his conscience and temperament dictated. Yet this is very far from what happened. There were powerful reactions of tension and emotional strain in a substantial proportion of the participants. Persons were observed to sweat, tremble, stutter, bite their lips, and groan as they found themselves increasingly implicated in the experimental conflict. Some sense of the subjects' mood can be gotten from a transcript of their remarks at break-off point. Here are the remarks of two defiant subjects:

Is he banging? . . . Is he hurt out there? Well, I don't want to be responsible for anything that happens to him. No, I can't go on with it. I don't know whether he's all right or not. I mean he may have a heart condition or something; I wouldn't feel right doing it. He's banging for help. He's evidently in trouble or he wouldn't bang . . . I don't see any sense to this — to knocking him out or something. I just can't see it.

(Subject refuses to administer shocks)   [*Subject 0108*]

The man is banging. He wants to get out . . . I'm sorry. If the man wants to get out I'd just as soon stop . . . I don't want to administer any more [extremely excited] . . . I will gladly refund the check, but I will not harm this man . . . I'm sorry, I will not give him any more if he obviously wants to get out. There is no money in the world that will make me hurt another individual. [*Subject 010X*]

And here is a transcript from an obedient subject. He began the experiment calmly, but became increasingly tense as the experiment proceeded.

94

After administering the 150-volt shock, he began to address the experimenter in agitated tones:

150 volts delivered. You want me to keep going?
165 volts delivered. That guy is hollering in there. There's a lot of them here. He's liable to have heart condition. You want me to go?
180 volts delivered. He can't stand it! I'm not going to kill that man in there! You hear him hollering? He's hollering. He can't stand it. What if something happens to him? . . . I'm not going to get that man sick in there. He's hollering in there. You know what I mean? I mean I refuse to take responsibility. He's getting hurt in there. He's in there hollering. Too many left here. Geez, if he gets them wrong. There's too many of them left. I mean who is going to take responsibility if anything happens to that gentleman?
[The experimenter accepts responsibility.] All right.
195 volts delivered. You see he's hollering. Hear that. Gee, I don't know. *[The experimenter says: "The experiment requires that you go on."]* — I know it does, sir, but I mean — hugh — he don't know what he's in for. He's up to 195 volts.
210 volts delivered
225 volts delivered
240 volts delivered. Aw, no. You mean I've got to keep going up with the scale? No sir. I'm not going to kill that man! I'm not going to give him 450 volts! *[The experimenter says: "The experiment requires that you go on."]* — I know it does, but that man is hollering in there, sir . . .

Despite his numerous, agitated objections, which were constant accompaniments to his actions, the subject unfailingly obeyed the experimenter, proceeding to the highest shock level on the generator. He displayed a curious dissociation between word and action. Although at the verbal level he had resolved not to go on, his actions were fully in accord with the experimenter's commands. This subject did not want to shock the victim, and he found it an extremely disagreeable task, but he was unable to invent a response that would free him from *E*'s authority. Many subjects cannot find the specific verbal formula that would enable them to reject the role assigned to them by the experimenter. Perhaps our culture does not provide adequate models for disobedience.

One puzzling sign of tension was the regular occurrence of nervous laughing fits. In the first four conditions 71 of the 160 subjects showed definite signs of nervous laughter and smiling. The laughter seemed entirely out of place, even bizarre. Full-blown, uncontrollable seizures were observed for 15 of these subjects. On one occasion we observed a seizure so violently convulsive that it was necessary to call a halt to the experiment. In the postexperimental interviews subjects took pains to point out that they were not sadistic types and that the laughter did not mean they enjoyed shocking the victim.

In the interview following the experiment subjects were asked to indicate on a 14-point scale just how nervous or tense they felt at the point of maximum tension.

95

. . . Self-reports of this sort are of limited precision, and at best provide only a rough indication of the subject's emotional response. Still, taking the reports for what they are worth, it can be seen that the distribution of responses spans the entire range of the scale, with the majority of subjects concentrated at the center and upper extreme. . . .

How is the occurrence of tension to be interpreted? First, it points to the presence of conflict. If a tendency to comply with authority were the only psychological force operating in the situation, all subjects would have continued to the end and there would have been no tension. Tension, it is assumed, results from the simultaneous presence of two or more incompatible response tendencies (Miller, 1944). If sympathetic concern for the victim were the exclusive force, all subjects would have calmly defied the experimenter. Instead, there were both obedient and defiant outcomes, frequently accompanied by extreme tension. A conflict develops between the deeply ingrained disposition not to harm others and the equally compelling tendency to obey others who are in authority. The subject is quickly drawn into a dilemma of a deeply dynamic character, and the presence of high tension points to the considerable strength of each of the antagonistic vectors.

Moreover, tension defines the strength of the aversive state from which the subject is unable to escape through disobedience. When a person is uncomfortable, tense, or stressed, he tries to take some action that will allow him to terminate this unpleasant state. Thus tension may serve as a drive that leads to escape behavior. But in the present situation, even where tension is extreme, many subjects are unable to perform the response that will bring about relief. Therefore there must be a competing drive, tendency, or inhibition that precludes activation of the disobedient response. The strength of this inhibiting factor must be of greater magnitude than the stress experienced, else the terminating act would occur. Every evidence of extreme tension is at the same time an indication of the strength of the forces that keep the subject in the situation.

Finally, tension may be taken as evidence of the reality of the situations for the subjects. Normal subjects do not tremble and sweat unless they are implicated in a deep and genuinely felt predicament.

* * *

[In order to test the possible effects on obedience of the "background authority" of Yale University, a second set of experiments was run in Bridgeport, Connecticut.]

The purpose in relocating in Bridgeport was to assure a complete dissociation from Yale, and in this regard we were fully successful. On the surface, the study appeared to be conducted by Research Associates of Bridgeport, an organization of unknown character (the title had been concocted exclusively for use in this study).

The experiments were conducted in a three-room office suite in a somewhat run-down commercial building located in the downtown shopping area. The laboratory was sparsely furnished, though clean, and marginally

respectable in appearance. When subjects inquired about professional affilia-
tions, they were informed only that we were a private firm conducting research for industry.

* * *

A failure to obtain complete obedience in Bridgeport would indicate that
the extreme compliance found in New Haven subjects was tied closely to the
background authority of Yale University; if a large proportion of the subjects
remained fully obedient, very different conclusions would be called for.

As it turned out, the level of obedience in Bridgeport, although somewhat
reduced, was not significantly lower than that obtained at Yale. A large proportion of the Bridgeport subjects were fully obedient to the experimenter's
commands (48 percent of the Bridgeport subjects delivered the maximum
shock vs. 65 percent in the corresponding condition at Yale).

How are these findings to be interpreted? It is possible that if commands
of a potentially harmful or destructive sort are to be perceived as legitimate
they must occur within some sort of institutional structure. But it is clear from
the study that it need not be a particularly reputable or distinguished institution. The Bridgeport experiments were conducted by an unimpressive firm
lacking any credentials; the laboratory was set up in a respectable office
building with title listed in the building directory. Beyond that, there was no
evidence of benevolence or competence. It is possible that the *category* of institution, judged according to its professed function, rather than its qualitative
position within that category, wins our compliance. Persons deposit money
in elegant, but also in seedy-looking banks, without giving much thought to
the differences in security they offer. Similarly, our subjects may consider one
laboratory to be as competent as another, so long as it *is* a scientific laboratory.

It would be valuable to study the subjects' performance in other contexts
which go even further than the Bridgeport study in denying institutional support to the experimenter. It is possible that, beyond a certain point, obedience
disappears completely. But that point had not been reached in the Bridgeport
office: almost half the subjects obeyed the experimenter fully.

FURTHER EXPERIMENTS

We may mention briefly some additional experiments undertaken in the
Yale series. A considerable amount of obedience and defiance in everyday
life occurs in connexion with groups. And we had reason to feel in the light
of many group studies already done in psychology that group forces would
have a profound effect on reactions to authority. A series of experiments was
run to examine these effects. In all cases only one naïve subject was studied
per hour, but he performed in the midst of actors who, unknown to him, were
employed by the experimenter. In one experiment (Groups for Disobedience)
two actors broke off in the middle of the experiment. When this happened 90
percent of the subjects followed suit and defied the experimenter. In another
condition the actors followed the orders obediently; this strengthened the

experimenter's power only slightly. In still a third experiment the job of pushing the switch to shock the learner was given to one of the actors, while the naïve subject performed a subsidiary act. We wanted to see how the teacher would respond if he were involved in the situation but did not actually give the shocks. In this situation only three subjects out of forty broke off. In a final group experiment the subjects themselves determined the shock level they were going to use. Two actors suggested higher and higher shock levels; some subjects insisted, despite group pressure, that the shock level be kept low; others followed along with the group.

Further experiments were completed using women as subjects, as well as a set dealing with the effects of dual, unsanctioned, and conflicting authority. A final experiment concerned the personal relationship between victim and subject. These will have to be described elsewhere, lest the present report be extended to monographic length.

It goes without saying that future research can proceed in many different directions. What kinds of response from the victim are most effective in causing disobedience in the subject? Perhaps passive resistance is more effective than vehement protest. What conditions of entry into an authority system lead to greater or lesser obedience? What is the effect of anonymity and masking on the subject's behavior? What conditions lead to the subject's perception of responsibility for his own actions? Each of these could be a major research topic in itself, and can readily be incorporated into the general experimental procedure described here.

**LEVELS OF OBEDIENCE
AND DEFIANCE**

One general finding that merits attention is the high level of obedience manifested in the experimental situation. Subjects often expressed deep disapproval of shocking a man in the face of his objections, and others denounced it as senseless and stupid. Yet many subjects complied even while they protested. The proportion of obedient subjects greatly exceeded the expectations of the experimenter and his colleagues. At the outset, we had conjectured that subjects would not, in general, go above the level of "Strong Shock." In practice, many subjects were willing to administer the most extreme shocks available when commanded by the experimenter. For some subjects the experiment provides an occasion for aggressive release. And for others it demonstrates the extent to which obedient dispositions are deeply ingrained, and are engaged irrespective of their consequences for others. Yet this is not the whole story. Somehow, the subject becomes implicated in a situation from which he cannot disengage himself.

The departure of the experimental results from intelligent expectation, to some extent, has been formalized. The procedure was to describe the experimental situation in concrete detail to a group of competent persons, and to ask them to predict the performance of 100 hypothetical subjects. For purposes of indicating the distribution of break-off points judges were provided with a diagram of the shock generator, and recorded their predictions before being informed of the actual results. Judges typically underestimated the amount of obedience demonstrated by subjects.

In *Figure 3*, we compare the predictions of forty psychiatrists at a leading medical school with the actual performance of subjects in the experiment. The psychiatrists predicted that most subjects would not go beyond the tenth shock level (150 volts; at this point the victim makes his first explicit demand to be freed). They further predicted that by the twentieth shock level (300 volts; the victim refuses to answer) 3.73 percent of the subjects would still be obedient; and that only a little over one-tenth of one percent of the subjects would administer the highest shock on the board. But, as the graph indicates, the obtained behavior was very different. Sixty-two percent of the subjects obeyed the experimenter's commands fully. Between expectation and occurrence there is a whopping discrepancy.

Why did the psychiatrists underestimate the level of obedience? Possibly, because their predictions were based on an inadequate conception of the determinants of human action, a conception that focuses on motives *in vacuo*. This orientation may be entirely adequate for the repair of bruised impulses as revealed on the psychiatrist's couch, but as soon as our interest turns to action in larger settings, attention must be paid to the situations in which motives are expressed. A situation exerts an important press on the individual. It exercises constraints and may provide push. In certain circumstances it is not so much the kind of person a man is as the kind of situation in which he is placed, that determines his actions.

Many people, not knowing much about the experiment, claim that subjects who go to the end of the board are sadistic. Nothing could be more foolish as an overall characterization of these persons. It is like saying that a person thrown into a swift-flowing stream is necessarily a fast swimmer, or that he has great stamina because he moves so rapidly relative to the bank. The context of action must always be considered. The individual, upon entering the laboratory, becomes integrated into a situation that carries its own momentum. The subject's problem then is how to become disengaged from a situation which is moving in an altogether ugly direction.

The fact that disengagement is so difficult testifies to the potency of the forces that keep the subject at the control board. Are these forces to be conceptualized as individual motives and expressed in the language of personality dynamics, or are they to be seen as the effects of social structure and pressures arising from the situational field?

A full understanding of the subject's action will, I feel, require that both perspectives be adopted. The person brings to the laboratory enduring dispositions toward authority and aggression, and at the same time he becomes enmeshed in a social structure that is no less an objective fact of the case. From the standpoint of personality theory one may ask: What mechanisms of personality enable a person to transfer responsibility to authority? What are the motives underlying obedient and disobedient performance? Does orientation to authority lead to a short-circuiting of the shame-guilt system? What cognitive and emotional defenses are brought into play in the case of obedient and defiant subjects?

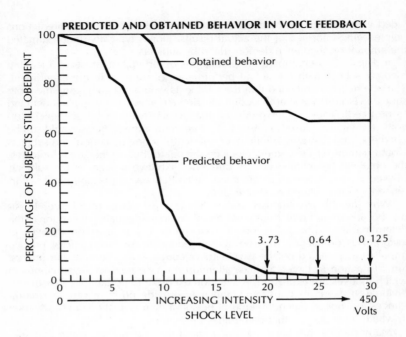

PREDICTED AND OBTAINED BEHAVIOR IN VOICE FEEDBACK

The present experiments are not, however, directed toward an exploration of the motives engaged when the subject obeys the experimenter's commands. Instead, they examine the situational variables responsible for the elicitation of obedience . . .

POSTSCRIPT

Almost a thousand adults were individually studied in the obedience research, and there were many specific conclusions regarding the variables that control obedience and disobedience to authority. . . .

There are now some other generalizations I should like to make, which do not derive in any strictly logical fashion from the experiments as carried out, but which, I feel, ought to be made. They are formulations of an intuitive sort that have been forced on me by observation of many subjects responding to the pressures of authority. The assertions represent a painful alteration in my own thinking; and since they were acquired only under the repeated impact of direct observation, I have no illusion that they will be generally accepted by persons who have not had the same experience.

With numbing regularity good people were seen to knuckle under the de-

100

mands of authority and perform actions that were callous and severe. Men who are in everyday life responsible and decent were seduced by the trappings of authority, by the control of their perceptions, and by the uncritical acceptance of the experimenter's definition of the situation, into performing harsh acts.

What is the limit of such obedience? At many points we attempted to establish a boundary. Cries from the victim were inserted; not good enough. The victim claimed heart trouble; subjects still shocked him on command. The victim pleaded that he be let free, and his answers no longer registered on the signal box; subjects continued to shock him. At the outset we had not conceived that such drastic procedures would be needed to generate disobedience, and each step was added only as the ineffectiveness of the earlier techniques became clear. The final effort to establish a limit was the Touch-Proximity condition. But the very first subject in this condition subdued the victim on command, and proceeded to the highest shock level. A quarter of the subjects in this condition performed similarly.

The results, as seen and felt in the laboratory, are to this author disturbing. They raise the possibility that human nature, or—more specifically—the kind of character produced in American democratic society, cannot be counted on to insulate its citizens from brutality and inhumane treatment at the direction of malevolent authority. A substantial proportion of people do what they are told to do irrespective of the content of the act and without limitations of conscience, so long as they perceive that the command comes from a legitimate authority. If in this study an anonymous experimenter could successfully command adults to subdue a fifty-year-old man, and force on him painful electric shocks against his protests, one can only wonder what government, with its vastly greater authority and prestige, can command of its subjects. There is, of course, the extremely important question of whether malevolent political institutions could or would arise in American society. The present research contributes nothing to this issue. . . .

Is Milgram considering precisely the same phenomenon as described in the Arthur Koestler excerpt in the preceding chapter? (See Milgram's footnote 4.)

Milgram's material may bear significantly on the mechanism by which an order to kill a human being might be carried out. Does it bear at all on the mechanism by which such an order might be given? Where else might you look for materials on the latter question?

What was the effect on Milgram's experimental results of the different variables he used? Note especially the effect of the following variables. on the subject's willingness to administer the "shock": First, the nearness of the experimenter who was giving the command *increased* the likelihood of obedience; second, the nearness of the person who was receiving the "shock" *decreased* the likelihood of obedience. Would Milgram's results suggest that there is the same like-lihood of obedience from an infantryman in a bayonet charge as there is from a bombardier on a B-52 mission? What variables can you identify in the B-52 situation that, according to Milgram's results, might make the bombardier more likely to obey his orders?

What experimental extensions of Milgram's work would you like to see? Would you like to see results from groups of subjects who pos-sessed particular characteristics — that is, the same age, race, religion, sex, educational level, section of the country, or rural or urban setting? What significance might experiments with each of these spe-cial groups have? Do you think the Army might be interested in com-parative results from a group 19 years old without any college train-ing and a group 23 years old with four years of college? Would it be useful to have parallel experiments carried out in Russia, Germany, France, and other countries? Do you see any methodological problems if the experiment becomes too well known?

The need for further research can be seen in the fact that "forty psychiatrists at a leading medical school" predicted that only one tenth of one percent of the subjects would administer the highest shock, while 62 percent of the subjects actually did so. Does this dis-crepancy suggest possible shortcomings in the theoretical tools used by modern psychiatry to explain mechanisms of group aggression?

To really bring home the impact and the content of these experi-ments, it is strongly recommended that the 45-minute film *Obedi-ence*, footage from the actual Milgram experiments, be seen. The screams are fully as terrifying, and the subjects' obedience fully as spine-chilling, as Milgram describes them.

Following Orders on the Battlefield

Can Milgram's results be transferred directly to actual warfare? Consider the following account, adapted from Brigadier General S. L. A. Marshall's *Men Against Fire*,[2] concerning empirical research done by him during World War II. Marshall held "post-combat mass interviews" with some 400 companies of infantrymen in the European and Pacific combat areas. His central finding was that

. . . On an average not more than 15 percent of the men had actually fired at the enemy positions or personnel with rifles, carbines, grenades, bazookas,

BARs, or machine guns during the course of an entire engagement. . . . The best showing that could be made by the most spirited and aggressive companies was that one man in four had made at least some use of his fire power.

The commanders were amazed, but in every case were convinced of the truth of the reports by the end of the interviewing session. The engagements took place in all kinds of settings, mostly "where it would have been possible for at least 80 percent of the men to fire."

Low percentage of "aggressive" soldiers. The initial interviewing, done in the Gilbert Islands in late 1943, had shown that only 36 men out of an entire battalion had fired in the course of repelling a series of Japanese "banzai" attacks. Most of the firers were "heavy weapons men," with "[t]he really active firers" usually being "in small groups working together." Further interviewing in both Europe and the Pacific showed consistently the average of 15 percent and the maximum of 25 percent firing any weapon at all at the enemy. (To be counted as firing in these results, a man had only to fire once or twice in the general direction of the enemy, not to fire persistently; however, it appears, from what Marshall says, that most of those who fired at all tended to fire persistently.)

Moreover, the percentage was not increased even when the action lasted several days. The same fifteen men out of each 100 fired, while the others did not. Furthermore, it tended to be the *same* fifteen in engagement after engagement. Out of those who did fire, the men with the heavy weapons—Browning Automatic Rifle (BAR), flamethrower, and bazooka—were generally among the firers. Thus the ordinary rifleman was found to fire his weapon very infrequently in any given engagement of World War II. But those back of the lines and using crew-served weapons, such as artillery, were found to have no such problem. "There, the group will keep them going," Marshall remarks, "a well-fixed principle in human nature."

Tactics to increase rate of fire. The average did not change appreciably with the combat-seasoning of the troops, with the nature or extent of enemy attacks, with the theatre of combat (that is, the ratio of firers to non-firers was the same against the Japanese as against the Germans), or with any other identifiable variable. An NCO or officer standing virtually over a man's shoulder could make him fire his weapon, but this was generally impractical. Finding ways of getting men to fire without close supervision was considered by Marshall to be a critical problem of training, selection, and motivation. Marshall saw drilling and discipline as having no assured correlation with willingness to fire; many of those who fired their weapons were lazy, unruly, and disorderly outside of combat, although a majority of those firing fit the usual mold of discipline. Because of this lack of correlation, Marshall rejects the yardsticks of "loyalty and obedience" as the means of predicting whether or not a soldier would fire in battle.

Marshall offers a number of possible suggestions for increasing the rate of fire. Junior leaders should, of course, encourage men to find good firing positions and should give direct orders to fire, so far as possible. Those who still hold back could sometimes be put on artillery crews, or could be given heavy one-man weapons like the BAR or flame-thrower. Marshall remarks that he has seen "many cases" where such a change made a firer out of a non-firer. He surmises that the cause is "self-pride and the ego," noting that a rifleman may tend to feel anonymous and to think that he is not being asked to perform any important task.

Beyond this, Marshall sees the non-firing as resulting from deep cultural inhibitions against killing. He notes that studies of combat fatigue cases in the European theatre of action showed that "fear of killing, rather than fear of being killed," was the chief cause, with the fear of failure (again, not the fear of being killed) running "a strong second." As one response to this inhibition, he urges that the emphasis in training be shifted away from target-firing to massed free fire, directed against features like an embankment or trees. This, he believes, may help "free the rifleman's mind" by disassociating the act of firing from the human being as target.

Marshall compared with Milgram. What do you think of this statement: "Marshall's data shows that Milgram's results are not transferable to actual combat. Only 15 to 25 percent of infantry soldiers engaged in World War II would even fire their weapons in the general direction of the enemy. Most men will not kill under orders, even in the face of military discipline." Are Marshall's results wholly inconsistent with Milgram's? Perhaps there are important differences in the setting of the two "experiments" that may explain the apparent differences in results. Considering the effects of an NCO or officer standing at a man's shoulder, do you see a possible relationship between the results? Whose "discipline" was generally stronger, the Army's or Milgram's? Is there any comparison between the graduated nature of the responses ordered in Milgram's experiment, and the new method of training for firing recommended by Marshall?

In what major areas do the results of the two research projects appear to be mutually confirming? What were Marshall's results on crew-served weapons (that is, artillery, and presumably also machine guns)? Consider Milgram's results in the special series of experiments in which the subject acted as a member of a group.

How to encourage soldiers to kill.   What about Marshall's results showing that those bearing "special" one-man weapons (such as BARs or flamethrowers) used them much more frequently than the riflemen used their weapon? How would you explain this difference? If the explanation is that these "special" weapons men and their actions were more visible, or that the officers were more likely to "keep an eye" on them, would this fact be consistent or inconsistent with Milgram's results? Marshall suggests the difference may have to do with "self-pride and the ego." Might the behavior of the "special" weapons men thus have little or nothing to do with obedience to commands? Do you think it might make an overall difference in the combat results if "special" weapons men were drafted and immediately assigned as such, instead of being picked out of a larger unit undergoing training or even picked out subsequently, on the battlefield? What means might be devised for telling in advance whether a man will fire his weapon? Marshall describes a group of habitual troublemakers in training, some of whom turned out to be among those who fired their weapons regularly. Would Milgram's work furnish the basis for understanding the behavior of these men? If not, where would you look for an explanation?

The Army switched, late in World War II, to a training system that emphasized "protect your buddy" and "protect the integrity of your unit," instead of "kill the enemy," in urging soldiers to make maximum use of firepower. Do Milgram's results make it seem at all likely that this change in tactics could make a difference? Consider the passage on "Tensions," pages 94–96. More recently, the Army has been experimenting with an approach to a basic training that emphasizes the "carrot" rather than the "stick." Instead of being "chewed out" when he does something wrong, the basic trainee is rewarded when he does it right, for example with points that can be cumulated towards a week-end pass. Do you think this technique is likely to result in increased use of fire-power? Decreased use of fire-power? If you need more data to be sure of an answer, how might it be developed? Consider, in this regard, the differences in viewpoint between the Army and the Marines, reflected in the following news item.[4]

There'll be hot soup on the firing range, a leisurely atmosphere at chow time and eight hours of sleep for Army recruits who are to be treated with dignity and addressed as "soldier," not "dud" or "eight-ball."

Profane language is out; so is hazing, harassment and mass punishment.

It's all part of a new look in basic training spelled out in 16 pages of revised Army regulations to improve the treatment of recruits and make their life more comfortable.

The changes, in the works for months, are not an attempt "to pamper or coddle trainees," but should, instead, help turn out a more "disciplined, highly motivated soldier," the regulations say.

On the other hand, Marine Corps Commandant Leonard F. Chapman takes an opposite view and believes Marine training should be "tightened up and toughened up."

"The object of recruit training," Chapman said recently, "is to instill discipline and other virtues of loyalty and patriotism and to put recruits under physical and mental strains to see if they can stand up to it."

Under the Army's regulations, recruit training "is to be devoid of harassment, and respect of the dignity of the individual trainee will be clearly evident at all times."

Concentration camps and atomic bombings. Consider certain other types of lethal violence from World War II. In *Young Radicals,* the psychologist Kenneth Keniston makes the following statement:[3]

. . . At Auschwitz and the other Nazi concentration camps, more than six million Jews were systematically exterminated. Although their executioners were sometimes brutal sadists, acts of personal cruelty were the least momentous part of the extermination of European Jewry. Even more impressive are the numbers of "decent," well-educated Germans (who loved their wives, children, and dogs) who learned to take part in, or blind themselves to, this genocide. Murder became depersonalized and dissociated, performed by a System of cold, efficient precision whose members were only following orders in doing a distasteful job well. Bureaucracy, technology, and science were linked in the service of death. Evil became "banal," in Hannah Arendt's words; it was impersonal, dissociated from its human perpetrators, and institutionalized in an efficient and "scientific" organization. . . .

Keniston goes on to point out that the atomic bombing of Hiroshima and Nagasaki by the United States was probably unnecessary, and that while Germany had done the unthinkable, "Hiroshima demon-

*Reprinted courtesy of Associated Press Newsfeatures.

strated how simple, clean, and easy (from the point of view of the perpetrator) doing the unthinkable could be."[4] Are Keniston's comments consistent with Milgram's results? With Marshall's as well, keeping in mind the results on crew-served weapons? Hiroshima, Nagasaki, and the fire-bombing of Dresden, all largely non-strategic attacks on predominantly civilian targets, killed perhaps a quarter-million people, while Hitler's gas chambers killed six million Jews. But are there distinctions between these horrendous acts in addition to those that turn on number alone? Consider at least the possible bearing of the following four points: (i) the American attacks on Hiroshima, Nagasaki, and Dresden were at least justified at the time in terms of an avowed military function—shortening the war—and most of the people involved apparently believed this justification, while Hitler's slaughter of the Jews was never justified on any war-related basis, but rather with a quasi-religious ideology of "purifying the race;" (ii) the attacks were also by military organizations using weapons of war, not a separate operation using gas ovens; (iii) the attacks were brief, discrete actions, whereas the slaughter of the Jews went on continuously for nearly five years; and (iv) the bombings, of course, were at a distance, and the victims were not in direct view of the bombers. Which, then, may be the more frightening demonstration of the power of Milgram's thesis?

Possible extensions of Marshall's work. It could be very useful to do an extension of Marshall's work in Vietnam today, among South Vietnamese and captured Vietcong as well as among American troops. Do you think that riflemen in Vietnam behave the same as their counterparts in World War II? What are possible sources of differences? Would it be possible to develop an approximate answer to this, by techniques that could be employed in a college community? If you wished to get the highest proportion of candid responses to questions concerning an individual's own participation—as distinct from his general observations of behavior—would you use face-to-face interviews, or unmarked questionnaires that could be returned by mail? If face-to-face interviewing in a group situation biased Marshall's results, in which direction would bias be likely—*more* or *fewer* people saying they had fired their weapons than had actually fired them?

Implications of Marshall's work. Do you find it significant that Marshall found little variation between different units, or under widely different conditions of battle? Why? That he got little variation in result between the European and Pacific theaters of combat? Why? One possible explanation for these results is that the soldiers had a concept of themselves as a solid "in-group" as against a hostile "out-group," and that this concept was strong enough to override any other factor that might have influenced combat behavior against the Germans and Japanese.

If Milgram and Marshall provide evidence of a group dynamic process that explains most large-scale killing in terms that have nothing to do with subjective anger or rancor on the part of the actors, then it appears that *man as a species is not notably more "violent"— in the sense of killing with subjective anger or rancor—than the primates or other animal species, even as they behave in the wild state.* Recall that Richardson's data shows that only about one person in 400 could be expected to die as a victim of murder. Corresponding to each of these victims must be approximately one murderer, since there are only a few murders done by more than one murderer, and these are balanced by single murderers who have more than one victim. Assuming that all of those murdered were victims of "rancorous" violence, *it would therefore mean that one human being out of every four hundred in the population would kill another human being in an act of rancorous or angry violence sometime in his thirty or forty active years of lifetime.* To put it another way: an "average" person would live through 400 active lifetimes—perhaps 14,000 years or over 5,000,000 days—before he came to a single day when he was moved to kill another man out of subjective anger or rancor. Even adding all those killed intentionally in riot or revolution would not increase the rate to more than one person in 250, and the increase would not represent generalized behavior but would be chiefly confined to a half-dozen countries.

Thus, an adequate model for explaining most *organized* group killing in terms other than rancor would bring the data for *all other* human lethal aggression well within the range of the results from the naturalists' observations of "pacific" animals.

Do Marshall and Milgram between them seem to explain a significant part of the dynamics of modern warfare? Or do their findings apply only to the significant but limited area of actual combat? Do they explain why wars *start?* Does their work seem as likely to apply to a guerrilla insurrection as to a classic "war"? To a riot? If not, why not?

Leadership and Lethal Conflict

The two previous sections have examined some of the mechanisms by which the rank and file may be mobilized by their leaders to commit deadly aggression. Now we shall deal with the question of why the leaders (not the intermediate leaders, who also may be carrying out orders, but the highest leaders, who make policy) may initiate deadly aggression. What motivates those at the very top of the command structure to give their commands? Desmond Morris, the naturalist from whose book, *The Human Zoo,* we quoted previously, offers this variegated analysis:[5]

In any organized group of mammals, no matter how cooperative, there is always a struggle for social dominance. As he pursues this struggle, each adult individual acquires a particular social rank, giving him his position, or status, in the group hierarchy. The situation never remains stable for very long, largely because all the status strugglers are growing older. When the overlords, or 'top dogs,' become senile, their seniority is challenged and they are overthrown by their immediate subordinates. There is then renewed dominance squabbling as everyone moves a little farther up the social ladder. At the other end of the scale, the younger members of the group are maturing rapidly, keeping up the pressure from below. In addition, certain members of the group may suddenly be struck down by disease or accidental death, leaving gaps in the hierarchy that have to be quickly filled.

The general result is a constant condition of *status tension.* Under natural conditions this tension remains tolerable because of the limited size of the social groupings. If, however, in the artificial environment of captivity, the group size becomes too big, or the space available too small, then the status 'rat race' soon gets out of hand, dominance battles rage uncontrollably, and the leaders of the packs, prides, colonies or tribes come under severe strain. When this happens, the weakest members of the group are frequently hounded to their deaths, as the restrained rituals of display and counter-display degenerate into bloody violence.

There are further repercussions. So much time has to be spent sorting out the unnaturally complex status relationships that other aspects of social life, such as parental care, become seriously and damagingly neglected.

If the settling of dominance disputes creates difficulties for the moderately crowded inmates of the animal zoo, then it is obviously going to provide an even greater dilemma for the vastly overgrown super-tribes of the human zoo. The essential feature of the status struggle in nature is that it is based on the *personal* relationships of the individuals inside the social group. For the primitive human tribesman the problem was therefore a comparatively simple one, but when the tribes grew into super-tribes and relationships became increasingly impersonal, the problem of status rapidly expanded into the nightmare of super-status.

Before we probe this tender area of urban life, it will be helpful to take a brief look at the basic laws which govern the dominance struggle. The best way to do this is to survey the battlefield from the viewpoint of the dominant animal.

If you are to rule your group and to be successful in holding your position of power, there are ten golden rules you must obey. They apply to all leaders, from baboons to modern presidents and prime ministers. The ten commandments of dominance are these:

* * *

2. *In moments of active rivalry you must threaten your subordinates aggressively.*

At the slightest sign of any challenge from a subordinate baboon, the group leader immediately responds with an impressive display of threatening behaviour. There is a whole range of threat displays available, varying from those motivated by a lot of aggression tinged with a little fear to those motivated by a lot of fear and only a little aggression.

3. *In moments of physical challenge you (or your delegates) must be able forcibly to overpower your subordinates.*

If a threat display fails, then a physical attack must follow. If you are a baboon boss this is a dangerous step to take, for two reasons. Firstly, in a physical fight even the winner may be damaged, and injury is more serious for a dominant animal than for a subordinate. It makes him less daunting for a subsequent attacker. Secondly, he is always outnumbered by his subordinates, and if they are driven too far they may gang up on him and overpower him in a combined effort. It is these two facts that make threat rather than actual attack the preferred method for dominant individuals.

The human leader overcomes this to some extent by employing a special class of 'suppressors.' They, the military or police, are so specialized and professional at their task that only a general uprising of the whole populace would be strong enough to beat them. In extreme cases, a despot will employ a further, even more specialized class of suppressors (such as secret police), whose job it is to suppress the ordinary suppressors if they happen to get out of line. By clever manipulation and administration it is possible to run an aggressive system of this kind in such a way that only the leader knows enough of what is happening to be able to control it. Everyone else is in a state of confusion unless they have orders from above and, in this way, the modern despot can hold the reins and dominate effectively.

* * *

5. *You must suppress squabbles that break out between your subordinates.*

110

If a baboon leader sees an unruly squabble taking place he is likely to interfere and suppress it, even though it does not in any way constitute a direct threat to himself. It gives him another opportunity of displaying his dominance and at the same time helps to maintain order inside the group. Interference of this kind from the dominant animal is directed particularly at squabbling juveniles, and helps to instil in them, at an early age, the idea of a powerful leader in their midst.

The equivalent of this behaviour for the human leader is the control and administration of the laws of his group. The rulers of the earlier and smaller super-tribes were powerfully active in this respect, but there has been increasing delegation of these duties in modern times, due to the increasing weight of other burdens that relate more directly to the status of the leader. Nevertheless, a squabbling community is an inefficent one and some degree of control and influence has to be retained.

*   *   *

10. *You must take the initiative in repelling threats or attacks arising from outside your group.*

It is always the dominant baboon that is in the forefront of the defence against an attack from an external enemy. He plays the major role as the protector of the group. For the baboon, the enemy is usually a dangerous member of another species, but for the human leader it takes the form of a rival group of the same species. At such moments, his leadership is put to a severe test, but, in a sense, it is less severe than during times of peace. The external threat, as I pointed out in the last chapter, has such a powerful cohesive effect on the members of the threatened group that the leader's task is in many ways made easier. The more daring and reckless he is, the more fervently he seems to be protecting the group who, caught up in the emotional fray, never dare question his actions (as they would in peace-time), no matter how irrational these actions may be. Carried along on the grotesque tidal-wave of enthusiasm that war churns up, the strong leader comes into his own. With the greatest of ease he can persuade the members of his group, deeply conditioned as they are to consider the killing of another human being as the most hideous crime known, to commit this same action as an act of honour and heroism. He can hardly put a foot wrong, but if he does, the news of his blunder can always be suppressed as bad for national morale. Should it become public, it can still be put down to bad luck rather than bad judgment. Bearing all this in mind, it is little wonder that, in times of peace, leaders are prone to invent, or at least to magnify, threats from foreign powers that they can then cast in the role of potential enemies. A little added cohesion goes a long way.

These, then, are the patterns of power. I should make it clear that I am not implying that the dominant baboon/human ruler comparison should be taken as meaning that we evolved from baboons, or that our dominance behaviour evolved from theirs. It is true that we shared a common ancestor with baboons, way back in our evolutionary history, but that is not the point.

The point is that baboons, like our early human forbears, have moved out of the lush forest environment into the tougher world of the open country, where tighter group control is necessary. Forest-living monkeys and apes have a much looser social system; their leaders are under less pressure. The dominant baboon has a more significant role to play and I selected him as an example for this reason. The value of the baboon/human comparison lies in the way it reveals the very basic nature of human dominance patterns. The striking parallels that exist enable us to view the human power game with a fresh eye and see it for what it is: a fundamental piece of animal behaviour. But we must leave the baboons to their simpler tasks and take a closer look at the complications of the human situation.

For the modern human leader there are clearly difficulties in performing his dominant role efficiently. The grotesquely inflated power which he wields means that there is the ever present danger that only an individual with an equally grotesquely inflated ego will successfully be able to hold the super-tribal reins. Also, the immense pressures will easily push him into initiating acts of violence, an all-too-natural response to the strains of super-status. Furthermore, the absurd complexity of his task is bound to absorb him to such an extent that it inevitably makes him remote from the ordinary problems of his followers.

*   *   *

Despite the great burdens of present-day leadership and despite the daunting fact that an ambitious male member of a modern super-tribe has a chance smaller than one in a million of becoming the dominant individual of his group, there has been no observable lessening of desire to achieve high status. The urge to climb the social ladder is too ancient, too deeply ingrained to be weakened by a rational assessment of the new situation.

Throughout the length and breadth of our massive communities there are, then, hundreds of thousands of frustrated, would-be leaders with no real hope of leading. What happens to their thwarted ladder-climbing? Where does all the energy go? They can, of course, give up and drop out, but this is a depressing condition. The flaw in the social dropout's solution is that he does not really drop out at all: he stays put and pours scorn on the rat race that surrounds him. This unhappy state is avoided by the great majority of the super-tribesmen by the simple device of competing for leadership in specialized sub-groups of the super-tribe. For some this is easier than others. A competitive profession or craft automatically provides its own social hierarchy. But even there the odds against achieving true leadership may be too great. This gives rise to the almost arbitrary invention of new sub-groups where competition may prove more rewarding. All kinds of extraordinary cults are set up—everthing from canary-breeding and train-spotting to UFO-watching and body-building. In each case the overt nature of the activity is comparatively unimportant. What is really important is that the pursuit provides a new social hierarchy where one did not exist before. Inside it a whole range of rules and procedures is rapidly developed, committees are formed and—most important of all—leaders emerge. A champion canary-breeder or body-builder would, in all probability, have no chance whatsoever of enjoying the heady fruits of dominance, were it not for his involvement in his specialized sub-group.

* * *

The setting up of specialist sub-groups is not the only solution to the super-status dilemma. Localized geographical pseudo-tribes also exist. Each village, town, city and county within a super-tribe develops its own regional hierarchy, providing further substitutes for thwarted super-tribal leadership.

On a smaller scale still, each individual has his own closely knit 'social circle' of personal acquaintances. The list of non-commercial names in his private phone-book or address-book gives a good indication of the extent of this kind of pseudo-tribe. It is particularly important because, as in a true tribe, all its members are personally known to him. Unlike a true tribe, however, all the members are not necessarily known to one another. The social groups overlap and interlock with one another in a complex network. Nevertheless, for each individual his social psuedo-tribe provides one more sphere in which he can assert himself and express his leadership.

Another major super-tribal pattern that has helped to split the group up without destroying it has been the system of social classes.

* * *

. . . A new super-tribal splitting system . . . has recently developed. Age classes are emerging. A widening gap has appeared between what we must now call a young-adult pseudo-tribe and an old-adult pseudo-tribe. The former possesses its own customs and its own dominance system which are increasingly distinct from those of the latter.

* * *

The sobering lesson to be learnt from all this is that the ancient biological need of the human species for a distinct tribal identity is a powerful force that cannot be subdued. As fast as one super-tribal split is invisibly mended, another one appears. Well-meaning authorities talk airily about "hopes for a global society." They see clearly the technical possibility of such a development, given the marvels of modern communication, but they stubbornly overlook the biological difficulties.

A pessimistic view? Certainly not. The prospects will remain gloomy only as long as there is a failure to come to terms with the biological demands of the species. Theoretically there is no good reason why small groupings, satisfying the requirements of tribal identity, should not be constructively interrelated inside thriving super-tribes which, in turn, constructively interact to form a massive, global mega-tribe. Failures to date have largely been due to attempts to *suppress* the existing differences between the various groups, rather than to improve the nature of these differences by converting them into more rewarding and peaceful forms of competitive social interaction. Attempts to iron out the whole world into one great expanse of uniform monotony are doomed to disaster. This applies at all levels, from break-away nations to tear-away gangs. When the sense of social identity is threatened, it fights back. The fact that it has to fight for its existence means, at the least, social upheaval and, at the worst, bloodshed.

As the super-tribes became bigger and bigger, the task of ruling the sprawling, teeming populations became greater, the tensions of overcrowding grew, and the frustrations of the super-status race became more intense. There was more and more pent-up aggression, looking for an outlet. Inter-group conflict provided it on a grand scale.

For the modern leader, then, going to war has many advantages that the Stone-Age leader did not enjoy. To start with, he does not have to risk getting his face bloody. Also, the men he sends to their deaths are not personal acquaintances of his: they are specialists, and the rest of society can go about its daily life. Trouble-makers who are spoiling for a fight, because of the super-tribal pressures they have been subjected to, can have their fight without directing it at the super-tribe itself. And having an outside enemy, a villain, can make a leader into a hero, unite his people and make them forget the squabbles that were giving him so many headaches.

It would be naive to think that leaders are so super-human that these factors do not influence them. Nevertheless, the major factor remains the urge to maintain or improve inter-leader status. The out-of-phase progress of the different super-tribes that I mentioned earlier is undoubtedly the greatest problem. If, because of its natural resources or its ingenuity, one super-tribe gets one jump ahead of another, then there is bound to be trouble. The advanced group will impose itself on the backward group in one way or another and the backward group will resent it in one way or another. An advanced group is, by its very nature, expansive, and simply cannot bear to leave things alone and mind its own business. It tries to influence other groups, either by dominating them or by *helping* them. Unless it dominates its rivals to the point where they lose their identities and are absorbed into the advanced super-tribal body (which is often geographically impossible), the situation will be unstable. If the advanced super-tribe helps other groups and makes them stronger, but in its own image, then the day will dawn when they are strong enough to revolt and repel the super-tribe with its own weapons and its own methods.

While all this is going on, the leaders of other powerful, advanced super-tribes will be watching anxiously to make sure that these expansions are not too successful. If they are, then *their* inter-group status will begin to slip.

All this is done under a remarkably transparent but nevertheless persistent cloak of ideology. To read the official documents, one would never guess that it was really the pride and status of the leaders that were at stake. It is always, apparently, a matter of ideals, moral principles, social philosophies or religious beliefs. But to a soldier staring down at his severed legs, or holding his entrails in his hands, it means only one thing: a wasted life. The reason why it was so easy to get him into that position was that he is not only a potentially aggressive animal, but also an intensely co-operative one. All that talk of defending the principles of his super-tribe got through to him because it became a question of helping his friends. Under the stress of war, under the

114

direct and visible threat from the out-group, the bonds between him and his battle companions became immensely strengthened. He killed, more not to let them down than for any other reason. The ancient tribal loyalties were so strong that, when the final moment came, he had no choice.

Given the pressures of the super-tribe, given the global overcrowding of our species, and given the inequalities in progress of the different super-tribes, there is little hope that our children will grow up to wonder what war was all about. The human animal has got too big for its primate boots. Its biological equipment is not strong enough to cope with the unbiological environment it has created. Only an immense effort of intellectual restraint will save the situation now.

* * *

What is it that makes a human individual one of "them," to be destroyed like a verminous pest, rather than one of "us," to be defended like a dearly beloved brother? What is it that puts him into an out-group and keeps us in the in-group? How do we recognize "them"? It is easiest, of course, if they belong to an entirely separate super-tribe, with strange customs, a strange appearance and a strange language. Everything about them is so different from "us" that it is a simple matter to make the gross over-simplification that they are *all* evil villains. The cohesive forces that helped to hold their group together as a clearly defined and efficiently organized society also serve to set them apart from us and to make them frightening by virtue of their unfamiliarity. Like the Shakespearean dragon, they are "more often feared than seen."

Such groups are the most obvious targets for the hostility of our group. But supposing we have attacked them and defeated them, what then? Supposing we dare not attack them? Supposing we are, for whatever reason, at peace with other super-tribes for the time being: what happens to our in-group aggression now? We may, if we are very lucky, remain at peace and continue to operate efficiently and constructively within our group. The internal cohesive forces, even without the assistance of an out-group threat, may be sufficiently strong to hold us together. But the pressures and stresses of the super-tribe will still be working on us, and if the internal dominance battle is fought too ruthlessly, with extreme subordinates experiencing too much suppression or poverty, then cracks will soon begin to show. If severe inequalities exist between the sub-groups that inevitably develop within the super-tribe, their normally healthy competition will erupt into violence. Pent-up sub-group aggression, if it cannot combine with the pent-up aggression of other sub-groups to attack a common, foreign enemy, will vent itself in the form of riots, persecutions and rebellions.

* * *

In some way we must tackle, at the roots, those conditions I referred to that are ripening us so effectively for inter-group violence.

115

I have already discussed these conditions, but it will help to summarize them briefly. They are:

1. The development of fixed human territories.
2. The swelling of tribes into over-crowded super-tribes.
3. The invention of weapons that kill at a distance.
4. The removal of leaders from the front line of battle.
5. The creation of a specialized class of professional killers.
6. The growth of technological inequalities between the groups.
7. The increase of frustrated status aggression within the groups.
8. The demands of the inter-group status rivalries of the leaders.
9. The loss of social identity within the super-tribes.
10. The exploitation of the co-operative urge to aid friends under attack.

The one condition I have deliberately omitted from this list is the development of differing ideologies. As a zoologist, viewing man as an animal, I find it hard to take such differences seriously in the present context. If one assesses the inter-group situation in terms of actual behaviour, rather than verbalized theorizing, differences in ideology fade into insignificance alongside the more basic conditions. They are merely the excuses, desperately sought for to provide reasons high-sounding enough to justify the destruction of thousands of human lives.

Examining the list of the ten more realistic factors it is difficult to see where one can begin to seek improvement in the situation. Taken together, they appear to offer an absolutely cast-iron guarantee that man will for ever be at war with man.

Main motives of leaders. How clearly does Morris delineate the factors that he believes cause leaders to command their followers to engage in lethal group conflict? The following are perhaps the most important of the factors he lists:

An intense status struggle through which the leader achieves his position at the top of a "super-tribe" that may number in the millions. This status struggle is a weeding-out process through which the super-tribe gets leaders who are enormously power-conscious and power-hungry.

A basic human leadership role, requiring the characteristics of dominance and the ability to act decisively to keep group order and maintain self-defense, which evolved because of the needs for defense against predators in the open country.

The need of each super-tribal leader to preserve pride and status vis-à-vis the leaders of other super-tribes.

The removal of certain former constraints on the leader's actions,

116

since the super-tribal leader need not fear personal injury and very rarely sends his own friends out to engage in lethal combat.

Is Morris' further analysis of why the followers obey the leaders clear? Does he seem to alternate in this analysis among several quite different factors, including (i) physical over-crowding, (ii) the frustrations of status-seeking, which generate aggression, and (iii) the cohesiveness among group members engaged in a common struggle? Are there some significant difficulties with this analysis? We have already noted that overcrowding, alone, does not seem a sufficient variable to supply a universal explanation for the actual behavior of various societies. (The Netherlands, post-war Japan, and Hong Kong are crowded societies with low levels of lethal conflict; despite recent events, India could be added.) Status-seeking frustrations would appear, on Morris' own account, to be at least as much a function of particular kinds of cultural structures as of over-crowding — although this does not negate the possibility that much aggression may be aroused by over-crowding. Cohesiveness seems a rather different kind of factor, similar to that described by Arthur Koestler in an earlier excerpt.

Does Morris appear to go far beyond his evidence when he states that his ten listed factors, taken together, "appear to offer an absolutely cast-iron guarantee that man will forever be at war with man"? Is his conclusion weakened by the existence of some reasonably sizeable "super-tribes" that have experienced relatively little lethal conflict of any form in the modern era? (Switzerland and Sweden are examples; although their suicide rates are high, this fact should have little bearing on the operation of the factors that Morris describes.) Does Morris' pessimism turn on a view that some of the factors listed above are physiologically built-in to the species? If so, is this a supportable conclusion? In an earlier book, *The Naked Ape*, Morris says that when earliest man moved out from the forests to the open country and "became a co-operative hunter with a fixed home base," he had to modify "the typical primate system . . . to match his adopted carnivore role." One major modification was that[6]

[W]ithin the group the tyrannical hierarchy system of the usual primate colony had to be modified considerably to ensure full co-operation from the weaker members when out hunting. But it could not be abolished altogether. There had to be a mild hierarchy, with stronger members and a top leader, if firm decisions were going to be taken, even if this leader was obliged to

117

take the feelings of his inferiors more into account than his hairy, forest-dwelling equivalent would have to do.

But now, in *The Human Zoo,* Morris says that "The point is that baboons, like our early human forbears, have moved out of the lush forest environment into the tougher world of the open country, where *tighter* group control is necessary. Forest-living monkeys and apes have a much *looser* social system; their leaders are under less pressure. The dominant baboon has a *more significant* role to play and I selected him as an example for this reason. The value of the baboon/human comparison lies in the way it reveals the very basic nature of human dominance patterns" [italics added].

Well, then, is the domination of the human leader supposed to be more or less tyrannical than that of the forest-dwelling apes? Is there a reduction of power, in the human leader, from the forest's "tyrannical hierarchy" to "a mild hierarchy, with stronger members;" or is there an increase, from a "much looser social system" to one with "tighter group control" and "a more significant role" for the leader to play than among the forest primates? The trouble is that, in books published two years apart, Morris takes *both* stands. Nothing could illustrate more dramatically the paucity of evidence on what, if anything, is biologically built into man by way of social dominance patterns. Nothing could show better the extent of the leap in the dark that Morris must take in arguing that the baboon "reveals the very basic nature of human dominance patterns," or of the further leap in the dark in equating leading a few dozen baboons (never in lethal conflict with other baboons) with the "basic nature" of what a human leader does, including leading his country into war.

Despite strong reservations about Morris' conclusions, it seems fair to make the following statements:

First, some degree of hierarchical structuring occurs in all primates and virtually all higher animals, and whether or not the physiological basis for such structuring is weaker or stronger in man than in the forest-dwelling apes — and indeed, even if the basis is entirely learned behavior and not at all physiological — it seems that the formation of tribal hierarchies is an extremely pervasive pattern, likely to be of significance in man.

Second, Morris' perfectly accurate statement that "an ambitious male member of a modern super-tribe has a chance smaller than one in a million of becoming the dominant individual of his group" is of potentially great significance. This would seem true whether the factors that propelled the leader upward lay in his one-in-a-million physiological characteristics, or his one-in-a-million upbringing or environmental background.

A Survey of Theories of Death-Dealing Behavior in Man

The preceding two chapters of this book have presented a considerable array of materials on human aggression. One thing seems clear: If we wish to consider the proffered explanations rationally, we must have some agreement on what we mean by "aggression." Storr and Freud, for example, mean vastly different things by "aggression"; Storr means "virtually all energized activity," while Freud means an impulse to destroy or cause death.

Since this volume is concerned with conflict, and particularly with lethal conflict, it seems appropriate to define human "aggression" in these terms: *"conduct whose deliberate end is to kill or cause serious injury to another human being."* The various views as to the causes of such behavior are the subject of this section.

There are a number of separate identifiable theories, which for convenience can be laid out in very rough categories, as in the following table, along the "nature-nurture" continuum. In columns I and II are views that most strongly emphasize the innate or genetic causes of death-dealing conduct, and in columns III and IV are the views that emphasize the importance of cultural or environmental factors. It should be stressed that many of these views are not, according to their terms, mutually exclusive, and that a *combination* of explanations may be needed to fit the many patterns of lethal aggression:

THEORIES THAT TEND TO EMPHASIZE:

I INNATE OR GENETIC DETERMINANTS OF AGGRESSION, OF A KIND RATHER CONSTANT FOR ALL PEOPLE AND ALL CULTURES	II INNATE OR GENETIC DETERMINANTS OF AGGRESSION, BUT OF A KIND INTERACTING WITH A SPECIFIC ENVIRONMENTAL SETTING
Freud's *"death instinct"* Lorenz' *hydraulic-accumulator* model	*Attack and self-defense* reaction *Affirmative propensity* for minimum food and territory *Status-seeking* by leaders (one interpretation)

119

III ENVIRONMENTAL DETERMINANTS OF AGGRESSION, OF A KIND RATHER CONSTANT FOR ALL PEOPLE AND ALL CULTURES	IV ENVIRONMENTAL DETERMINANTS OF AGGRESSION, OF A KIND TENDING TO RELATE TO SPECIFIC INDIVIDUALS OR SPECIFIC CULTURES
Storr's *infantile-dependency* model *Universal-reaction* model; Freud's "Oedipus complex"	*Brain damage* to a specific individual Generalized model of *frustration–aggression* *Stress* from crowding, noise, over-stimulation *Boredom* model, under-stimulation *Acquisitiveness,* under cultural norms *Status-seeking* by leaders (another interpretation) *Ideology* model *Imitation* model Milgram's *command and obedience* model

Here, in summary, is a recapitulation and comparison of these various explanatory models:

The death instinct is the classic Freudian view of a stream of instinctive energy specifically directed towards destructive behavior. It is perhaps not irrelevant that Freud's psychological interpretation of the causes of war and other death-dealing group behavior was often the *only* view offered during the forties and fifties, when many scholars of the past decade attended universities. Thus, many scholars who write incidentally or peripherally about lethal conflict, without any special expertise in the subject, assume that Freud's view is correct. It is obvious without any particularly searching analysis, that much of our contemporary literature and scholarship is casually permeated with the Freudian view, in spite of the lack of supporting evidence for this view. William Golding's widely read novel *Lord of the Flies,* for example, seems based on assumptions about human psychology that are closely related to Freud's views (although one *could* offer alternative interpretations of Golding's psychological assumptions). Judging from actual experimental literature, one would expect quite different results from Golding's group of boys, cast up wrecked on a tropical island without adult supervision. For example, one likely outcome of this situation would be a passive, gradual social disintegration, catatonia, and death, in the absence of adult direction. These developments are, of course, far less dramatic than Golding's scenario of primitive aggression, cannibalism, and man-hunting. But from the standpoint of modern psychology, Golding's story seems one of the least likely outcomes.

The "hydraulic" model. This is essentially the Lorenz view. "Aggression" involves attack on other members of the species, but with an ordinarily positive function, and without any specific direction towards destruction or killing. As in Freud, the "hydraulic" notion emphasizes that this innate aggressive energy accumulates, and that an outlet for it must be found. But Lorenz adds a second instinct, one which is aimed at automatically *inhibiting* the dealing of the death-blow. This — the theory runs — is very weak in man, since in his natural state he is not ordinarily capable of dealing a deathblow during the time in which he is physiologically mobilized for maximum aggressive conduct (that is, before an unarmed man can dispatch an opponent he will probably "cool off," or the opponent will decamp). Man has only become capable of dealing a rapid deathblow with the onset of technology.

Attack and self-defense model. This highly modified version of the Lorenz view accepts an innate propensity to defend oneself (and, perhaps, also one's family and land) against attack or threat of attack, but this thesis purports to explain death-dealing behavior in only a limited range of situations. Also, it is not a "hydraulic" model. This defensive instinct will be triggered by appropriate circumstances, but there is no continuous accumulation of energy that must be "worked off" or "got rid of." Broadened to take account of numerous cultural features, this becomes what we may call the *fear model.*

Affirmative-propensity model. This can be viewed as another marked modification of Lorenz, in which certain object-directed innate behavior moves toward a few essentials (such as food and perhaps territory); if blocked or prevented, these drives may lead to lethal violence. Like the idea of *defending* essentials that one already has, this behavior model applies in only a limited range of situations.

Status model. Discussed below.

The frustration model. (This is taken out of "order" on our nature–nurture continuum because it facilitates discussion of other viewpoints.) This is a very popular model for explaining all kinds of aggression, including lethal aggression. It was introduced by J. Dollard and three other authors in *Frustration and Aggression,* published in 1939. One recent paper comments:[8]

"There seems to be little doubt that frustration is a major stimulus for provoking aggressive responses, but it is debatable whether the original formulation that all aggression stems from frustration, or that aggression always follows frustration is accurate." . . . One great difficulty with the theory is in defining "frustration." In some formulations, it is said that frustration is equivalent to the interruption or "blocking" of *any* ongoing activity, whether of child or adult. This definition makes it very difficult to identify specific factors causing frustration in the environment—and, of course, the theory very much emphasizes that the totality of the individual's external environment interacts with the instinctive capacity for aggression, causing specific kinds or levels of aggressive response. What causative events, for example, are to be looked for in lethal aggressive behavior? Subsequent refinements of the theory have considered possible effects of cumulative or persistent frustration, and also introduced the useful notion of a "threshhold" of frustration; that is, different individuals will tolerate differing degrees of interference or interruption before responding with a given level of aggressive behavior. In some environments and for some individuals, especially where there has been an accumulation of frustrating incidents, the "threshhold" can be very low—prisoners have been known to stab a fellow inmate for failing to pass the salt.

The infantile-dependency model. This view, which is expressed in the Storr excerpt, starts with only a very generalized assumption about innate patterns of behavior, but assumes that these innate propensities are nearly always subjected to an early environment in which the infant feels great dependency and is frustrated in his attempts at independent activity. This early frustration causes part of the instinctive energy to be transformed into "hate," with potentially lethal consequences. Storr is not completely clear as to whether this energy thereafter accumulates "hydraulically," specifically reserved for the purposes of hating and requiring constant discharge; or merely remains a latent pattern until triggered by some outside event; or perhaps builds to, then holds at, some relatively constant level. In this model, there is a clear interplay between instinctive and early environmental factors. Storr also refers to the mechanism of "projection," by which one's own hatred may be attributed to another person or group. This seems less an independent cause of death-dealing behavior than a mechanism that may be associated with the ultimate channeling of rage or anger arising out of any of the basic models.

"Universal-reaction" model. The infantile-dependency theory described by Storr can be taken as a special case of "frustration-aggression," emphasizing the persisting and fundamental role of severe frustrations experienced in infancy, and thus emphasizing frustration suffered at a particular *time* of life as conditioning the behavior Storr calls "hate." However, by emphasizing such common features of environment (the presence of the parent and the relatively small size and helplessness of the infant), this theory differs from the usual "frustration" model in suggesting universal interactions between the human organism and basic environmental features (which do *not* vary from culture to culture) as laying the basis for lethally aggressive behavior — not for *immediate* lethal aggression, but for a reaction that may be years delayed. This kind of mechanism is also found in pronounced form in classic Freudian theory, which posits the existence of a child's "Oedipal wish" to kill its father and marry its mother. Freud clearly considered the Oedipal situation to be a feature of any environment in which a child is principally attached to a male-female pair.

Brain damage model. This is the model suggested by the Boston group for some aggressive acts, discussed briefly on pages 79–80.

Stress model. This is a close parallel to the frustration-aggression model, but tends to emphasize the *direct physiological* consequences of unusual or extreme environmental conditions, rather than the intermediating psychological response to events which interrupt, forestall, or rechannel activity. This model thus looks particularly to environmental conditions such as crowding, isolation, and noise as affecting or eliciting an aggressive response. The prison example cited under "frustration" might also be explained by this means (emphasizing the overcrowding) or by a combination of the two models (overcrowding, plus a series of specific frustrations likely to arise in that particular kind of overcrowded environment). Previous excerpts from Desmond Morris and others have suggested that this model is highly significant for animals, and may be significant for man.

Boredom model. Another parallel to the "frustration-aggression" model is boredom. The writer Arthur Miller pointedly describes the effects that an extreme lack of challenge, direction, or meaningful stimuli can have on human beings [from "The Bored and the Violent," *Harper's* (1962) p. 50[9]].

The delinquent is stuck with his boredom, stuck inside it, stuck to it, until for two or three minutes he "lives"; he goes on a raid around the corner and feels the thrill of risking his skin or his life as he smashes a bottle filled with gasoline on some other kid's head. In a sense, it is his trip to Miami. It makes his day. It is his shopping tour. It gives him something to talk about for a week. It is *life*. Standing around with nothing coming up is as close to dying as you can get. Unless one grasps the power of boredom, the threat of it to one's existence, it is impossible to "place" the delinquent as a member of the human race.

This model may have particular significance in a society such as ours, where we grow up accustomed to a constant stream of events and stimulations: travel, new people, television, moving to new cities, changing schools, getting a car at sixteen, and many other things that are rare events in most human cultures. This experience may create a set of psychological expectations, and perhaps even lead to physiological adaptations, by which a constant high level of stimulation is required to prevent boredom. In a sense, it may be said that living in our culture typically creates a "low boredom threshhold." Just "a-settin' and a-whittlin' " is not enough to keep the average teenage male from being driven up the wall. For most, there are a variety of activities available (sports, parties, cars, and girls), but these are not available, or adequate, for all.

Acquisitiveness model. This is the view that lethal aggression may result from an individual's or group's effort to acquire objects on which they place some value for cultural reasons (environmentally acquired tastes for jewelry or horses, and also "tastes" for more food or territory, to the extent that one rejects the model of an instinctive "affirmative propensity"). In its chief implications for violence, this is really a special case of the "frustration-aggression" model: interference with the ongoing activity of seeking to acquire the object leads to an aggressive response. If for some environmental reason the individual places an extremely high value on the object, it is possible that lethal violence will follow.

Status model. This is one which Desmond Morris considers especially relevant in explaining the aggressive posture of leaders, and is the first among the theories that we have considered to focus specifically and differentially on why *leaders* may lead their followers into lethal conflict. Morris seems to regard a "status drive" as substantially built-in to human physiology, an "instinct" for achieving the highest status possible, if you will. In the gigantic "super-tribal"

124

communities there are now very few highest-status positions per capita of the human population; there are enormous frustrations and set-backs in trying to achieve such a position; and those who reach the highest positions are likely to have a particularly strong status-drive, honed razor-sharp by the competition. These leaders, in the course of protecting their power and seeking to extend it further, may come into conflict with other leaders and lead the whole "super-tribe" into large-scale lethal conflict.

Some, emphasizing the genetic interpretation of Morris' view, may point to the almost universal seeking of status and the establishment of a "pecking order" in groups of higher animals and primates. Others, still genetically oriented, may urge that being more careful with the evidence requires us to speak of an "identity drive" rather than a "status drive" among animals—that is, a process in which animals attempt to achieve a high status, but their primary need is to achieve a defined status, whether high or low, within the group. On this view, the absence of a clear-cut social structure in modern societies, the presence of overlapping and confusing roles that often lead to con-stant changes in status position vis-à-vis various groups within which the individual moves (and sometimes to no status at all, as in the anonymity of riding the subway or standing in a line), all intensely frustrate the built-in need to have a clearly defined position within the group. Again, leaders might be expected to have a particularly strong drive both to achieve high status and to define some unam-biguous status for themselves.

Using either of these views—"status drive" or "identity drive"—one would have some explanation not only for the leaders' aggressive behavior but for that of their followers. The followers would be primed for aggressive conduct if they were frustrated in their ongoing efforts to achieve status or identity. Possibly this theory could offer some explanation of such violent behavior as that of Napoleonic France after the revolution and that of Hitlerite Germany after the debacles of World War I, hyper-inflation, and depression. In both societies, the existing social order had been turned upside down, and "all bets were off" on status and identity as previously perceived. On this view, a society that has just undergone a really sweeping internal upheaval, far from being likely to "turn inward" and "heal its wounds," may be a particularly dangerous factor on the international scene.

Another view of the "status" theory would be closer to the non-genetic explanations of aggression. This view would simply emphasize that those who reach leadership positions in a very large society are likely to be self-selected individuals who, because of a variety of special environmental factors in their own lives, are among the most competitive, power-hungry, and status-seeking individuals in that society. Thus they would be far more likely than an individual chosen at random from that society to protect their perceived power and status, and quite possibly to attempt to extend it, by extreme means. While this interpretation does not seek to explain the *followers'* behavior, the search for rôle and identity—and perhaps for at least a sufficient degree of status so that one doesn't get "dumped on" by everyone else—can be separately considered a pervasive cultural phenomenon. The frequent failure to attain this identity in some complex societies then becomes an important added source of "frustration" aggression.

It is probably some version of these views on the "specialness" or greater intensity of leaders' aggression that underlies suggestions for ending lethal conflict, ranging from "let the leaders fight each other" to opposition to proposals for an ABM defense around Washington.

As applied to persons other than leaders, the "status" model may overlap the "infantile dependency" model as an explanation for aggression apparently elicited by situations of substantial downgrading or denial of social position.

Ideology model. This is along the lines of the view suggested by Arthur Koestler, emphasizing environment and group influences, particularly those in the form of religious or political ideas. In Koestler's view, the operation of this mechanism may also involve an instinctive component, but it is quite unlike the instinctive component suggested in *any* of the preceding theories: a tendency to cleave together, to seek solidarity with the group; a "herd instinct" rather than a "death instinct." (Indeed, to the extent that a particular interpretation of Koestler's views de-emphasizes specific ideas in favor of pure cooperation in physical action, we may speak instead of a *"cooperation model."*) This model seems more appropriate to explain lethal aggression by groups than lethal aggression by individuals. The inward psychological state of the individual committing the lethal act in accordance with the ideology of the group—again in contrast to all of the previously described models—is not one of hate, rage, or fear, but is instead "assenting" or "energetic" or "enthusiastic." Such an individual may say, "I kill you in sorrow and not in anger."

126

(There is a variant model which might be termed "fanaticism;" this model is a combination of the Koestler model with any of those preceding models that might explain a subjective state of hate or rage. In this model, a lethal act grows out of an articulated ideology *and* hatred for the victim. This model may describe the state of mind of many political assassins.)

Imitation model. This view is a first cousin of Koestler's, emphasizing the features of environment that display or approve of lethal violence in certain circumstances, but this viewpoint does not emphasize the ideological factors as motivating group behavior to the extent that Koestler does (for example, this view might emphasize that a group of soldiers in battle "helps the outfit," doing what everybody else is observed to do and imitating the remembered actions of thousands of movie and TV soldiers, but would not emphasize that they are "fighting for the flag").

The imitation model may be of growing significance in American society today, where the role of the "revolutionary" may have now achieved a degree of separate identification for many high school and college students who come from substantial middle-class backgrounds and do not have in great degree the other personal indicia of proclivity to extreme violence. It may be that we will shortly see the full flowering of what David Riesman described in *The Lonely Crowd* as a shift among younger persons from values and behavior patterns largely derived from parents to values and behavior patterns largely derived from their own peers—from "inner direction" to "other direction." If so, the establishment of a recognized "revolutionary" pattern of behavior among certain respected members of the same age group may hold strong attraction, without further reason, for some significant fraction of the revolutionaries' peers. It may, in fact, come to be regarded by some as just "doing your thing" in a way that is romantic, dashing, or highly stimulating—like a pilot, Marine, or racing-driver, for example—without the imitator fully coming to grips with the implications or special potentials for lethal violence of the role he has assumed. There may be potent possibilities for combination of this model with the "boredom" model.

Command and obedience model. This, of course, is the model suggested by Milgram's experiments. It emphasizes one element of the external environment: the presence of a specific authority-figure telling the subject to go out and kill. Like the three preceding models, it is particularly appropriate for explaining group behavior like war, although not very helpful in describing individual lethal acts (except, perhaps, for a Mafia "contract"). It is also a first cousin to Koestler's view. (Extending the example of the soldiers, two paragraphs previous, this view would emphasize that a group of soldiers in battle were "following orders.") Like the "ideology" and "imitation" models, this is closely complementary to the "status" model; it suggests why followers follow to counterpoint the latter's suggestion of why leaders lead.

Two "non-starters" in terms of further separate models for lethal aggression would appear to be behavioristic "learning theory" models (i.e., that one learns to kill because it brings benefits) and "displacement of hunting behavior" (i.e., that man has an instinct to hunt prey of other species, and not being able to exercise it, kills human beings instead). The "hunting behavior" theory goes aground on the same shoals as does Freud's "death instinct" — the wide variations in actual death-dealing behavior from society to society, plus the lack of any evidence of an inverse correlation between the extent to which people go hunting and the extent to which they carry out death-dealing acts — although the "death instinct" *is* included on the main list above, because of its significant role in the intellectual history of this century. The "learning theory" model may be useful for a few acts of *non*-lethal violence: for example, the armed robber who succeeds in his first robbery attempt may have his patterns of behavior "reinforced" and be more likely to commit additional robberies. But very few murderers commit more than one murder, and any learning process associated with the act is likely to be "aversive conditioning" rather than reinforcement — a sense of horror and rejection by any witnesses, the terror of "hiding out" and of being the subject of an intense manhunt. There may be a few exceptions (rare multiple murderers who relish publicity; or group behavior in armies which have come to associate killing with personal booty and free sexual enjoyment of the female population). But the chief modern exception — where one may be said to "learn" to kill — is a mechanism already included in the "command and obedience" model above: cases of group military behavior where there is "reinforcing" approval from the command figure if the lethal act is carried out and immediate disapproval where it is not carried out. Except for minor exceptions, therefore, the "learning" model seems redundant with what has already been set forth.

Multiple models for one situation. The preceding models may combine in various ways to suggest overall explanations for conduct that turns into lethal conflict. Consider, for example, the Morris excerpt. Which of our models can be said to figure in his list? What elements of Morris' list, and which of the applicable models, might best describe, say, the Russian invasion of Czechoslovakia in 1968? Which would be likely to describe an armed resistance by the Czech army, if resistance had occurred?

Is the existence of possible multiple causes, as in the Morris excerpt, discouraging? Perhaps some generalized hope may be gleaned from the fact that bacteriologists and parasitologists are delighted when they find that a particular germ or parasite has a complex life cycle, because they know that if they can find some means of attacking any step in the life cycle they can destroy the organism. Which of the elements in Morris' list seem most susceptible to deliberate human control?

Application of models to situations. Considering the last sentence of description of the "acquisitiveness model," may there be a special significance to this view when the "individual" is a national leader, and the "object" sought is oil or territory? Do you think that a complete international cut-off of trade with communist China would be an effective peace-keeping measure? Concerning the relative importance of this and the "affirmative-propensity" model, note that people in many parts of India, and in some other cultures, will often quietly starve to death, sometimes with a food-vendor's cart just a few feet away, without even attempting to steal food, let alone engaging in lethal violence to obtain it. What factors, in terms of the models, might be capable of changing this passivity?

Which of the models might help to explain the state of mind of a revolutionary guerrilla leader? Of the men he led? Does the model for such a leader's behavior have to be the same as that for his men's behavior? Might they be the same? Would you expect that the model describing the rank-and-file guerrilla's lethal behavior might be different than that describing the lethal behavior of the foot-soldiers on the other side? Would it affect your answer to the foregoing if the question concerned, specifically, a guerrilla fighting under Fidel Castro in Cuba in 1958, that guerrilla being an ex-plantation worker to whom Castro promised his own piece of land (although the promise was not kept); and a regular soldier, drafted into Batista's army, who also had formerly been a plantation worker?

From what you know of the events by way of general information, how would you assess the application of the models to the following events:

The 1967 riots in the big-city black ghettoes of Detroit and Newark. (To begin with, it seems that the models that have the greatest applicability to homicide by individuals — such as intense frustration — would also be likely motives for relatively unplanned, unstructured lethal group actions, such as riots. However, these same motives would not necessarily be accurate descriptions of highly structured group actions, such as wars. Nevertheless, might an "ideology" or "cooperation" model often be a useful element of explanation in *both* riots and wars?)

The demonstrations, and the killing of four students, at Kent State in May 1970.

The United States decision to send troops to Vietnam in 1965. In this connection, what model or models might fit the behavior of President Johnson? If you give him, in every respect, the benefit of the doubt, what models might fit? What models might fit the behavior of the troops? Would the same model apply to an infantryman looking for a sniper and a B-52 bombardier dropping his bombs? What might the difference be? What about the troops who committed the massacre at My Lai? If a pilot interviewed after a bomb run explained that it was "just a job," what model or models might apply to his lethal behavior?

Inhibitions against lethal conflict. If a population is overwhelmingly hostile to a war, do some of the models become inoperative? Do some of the models have "mirror images" that may restrain, rather then enhance, the propensity for lethal aggressive conduct? Lorenz and others suggested there may be some degree of biological inhibition of lethal conduct, and all writers agree that there are vitally important cultural or environmental inhibitions. For example, extreme aggression is normally discouraged in the growing child by various forms of parental behavior — corporal punishment, other forms of punishment, withholding of affection, reward, and reasoning. Is extreme corporal punishment likely to be a good way to teach a child to be nonviolent? Actual models of parental behavior, as well as the behavior of other persons in the immediate environment, are likely to have substantial impact. Take an example of two children, one living in Tribe A and one in Tribe B. In Tribe A the child's father has a dispute with a member of a neighboring village over a yam patch,

130

kills the neighbor, perhaps before the assembled members of both villages, and is subsequently rewarded by praise and feasting. In Tribe B, the father involved in a similar dispute goes to the village elders, who decree a judgment that both parties observe. Naturally the child in Tribe A is going to grow up with very different ideas from the child in Tribe B as to appropriate dispute-settlement techniques. Also important as an inhibitor, of course, is a firmly and repeatedly expressed parental or cultural prohibition against killing. Certainly such a prohibition makes it less likely that this individual will, in later life, readily follow modes of lethal conduct such as those described in the "ideology" of "obedience" models, and would appear likely to limit the effect of a wide range of the models. (Which most, and which least, would you suppose?) What other cultural or environmental factors may reduce the amount of lethal behavior?

If there were any degree of instinctive inhibition against dealing a death-blow, as suggested by Lorenz, would it be more likely to operate in a bayonet charge or a B-52 raid? How much influence could it have over the man "pushing the button" for nuclear holocaust in Washington or Moscow? Would you be surprised to learn that one Asian commander, when his troops were about to engage in hand-to-hand combat with bayonets, always ordered them to remove their shirts?

To the extent that there is a major inhibition (whether genetic or cultural) against lethal aggression, an important process for a potentially aggressive group is that of *dehumanizing* a potential enemy. What factors may contribute to the process of dehumanization? What factors may slow it down or reverse it?

Using models for prevention of conflict. If you believed that Lorenz's "hydraulic" model was a valid general explanation of aggressive behavior, would you see reasons for encouraging children to watch violent TV shows and play with "war" toys? What if you were particularly concerned with the "imitation" model? Can you think of possible experiments that might indicate which model you *should* be most concerned with? Perhaps viewing TV or film violence could provide a mild discharge or displacement of the tendency to lethal aggression for *some* people (for example, children, who might not have sufficiently detailed fantasies for discharge, or adults who were too inhibited to fantasize about aggression), while for certain *other* people it might provide models to imitate, and for most—as one recent study indicates—it might have no effect at all.

131

The various models suggest the existence of various objects or goals of aggressive behavior which, if achieved, will terminate the behavior, at least temporarily. For each model, how far can you go in identifying the kind of action or achievement which would satisfy the need? Does this process of identification help to evaluate how easy or difficult it would be to end, or prevent the recurrence of, certain conflicts or types of conflicts? Consider, in this connection, the conflicts listed on page 130.

The brain damage model is one that does not involve a goal or object to be reached or obtained by aggression. But is the problem of preventing lethal aggression stemming from this cause one which, on the whole, should be least amenable or most amenable to specific, definitive solution? Why?

Role of public opinion in conflict. A factor sometimes associated with entry into conflicts, or with their vigorous prosecution, is a broad public outcry. While the public is not directly involved in carrying out lethal violence, their state of feeling may in some cases be understood by reference to one or more of the above models. How might you relate the public outcry "Avenge the Maine" (about the sinking of the battleship *Maine* in Havana Harbor in 1898), which helped lead to the Spanish-American War, to the above models? How about "Free the slaves," before the Civil War? How about "the only good Indian is a dead Indian," in relation to the extensive warfare with the Indian tribes during America's westward expansion? Is command from the top generally sufficient to start a major war, or would you expect some degree of public enthusiasm to be present? (Depending on the sophistication and degree of centralized control of the communications apparatus in a particular society, the outcry, however, may itself be largely "manufactured" by the leaders.) Moreover, the supportive climate of public opinion may sometimes simply be a relatively easily established reflection of Koestler's "ideology" model, or an almost-festive shedding of boredom, rather than a deeply-felt rage or hatred toward the supposed enemy.

Might the need for *some* public support in the prosecution of a war nonetheless be significant in predicting, or even preventing, the outbreak of lethal conflict? Do you find it ominous that the Chinese press has reiterated that they would resolutely defend their homeland and "bury the invaders on the spot" if invaded by the "revisionist stooges" of the Kremlin? Does the development of super-weapons, like the hydrogen warhead delivered by an ICBM, make the factor of public outcry more important? Less important? How might one hope to test the view that public outcry *is* associated with war-making?

Models applied to long-term oppression. In Chapter 1 we refer to "long-time-line oppression," lethal results caused by what appear to be attitudes of neglect or indifference (such as those that cause, at least in significant part, high non-white infant death rates in the United States). Does the "status" model appear in any ways significant in explaining such occurrences (in that some whites feel that blacks should be of lower status than themselves)? The "command" model (in terms of accepting priorities or courses of action laid down by leaders)? The "ideology" or "cooperation" model (in so far as there may be in-group formation by whites against an out-group of blacks)? The "acquisitiveness" model (in the sense of whether the benefits that can be provided through limited resources will be allocated to luxuries for a dominant group or necessities for a non-dominant one)?

Models applied to leaders' role. If the leadership role is of great importance in most large-scale lethal conflict, what variety of measures can you imagine, besides the two mentioned at the end of the section on the "status" model, that might generally discourage leaders from ordering the initiation of such conflict? It may help to think in terms of three rough categories: first, measures to select leaders with less push towards seeking status; second, measures to reduce the threats to leaders' status; and third, measures to create a *greater* threat to leaders' status if they initiate conflict than if they don't.

May the command-and-obedience phenomenon operate even in group violence as unplanned and unstructured as a riot? That is, does even a riot depend on a significant degree of leadership? Or in this situation would it be more accurate to say that the leaders provide an example of behavior to imitate, rather than a command to obey? Assuming that at least some of the Milgram and Marshall findings are applicable whether the leaders command or provide models, would we think it was important, not only in organized groups, but also in relatively unstructured group violence situations (as in riots and violent protests), that there be at least some minimum number of leaders present in a crowd of a given size? In *Crowds and Power,* Conavetti suggests that a certain number of "crystals," or leaders, around whom the crowd can form and act, are needed, and the available observations seem to confirm this view. Why would this appear to follow, if the Milgram and Marshall data were relevant?

FOOTNOTES, CHAPTER 3

[1] Stanley Milgram, "Some Conditions of Obedience and Disobedience to Authority," *Human Relations*, Vol 18, No. 1 (February 1965), pp. 57–75.

[2] S. L. A. Marshall, *Men Against Fire* (New York: William Morrow & Company, 1947).

[3] Kenneth Keniston, *Young Radicals* (New York: Harcourt Brace Jovanovich, Inc., 1968), p. 249.

[4] Keniston, *Young Radicals*, p. 249.

[5] Associated Press, in *Seattle Times*, October 11, 1970.

[6] Desmond Morris, *The Human Zoo* (New York: Dell Publishing Co., Inc., 1969), pp. 41–42, 45–47, 49, 53–54, 56–58, 60–61, 128–31, 151–52.

[7] Desmond Morris, *The Naked Ape* (New York: McGraw Hill Book Company, 1967), p. 148.

[8] Louis S. B. Leakey, in *Aggression and Defense*, ed. Clemente and Lindsley (University of California Press, 1967) p. 4.

[9] Ralph L. Holloway, Jr., "Human Aggression: The Need for a Species-Specific Framework," in *War: The Anthropology of Armed Conflict and Aggression*, ed. Fried, Harris and Murphy (Garden City, N.Y.: The Natural History Press, 1967), p. 39.

[10] Arthur Miller, "The Bored and the Violent," *Harper's*, 225 (1962), p. 50.

4

Motives for Conflict:

Prehistoric and primitive societies

If animals other than man do not wage war, when did war begin? Are there any primitive societies still in existence that do not engage in warfare? In this chapter we move on from the theoretical frameworks, analogies, and laboratory experiments of the naturalist, the biologist, and the psychologist. We go to the paleontologist, the archeologist, the historian, and the anthropologist to review the traces and records left by evolving humankind during its two million years upon this planet.

Prehistoric Man: The Myth of Savagery

The following is from Ashley Montagu's *The Human Revolution:*[1]

It has already been pointed out that among the apes, in a forest environment, food gathering is easy; all can provide for themselves except the small infants, who are nursed by the mothers and suckled by them for several years and fed plant foods, until the young are able to forage for themselves. The adult males, and the dominant male, do not under these conditions provide food for the females and their young. With the shift into the savannas and the extension of food gathering to small slow-moving and juvenile animals, foraging would continue among the females, until with the development of hunting the economic activities of the sexes would become asymmetrically emphasized. A hominid infant is not conveniently carried on a hunting expedition; he is too large, too dependent, he may cry at an inappropriate moment and scare the game away, and he may be endangered. Furthermore, there may be other siblings who require the mother's care. Nor are pregnancy and parturition compatible with hunting. For all these reasons, and the additional ones, that she cannot run as fast as the male, and because she is muscularly less powerful than he, the female cannot be as effective a hunter. Hunting would therefore become an exclusively male occupation. In this way the first economic division of labor would come into being between the sexes. The female would remain the food gatherer, and the male would become the hunter.

The division of labor between the sexes resulting from the development of hunting, in addition to food gathering, as a way of life led to the most substantive of cultural changes. The male now becomes the provider of animal foods for the female and her young; the female provides the male with the vegetable foods. Thus cooperation and mutual aid in subsistence activities are established, and become an indispensable condition and pattern of human behavior. Food sharing is one of the most significant characteristics of man. Indeed, quite early in the evolution of man it became a vital necessity. Sharing became a way of life, and to this day the sharing of food has remained a ritual evidence of friendship and a token of involvement in the other's welfare. The willingness to share, generosity, would therefore have become a trait which would have both a high natural and social selective value, since it would substantially contribute toward the survival of the group. Mutual aid, cooperation, and generosity would take on significances far beyond the meaning they may have had at the anthropoid level.

The shift in meaning, during the nineteenth century, from the eighteenth-century conception of nature as harmony and design to nature as struggle brought about the eclipse of the concept of harmony as an ideal of human relations, and saw the emergence of the idea that what is just is determined by the arbitrament of force, the survival of the fittest.

Traditional conceptions concerning the innate depravity of man's nature, and the transformation, during the nineteenth century, of this doctrinal teaching into a bulwark of the Darwinian theory of evolution, have led to the belief in our own time that since man's ancestors were "wild animals" resembling the gorilla and chimpanzee, early man must have partaken to a great degree of this wildness. "The wild," "the jungle," "prehistoric man," "Neanderthal man," "the savage," and similar pejoratively used terms have served to condition the thinking of educated people and others for the last hundred years. To behave like a "Neanderthal" meant to behave like a "brute." And the "savage," of course, was very savage, indeed, preserving in his "savage" behavior something of the character of "prehistoric man." Learned scientists were quite as much affected by the traditional and tough Darwinian points of view as was the layman. Hence, when Neanderthal man's skeleton was found, it was reconstructed not in accordance with the anatomical functional traits it exhibited, but in accordance with its reconstructor's, Professor Marcellin Boule's, conception of what such a prehistoric man *ought* to look like! And so, for several generations, the world has had perpetrated upon it a creature called "Neanderthal man," characterized by a bestial face, a bull neck, knock-knees, and a stooping gait, usually holding a club in one hand and dragging a female by her hair with the other. This travesty of the facts met with ready acceptance since it was congenial to the intellectual temper of the times, even as it is to ours. Because they are so emotionally satisfying, such ideas will not soon be replaced by the facts. Man is a mythmaking animal who prefers to live with the myths that keep him comfortable rather than with the facts that enjoin him to think.

If some scientists have served to keep such myths alive, what may be said of the numinous-luminous school of popular-science writers? One thing that can certainly be said of them is that they faithfully reflect the ideas of their time. Indeed, it is in the works of such contemporary writers that we are most likely to find the orthodox beliefs faithfully reproduced. A typical example of such a work is entitled *Prehistoric Man*, by Charles Knight. This work is representative of views concerning prehistoric man that are widely held at the present time. Mr. Knight, who for many years was the distinguished artist at the American Museum of Natural History, takes a Hobbesian view of prehistoric man. For him the life of early man was poor, nasty, brutish, and short. Every man's hand was set against every other man's, and all the creatures of the earth seemed to have lived in a perpetual state of strife or warfare. This is not altogether surprising, since Darwin's favorite phrase in this connection was "the warfare of nature." According to Mr. Knight, "one never knew on retiring whether one would actually be there when morning broke." "The facts show now that a bitter struggle for supremacy has been going on ever since our old world was created." "Man had constructive ideas. He *wanted* things, and if his neighbors had a specially comfortable shelter in which to hide at night, envious thoughts arose and at times he was able to drive them out of the coveted retreat and occupy it himself." "How easy it was to sneak up on an enemy in a neighboring clan and in the dense jungle and tap him none too gently on his thick skull with a heavy club or a piece of sharp stone!" "We have no doubt that it often became a question of who was who in the jungle retreats, and that fierce battles were the result of any chance meetings between our unsavoury antecedents when tribal or family differences were involved." And so on throughout this bloodthirsty book about the purely mythical "fiery little brutes" who have been conjured, not so much out of the pigments of Mr. Knight's imagination, as out of the orthodox viewpoint on these matters.

Among the purposes served by myths is the justification of the ways of man or of a particular variety of man to other varieties of the kingdom of animated nature. In the same manner myths idealize certain forms of social conditions and justify their maintenance. The myth of "bestial" prehistoric man is of the same nature as the myth of the "savage" or the myth of the "beast," or "the gorilla." Are any of these creatures what we have been led to believe they are by countless "mythologists" masquerading as "authorities," and perpetrating their various ignorances upon an only too willing audience? The answer is that they are not. The "savage" is not savage, the "beast" is not a beast, and the "gorilla" is not, as Mr. Knight and others would have us believe, of "a very cantankerous and irascible disposition, which is part of his ferocious make-up." The very contradictory of all these statements is the truth. "Savages" live cooperatively with one another, and, with few exceptions, seldom bother anyone. Men behave like "beasts" in highly civilized societies, but the beasts of the field do not. As for the gorilla, far from being "very cantankerous and irascible" and "ferocious," it is a very quiet, amiable, and unquarrelsome creature, as innumerable authorities who have observed it both at first hand in its native habitat and under captive conditions have testified. Gorillas have never been observed fighting with one another nor have chimpanzees or orangutans.

So deeply ingrained in our culture is the belief in prehistoric man's belligerent nature that whenever any evidence is presented that could possibly be interpreted as supporting that belief, it is at once so interpreted. Thus, in his book *Adventures with the Missing Link,* published in 1959, Professor Raymond Dart has a chapter entitled "The Antiquity of Murder." This is a promising beginning. In this chapter Dart draws attention to the fact that an adolescent jaw of *Australopithecus prometheus,* found at Makapansgat, had been split on both sides and all the front teeth "knocked out." "This dramatic specimen," he writes, "instantly prompted me to study the murderous and apparently cannibalistic manner of life of these violent creatures."

But is the assumption that this adolescent australopithecine was murdered necessary? Could not the blow, if it was delivered by another australopithecine, have been accidental? The question has never been asked. It did not have to be, for if the answer to a question is already known, it is scarcely necessary to ask it. Even professors are not immune from reasoning from unwarranted assumptions to foregone conclusions. Why think of so lackluster an explanation as an "accident" when the more dramatic "murder" is so much more in keeping with the orthodox manner of dealing with these matters. But then there are "the casts of the insides of several man-ape skulls found at Sterkfontein (which) shows that they too had been shattered shortly before death by skull-smashing shocks." Some skulls had had the bones broken from within outward, and this suggests that the brains may have been eaten. This is accompanied by an illustration showing "Australopithecines fighting with bone club and dagger."

138

Let it be supposed for a moment that Dart's *anatomical* interpretations of the skull fractures are correct; does it necessarily follow that his interpretation of the skull fractures is correct, does this necessarily imply that his interpretation of the causes of those fractures is also correct? It does not, for the damage may have been produced in a variety of different ways. But let it further be supposed that the damage was deliberately produced by other australopithecines, and that they ate the brains, and possibly even other parts of other australopithecines; does this, then, necessarily mean that the australopithecines were habitual murderers and cannibals? It does not, any more than it means that any group of men are habitual murderers and cannibals when as a result of famine and starvation they resort to murder and cannibalism. It has happened in our own time among the most civilized of people, and it will happen again. Does this prove that man is murderous and cannibalistic by nature? It does not. Ritual cannibalism is another possible explanation.

It is highly probable that on occasion, as men at similar times have done, australopithecines may have resorted to murder and cannibalism when famine and starvation drove them to it, but even the evidence of Dart's own findings, and the numerous australopithecine finds made elsewhere in Africa, indicate that, if it occurred at all, this was the exceptional rather than the usual form of behavior. The australopithecines, like most other prehistoric men, have become victims of the myth of the "beast." Let no one be deceived by it.

Yet another addition to the myth of the "beast" has been produced from Olduvai. The left parietal or dome bone of the 11- or 12-year-old child found at the oldest site at Olduvai showed a break at the point of impact with radiating fractures. It need not be added that this has been interpreted by its discoverer, Dr. L. S. B. Leakey, as constituting evidence that the child had been murdered. "I think it reasonable to say," writes Dr. Leakey in the October 1961 issue of the *National Geographic*, "that the child received — and probably died from — what in modern police parlance is known as 'a blow from a blunt instrument.'" The "modern police parlance" is an elegant touch; it provides just the "right" decor. The truth is, of course, that one cannot say what that fractured right parietal was due to, but it does lend a dramatic element to the story to introduce the "murder" motif once more, and since that motif is perfectly acceptable to almost everyone, the explanation passes without criticism.

In April 1965 Dr. Leakey claimed that three distinct species of man overlapped in time and were living within a range of 100 miles of each other in East Africa, namely, *Zinjanthropus, Homo habilis,* and "Chellean" man (or the LLK skull, as Leakey prefers to call it from the site at which it was found). These three "species" of man were, according to Dr. Leakey, in competition with one another. "The time has come," he said at a symposium on the origin of man held at the University of Chicago, "to get away from the 1, 2, 3, 4 idea of man's development. Man developed just like the animals did, with various species living side by side until the weaker died out or were annihilated, leaving the stronger until eventually modern man emerged" (*Science News Letter,* 17 April 1965, p. 243).

Altogether apart from the doubtful validity of the claim for these forms as three different species, the suggestion that the competition was of a combative kind, with the weaker succumbing to the stronger, is based on nothing more than the nineteenth-century manner of thinking about competition. There is no evidence whatever for such competition. It requires to be pointed out that cooperation is also a form of competition, and that as such it undoubtedly played a highly significant role in the evolution of man. What is most likely is that, if the members of these three different groups ever met, they did what peoples have always done: they interbred, and by such hybridization formed a common gene pool, resulting in descendants somewhat different from the original hybridizing forms. Although we observe the results of it virtually every day among us, there is a marked tendency to shy away from any consideration of hybridization as an important factor in the evolution of man. Possibly this evasive behavior has some connection with the fact that hybridization, "race mixture," has quite unjustifiably been given a bad name. Certainly there are many among us who prefer to think of man's evolution as unsullied by "mongrelization." But this is a modern prejudice. It suits the book of such thinkers to believe that the "higher" forms exterminated the "lower" forms, so that by a series of such progressive exterminations the "higher" forms gradually replaced the "lower." It is such thinking that gave rise to the belief, still prevalent among some anthropologists, that Neanderthal man, instead of contributing to the evolution of modern man through the usual processes of evolution, including hybridization, was in fact exterminated by him. There is no more evidence for this extermination theory than there is for it in the case of Leakey's East African forms. When the final story of man's evolution comes to be written, it will probably be seen to have been, among other things, a history of increasing migrations and "mongrelizations." All of us are mongrels, and we are all the better for being so.

It is a prejudice, inherited from earlier generations of thinkers, influenced by the combative "survival of the fittest" schools of thought, that "higher" forms replaced "lower" forms of man by extermination. It is at the present time quite impossible to speak with certainty upon the subject, but it seems highly improbable that extermination played any role whatever in the evolution of man, and that hybridization and cooperation played a highly significant role in that evolution.

A definition of war. Let us take, as a rough definition of "war," "a group activity, carried on by members of one community against members of another community, in which it is the primary purpose to inflict serious injury or death on multiple nonspecified members of that other community, or in which the primary purpose makes it highly likely that serious injury or death will be inflicted on multiple nonspecified members of that community in the accomplishment of that primary purpose." We are thus identifying war as (1) a group undertaking; (2) directed not internally, but against a second community; (3) directed not against one individual or a specific family, but against any members of the opposing community—or at least any

140

armed, adult, male members—who "get in the way" or offer resistance; and (4) aimed either at killing members of the other community, or at some goal that makes it likely they will have to be killed in accomplishing it. This definition clearly excludes the murder of one man by another or a group attack on a specific individual or family, as in a blood feud or a revenge killing; we are trying here to focus on relatively impersonal group violence. But this definition does include situations where the aim of the attack itself is not killing, but is such that the attackers reasonably expect to have to kill in order to achieve their object; for example, seizing lands or women, or taking slaves from another group. In certain societies, the effort to take revenge on a specific individual will also generally necessitate the killing of non-specified individuals.

This definition could be varied in many minor ways, but it gives us a functional criterion for distinguishing war, or relatively impersonal group lethal violence, from individual or personal violence. (Depending on definitions of "community" or "group," this definition of war could also include none, some, or all of the events we call civil wars or insurgencies.)

No war in prehistoric times. There is little evidence of either warfare or more personalized forms of lethal violence in early human prehistory. The excerpt by Ashley Montagu discusses what there is: occasional indications of a broken skull, which could represent either death by accident or death by design; a reasonable surmise of cannibalism when food became extremely scarce. But there is no basis for supposing that there was either widespread group violence or widespread individual violence by man against man in early prehistory. William Golding, in his novel *The Inheritors,* pictures an emerging society of Cro-Magnon (around 30,000 B. C.) that makes fierce, incessant war upon groups of Neanderthal men, who are depicted by the author as meek and nonaggressive. In terms of evidence, this is a purely poetic vision.

Since Cro-Magnon apparently had much more varied tools, he may have hunted the game on which the Neanderthal largely depended so much more successfully that in harder years the Neanderthal died off.

The origins of war. Through most of the Paleolithic and Mesolithic periods (to around 4,500 B. C.), human communities lived principally by hunting. William H. McNeill, in *The Rise of the West,* suggests[2] that

141

. . . it is likely that Paleolithic men lived in small groups of not more than twenty to sixty persons. Such communities may well have been migratory, returning to their caves or other fixed shelter for only part of the year.

But Morris, in Chapter 3, suggests that most of the time was spent within a fixed hunting territory. The evidence appears inconclusive.

Some have speculated that the kind of complex, cooperative organization necessary for the hunting of large animals (and perhaps also the emotional bonds and sense of enthusiasm and accomplishment of the hunting party) could have led to warfare against other groups. Such warfare would not have been motivated by Freudian or Lorenzian "aggression," but rather by a combination of the "command" factor and a very simple form of "ideology (cooperation)" with some basic form of "acquisitiveness," as these theories were identified in Chapter 3. The cause of the conflict, this line of speculation runs, might have been overlapping hunting territories, especially in years when game was scarce; sometimes the man from another group might himself have been hunted as prey, with cannibalism the object, and warfare resulted when others of his group came to his defense. Or, in a community as small as twenty to sixty persons, accident or disease could easily have reduced the female population of the group to a number smaller than the male population; and raids to seize women, with ensuing warfare, might have resulted. However, all this is pure speculation, and the available data from numerous paleontological finds, as Montagu states, "indicate that, if it [lethal conflict] occurred at all, this was the exceptional rather than the usual form of behavior."

L. S. B. Leakey, criticized by Montagu in the excerpt, had substantially altered his views by 1971, when he told a scientific convention, according to the *New York Times*,[3] that, over the two million years of human evolution, there was no archeological evidence of murder or war until some 40,000 years ago. " 'Then, about 40,000 years ago,' " the *Times* quotes him, " 'everything changed.' " " 'Violence began,' " according to Leakey, when man learned how to make fire, and acquired the leisure " 'to invent abstract words like love and hate and jealousy.' " This violence then increased, Leakey suggested, as growing population pressed on territory and other resources.

Towards the end of the Mesolithic period, major changes began to occur here and there through the advent of agriculture and animal husbandry, particularly agriculture. "The grain-centered agriculture of the Middle East provided the basis for the first civilized societies," [4] beginning around 6,500 B. C. Grain was cultivated on partially cleared forest land, in a pattern that might involve periodic movement from field to field, but that attached a group to the soil of a single area for several years. With new control over the size of the food supply, communities could grow more populous, and McNeill suggests a distinction between these agricultural communities and the emerging pastoral communities where newly domesticated animals were supporting the hunters-turned-herdsmen. [5]

Archeological remains from early Neolithic villages suggest remarkably peaceable societies. As long as cultivable land was plentiful, and as long as the labor of a single household could not produce a significant surplus, there can have been little incentive to war. Traditions of violence and hunting-party organization, presumably withered in such societies, to be revived only when pastoral conquest superimposed upon peaceable villagers the elements of warlike organization from which civilized political institutions without exception descend.

On the other hand, he says,

Among predominantly pastoral peoples, however, religious-political institutions took a quite different turn. To protect the flocks from animal predators required the same courage and social discipline which hunters had always needed. Among pastoralists, likewise, the principal economic activity — focused, as among the earliest hunters, on a parasitic relation to animals — continued to be the special preserve of menfolk. Hence a system of patrilineal families, united into kinship groups under the authority of a chieftain responsible for daily decisions as to where to seek pasture, best fitted the conditions of pastoral life. In addition, pastoralists were likely to accord importance to the practices and discipline of war. After all, violent seizure of someone else's animals or pasture grounds was the easiest and speediest way to wealth and might be the only means of survival in a year of scant vegetation.

Moreover, as agriculturists began to create surpluses, both in food and, through trade, in other material possessions, pastoralists may have found it tempting to attack the agricultural communities.

There are, however, many sharp dissenters from these views today, and it should be noted that the preceding passage is highly speculative except for the concrete data, "Archeological remains from early Neolithic villages suggest remarkably peaceable societies." Interestingly, McNeill does not seem entirely consistent. Why, for example, should the agriculturalist respect another's grain, anymore than the herdsman should respect another's animals, in a bad year? As for shortages affecting the basic needs of the two types of communities, evidence can be mustered for the hypothesis that agriculturalists in some areas ran short of forest lands and began to push into pastoral grazing lands for cultivation. Possibly, too, grain cultivation was subject to a greater risk of famine — pastoralists could move their herds away from a drought area, and could often salvage more from the ravages of nature by killing their animals than the farmer could when his unripened grain withered in the fields. Thus the agriculturalist might be under greater pressure, on occasion, to raid the herdsman, than vice versa. Hence, when shortages developed, if there was an aggressor, it may often have been the agriculturalist. It was, after all, Cain, the tiller of soil, who slew Abel, the keeper of sheep, in one of the earliest of cautionary tales.

Materials from later pre-history are thus inconclusive on the exact nature and frequency of intergroup hostilities, but they generally indicate that communities in possession of sufficient quantities of the things that they thought important did not commonly make war upon other communities; while those that were lacking in the things that they thought important may sometimes have made war to get them.

One source of inference of the peacefulness of early man is found in his art. Virtually all known societies that have graphic art and that also engage in lethal conflict depict their conflicts in their art. Despite the prolific cave paintings of the Cro-Magnon period (in France alone, more than seventy caves with Cro-Magnon art on the walls have been discovered, dating roughly from 30,000 B. C. to 10,000 B. C.), there seems to be no depiction of violence by men against men; the hunting of *animals* is the sole use portrayed for tools. With a sampling that undoubtedly includes the work of hundreds of separate artists, it would seem almost inevitable that if some major battle had occurred during the lifetimes of even a handful out of their number, there would have been some pictorial record left behind. So far as I am aware, not until the advent of the bow and arrow — sometime subsequent to 10,000 B. C. — does a cave painting appear (in a cave in Spain) in which men are shown fighting other men.

There is, in any event, clearly no record of general warfare or unabated savagery, and the vast majority of early men seem to have led an extremely pacific existence.

Misconceptions of early man's savagery. It is hard to appreciate the extent to which this more recently developed evidence departs from the terrifying poetic visions of human pre-history that dominated the early years of this century. Freud, for example, combines psychoanalytic theory with turn-of-the-century Darwinian thinking to develop his theory of the "Oedipus wish" in *Totem and Taboo,* written in 1919.[6]

But if we associate the translation of the totem as given by psychoanalysis, with the totem feast and the Darwinian hypothesis about the primal state of human society, a deeper understanding becomes possible and a hypothesis is offered which may seem fantastic but which has the advantage of establishing an unexpected unity among a series of hitherto separated phenomena.

The Darwinian conception of the primal horde does not, of course, allow for the beginning of totemism. There is only a violent, jealous father who keeps all the females for himself and drives away the growing sons. This primal state of society has nowhere been observed. The most primitive organization we know, which today is still in force with certain tribes, is *associations of men* consisting of members with equal rights, subject to the restrictions of the totemic system, and founded on matriarchy, or descent through the mother. Can the one have resulted from the other, and how was this possible?

By basing our argument upon the celebration of the totem we are in a position to give an answer: "One day the expelled brothers joined forces, slew and ate the father, and thus put an end to the father horde. Together they dared and accomplished what would have remained impossible for them singly. Perhaps some advance in culture, like the use of a new weapon, had given them the feeling of superiority. Of course these cannibalistic savages ate their victim. This violent primal father had surely been the envied and feared model for each of the brothers. Now they accomplished their identification with him by devouring him and each acquired a part of his strength. The totem feast, which is perhaps mankind's first celebration, would be the repetition and commemoration of this memorable, criminal act with which so many things began, social organization, moral restrictions and religion.

He adds this footnoted comment:

The seemingly monstrous assumption that the tyrannical father was overcome and slain by a combination of the expelled sons has also been accepted by Atkinson as a direct result of the conditions of the Darwinian primal horde. "A youthful band of brothers living together in forced celibacy, or at most in polyandrous relation with some single female captive. A horde as yet weak in their impubescence they are, but they would, when strength was gained with time, inevitably wrench by combined attacks, renewed again and again, both wife and life from the paternal tyrant" (*Primal Law,* pp. 220–21).

Despite the utter inconsistency of these visions with the modern evidence from the paleontologists' diggings and the ethologists' observation of behavior in primates and other animals, elements of them still permeate our popular culture and literature. Clearly, perpetration of this view by the media — let alone by some universities, outside of the literature curriculum — is as utterly irresponsible as 1930 Hollywood's portrayal of the black man as stupid, indolent, and cowardly. Perpetuating an illusion of human nature and behavior as innately destructive contributes to an underlying sense of futility, hopelessness, and inevitability. In a peculiar sense, it creates a "racism" directed at the whole human race.

Lethal Conflict in Primitive Societies

As we have seen, lethal conflict in prehistoric society appears to have been quite infrequent, on all available evidence. When we turn to consideration of contemporary primitive societies, a more mixed picture emerges.

Causes of war in primitive societies. Lethal conflict among groups occurs for a vast range of apparent reasons in primitive societies,* and in some it does not occur at all (in some, but fewer, even murder is unknown). The Yanonamö villages of eastern Venezuela engage in constant lethal conflict with one another for the purpose of acquiring women, who are paradoxically in short supply largely because manly virtues of the fierce warrior are extolled and infanticide is practiced on females — while everyone wants a grown one, no one wants to raise one. Many Plains Indian tribes raided others for horses, frequently with lethal consequences. While there are some indications that those with fewer horses per capita tended to raid those with more, it seems that raiding among the Ruwala Bodawin camel breeders in Africa was largely by strong tribes greedily seizing still more camels from the

*"Primitive" is of course a reference to certain features of cultural complexity, such as possession of a written language, and not a judgment as to relative worth.

146

weak tribes that needed them more. The Mae Enga of the New Guinea highlands carried on warfare when one group found itself shorter of land than its neighbor; the Zulu tribes of Africa went to war for women and cattle (and later, under the chief Shaka, to acquire control of land and people in an almost imperial way).

The goal of fighting for cattle, horses, land, women, and other goods might vary in a given case from the simple satisfaction of the greed for those goods motivated by social norms, to rough equalization with other groups of per capita possession, to attainment of the minimal essentials needed for survival. Depending on the goal, the group may appear to have been following largely the "acquisitiveness" model, the "status" model, or the "affirmative-propensity" model (all described in the last section of Chapter 3). Such patterns of lethal conflict directed toward obtaining various material goods or captives occur widely among groups of primitive peoples, although they are *by no means* universal.

Another widespread form of conflict is represented by group action to revenge raids by another group, or in reprisal for rape or murder by a member of another group. What might frequently be explained by a relatively straightforward "self-defense" model becomes clouded, however, when lethal group conflict takes place to revenge a mere insult. Even further removed from clearcut self-defense is the "blood revenge" of the Jibaro Indians of eastern Ecuador. This lethal aggression often grows out of a wholly fanciful perception that a member of another group has killed a member of one's own group by sorcery. These attacks are clearly not motivated by greed, either, for the sole acquisition, in constant lethal conflict, is the shrunken heads of the slain enemy. Still further from self-defense is the case of the New Guinea native who told an anthropologist that he had organized a raiding party against another group simply because his wife had taunted him and made his "belly hot with anger." Certainly this last case appears to be a classic example of the "frustration–aggression" model.

Again, the Kwakiutl tribe in British Columbia would carry out raids, sometimes with lethal consequences, to acquire goods that they then gave away or destroyed in potlatches (not, perhaps, very far removed from our large-scale social function, except that the liquor, caviar, and dance-bands are acquired without blood-letting). Various Plains Indian tribes required lifting a scalp as part of the proof of manhood; among some of these tribes, "counting coup" by touching a live enemy was more highly regarded than lifting a scalp, because it was more dangerous. These examples probably fall under the "status" model of aggression. The status theory is at least a secondary explanation for the warriors of the Yanonamö, the Zulu empire-builders, and a good deal of other lethal group conflict in primitive tribes. And the effectiveness of group action for these various ends may generally require us to include the "ideology," "cooperation," and "imitation" models in the explanations for these conflicts.

The data from cultural anthropology thus serves to reinforce the impression that lethal conflict results from highly varied conduct, variously motivated. Moreover, it once more confirms that we are *not* dealing with a physiological constant or a "biological necessity," for some primitive societies indeed have no wars. Does this fact hold out hope that all war, and perhaps all lethal conflict, can eventually be "cured"?

Societies without war. Consider Margaret Mead's "Warfare Is Only an Invention — Not a Biological Necessity," a now-classic essay published in 1940, in the very teeth of the Darwinian and Freudian views that held such wide sway at the time:[7]

Is war a biological necessity, a sociological inevitability, or just a bad invention? Those who argue for the first view endow man with such pugnacious instincts that some outlet in aggressive behavior is necessary if man is to reach full human stature. It was this point of view which lay back of William James's famous essay, "The Moral Equivalent of War" (*supra*), in which he tried to retain the warlike virtues and channel them in new directions. A similar point of view has lain back of the Soviet Union's attempt to make competition between groups rather than between individuals. A basic, competitive, aggressive, warring human nature is assumed, and those who wish to outlaw war or outlaw competitiveness merely try to find new and less socially destructive ways in which these biologically given aspects of man's nature can find expression. Then there are those who take the second view: warfare is the inevitable concomitant of the development of the state, the struggle for land and natural resources of class societies springing not from the nature of man, but from the nature of history. War is nevertheless inevitable unless we change our social system and outlaw classes, the struggle for power, and possessions; and in the event of our success warfare would disappear, as a symptom vanishes when the disease is cured.

One may hold a sort of compromise position between these two extremes; one may claim that all aggression springs from the frustration of man's biologically determined drives and that, since all forms of culture are frustrating, it is certain each new generation will be aggressive and the aggression will find its natural and inevitable expression in race war, class war, nationalistic war, and so on. All three of these positions are very popular today among those

148

who think seriously about the problems of war and its possible prevention, but I wish to urge another point of view, less defeatist, perhaps, than the first and third and more accurate than the second: that is, that warfare, by which I mean recognized conflict between two groups *as groups,* in which each group puts an army (even if the army is only fifteen pygmies) into the field to fight and kill, if possible, some of the members of the army of the other group — that warfare of this sort is an invention like any other of the inventions in terms of which we order our lives, such as writing, marriage, cooking our food instead of eating it raw, trial by jury, or burial of the dead, and so on. Some of this list anyone will grant are inventions: trial by jury is confined to very limited portions of the globe; we know that there are tribes that do not bury their dead but instead expose or cremate them; and we know that only part of the human race has had the knowledge of writing as its cultural inheritance. But, whenever a way of doing things is found universally, such as the use of fire or the practice of some form of marriage, we tend to think at once that it is not an invention at all but an attribute of humanity itself. And yet even such universals as marriage and the use of fire are inventions like the rest, very basic ones, inventions which were, perhaps, necessary if human history was to take the turn that it has taken, but nevertheless inventions. At some point in his social development man was undoubtedly without the institution of marriage or the knowledge of the use of fire.

The case for warfare is much clearer because there are peoples even today who have no warfare. Of these the Eskimos are perhaps the most conspicuous examples, but the Lepchas of Sikkim described by Geoffrey Gorer in *Himalayan Village* are as good. Neither of these peoples understands war, not even defensive warfare. The idea of warfare is lacking, and this idea is as essential to really carrying on war as an alphabet or a syllabary is to writing. But, whereas the Lepchas are a gentle, unquarrelsome people, and the advocates of other points of view might argue that they are not full human beings or that they had never been frustrated and so had no aggression to expand in warfare, the Eskimo case gives no such possibility of interpretation. The Eskimos are not a mild and meek people; many of them are turbulent and troublesome. Fights, theft of wives, murder, cannibalism, occur among them — all outbursts of passionate men goaded by desire or intolerable circumstance. Here are men faced with hunger, men faced with loss of their wives, men faced with the threat of extermination by other men, and here are orphan children, growing up miserably with no one to care for them, mocked and neglected by those about them. The personality necessary for war, the circumstances necessary to goad men to desperation are present, but there is no war. When a traveling Eskimo entered a settlement, he might have to fight the strongest man in the settlement to establish his position among them, but this was a test of strength and bravery, not war. The idea of warfare, of one *group* organizing against another *group* to maim and wound and kill them was absent. And, without that idea, passions might rage but there was no war.

But, it may be argued, is not this because the Eskimos have such a low and undeveloped form of social organization? They own no land, they move from place to place, camping, it is true, season after season on the same site, but this is not something to fight for as the modern nations of the world fight for land and raw materials. They have no permanent possessions that can be looted, no towns that can be burned. They have no social classes to produce stress and strains within the society which might force it to go to war outside. Does not the absence of war among the Eskimos, while disproving the biological necessity of war, just go to confirm the point that it is the state of development of the society which accounts for war and nothing else?

We find the answer among the pygmy peoples of the Andaman Islands in the Bay of Bengal. The Andamans also represent an exceedingly low level of society; they are a hunting and food-gathering people; they live in tiny hordes without any class stratification; their houses are simpler than the snow houses of the Eskimo. But they knew about warfare. The army might contain only fifteen determined pygmies marching in a straight line, but it was the real thing none the less. Tiny army met tiny army in open battle, blows were exchanged, casualties suffered, and the state of warfare could only be concluded by a peace-making ceremony.

Similarly, among the Australian aborigines, who built no permanent dwellings but wandered from water hole to water hole over their almost desert country, warfare — and rules of "international law" — were highly developed. The student of social evolution will seek in vain for his obvious causes of war, struggle for lands, struggle for power of one group over another, expansion of population, need to divert the minds of a populace restive under tyranny, or even the ambition of a successful leader to enhance his own prestige. All are absent, but warfare as a practice remained, and men engaged in it and killed one another in the course of a war because killing is what is done in wars.

From instances like these it becomes apparent that an inquiry into the causes of war misses the fundamental point as completely as does an insistence upon the biological necessity of war. If a people have an idea of going to war and the idea that war is the way in which certain situations, defined within their society, are to be handled, they will sometimes go to war. If they are a mild and unaggressive people, like the Pueblo Indians, they may limit themselves to defensive warfare, but they will be forced to think in terms of war because there are peoples near them who have warfare as a pattern, and offensive, raiding, pillaging warfare at that. When the pattern of warfare is known, people like the Pueblo Indians will defend themselves, taking advantage of their natural defenses, the mesa village site, and people like the Lepchas, having no natural defenses and no idea of warfare, will merely submit to the invader. But the essential point remains the same. There is a way of behaving which is known to a given people and labeled as an appropriate form of behavior; a bold and warlike people like the Sioux or the Maori may label warfare as desirable as well as possible, a mild people like the Pueblo Indians may label warfare as undesirable, but to the minds of both peoples the possibility of warfare is present. Their thoughts, their hopes, their plans are oriented about this idea — that warfare may be selected as the way to meet some situation.

So simple peoples and civilized peoples, mild peoples and violent, assertive peoples, will all go to war if they have the invention, just as those peoples who have the custom of dueling will have duels and peoples who have the pattern of vendetta will indulge in vendetta. And, conversely, peoples who do not know of dueling will not fight duels, even though their wives are seduced and their daughters ravished; they may on occasion commit murder but they will not fight duels. Cultures which lack the idea of the vendetta will not meet every quarrel in this way. A people can use only the forms it has. So the Balinese have their special way of dealing with a quarrel between two individuals: if the two feel that the causes of quarrel are heavy, they may go and register their quarrel in the temple before the gods, and, making offerings, they may swear never to have anything to do with each other again. . . . But in other societies, although individuals might feel as full of animosity and as unwilling to have any further contact as do the Balinese, they cannot register their quarrel with the gods and go on quietly about their business because registering quarrels with the gods is not an invention of which they know.

Yet, if it be granted that warfare is, after all, an invention, it may nevertheless be an invention that lends itself to certain types of personality, to the exigent needs of autocrats, to the expansionist desires of crowded peoples, to the desire for plunder and rape and loot which is engendered by a dull and frustrating life. What, then, can we say of this congruence between warfare and its uses? If it is a form which fits so well, is not this congruence the essential point? But even here the primitive material causes us to wonder, because there are tribes who go to war merely for glory, having no quarrel with the enemy, suffering from no tyrant within their boundaries, anxious neither for land nor loot nor women, but merely anxious to win prestige which within that tribe has been declared obtainable only by war and without which no young man can hope to win his sweetheart's smile of approval. But if, as was the case with the Bush Negroes of Dutch Guiana, it is artistic ability which is necessary to win a girl's approval, the same young man would have to be carving rather than going out on a war party.

In many parts of the world, war is a game in which the individual can win counters—counters which bring him prestige in the eyes of his own sex or of the opposite sex; he plays for these counters as he might, in our society, strive for a tennis championship. Warfare is a frame for such prestige-seeking merely because it calls for the display of certain skills and certain virtues; all of these skills—riding straight, shooting straight, dodging the missiles of the enemy and sending one's own straight to the mark—can be equally well exercised in some other framework and, equally, the virtues—endurance, bravery, loyalty, steadfastness—can be displayed in other contexts. The tie-up between proving oneself a man and proving this by a success in organized killing is due to a definition which many societies have made of manliness. And often, even in those societies which counted success in warfare a proof of human worth, strange turns were given to the idea, as when the plains Indians gave their highest awards to the man who touched a live enemy rather than to the man who brought in a scalp—from a dead enemy—because the latter was less risky. Warfare is just an invention known to the majority of human societies by which they permit their young men either to accumulate prestige or avenge their honor or acquire loot or wives or slaves or sago lands or cattle or appease the blood lust of their gods or the restless souls of the recently dead. It is just an invention, older and more widespread than the jury system, but none the less an invention.

151

But, once we have said this, have we said anything at all? Despite a few instances, dear to the hearts of controversialists, of the loss of the useful arts, once an invention is made which proves congruent with human needs or social forms, it tends to persist. Grant that war is an invention, that it is not a biological necessity nor the outcome of certain special types of social forms, still, once the invention is made, what are we to do about it? The Indian who had been subsisting on the buffalo for generations because with his primitive weapons he could slaughter only a limited number of buffalo did not return to his primitive weapons when he saw that the white man's more efficient weapons were exterminating the buffalo. A desire for the white man's cloth may mortgage the South Sea Islander to the white man's plantation, but he does not return to making bark cloth, which would have left him free. Once an invention is known and accepted, men do not easily relinquish it. The skilled workers may smash the first steam looms which they feel are to be their undoing, but they accept them in the end, and no movement which has insisted upon the mere abandonment of usable inventions has ever had much success. Warfare is here, as part of our thought; the deeds of warriors are immortalized in the words of our poets, the toys of our children are modeled upon the weapons of the soldier, the frame of reference within which our statesmen and our diplomats work always contains war. If we know that it is not inevitable, that it is due to historical accident that warfare is one of the ways in which we think of behaving, are we given any hope by that? What hope is there of persuading nations to abandon war, nations so thoroughly imbued with the idea that resort to war is, if not actually desirable and noble, at least inevitable whenever certain defined circumstances arise?

In answer to this question I think we might turn to the history of other social inventions, and inventions which must once have seemed as firmly entrenched as warfare. Take the methods of trial which preceded the jury system: ordeal and trial by combat. Unfair, capricious, alien as they are to our feeling today, they were once the only methods open to individuals accused of some offense. The invention of trial by jury gradually replaced these methods until only witches, and finally not even witches, had to resort to the ordeal. And for a long time the jury system seemed the one best and finest method of settling legal disputes, but today new inventions, trial before judges only or before commissions, are replacing the jury system. In each case the old method was replaced by a new social invention. The ordeal did not go out because people thought it unjust or wrong; it went out because a method more congruent with the institutions and feelings of the period was invented. And, if we despair over the way in which war seems such an ingrained habit of most of the human race, we can take comfort from the fact that a poor invention will usually give place to a better invention.

For this, two conditions, at least, are necessary. The people must recognize the defects of the old invention, and someone must make a new one. Propaganda against warfare, documentation of its terrible cost in human suffering and social waste, these prepare the ground by teaching people to feel that warfare is a defective social institution. There is further needed a belief that social invention is possible and the invention of new methods which will render warfare as out of date as the tractor is making the plow, or the motor

152

car the horse and buggy. A form of behavior becomes out of date only when something else takes its place, and, in order to invent forms of behavior which will make war obsolete, it is a first requirement to believe that an invention is possible.

At another point, in *Sex and Temperament in Three Primitive Societies*, Dr. Mead describes some of the characteristics that may make the mountain Arapesh of New Guinea a pacific, unwarlike people.[8]

. . . The men spend over nine-tenths of their time responding to other people's plans, digging in other people's gardens, going on hunting-parties initiated by others. The whole emphasis of their economic lives is that of participation in activities others have initiated, and only rarely and shyly does anyone tentatively suggest a plan of his own.

This emphasis is one factor in the lack of political organization. Where all are trained to a quick responsiveness to any plan, and mild ostracism is sufficient to prod the laggard into co-operation, leadership presents a different problem from that in a society where each man pits his own aggressiveness against that of another. If there is a weighty matter to be decided, one that may involve the hamlet or a cluster of hamlets in a brawl or accusations of sorcery, then the decision is arrived at in a quiet, roundabout, and wholly characteristic fashion. Suppose for instance that a young man finds that a pig belonging to a distant village has strayed into his garden. The pig is a trespasser, meat is scarce, he would like to kill it. But would it be wise to do so? Judgment must be made in terms of all kinds of relationships with the pig's owners. Is a feast pending? Or is a betrothal still unsettled? Does some member of his own group depend upon the pig's owner for assistance in some ceremonial plan? All these things the young man has not the judgment to decide. He goes to his elder brother. If his elder brother sees no objection to killing the pig, the two will take counsel with other elder male relatives, until finally one of the oldest and most respected men of the community is consulted. Of such men every locality with a population of one hundred and fifty to two hundred has one or two. If the big man gives his approval, the pig is killed and eaten and no censure will fall upon the young man from his elders; everyone will stand together to defend their bit of legal piracy.

Warfare is practically unknown among the Arapesh. There is no head-hunting tradition, no feeling that to be brave or manly one must kill. Indeed, those who have killed men are looked upon with a certain amount of discomfort, as men slightly apart. It is they who must perform the purificatory ceremonies over a new killer. The feeling towards a murderer and that towards a man who kills in battle are not essentially different. There are no insignia of any sort for the brave. There is only a modicum of protective magic which can be used by those who are going into a fight: they may scrape a little dust from their fathers' bones and eat it with areca-nut and magic herbs. But although actual warfare—organized expeditions to plunder, conquer, kill, or attain glory—is absent, brawls and clashes between villages do occur, mainly over women. The marriage system is such that even the most barefaced elopement of a betrothed or married woman must be phrased as an abduction and, since an abduction is an unfriendly act on the part of another group, must be avenged. This feeling for righting the balance, for paying back evil for evil, not in greater measure, but in exact measure, is very strong among the Arapesh. The beginning of hostilities they regard as an unfortunate accident; abductions of women are really the result of marital disagreements and the formation of new personal attachments, and are not unfriendly acts on the part of the next community. So also with pigs, since people attempt to keep their pigs at home. If the pigs stray, it is a bad accident, but if a pig is killed, it should be avenged.

All such clashes between hamlets start in angry conversation, the aggrieved party coming, armed but not committed to fighting, into the village of the offenders. An altercation follows; the offenders may justify or excuse their conduct, disclaim any knowledge of the elopement, or deny having known the ownership of the pig—it had not had its tail cut yet, how could they know it was not a bush pig? and so on. If the aggrieved party is protesting more as a matter of form than from real anger, the meeting may end in a few harsh words. Alternatively, it may progress from reproach to insult, until the most volatile and easily angered person hurls a spear. This is not a signal for a general fracas; instead everyone notes carefully where the spear—which is never thrown to kill—hits, and the next most volatile person of the opposite party throws a spear back at the man who hurled the first one. This in turn is recorded during a moment of attention, and a return spear thrown. Each reprisal is phrased as a matter of definite choice: "Then Yabinigi threw a spear. He hit my cross-cousin in the wrist. I was angry because my cross-cousin was hit and I threw a spear back and hit Yabinigi in the ankle. Then the mother's brother of Yabinigi, enraged that his sister's son had been wounded, drew back his arm and hurled a spear at me which missed," and so on. This serial and carefully recorded exchange of spears in which the aim is to wound lightly, not to kill, goes on until someone is rather badly wounded, when the members of the attacking party immediately take to their heels. Later, peace is made by an interchange of rings, each man giving a ring to the man whom he has wounded.

If, as occasionally happens, someone is killed in one of these clashes, every attempt is made to disavow any intention to kill: the killer's hand slipped; it was because of the sorcery of the Plainsmen. Almost always those on the other side are called by kinship terms, and surely no man would willingly have killed a relative. If the relative killed is a near one, an uncle or a first cousin, the assumption that it was unintentional and due to sorcery is regarded as established, and the killer is commiserated with and permitted to mourn whole-heartedly with the rest. If the relative is more distant, and the possibility of genuine intent more open, the killer may flee to another community. No blood feud will follow, although there may be an attempt to subsidize the sorcery of the Plainsmen against him. But in general sorcery deaths are avenged with sorcery deaths, and all killings within the locality or within avenging distance are regarded as too aberrant, too unexpected and inexplicable, for the community to deal with them. . . .

The general policy of Arapesh society is to punish those who are indiscreet enough to get involved in any kind of violent or disreputable scene, those who are careless enough to get hurt in hunting, or stupid enough to let themselves become the butt of public vituperation from their wives. In this society unaccustomed to violence, which assumes that all men are mild and co-operative and is always surprised by the individuals who fail to be so, there are no sanctions to deal with the violent man. But it is felt that those who stupidly and carelessly provoke violence can be kept in order. In mild cases of offence, as when a man has been one member of a fighting group, his individual mother's brother calls out for payment. After all, the poor sister's son has already suffered a wound and loss of blood. But if instead he has got himself involved in an undignified public disputation with a wife, or with a young relative who has been overheard by others to insult him, then the whole men's group of the hamlet or cluster of hamlets may act, still instigated by the mother's brothers, who are the official executors of the punishment. The men's group will take the sacred flutes, the voice of the *tamberan* — the supernatural monster who is the patron of the men's cult — and going by night to the house of the offender, play his wife and himself off the premises, break into his house, litter his house-floor with leaves and rubbish, cut down an areca-palm or so, and depart. If the man has been steadily falling in the esteem of the community, if he has been unco-operative, given to sorcery, bad-tempered, they may take up his fire-place and dump it out, which is practically equivalent to saying that they can dispense with his presence — for a month at least. The victim, deeply shamed by this procedure, flees to distant relatives and does not return until he has obtained a pig with which to feast the community, and so wipe out his offence.

But against the really violent man the community has no redress. Such men fill their fellows with a kind of amazed awe; if crossed they threaten to burn down their own houses, break all their pots and rings, and leave that part of the country for ever. Their relatives and neighbours, aghast at the prospect of being deserted in this way, beseech the violent man not to leave them, not to desert them, not to destroy his own property, and placate him by giving him what he wishes. It is only because the whole education of the Arapesh tends to minimize violence and confuse the motivations of the violent that the society is able to operate by disciplining those who provoke and suffer from violence rather than those who actually perpetrate it.

With work a matter of amiable co-operation, and the slight warfare so slenderly organized, the only other need that the community has for leadership is for carrying out large-scale ceremonial operations. Without any leadership whatsoever, with no rewards beyond the daily pleasure of eating a little food and singing a few songs with one's fellows, the society could get along very comfortably, but there would be no ceremonial occasions. And the problem of social engineering is conceived by the Arapesh not as the need to limit aggression and curb acquisitiveness, but as the need to force a few of the more capable and gifted men into taking, against their will, enough responsibility and leadership so that occasionally, every three or four years or at even rarer intervals, a really exciting ceremonial may be organized. No one, it is assumed, really wants to be a leader, a "big man." "Big men" have to plan, have to initiate exchanges, have to strut and swagger and talk in loud

155

voices, have to boast of what they have done in the past and are going to do in the future. All of this the Arapesh regard as most uncongenial, difficult behaviour, the kind of behaviour in which no normal man would indulge if he could possibly avoid it. It is a rôle that the society forces upon a few men in certain recognized ways.

* * *

The continual moving about from one place to another has its reverberation in the children's lives. They are not accustomed to large enough groups to play group games; instead each child clings close to an adult or an older brother or sister. The long walks from one garden to another, or from garden-house to village, tire them out, and arrived at the end of the journey, while the mother cooks the supper and the father sits and gossips with the other men, the children sit about, bubbling their lips. Games are hardly ever played. Little children are only allowed to play with each other as long as they do not quarrel. The minute there is the slightest altercation the adult steps in. The aggressor — or both children if the other child resents the attack — is dragged off the scene of battle and held firmly. The angry child is allowed to kick and scream, to roll in the mud, to throw stones or firewood about on the ground, but he is not allowed to touch the other child. This habit of venting one's rage at others upon one's own surroundings persists into adult life. An angry man will spend an hour banging on a slit gong, or hacking with an ax at one of his own palm-trees.

The whole training of the little children is not to teach them to control emotion, but to see that its expression harms no one but themselves.

* * *

. . . Temper tantrums are almost always motivated by some insecurity or rejection point. A child is refused a request, is not permitted to accompany someone, is given a push or spoken to roughly by an older child, is rebuked, or, most important of all, is refused food. The tantrums that follow a refusal of food are the most numerous and the most interesting because the child is not to be placated by a subsequent offer of food. The refusal of the longed-for coconut or piece of sugar-cane has set off a whole train of response, far in excess of any power that the mere food has to stop it, and the child may weep for an hour, the helpless victim of a repeat situation in which the parent is equally powerless. These tantrums over rejection serve to channel anger as response to a hostile act on the part of another, and the definite training against aggressiveness towards other children completes this pattern.

The parental disapproval of fighting among children is always reinforced by rebukes couched in terms of relationship: "Would you, the younger brother, hit him who is first-born?" "Would you, his father's sister's son, hit your mother's brother's son?" "It is not right that two cousins should struggle with one another like little dogs." Children get no schooling in accepting harshness, in what we are accustomed to call good sportsmanship, that willingness to take it on the chin which is believed to be more consonant with the masculine temperament in our society. Arapesh small boys are as protected

156

from aggression and struggle, from rude disciplinary measures on the part of older children and irritated parents, as is the most tenderly reared and fragile little daughter among ourselves. As a result, Arapesh boys never develop "good sportsmanship"; their feelings are intolerably wounded by a blow, or even a harsh word. The slightest gibe is taken as an expression of unfriendliness, and grown men will burst into tears at an unfair accusation.

They carry into adult life the fear of any rift between associates. The culture has a few external symbolic ways in which a genuine rift can be expressed, public signs of a disagreement that can be set up to handle the situation without actual personal clash between the individuals concerned. These are seldom used. . . .

The fear and discomfort resulting from any expression of anger is further worked into the pattern of sorcery. An angry person may not hit another, he may not resort to any thorough-going abuse of another. But one may, in retailiation, take on for a moment the behaviour that is appropriate not to a relative and a member of the same locality, but to a Plainsman, a stranger and an enemy. Arapesh children grow up dividing the world into two great divisions: *relatives,* which division includes some three to four hundred people, all the members of their own locality, and those of villages in other localities which are connected with them or their relatives by marriage, and the long lines of the wives and children of their father's hereditary trade-friends; and *strangers* and *enemies,* usually formalized as *waribim,* Plainsmen, literally, "men from the river-lands." These Plainsmen play in the children's lives the dual rôle of the bogyman to be feared, and the enemy to be hated, mocked, outwitted, upon whom all the hostility that is disallowed in the group is actively displaced. . . .

* * *

To return again to the play-training of the children: as children grow older and play games, they play none that encourage aggressiveness or competition. There are no races, no games with two sides. Instead they play at being opossums or at being kangaroos, or one is a sleeping cassowary that the others startle. Many of the games are like the kindergarten games of very little children, singing games in which some simple pantomime like an imitation of sago-cutting accompanies the traditional words. And even these games are played very seldom. More often the times when children are together in large enough groups to make a game worth while are the occasions of a feast, there is dancing and adult ceremonial, and they find the rôle of spectatorship far more engrossing. . . .

* * *

. . . We have seen how they lack the conception of human nature as evil and in need of strong checks and curbs, and the way in which they conceive the differences between the sexes in terms of the supernatural implications of male and female functions and do not expect any natural manifestations of these differences in sex-endowment. Instead they regard both men and women as inherently gentle, responsive, and co-operative, able and willing to

157

subordinate the self to the needs of those who are younger or weaker, and to derive a major satisfaction from doing so. They have surrounded with delight that part of parenthood which we consider to be specially maternal, the minute, loving care for the little child and the selfless delight in that child's progress towards maturity. In this progress the parent takes no egotistic pleasure, makes no excessive demands for great devotion in this world, or for ancestor-worship in the next. The child to the Arapesh is not a means by which the individual ensures that his identity will survive his death, by which he maintains some slight and grasping hold upon immortality. In some societies the child is a mere possession, perhaps the most valuable of all, more valuable than houses and lands, pigs and dogs, but still a possession to be counted over and boasted of to others. But such a picture is meaningless to the Arapesh, whose sense of possession even of the simplest material objects is so blurred with a sense of the needs and obligations of others as to be almost lost.

To the Arapesh, the world is a garden that must be tilled, not for one's self, not in pride and boasting, not for hoarding and usury, but that the yams and the dogs and the pigs and most of all the children may grow. From this whole attitude flow many of the other Arapesh traits, the lack of conflict between old and young, the lack of any expectation of jealousy or envy, the emphasis upon co-operation. Co-operation is easy when all are whole-heartedly committed to a common project from which no one of the participators will himself benefit. Their dominant conception of men and women may be said to be that of regarding men, even as we regard women, as gently, carefully parental in their aims.

Furthermore, the Arapesh have very little sense of struggle in the world. Life is a maze through which one must thread one's way, battling neither with demons within nor demons without, but concerned always with finding the path, with observing the rules that make it possible to keep and find the path. . . .

* * *

In their attitudes towards egotism of any sort, either of the type that seeks recognition and applause or of the type that attempts to build up a position through possessions and power over others, the Arapesh . . . reward the selfless child, the child who is constant in running hither and yon at the beck and call of others; they disapprove of and reprove the other types, as children and as adults. . . . There are certain types of individuals—the violent, the jealous, the ambitious, the possessive, the man who is interested in experience or knowledge or art for its own sake—for whom they definitely have no place.

* * *

More often, the violent, aggressive boy, the boy who in a head-hunting, warlike society would be covering himself with glory, the boy who in a culture that permitted courtship and conquest of women might have had many broken hearts to his credit, becomes permanently inhibited in his late adolescence. This was so with Wabe. Tall, beautifully built, the heir of one of the

158

most gifted family lines in Arapesh, Wabe at twenty-five had retired from taking any active interest in his culture. He would help his younger brother, Ombomb, a little, he said, but what was the use, everything was against him. . . . One war-party, one good fight, one chance for straight, uncomplicated initiative, might have cleared the air. But there was none. He began to believe that other men were trying to seduce his wives. People laughed, and when the accusation was repeated, they grew a little remote. He decided that his gardening partners were using black magic for theft—a magic that is a mere matter of folk-lore and of which no one knows the formulas—on his yam-gardens. . . . His behaviour was jerky, irrational, changeable, his temper dark and sullen. He was a definite liability to his society, he who had the physique and the intelligence to have been very useful to it. His capacity to lead was high. . . .

Of all the men in the locality of Alitoa, he was the one who approached most strongly to a western-European ideal of the male, well built, with a handsome face with fine lines, a well-integrated body, violent, possessive, arbitrary, dictatorial, positively and aggressively sexed. Among the Arapesh, he was a pathetic figure.

* * *

The violent aberrant personalities, either men or women, have therefore a very difficult time among the Arapesh. They are not subjected to the rigid discipline that they would receive among a people who deal seriously with such temperaments. A woman like Amitoa who murders her child continues to live on in a community; similarly a Suabibis man who murdered a child in revenge for his own son's fall from a tree was not disciplined by the community, nor by the child's relatives, because they lived too far away. The society actually gives quite a good deal of leeway to violence, but it gives no meaning to it. With no place for warfare, for strong leadership, for individual exploits of bravery and strength, these men find themselves treated as almost insane. . . . Intellectually they are lost to their society, always seeking to project their own violent and aberrant temperamental choices upon it. If in addition circumstances are adverse, if their pigs die or their wives miscarry or the yams fail, far from being merely a loss to society, they may become a menace, and substitute overt murderous activity for glowering suspicion and impotent rage.

* * *

The Western reader will realize only too easily how special an interpretation the Arapesh have put upon human nature, how fantastic they have been in selecting a personality type rare in either men or women and foisting it as the ideal and natural behaviour upon an entire community. It is hard to judge which seems to us the most utopian and unrealistic behaviour, to say that there are no differences between men and women, or to say that both men and women are naturally maternal, gentle, responsive, and unaggressive.

159

Characteristics of primitive societies correlated with warfare. A Cross-Cultural Summary is a compilation by Robert B. Textor, in the form of a computer printout, of a huge number of collected observations by cultural anthropologists, missionaries, and others. This compilation compares features found in thirty-four primitive cultures "where warfare is prevalent" with features found in nine primitive cultures "where warfare is not prevalent." (There is a subsequent, overlapping but not identical listing of eight primitive cultures "where warfare is common or chronic" and twenty-four "where warfare is rare or infrequent"—but with no additional printout of correlating features.) The following features are correlated with the prevalence or non-prevalence of warfare to a degree that could occur by chance less than one out of twenty times. Correlation, of course, is not causation. *Both* warfare and the listed feature could be common results of some underlying cause, or warfare could *cause* the other, rather than vice versa.* Where all of the societies in either group exhibit the particular features, the characteristic has been preceded by the italicized words *in all*.

THIRTY-FOUR CULTURES WHERE WARFARE *IS* PREVALENT ARE FAIRLY STRONGLY CORRELATED WITH THESE CHARACTERISTICS	NINE PRIMITIVE CULTURES WHERE WARFARE IS *NOT* PREVALENT ARE FAIRLY STRONGLY CORRELATED WITH THESE CHARACTERISTICS
outside East Eurasia	located in East Eurasia
settlements fixed	settlements non-fixed
not the case that settlements are non-fixed and movement is nomadic	settlements are non-fixed and movement is nomadic
husbandry of some kind—caring for cows, sheep, etc.—is present	husbandry is absent
metal working is present	*in all,* metal working is absent
weaving is present	weaving is absent
a city or town is present, or the average community size is fifty or greater	*in all,* no city or town is present, and the average community size is smaller than fifty
the level of political integration is "the large state, the little state, or the minimal state"	*in all,* the level of political integration is the autonomous community, or the family
"heirarchies are more complex than the 'simplest,' that is,	"hierarchies are the 'simplest;' that is, where there are only

*For example, there may be a fairly close correlation between the height of a child, among other children of its age and sex, and the height of its parents. But the parents' height does not cause the child's: rather the child's height and the parents' height are caused by a common genetic constituent. And for an example of the second case, gasoline rationing is likely during large-scale modern wars. But the war causes the rationing, not vice versa.

more complex than two local levels with no national levels" class stratification is present slavery is present

*

*

the taboo against sexual relations after childbirth lasts longer than six months
"the early sexual satisfaction potential is low"
in all, "the child's inferred anxiety over non-performance of achievement behavior is high"
"military glory is strongly or moderately emphasized"
"bellicosity is extreme"

where games are present, they include games of chance
where games are present, they include others besides games of skill
there is a high composite self-love index
"boastfulness is extreme"

two local levels with no national levels"
class stratification is absent
slavery is absent
in all, there is moderate, little, or negative emphasis on "invidious display of wealth"
in all, "the level of social sanction is public property sanction or private settlement, rather than public corporeal sanction"
in all, the taboo against sexual relations after childbirth lasts six months or less
in all, "the early sexual satisfaction potential is high"
"the child's inferred anxiety over non-performance of achievement behavior is low"
"military glory is negligibly emphasized"
in all, "bellicosity is moderate or negligible"
in all, no games of chance

in all, where games are present, they include only games of skill

in all, there is a low "composite narcissism index"
in all, "boastfulness is moderate, negligible, or unreported"

Even apart from the fact that these features are only *correlated* with warfare or peacefulness, and do not necessarily express *causal* relationships, there are numerous other reasons why this list is not a readily usable "recipe" for avoiding wars or lethal group violence. We shall explore some of these reasons shortly. The printout, however, is intriguing because of its contrasts, particularly those underlining certain features of the nine non-warlike primitive societies. These key features appear similar to many features of the early prehistoric societies discussed earlier in this chapter. The non-warlike communities

*In these cases, roughly opposite characteristics are displayed with a frequency that could occur by chance as often as one time out of ten.

tend to be nomadic hunter-gatherers, not living in fixed settlements and not engaged in husbandry. They live in small, politically autonomous groups of fifty or less, as we believe Paleolithic man to have done. Hierarchies are simple, without class stratification or slavery. Metal working and weaving are also absent.

Additionally, there is little pressure in these peaceful cultures for "achievement," negligible emphasis on military glory, little boastfulness or bellicosity, and little display of wealth. Early sexual satisfaction is high, and the post-partum taboo is limited or absent. Public physical punishment for social offenses is absent. Where there are games, they are games of skill, not games of chance.

Were we to put these features of primitive societies into the terms of our previous models for lethal aggressive behavior, would it be fair to say that these peaceable peoples are societies with little frustration over property, status, or sex? Also, that they have no strong hierarchy to order them into combat, and that they provide neither models of violent behavior for emulation, nor an ideology or value system favoring violence?

Descriptions of some of the nine societies suggest even less violence than Margaret Mead's mountain Arapesh. For example, the Semang of the Malay Peninsula carried on no warfare either among themselves or with the Sakai or the Malays. When the Malays harassed them, they simply ran away. They believed that the Semang deity punished violations of a number of social and religious taboos, but not murder, manslaughter, or theft. "The reason given," notes the German anthropologist Paul Schebesta, who studied the Semang, "was that these crimes are unknown." Semang parents did not punish their children; rather the mother would yell and scold, while the father used his "thunder call." The Semang were also completely unspecialized in labor or occupation. The men sometimes cooked, while the women sometimes did heavy work and both played equal roles in child care. There was no known case of suicide among them, and Schebesta notes, "they do not even know what it means." (It appears that the Hopi Indians of the Southwestern United States were similarly unable even to grasp the concept of homicide. To them a question about murder was as meaningless as, "What happens when a member of your tribe 'plkts' someone?")

Comparison of lethal violence in primitive and civilized societies. However, at least short of the most extreme examples—as where the very idea of homicide is unknown—one *very* strong caution has to be

162

offered about drawing inferences from anthropological descriptions of societies as "nonviolent" or "peaceful" or "not warlike." Considering in this context the mountain Arapesh, is such a society really *more* "peaceful," as one might infer, than Britain, India, or the United States? Typically, even anthropologists' strongest judgments of "peacefulness" have been based on observations of communities totalling a few score up to perhaps 1000 individuals, in which no lethal conflict, or "only" one or two killings, occurred over an observation period of anywhere from one to ten years. Consider a village of 400 people in which an anthropologist lives for five years. Down the river there is a second village with, say, 300 people in it. In the second year, there is a dispute between families in the two villages over a yam patch, and one man dies of spear wounds. In the fifth year, a woman in the larger village is killed by her wild, culturally marginal husband. These are the only two instances of lethal conflict in the five years, and the anthropologist describes the culture as basically very "peaceful." Now, statistically, there have been two killings in a population of 700 over five years. Considering only one of the killings as "murder," and even using the whole population of 700 for calculation, this amounts to a homicide rate of 0.2 per 700 in *one* year, or *about 29 per 100,000*. Considering the other death as "internal group violence," the rate is also 0.2 per 700 for each single year, or multiplied by 13 to match the 13-year data in the Yale data (page 17), about 3,770 per 1,000,000 population over a 13-year period. In terms of both homicide and group violence data for civilized societies, *these are high figures*. Remember that, World War I and II apart, the chances of an individual's life ending through lethal violence, according to Richardson's worldwide data, were substantially *less than one in one hundred* over the period 1820–1945. Yet, in five years, our hypothetical anthropologist has reported two out of a population of 700 killed by lethal violence. This data suggests that, of all of those now alive in the two villages fully fifteen or twenty will eventually die of lethal violence—between *two and three* out of every hundred. Certainly, our anthropologist has not painted a picture of savagery and ferocity, and the appellation "peaceful" may seem quite appropriate for this society. But then our civilized societies, on any statistical comparison, must be viewed as fully as "peaceful," and indeed as substantially more so. (Compare here the discussion on p. 110.)

The ultimate point is simply this: If one takes all modern lethal violence, apart from World Wars I and II (the figures since 1945 have

163

probably been *lower* than the 126-year average, exclusive of the two wars), then an anthropologist who observed comparably peaceful behavior in a community of 700 *would see not much more than one killing in that community each decade.* There are, I believe, extremely few primitive societies about which any comparable declaration can be made. Certainly there are *none*—even the Hopi or the Semang—for which one could be *sure* that murder is as infrequent as in Norway or Ireland, where there is fewer than one murder for every 400,000 people per year (in communities with a steady population of 700, the rate would be statistically equivalent if *one* murder occurred in a period of 571 years!). Thus, the anthropological data may be useful in comparing primitive communities *among themselves,* and to that extent helpful in suggesting factors that might assist in making modern societies more "peaceful." But it is virtually impossible to say, attempting direct comparison, that a given primitive society is comparatively *more* "peaceful" than a particular modern society.

It may also be said that the frequency of deaths from all lethal conflict in *warlike* primitive societies generally far *exceeds* that in modern societies, although there may be some exceptions, such as in Russia and Germany during World War II. Among the Yanonamö, for example, interviews indicated that *fifteen percent* of all deaths (among a group of 240 adult ancestors of those being interviewed) had been due to warfare, and this rate appears to have been steady for generation after generation. This is over twelve times the overall civilized rate, *including* the two world wars. Another 0.8 percent of Yanonamö deaths were due to club fights, which represent the "homicide" category. (It will be recalled from Richardson's data that about one death in four hundred, or 0.25 percent of all deaths, was due to homicide.)

Looking back on our discussion at the beginning of this chapter, it must *also* be said that, given the various paleontological finds, we can surely regard prehistoric man as highly "peaceful" in the sense of not being regularly engaged in the killing of his own kind, and essentially in the same sense that a village of 700 in which only one death occurs by lethal violence in a decade is a peaceful society. But modern man *is just as, or more, peaceful,* excluding the large-scale, highly organized violence that is not accompanied by rancor or anger.

Application from peaceful tribes to modern society. As for "nonrancorous" organized warfare, in which most of the contemporary deaths from lethal violence occur, it may unfortunately be true that primitive societies offer the *least* directly applicable "recipes." Even if certain of their characteristics appeared likely to make *us* less "war-like," most of the applications would have to be regarded as very long-term or utopian. Study of modern societies may also suggest that major changes in family structure, child-rearing practices, decision-making processes, and methods for selecting leaders may all be necessary for the elimination of large-scale group conflict. But many of these measures would require a very extended period of time for their public acceptance and implementation. We shall, indeed, consider the long-range "utopian" measures at the end of this book as desirable, but not as an immediate program: one may view great changes in the patterns of energy consumption, travel, and industrialization as the ultimate approach to pollution, but over the next decade or two our greatest hope will lie with less ambitious measures, such as the development of a non-polluting automobile engine. Moreover, utopian changes must be undertaken with complete awareness of the total environment in which they will operate. For instance, supposing a single family or group of families were to raise their sons as the Arapesh do, "as protected from aggression and struggle, from rude disciplinary measures on the part of older children and irritated parents, as is the most tenderly reared and fragile little daughter among ourselves." Such individuals could not be let loose in our present society — even assuming a sufficient previous insulation in the process of child-rearing, which is highly doubtful — if "their feelings are intolerably wounded" by even "a harsh word," or if "[t]he slightest gibe is taken as an expression of unfriendliness." They could not "carry into adult life the fear of any rift between associates." To raise a child in this way in any twentieth-century culture would be intolerably cruel. Short of such extremes, of course, there are many perfectly practical changes in emphasis and values: rejection of bellicosity and "warrior virtues," downgrading of material possessions, or changes in perceptions of male-female differences. Even a measure such as de-emphasizing achievement orientation in child-rearing would have to be very carefully considered, for there is undoubtedly a need for generations of politicians, scholars, and doers strongly motivated to achieve a peaceful, pollution-free, and happy world, possibly in competition with "achievers" who are *not* so motivated.

It seems worth emphasizing once more that despite all the crowded, stressful, competitive conditions of the "human zoo," man in contemporary society *has* succeeded in achieving a means of dealing with angry or rancorous acts of lethal violence by which we *do not* come off significantly the worse in comparison with "peaceful" animals, "peaceful" prehistoric man, or "peaceful" primitive tribes. One homicide per approximately 5,000,000 active man-days of living falls well to the "peaceful" side of any reasonable operational definition of "peaceful" versus "ferocious" behavior. When one considers the existence of the gun, the violent media, the psychotic, the brain-damaged, the children who are grotesquely raised and those who are not raised at all, the figure seems remarkably low.

If you closely observed one hundred New Yorkers or Londoners or Muscovites in their natural habitat for twenty years, the odds are very good that you would not see any of them, at any time, kill another human being in anger. Chances are several times better, however (probably between three and five times better), that you would see one of them do the final act that killed another human being while "doing his job" as part of an organized group effort—the bombardier, for example, releasing a load of bombs in wartime—and several times better still that you would see one or more engaged in the group effort that led up to that final act.

FOOTNOTES, CHAPTER 4

[1] Ashley Montagu, *The Human Revolution* (Cleveland: The World Publishing Co., 1965), pp. 95–96, 149–56.

[2] William H. McNeill, *The Rise of the West* (Chicago: The University of Chicago Press, 1963), p. 23.

[3] *The New York Times.* Dec. 29, 1971, p. 18.

[4] McNeill, *The Rise of the West*, p. 27.

[5] McNeill, *The Rise of the West*, pp. 27–8.

[6] Sigmund Freud, *Totem and Taboo* (New York: Random House, Inc., 1938), pp. 915–16.

[7] Margaret Mead, "Warfare Is Only an Invention—Not a Biological Necessity," in *Asia*, XL (1940), pp. 402–5.

[8] Mead, *Sex and Temperament in Three Primitive Societies* (New York: William Morrow and Company, Inc., 1935), pp. 40–44, 64–70, 135–36, 143–44, 146–47, 154, 157, Laurel edition.

5

War and Revolution:

The contemporary world

We have seen little evidence of lethal group conflict in Neolithic and earlier human societies—perhaps it occurred sporadically, during famine. But even if this rare lethal group conflict under extreme conditions were genetically "programmed" most reasons for lethal group conflict were invented and then emulated by human societies, one by one, over millennia. Thus, even those current societies that we call "primitive" often engage in such conflict not only for food or cattle or land, but for reasons ranging from material plunder, to fancied perceptions of insult or attack, to the pride of warriors or of their leaders, and so on down a long list.

When one considers the group conflicts of complex modern societies—and Richardson's data shows that it is in large-scale group conflict that most of the deaths through human aggression occur—a number of questions arise. Has the list of reasons for such conflict continued to grow even longer as primitive societies developed into more complex ones? (Consider the discussion of Richardson's factors, page 40.) Or are there, at least, certain focal models that explain many or even most such conflicts?

Internal Conflict

Are the reasons for internal revolution different, on the whole, than those for wars between nations? Are the reasons for internal group conflict even different depending on whether the insurgency is urban or rural, is in an early or late stage, comprehends a distinct geographic region, or is generalized throughout the society? We turn first to an examination of the wellsprings of such internal conflict.

Relative deprivation and internal violence. Consider the following formulation by Louis Coser, who has written extensively on conflict, from a sociologist's perspective, in *Violence and the Social Structure.*[1]

The notion of relative deprivation has been developed in recent sociological theorizing to denote the deprivation that arises not so much from the absolute amount of frustration as from the experienced discrepancy between one's lot and that of other persons or groups which serve as standards of reference. Whether or not superordinate groups or persons are taken as standards of reference by subordinate groups or individuals depends, at least in part, on whether the unequal distribution of rights and privileges is considered illegitimate by them. Negatively privileged groups or individuals may not develop the awareness that they are deprived of rights and privileges. In a caste society, for example, members of the lower caste, considering this system justified for religious reasons, may not feel frustrated by it. If the privileges of the superordinate groups are not considered legitimately attainable by their subordinates, lower-status people compare themselves only with each other and not with members of higher status groups.

In contrast, in societies such as ours, in which upward social mobility is said to be accessible to all, yet where in fact mobility is blocked for significant sections of the population, the bottom dogs in the status hierarchy compare their lot to that of the top dogs. Persons measure their status and the deprivations which it entails against the superior rights and privileges that they visualize as being enjoyed by the superordinate strata. Thus it stands to reason that, for example, American Negroes are especially frustrated because they contrast the success ideology inculcated by schools and mass media to the reality of continued discrimination. Hence among them, as among other low-status groups discussed so far, relative deprivation is likely to be high. This helps to account for their higher homicide rates more adequately than the notion of absolute deprivation, for it clarifies the fact that in social structures which do not institutionalize social mobility, homicide rates do not necessarily follow the American pattern.

The notion of relative deprivation also helps us understand why other low-status categories, such as women and the young, do not show high homicide rates. To put the matter in a nutshell: the young know that they will grow older, move up in the age hierarchy, and enjoy the perquisites of higher age status in the future; hence their lower relative deprivation. Women similarly do not tend to feel relatively deprived but for opposite reasons: equality with men seems unattainable, and different status between the sexes seems legitimate to both sexes. This accounts for the fact that women experience smaller degrees of relative deprivation. The young tend to accept the higher status of their elders because they know that one day they will be like them. Women accept the higher status of men because they believe that they will never be like them. Thus assurance of success just as assurance of lack of success may equally shield one against a sense of frustration. Similarly, sectarian subgroups who have withdrawn from involvement with the larger society in the name of a set of exclusive values do not compare their lot with that of members of the outside world and hence do not feel deprived.

This reasoning seems to account adequately for the fact that although women occupy lower statuses vis-à-vis men, their homicide rate is distinctly lower. (Of all city arrests for murder and non-negligent manslaughter in 1961, 834 were women and 3,791 were men.) It also explains why the young, although having lower status positions than their elders, still have relatively low homicide rates. (Only 8.3 percent of the city arrests for murder and non-negligent manslaughter in 1961 were under eighteen years of age and only 32.7 percent under twenty-five years.)

Is Coser's explanation a model for lethal aggression different from those described in Chapter 3? Or is he simply refining our understanding of the concept of "frustration," and reminding us that it is *not* a biological absolute — it *is* tied to the expectations and desires of a particular individual, in a particular society, at a particular time? However, Coser does not mention that there may also be relative deprivation in terms of *status* (see Chapter 3) as well as material goods.

Consider, again, the extract from Robert McNamara's "Montreal speech" in Chapter 1, and the comments which follow it. Does McNamara suggest that internal lethal violence is predictable on the basis of per capita gross national product? Is Coser inconsistent with McNamara? Is McNamara saying that a low income of, say, $100 per year, represents an "absolute" level of frustration, to which all individuals will react alike? Or are there additional reasons, cultural, *but common to many cultures,* why many people in many societies in 1960 and 1970 would feel strong relative deprivation with an income of only $100? Some of these reasons are the ubiquitousness of Marxist/Leninist/Maoist ideologies, the increase of literacy, and the spread of radio and other forms of communication that traverse national boundaries. Feelings of relative deprivation might depend, moreover, on whether there were other people, highly visible in the society, who had an income ten or one hundred times as great. They

169

might also depend upon what the relation between the wealthy people and those with low income was — for example, whether they were favored religious functionaries who received largely voluntary contributions, or factory owners who grew rich on the labor of their desperately impoverished workers.

Is Coser careful with his data? Note the data he uses to show that the young "have relatively low homicide rates." His data states that in the United States in 1961, persons 18 through 24 years of age accounted for 24.4 percent (32.7–8.3) of all city arrests for murders and non-negligent manslaughter. Actually, even after one excludes the very old and the very young from the total population, the 18 to 24 age group still accounted for a little *more* than its proportional share of the total, and this percentage has probably risen since 1961. However, the actual data is still consistent with Coser's theory of relative deprivation, if one keeps in mind two factors: first, his assumption that a *lower* 18 to 24 homicide rate would be explained by the fact that the young know they will "enjoy the prerequisites of higher age status in the future;" and second, that most homicides committed by the young are committed by young *blacks*.

Is it significant that McNamara discusses internal *group* violence, while Coser is speaking of homicide, or *individual* violence? Or should Coser's "relative deprivation" model of frustration also apply to such internal group violence as that reflected in riots, insurrections, and civil wars? It may seem at first that this view is contradicted by the lack of statistical correlations between the raw data showing, for various countries, the frequency of homicide and the frequency of deaths from internal group violence (see Chapter 1). Or are there many other factors that may determine whether a particular degree of frustration, at a particular time, in a given society will vent itself chiefly in homicide, chiefly in group violence, or chiefly in yet another form? If that were so, it is not surprising that we fail to find direct correlations in the raw data itself.

Can Coser be read to suggest that relative deprivation is the only, or at least the chief, basis for lethal violence within a country? Consider the possible application of other psychological models that we have discussed.

Can "relative deprivation" also be effectively felt by a population when it is deprivation relative to the affluence of persons in *other* societies? That is, can the same mechanism serve to motivate international conflict? If this motive seems less likely for war than for internal conflict, what does motivate conflict between nations? Even if relative deprivation does not directly move the mass of the population, can it affect the leader's sense of status or power? Is it possible that, with modern communications and propaganda techniques, a sense of "relative deprivation" on an international scale *might* be brought home to a whole population?

Land reform as a key to preventing internal violence. Are there particular aspects of relative deprivation that are especially likely to be causally related to large-scale internal violence? Focusing on twentieth-century revolutions, I have worked on several manuscripts on the problem of land reform — giving land ownership to peasants who currently make their living as tenants, sharecroppers, or plantation laborers. Here is an excerpt:*

It is important to realize that the less developed world is still predominantly agrarian; about three-fifths of the collective population of these countries, despite massive post-war migrations to the cities, still lives in the rural sector. There is enormous poverty in the rural sector in many of these countries, with the mass of people almost wholly excluded from the cash economy. One index of the deprivation of the rural sector of a given society — which is an index of social inferiority and political impotence as well as economic want — is the proportion of the population making its living as tenant farmers, share-croppers, or laborers on another's land. I have spent a good deal of time in the last three years developing data on the prevalence of this particular form of deprivation, and it yields some startling figures. If one takes the agrarian proportion of the total population in a given society (thus accounting for the weight that the rural sector has in the entire society) and multiplies it by the proportion of that agrarian population that is landless (tenant farmers, share-croppers, plantation laborers), one gets, quite simply stated, the percentage of the total population of that society that makes its living as landless peasants. This percentage furnishes what I have, for good reason, dubbed an "Index of Rural Instability." (See tables on next page.)

In fact, in most, if not all, of the societies that have undergone major revolutions in the twentieth century, at least a third of the *total* population was landless peasants.

This has been true in *all* of the Marxist revolutions, and has been made a part of revolutionary doctrine by the Chinese and Cubans (over half of the men who served with Castro in the Sierra Maestra were ex-plantation workers from Oriente province). Even in Russia, the land-to-the-peasants law was one of the two basic measures passed by the new Soviet in the first week of the October Revolution, and Lenin would almost certainly have failed without the support of the peasant militias. In Spain, Franco was provoked by the re-

*A somewhat different, and shorter, version of this manuscript was published in the Spring 1972 issue of *Foreign Policy* magazine, under the title "Land Reform and Foreign Aid."

**Landless peasants as an approximate percentage
of the total population**

Pre-revolutionary Mexico (pre-1911)	62%
Pre-revolutionary Bolivia (pre-1952)	60%
Pre-revolutionary China (pre-1949)	35–45%*
rice region only	42–58%
Pre-revolutionary South Vietnam (pre-1961)	42–58%
Pre-revolutionary Russia (pre-1917)	32–47%
Pre-revolutionary Cuba (pre-1959)	39%
Pre-civil war Spain (pre-1936)	over 33%

sults of the 1936 election, which demonstrated large-scale peasant support for the extreme radicals. Had the more moderate republican government not procrastinated through the early thirties in carrying out land reform measures, Franco might not have been able to intervene forcefully against the newly elected left. The failure of the moderate republicans in Spain thus paralleled that of Kerensky in Russia.

Other societies that have had serious peasant problems, short of completed revolution, have followed a similar pattern.

**Landless peasants as an approximate percentage
of the total population**

Central Luzon (Hukbalahap country: the average for the rest of the country, where the Huks have *not* been active, is under 30%)	50–57%
Java (where the communist PKI regularly won elections from 1955 until their abortive putsch of 1965)	50%
Eastern India (including West Bengal, where the communists have elected the state government and carried out waves of land seizures)	over 40%

Other places with relatively high percentages include northeastern Brazil (where one out of six South Americans lives), Nicaragua, Guatemala, Honduras, Nepal, Ethiopia, and Bangladesh.

By contrast, Thailand has around 20 percent and Cambodia under 10 percent landless peasants; figures which may be closely related to the slowness of any *indigenous* revolutionary movement to take hold in these countries.

*Where there is a range of figures, some peasants own some land but remain substantially reliant on other lands that they farm as tenants. The higher percentage figure is the result of considering them as though they were wholly tenants, the lower percentage figure is the result of considering them as though they were wholly owners.

Post-1953 Bolivia—where Che Guevara complained of the "stolid indifference" of the peasantry to his appeals—was only 5 percent landless peasants. . . .

In South Vietnam, certainly, the record is clear on the relation between the land tenure problem and rebellion. The Vietminh began distribution of French lands and the lands of absentee landowners in 1946, in the areas they controlled, and limited, rents on the rest of these lands to 15 percent (versus 33–50 percent previously), with credible penalties for over-collection. In 1954, they undertook an even more sweeping distribution, which was accompanied in 1954–55 with extensive violence in the North, aimed at landlords and ex-officials.

Diem had the opportunity, as historian Joseph Buttinger has pointed out, to carry out a democratic social revolution in the South that would have contrasted sharply and favorably with the difficulties of collectivization and the political repression in the North. Instead, he moved the other way. Landlords who had been dispossessed by the Vietminh were re-established during 1957 and 1958 under cover of a "rent control" law which was neither credible to the landlords nor enforceable, except for the purpose of getting the land occupant to re-acknowledge the landlord's rights. A minute redistribution of land took place under a complex law that permitted the landlords to retain enough land to hold at least 60 average tenant families.

The largely negative character of Diem's purported land reform was a major factor in letting the Vietcong establish a resurgent revolutionary movement among the peasantry: the "fish" could "swim in the sea."

In 1960, there were over one million South Vietnamese families—between six and seven million people out of a rural population of 11 million and a total population of 14–15 million—who were wholly or predominantly dependent on tenant farming. In the populous Mekong Delta, seven out of ten farm families were tenants. They farmed an average tract of four to five acres, and paid a third of the crop in rent, leaving them virtually no surplus. Having no effective security of tenure, they could be evicted virtually at will, and if there was a crop failure, rent remained payable in full. The landlord supplied neither inputs, credit, nor advice, but merely collected the rent when the annual harvest came in December and January.

The Vietcong promised land, and when they took over an area, they fulfilled the promise so far as all appearances were concerned. Larger landlords fled; absentees could not get in to collect their rents; and the few landlords who remained were subject to a strictly enforced limitation of 15 percent. It appeared to the former tenant that the Vietcong had given him surplus, security of tenure, and status.

Little wonder that all through the sixties the Vietcong used the recruiting appeal, "We have given you land, now give us your son." The well-publicized infusions of manpower from the North did not begin until 1965. Both before and after, the peasants of the South supplied 5,000–7,000 recruits a month to the Vietcong, an estimated three-fifths of them as volunteers or "soft-sell" enlistees. The peasants also supplied the famous guerrilla environment: intelligence reports, porters to carry in and bury supplies, and "safe" houses. They gave little or no support to Saigon.

The failures of government intelligence were humiliatingly underlined when multi-battalion Communist forces moved into position before Tet 1968, made elaborate logistical preparations, and nonetheless achieved almost complete surprise. Failures of intelligence continued to be apparent in the daily incidents, one of the most substantial sources of United States deaths, in which local guerrillas planted mines or booby traps and unwarned United States troops stumbled into them.

Saigon, in 1965 and 1966, issued decrees that formalized once more the right of landlords to reassert their titles to lands in newly "pacified" villages. Again, negative land reform drove tens of thousands of peasants into the arms of the National Liberation Front. The landlords rode into the villages, newly cleared and "secured" by the American innocents, literally on the jeeps that brought the ARVN back. Tenant farmers told Stanford Research Institute interviewers in 1967 that they regarded land ownership as a matter of crucial importance *five times as frequently* as they said the same thing about security. Clearly, the experience of being "saved from the Communists" meant something different to them than it meant to us.

Meanwhile, United States officials concentrated on tinkering with the political apparatus, while every excuse was found for not pushing grassroots reforms that might be unpalatable to elements of the ruling elite. The chief form of communication with the peasants remained the gun and the bomb.

Robert Sansom, a young member of Henry Kissinger's staff who was doing field work in Vietnam at the time of my own initial studies in 1967, put it most succinctly in *The Economics of Insurgency,* published in 1970:

> The basic reason land reform was not pursued was that U.S. officials did not believe that land-based grievances were important.

* * *

> The Americans offered the peasant a constitution; the Viet Cong offered him his land and with it the right to survive.

There were, certainly, important non-Communist models for reform in Mexico and Bolivia (whose current percentages of landless peasants are around 15 percent and 5 percent respectively, versus the figures shown earlier). Even more immediately, there were models in Japan and South Korea (where extensive land reform was, fortunately, carried out *before* the 1950 invasion by the North), and even in Taiwan — where, ten years too late, Chiang Kai-shek did what he should have done on the mainland and carried out a drastic land distribution to the Taiwanese tenant farmer. Significant, but lesser, land reforms were carried out in Iran and Venezuela, and by the British in response to the Malayan insurgency.

In the introductory chapter of a book on land reform that I am co-authoring with Barry Head, we note the following:

Finally, in showing the uses to which IRI [Index of Rural Instability] can be put, two further points should be made:

174

First, the basic concern here is with *revolutions*, rather than with palace coups or the other games of "musical chairs" played among governing elites. The prototypes are the twentieth century upheavals in Mexico, Russia, China, and Vietnam — conflicts that each caused over a million deaths and brought vast destruction, that revolved around issues of basic change in the economic and social structure of the societies, that brought wholly new faces to the role of leadership, and that, in the cases of Russia, China, and Vietnam, threatened great shifts along the fault-lines of international relations and involvement of the great powers.

Secondly, the development and use of IRI does not discount the possibility of revolution in an urban setting. But, unlike wars between nations, *all* protracted civil conflicts require genuine popular grievances. They muster their recruits despite the society's existing institutions and power structure, not because of them. How broadly the grievance is shared determines how great the chances are for bringing down the existing governmental structure, or at least for extending and intensifying the civil conflict. By themselves urban-based movements have not, over the course of the last century, presaged the really serious revolutinary threats. Certainly the Marxist revolutions were not based in the cities. The Russian workers needed, for their allies, the mass of discontented peasantry; in Vietnam, China, Cuba, the Philippines, Malaya, Guatemala, and Burma, the protracted conflict was almost wholly rooted in the countryside, and only there could the revolutionaries maintain areas of long-term control. On the other hand, having neglected to mobilize and build the conflict on their peasant support, the Communist putsch-makers of Indonesia failed in 1965; and in Algeria, the Arabs of the Casbah were wholly quelled, while the quasi-Marxist guerrillas of the countryside fought on.

Moreover, with the possible exceptions of the Czechoslovakian takeover in 1948 and the post–World War II struggle of the Zionist movement for Palestine, it can be strongly argued *that, among all conflicts that could reasonably be called "revolutions" during the last hundred years, whether or not Marxist in ideology, not one of those having a preponderantly urban base succeeded.*

The non-Communist revolutions in Mexico and Bolivia were essentially peasant uprisings. In Ireland in the early years of this century, the English were not only foreigners but absentee landlords occupying a position much like that of the French in Vietnam and Algeria forty years later. In Kenya and Malaya as well, the British were involved in conflicts where the land problem figured prominently. In Spain, scene of a civil conflict whose bloodiness rivaled fully earlier ones in Russia and Mexico, the agrarian problem was fundamental, but had been sidestepped by the moderate democratic regime of the early 1930s. . . . Perhaps the Zionist struggle against the British in Palestine after World War II has been the only instance of a *sustained* civil struggle (Czechoslovakia was a revolutionary *coup*) that had no major component of agrarian unrest. Indeed, it seems virtually impossible to find *any* such struggle not involving a land problem in any country without the additional problem of foreign rule. (The more recent Nigeria–Biafra conflict was along clear geographical-tribal lines, and much more like a traditional war between separate sovereign states than like a guerrilla war; it resembled the Korean

War much more than the war in Vietnam.) A protracted civil conflict without a major land question may be possible, but has hardly been typical.

Moreover, as to the prospects for sustained urban uprisings that have no massive support in the countryside, Martin Oppenheimer offers, in *The Urban Guerrilla*, evidence for his view that a black insurrection in the United States would almost certainly fail militarily. He describes six urban uprisings, each involving four factors that would confront a black-power insurrection: Each was "at minimum a guerrilla outbreak, backed by a significant sector of the local urban population;" each rising "developed into a rebellion which successfully took over an entire city or a large sector thereof;" in each, the rebels "were isolated, either acting totally alone, or effectively separated from outside support;" and in each, the government "continued to function effectively at least outside the city."[2] He then describes their fate:

CASE	DATES	CASUALTIES
The Paris Commune	March 28–May 28, 1871	20,000 to 30,000 dead versus 83 officers and 794 men of the Versailles government
The Easter Rising (Dublin)	April 24–29, 1916	No figures available
Shanghai, China	February 21–April 13, 1927	About 5,000 dead
Vienna, Austria	February 12–17, 1934	1,500 to 2,000 dead versus 102 Heimwehr
Warsaw Ghetto	April 19–May 15, 1943	Several thousand killed, 56,000 deported, versus about 20 Germans
Warsaw Uprising	July 31–October 2, 1944	100,000 to 250,000 dead

Against modern military and police techniques, the longest-lived of those urban rebellions lasted two months and three days: Again, on the recent historical record, it is *only* insurgencies with strong rural constituencies that have had staying power.

Do most of the societies that have carried out major non-Communist land reforms appear to have had a "strong hand" at the helm at the time? (Consider Japan and South Korea under American occupation just after the war; Chiang Kai-shek descending on Taiwan with the remains of his mainland army and administrative corps; the Shah in

Iran; and the position of the post-revolutionary regimes in Mexico and Bolivia.) Why might this be so? What difficulties might a less powerful regime that was "democratic" at the top—that is, ruled by a coalition of the rich and powerful—have? (Consider Marcos in the Philippines, Indira Gandhi in India, Frei in Chile.) Where might effective opposition to land reform come from? What would be the real basis for such opposition—why would the opponents oppose? Can you think of mechanisms by which such opposition might be placated or resolved? Or is it impossible for a society that is "democratic" at the top to carry out major land reform? Venezuela seems to fit the description, yet it carried out a substantial measure of land reform in 1958–64—how might this take place?

Can you formulate a reasonable response to this position: "We should not interfere with the internal affairs of any country. Land reform is such interference. Therefore, we should not support land reform." But there are many dynamics of "interference"—yeasty compounds of ideology, modern communications, and the cumulative experience of past twentieth-century revolutions—at large in the less developed world besides those that are reflected in United States foreign aid. Thus, consider in relation to the question just posed these further excerpts from the initial land-reform manuscript above:

The grass-roots shift in peasant support will, presumably, be most pronounced if the peasants think they are getting more from Saigon than from NLF land reform, not just that Saigon is doing less badly in comparison. But are they getting more? Or is the "more" at most the greater surface legitimacy of a Saigon-backed land title?

The answer to this question goes to the root of Robert Heilbroner's thesis that revolution and Marxist economic organization is, after all, "best" for the less-developed countries. If we just keep our hands off, he suggests, all will be for the best.

There are some major ethical questions raised by this viewpoint, of course: are we willing to see lethal violence used to effect social change, given any sort of plausible alternative that is non-violent? The Mexican, Russian, Chinese, and Spanish civil conflicts—the first three with very little active help from outside and the fourth *mostly* out of internal resources—killed more than a million people each. Does one wish that kind of violence on India or Brazil?

Again, are we willing to see the happiness and welfare of the present generation deliberately sacrificed as a means to make later generations supposedly happier or better off? This question is bound up, in turn, with whether one wishes to encourage the destruction of the existing managerial and professional class—not all or always monsters of iniquity, and perhaps deserving as individuals of at least some of the "due process" and presumption-of-innocence protections that we rightly insist upon in our own society.

And again, are we willing to see the rigorous repression of political and press freedoms that have accompanied all of the Marxist revolutions to date? When we discuss such repressions by the Saigon regime—and they are substantial and execrable—it seems only fair to point out that they are much worse, indeed virtually absolute, in North Vietnam or Czechoslovakia. (Indeed, they have been considerably worse in Pakistan and Greece).

But, assuming that one is *willing* to accept the violence, dislocation and repression that accompany a Marxist revolution, does the result really reflect the best alternative that can reasonably be offered *to the people* of the affected country? Certainly for the agricultural sector that predominates in such countries, I think the answer is that it is clearly not.

While Marxist revolutions have been built on the promise of land to the individual tenant or farm laborer, the promise has not been kept. Collectivization has followed within successively shorter periods after revolution in Russia (1917/28), China (1949/53), North Vietnam (1954/55), and Cuba (immediately). Let us ignore the violence that has accompanied collectivization—we are for the moment accepting revolutionary violence as a necessary means—and simply consider the lot of the peasant as a farmer.

In Russian agriculture, it took from 1928 to 1953 to recover the pre-collectivization level of farm production (and agriculture was much slower than industry in recovery after the war). Per capita production of grain today is barely higher than in tsarist times; private plots, comprising 3 percent of the cultivated land, were producing almost one fourth of the gross agricultural output at the end of the sixties including one fifth of Russia's meat and nearly half of its potato production. In recognition of the much higher motivation to produce on the private plots, a committee chaired by Brezhnev recommended last spring that the maximum size be increased from one-half acre to one and one-fourth acres.

Eastern European agriculture has had a parallel experience. Private plots dramatically out-produce collective acreage, and the collectivized farms must spend three to ten times as much in capital investment for a given increase in productivity as do comparable private farms in other European countries.

In China, rice and wheat production hardly increased at all from 1953 to the mid-1960s. Taiwan, having carried out non-Marxist land reform, increased its rice production by two-thirds during the same period; Japan and South Korea, which had likewise completed non-Marxist land reform, were also showing large gains. During China's "cultural revolution," many farmers in areas where there was dislocation tried to seize communal lands and turn them into private farms, and the Chinese experience with private plots parallels that in Russia.

For North Vietnam, data are very poor, but the experience appears to be roughly similar to that of China, and "self-criticism" on this issue has been intense.

In Cuba, total food production during the late 1960s was still below 1958 levels. The entire society had to be dislocated for the 1969–70 effort to reach

178

a record sugar harvest—the record was beaten, but the harvest fell over a million tons short of the goal. On the other hand, consider Mexico, whose major land reform began in the thirties on a non-Marxist model, and which has more than tripled agricultural production since then.

The evidence is strong indeed that most of the affected peasants have disliked the Marxist organization of agriculture in collectives, and that peasants affected by major non-Marxist land reform have consistently shown marked increases in motivation and productivity.

The effects, moreover, have not been confined to economics. A basic, simplified model of what the major non-Marxist land reforms have done may be visualized as follows:

A peasant previously paying one-third to one-half his crop in rent to a landlord no longer makes that payment.

He pays a smaller amount to the government for about ten years (in Vietnam, nothing) to cover all or most of the cost of acquiring the land from the landlord. In Taiwan, where peasants paid the highest price for their land of any of the reforms, net family income had doubled early in the repayment period and more than tripled following the last payment.

The balance between his pre-reform and post-reform incomes is surplus for the peasant's own use. Some is reinvested in agricultural inputs, the entire yield of which is now assured to the peasant.

The additional yield goes to the urban and export markets. Some of the surplus income is used for still further agricultural inputs, including small capital investments in tools or irrigation—overall production increases of 50 to 100 percent in the decade following reform have been typical. Other surplus income is used for consumer products such as transistor radios, clothing, or bicycles. Many of the demands for agricultural and consumer products can be met by local urban industry, and such demands encourage the growth of that industry. (Landlords may be encouraged or even required to invest a substantial fraction of the compensation received for the land in such industries.)

It now becomes important and relevant to have storage facilities for grain and optimum marketing and purchasing facilities. Cooperative village efforts, through taxation, borrowing, or profit-sharing investment, can mobilize part of the surplus for storage and other capital projects, and can mobilize joint buying and selling power in co-ops for fertilizer purchase, marketing, credit, and other ends.

Other portions of the surplus can be collectively mobilized for "social overhead." Wealth left in the village rather than siphoned off by landowners can be used for schools and dispensaries.

With more schools, and surplus available to support children through more years of schooling, literacy increases. Surplus, and freedom from landlord and moneylender political pressures, combine with greater literacy to increase the prospects for political activity. Ex-tenant farmers run for village office, and later for district and higher offices.

During this time, urban industry continues to grow, spurred by the demands of an increasingly prosperous countryside.

What *has* Thieu done about the land problem in Vietnam, if anything? If you had been faced with solving the land problem in late 1968, what would you have recommended? What has been done is described in the final chapter of this book.

If you had to solve the land problem in India or Brazil — through the present governments and avoiding lethal violence — what overall direction might your recommendations take? Again, some suggestions appear in the final chapter.

General factors related to internal violence. Is the data on land reform and revolutions consistent with what McNamara has said? With what Coser has said? Even if land-related grievances have given impetus to a number of twentieth century revolutions, does this necessarily mean that "frustration" by itself explains the consequent aggression? Consider the following excerpt from a joint Senate–House committee report on Latin America, issued in 1962.

> To the campesino (worker on the land) ownership of the land is more than a source of wealth. It is the source of prestige and political power and social justice. . . . It lets him share in the bundle of rights which have so long been the prerogative of the large landowner and denied to the landless. . . . The landless see in ownership of a piece of land a kind of job protection and assurance that, whatever happens, they will have food and shelter. . . . Through land ownership the landless hope for status in their communities, freedom to act and speak freely, the opportunity to see their children given an education, and the right to share in control over their government.

Does this suggest that other mechanisms as well as "frustration" would elicit aggressive behavior in the peasant or campesino? In certain cases, a lower, "colonial" status for the population may have been a contributing factor in insurrection. However, significant insurrections have usually occurred against colonial powers, in this century, only where the populace also had a substantial land-tenure grievance. Examples are the uprisings against the British in Ireland (after World War I), Kenya, and Malaya; against the French in Indochina and Algeria; and against the Dutch in Indonesia.

What is the relative importance of the "command and obedience model" (see Chapter 3), would you suppose, in determining combat behavior by the Vietcong on the one hand and the Saigon forces on the other? In describing the reasons for which a young peasant initially *joined* each of those forces in, say, 1967? We would generally expect the soldiers of a revolutionary movement to have the motivations described in "frustration," "acquisitiveness," and "fanatacism" models, as well as a sense of personal hostility towards the other side, but are these motives necessarily absent in the forces supporting an established government? Might the motivation of a revolutionary force be somewhat different if the revolutionaries had established stable control and administration of some part of the country for a period of time? What if a soldier from such an area were a "draftee," rather than a voluntary "enlistee"? Do you suppose that a 100 percent "enlistee" of the Vietcong would be a more effective soldier than a 100 percent "draftee" of the Saigon forces? Why? Is S. L. A. Marshall's data of any potential significance here? If the South Vietnamese government *did* succeed in carrying out a sweeping distribution of land to all of the tenant farmers, what changes, if any, might it bring about in the factors discussed in this paragraph? It is significant, in this regard, that the largest single group in the South Vietnamese armed forces have been drafted tenant farmers and sons of tenant farmers. How would their motivations be changed if the peasants believed that a Vietcong victory would probably bring ultimate collectivization?

Which of the following actions do you think might require a more solid, personal motivation on the part of the average fighting man, and thus be more difficult to initiate: a raid or war party in a primitive society, or a guerrilla war? Which would seem closer in motivation to the occasional lethal conflicts of prehistoric man?

If one were concerned with gaining the support of a peasant population, what other measures might be important besides land reform? Over the past two years, the Thieu government has armed over 1,000,-000 peasants in local force and militia units operating out of their home villages; conducted village elections, with the result that tenant farmers by early 1970 outnumbered landlords three to one on the elected village councils; and greatly expanded the availability of low-interest agricultural credit.

In relation to the causes of the internal conflict about which we have spoken, how relevant are responses such as "search-and-destroy" operations, B-52 bombings of the "Ho Chi Minh trail" or North Vietnam, defoliation, and clearing of populations out of "Vietcong-infested areas" and relocating them in refugee camps? (Which one of our "models" appears to be operating, incidentally, when we speak of an area as "infested" with the enemy?)

Are the grievances motivating severe internal conflict in a developed, urbanized society in any way similar to those in less developed societies? Since very basic grievances appear needed to motivate large-scale lethal group conflict within any existing organized society, it would seem reasonable to consider the availability of various resources essential to human beings over the coming decades. Without having studied detailed projections of figures on each of these resources, which of the following listed factors do you think might be most helpful in predicting internal conflict in either developed or less developed societies over the coming decades:

Population growth
Cultivable land per capita
Owned cultivable land per capita
Food production per capita
Deprivations of the second, third, or fourth items *relative to* other more favored groups in the society
Lower status positions through racial, caste, or religious discrimination
Housing space per capita
Jobs, versus unemployment or underemployment
Access to education
Deprivations of the seventh, eighth, or ninth factors *relative to* other, more favored groups in the society
Frequency of child-rearing techniques engendering severe frustration and rage in the infant
Frequency of an emphasis on "manly" virtues and competition, in a socially stratified society

Do any of the factors listed seem as likely to prove as powerful a *single* predictive tool for the developed societies as the combination of the third and fifth factors appears to be for the less developed societies?

War

What are the reasons underlying lethal group conflict between already separate geopolitical entities? Some suggestions from Richardson as to the apparent reasons for such conflicts, as well as for internal "quarrels," are given and commented upon briefly on pages 40–41. Consideration of the reasons for primitive warfare appears on pages 142–44. However, a closer examination of a few key conflicts may be more helpful than abstract discussion.

The Peloponnesian War. A strikingly "modern" system of political life and potential reasons for war can be seen clearly in the first objective historical account of a military conflict: Thucydides' history of the Peloponnesian War. This war was a terrible and wasting conflict fought among the Greek city-states, pitting Athens and her allies against Sparta (Lacedaemon) and her allies, during the last part of the fifth century B. C.

There are echoes of many familiar elements in the background of this war. There was a long history of conflict between Athens and Sparta. There was also a long history of conflict with the "barbarians" — the non-Greek-speaking people — of Persia and outlying areas. Among the functions served by these wars, as well as by some of the conflicts between the Greek city-states, was the acquisition of slaves. Athens and a number of other city-states, not including Sparta, used slaves to do the heavy work and make life more comfortable and pleasant for its free men. The older city-states had sent out an elaborate network of colonies to the many outlying islands, Sicily, and the Mediterranean coast of Asia Minor that bordered on the Persian empire. They were bound together with these colonies and other Greek city-states closer at hand in a network of treaties and protective alliances. Thucydides tells us:[3]

> The policy of Lacedaemon was not to exact tribute from her allies, but merely to secure their subservience to her interests by establishing oligarchies among them; Athens, on the contrary, had by degrees deprived hers of their ships, and imposed instead contributions in money on all except Chios and Lesbos.

Thus, it appears that each alliance was bound together by many factors significant to the two dominant city-states. The alliances provided the basis for trade and economic activity; the colonies could also serve as an outlet for excess population growth; Sparta's policy was to establish an oligarchical political system like her own within her allied states, while Athens leaned towards democracies, but was willing to allow other forms of government. Athens, however, generally collected direct revenues from her allies, as well as indirect revenues derived from monopolizing the largely sea-borne trade with her shipping. Athens was chiefly a sea power, Sparta a land power. Derived from the dominance of the two chief city-states (most directly in the features just quoted from Thucydides) was assuredly an enhancement of the power and status of their respective leaders.

183

The beginnings of the great war came with a squabble over a colony between Corinth, a part of Sparta's confederation of allies, and Corcyra, neutral and unallied. Corinth and Corcyra had the largest fleets, next to Athens, in a world where naval power was crucial to trade, communication, and defense. The passage below from Thucydides' history concerns the arguments made by the Corcyran delegates to the Athenians, urging them to form an alliance with Corcyra. After an initial victory and a series of skirmishes with Corinth, Corcyra had become concerned because Corinth had "spent the whole of the year after the engagement and that succeeding it in building ships, and in straining every nerve to form an efficient fleet" (p. 20) and because Corinth already had powerful allies — two features of a developing conflict 2400 years ago that seem strikingly modern. Where other particular modern parallels appear in the Corcyrans' arguments, I shall interpolate comments in brackets.[4]

Athenians! when a people that have not rendered any important service or support to their neighbours in times past, for which they might claim to be repaid, appear before them as we now appear before you to solicit their assistance, they may fairly be required to satisfy certain preliminary conditions. They should show, first, that it is expedient or at least safe to grant their request; next, that they will retain a lasting sense of the kindness. [The latter perhaps suggesting favorable trade, investment or other material benefits in a modern setting.] But if they cannot clearly establish any of these points, they must not be annoyed if they meet with a rebuff. Now the Corcyraeans believe that with their petition for assistance they can also give you a satisfactory answer on these points, and they have therefore despatched us hither. It has so happened that our policy as regards you, with respect to this request, turns out to be inconsistent, and as regards our interests, to be at the present crisis inexpedient. We say inconsistent, because a power which has never in the whole of her past history been willing to ally herself with any of her neighbours, is now found asking them to ally themselves with her. And we say inexpedient, because in our present war with Corinth it has left us in a position of entire isolation, and what once seemed the wise precaution of refusing to involve ourselves in alliances with other powers, lest we should also involve ourselves in risks of their choosing, has now proved to be folly and weakness. [Rejection of "isolationism."] It is true that in the late naval engagement we drove back the Corinthians from our shores single-handed. But they have now got together a still larger armament from Peloponnese and the rest of Hellas; and we, seeing our utter inability to cope with them without foreign aid, and the magnitude of the danger which subjection to them implies, find it necessary to ask help from you and from every other power. And we hope to be excused if we forswear our old principle of complete political isolation, a principle which was not adopted with any sinister intention, but was rather the consequence of an error in judgement. [Ours was not an "immoral neutralism," to use an old John Foster Dulles phrase.]

Now there are many reasons why in the event of your compliance you will congratulate yourselves on this request having been made to you. First, because your assistance will be rendered to a power which, herself inoffensive, is a victim to the injustice of others. [We are victims of aggression.]

Secondly, because all that we most value is at stake in the present contest, and your welcome of us under these circumstances will be a proof of good will which will ever keep alive the gratitude you will lay up in our hearts. Thirdly, yourselves excepted, we are the greatest naval power in Hellas. Moreover, can you conceive a stroke of good fortune more rare in itself, or more disheartening to your enemies, than that the power whose adhesion you would have valued above much material and moral strength, should present herself self-invited, should deliver herself into your hands without danger and without expense, and should lastly put you in the way of gaining a high character in the eyes of the world, the gratitude of those whom you shall assist, and a great accession of strength for yourselves? [This will be a militarily favorable alliance, like adding the strength of West Germany.]

You may search all history without finding many instances of a people gaining all these advantages at once, or many instances of a power that comes in quest of assistance being in a position to give to the people whose alliance she solicits as much safety and honour as she will receive. [This will be a mutual alliance of equal contributors, like France (formerly) and Germany and Britain in NATO.] But it will be urged that it is only in the case of a war that we shall be found useful. To this we answer that if any of you imagine that that war is far off, he is grievously mistaken, and is blind to the fact that Lacedaemon regards you with jealousy and desires war, and that Corinth is powerful there, — the same, remember, that is your enemy, and is even now trying to subdue us as a preliminary to attacking you. [The "domino theory" — do you want Lacedaemonian troops on the Acropolis?] And this she does to prevent our becoming united by a common enmity, and her having us both on her hands, and also to insure getting the start of you in one of two ways, either by crippling our power or by making its strength her own. [By conquering us, she can add our resources to her own: do you wish to look out on a hostile world?]

Now it is our policy to be beforehand with her — that is, for Corcyra to make an offer of alliance and for you to accept it; in fact, we ought to form plans against her instead of waiting to defeat the plans she forms against us. [That is, let's consider a preemptive strike; we'll attack first.]

If she asserts that for you to receive a colony of hers into alliance is not right, let her know that every colony that is well treated honours its parent state, but becomes estranged from it by injustice. [This is the War of 1812, we are the former Thirteen Colonies, she is England, and you are France.]

For colonists are not sent forth on the understanding that they are to be the slaves of those that remain behind, but that they are to be their equals. And that Corinth was injuring us is clear. Invited to refer the dispute about Epidamnus to arbitration, they chose to prosecute their complaints by war rather than by fair trial. And let their conduct towards us who are their kindred be a

185

warning to you not to be misled by their deceit, nor to yield to their direct requests; concessions to adversaries only end in self-reproach, [no appeasement; millions for defense, not one cent for tribute] and the more strictly they are avoided the greater will be the chance of security.

If it be urged that your reception of us will be a breach of the treaty existing between you and Lacedaemon, the answer is that we are a neutral state, and that one of the express provisions of that treaty is that it shall be competent for any Hellenic state that is neutral to join whichever side it pleases. [We grant that treaties are solemn obligations: but this action is consistent with all existing treaty language.] And it is intolerable for Corinth to be allowed to obtain men for her navy not only from her allies, but also from the rest of Hellas, no small number being furnished by your own subjects. [Corinth was getting rowers from all over for her enlarged navy by paying a large bounty: they are threatening your power over your own allies, causing a "rower drain" with their gold; if carried a step further, this argument becomes the threat of mass defection that needs a Berlin wall or some other drastic measure.]

While we are to be excluded both from the alliance left open to us by treaty, and from any assistance that we might get from other quarters, and you are to be accused of political immorality if you comply with our request. On the other hand, we shall have much greater cause to complain of you, if you do not comply with it; if we, who are in peril, and are no enemies of yours, meet with a repulse at your hands, while Corinth, who is the aggressor and your enemy, not only meets with no hindrance from you, but is even allowed to draw material for war from your dependencies. This ought not to be, but you should either forbid her enlisting men in your dominions, or you should lend us too what help you may think advisable. [If you are going to be neutral, you must not help *either* side; help them alone and you may find us your enemies.]

But your real policy is to afford us avowed countenance and support. The advantages of this course, as we premised in the beginning of our speech, are many. We mention one that is perhaps the chief. Could there be a clearer guarantee of our good faith than is offered by the fact that the power which is at enmity with you, is also at enmity with us, and that that power is fully able to punish defection. And there is a wide difference between declining the alliance of an inland and of a maritime power. For your first endeavour should be to prevent, if possible, the existence of any naval power except your own. [Proliferation of modern arms is a bad thing—a monopoly is best.] Failing this, to secure the friendship of the strongest that does exist. [A United States–Russian alliance is a reasonable road to world order.] And if any of you believe that what we urge is expedient, but fear to act upon this belief, lest it should lead to a breach of the treaty, you must remember that on the one hand, whatever your fears, your strength will be formidable to your antagonists; on the other, whatever the confidence you derive from refusing to receive us, your weakness will have no terrors for a strong enemy. You must also remember that your decision is for Athens no less than for Corcyra, and that you are not making the best provision for her interests, if at a time when you are anxiously scanning the horizon that you may be in readiness for the breaking out of the war which is all but upon you, you hesitate to attach to your side a place whose adhesion or estrangement is alike pregnant with the most vital consequences. For it lies conveniently for the coast-navigation in the direction of Italy and Sicily, being able to bar the passage of naval reinforcements from thence to Peloponnese, and from Peloponnese thither; and it is in other respects a most desirable station. [Corcyra is of great strategic importance.] To sum up as shortly as possible, embracing both general and particular considerations, let this show you the folly of sacrificing us. Remember that there are but three considerable naval powers in Hellas, Athens, Corcyra, and Corinth, and that if you allow two of these three to become one, and Corinth to secure us for herself, you will have to hold the sea against the united fleets of Corcyra and Peloponnese. But if you receive us, you will have our ships to reinforce you in the struggle. [Beware a Sino-Soviet rapprochement.]

The Athenians ultimately decided at a public assembly to join with Corcyra in "a defensive, not an offensive alliance," which would not violate the existing peace treaty. This, however, became an important addition to the train of events that shortly led to general war. At the most basic level, Thucydides suggests:[5]

The real cause I consider to be the one which was formally most kept out of sight. The growth of the power of Athens, and the alarm which this inspired in Lacedaemon, made war inevitable.

Once begun, the war continued twenty-one years. These city-states, tiny by modern standards (hardly any of the individual states had more than 100,000 free citizens), mobilized fully for the bloody conflict. Fleets were sunk; casualties of as many as 10,000 dead and wounded were suffered in a single battle; patterns of trade were destroyed; economies were shattered and political systems overturned, from oligarchy to democracy and back again. In the end, no one won, but the war put an end to the golden age of Greek culture, and the life of the city-states never again regained its full political and intellectual vigor.

On this tiny canvas, painted 2,400 years ago, we can see a panorama of many of the causes of modern war: patterns of trade and colonization are extended, partly for economic reasons and partly to achieve status for the leaders. Alliances arise out of these and other past relationships—out of ideologically formulated ties to the allies and out of certain material benefits from them. A need is felt to safeguard the alliances and the desirable economic relationships by ensuring the sufficiency of the dominant power's military position and the "credibility" of its network of guarantees. There is a tendency to accept a "worst feasible case" analysis of potential opposing powers' intentions in determining courses of action. Nonaligned or third powers have a built-in "judo" leverage to play on the dominant parties' fears. There is a tendency to form additional alliances and to arm and train for combat. The net draws tighter until the mutual "worst feasible case" assumptions of the powers, or the rash or deliberately precipitating acts of allies, or some leader's sense of threatened status, moves the whole system into war.

The role of ideology in international conflict. Of course, not all lethal conflicts between different geopolitical entities are as complex or cataclysmic as the Peloponnesian War. On the nature of wars over recent centuries, consider this passage from the Somervell abridgment of Toynbee's *A Study of History*:[6]

If we cast our minds back to the state of the Western World on the eve of the emergence of Industrialism and Democracy, we shall notice that at that time, in the middle of the eighteenth century, war was in much the same condition as slavery: it was manifestly on the wane, not so much because wars were less frequent—though even that fact could perhaps be statistically proved[1]—as because they were being conducted with more moderation. Our eighteenth-century rationalists looked back with distaste on a recent past in which war had been keyed up to a horrid intensity by the impact of the drive of religious fanaticism. In the latter part of the seventeenth century, however, this demon had been cast out, and the immediate effect was to reduce the evil of war to a minimum never approached in any other chapter of our Western history before or since. This age of relatively "civilized warfare" came to an end at the close of the eighteenth century when war began to be keyed up once again by the impact of Democracy and Industrialism. If we ask ourselves which of these two forces has played the greater part in the intensification of warfare during the last hundred and fifty years, our first impulse will probably be to attribute the more important role to Industrialism. But we should be wrong. The first of the modern wars in this sense was the cycle of wars inaugurated by the French Revolution, and on these wars the impact of Industrialism was inconsiderable and the impact of Democracy, French Revolutionary Democracy, all-important. It was not so much the military genius of Napoleon as the revolutionary fury of the new French armies that cut through the old-fashioned eighteenth-century defence of the unrevolutionized Continental Powers like a knife through butter and carried French arms all over Europe. If evidence for this assertion is required it can be found in the fact that the raw French levies had accomplished feats too hard for the professional army of Louis XIV before Napoleon appeared on the scene. And we may remind ourselves also that Romans and Assyrians and other keyed-up

[1]Though P. A. Sorokin, in the statistical evidence marshalled by him, finds that the incidence of war on the Western World was lighter, on the whole, in the nineteenth century than in the eighteenth (*Social and Cultural Dynamics*, vol. iii (New York 1937, American Book Co.), pp. 342 and 345–6).

militarist Powers of bygone ages have destroyed civilizations without the aid of any industrial apparatus, in fact with weapons that would have seemed rudimentary to a sixteenth-century matchlockman.

The fundamental reason why war was less atrocious in the eighteenth century than either before or since was that it had ceased to be a weapon of religious fanaticism and had not yet become an instrument of nationalist fanaticism. During this interval it was merely a "sport of kings." Morally, the use of war for this more frivolous purpose may be all the more shocking, but the effect in mitigating the material horrors of war is undeniable. The royal players knew quite well the degree of licence that their subjects would allow them, and they kept their activities well within these bounds. Their armies were not recruited by conscription; they did not live off the country they occupied like the armies of the Wars of Religion, nor did they wipe the works of peace out of existence like the armies of the twentieth century. They observed the rules of their military game, set themselves moderate objectives and did not impose crushing terms on their defeated opponents. On the rare occasions when these conventions were broken, as by Louis XIV in his devastations of the Palatinate in A. D. 1674 and A. D. 1689, such atrocities were roundly condemned not only by the victims but by neutral public opinion.

The classic description of this state of affairs comes from the pen of Edward Gibbon:

"In war the European forces are exercised by temperate and undecisive contests. The Balance of Power will continue to fluctuate, and the prosperity of our own or the neighbouring kingdoms may be alternately exalted or depressed; but these partial events cannot essentially injure our general state of happiness, the system of arts and laws and manners which so advantageously distinguish, above the rest of mankind, the Europeans and their colonists."

The author of this excruciatingly complacent passage lived just long enough to be shaken to the core by the beginning of a new cycle of wars which was to render his verdict obsolete.

Here again, our Western Society was in a happier posture in the Pre-Nationalistic Age of the eighteenth century. With one or two notable exceptions the parochial sovereign states of the Western World were not then the instruments of the general wills of their citizens but were virtually the private estates of dynasties. Royal wars and royal marriages were the two procedures through which conveyances of such estates, or of parts of them, from one dynasty to another were brought about, and, of the two methods, the latter was obviously to be preferred. Hence the familiar line in praise of the foreign policy of the House of Hapsburg: *Bella gerant alii; tu, felix Austria, nube.* ("Let others wage wars; you, happy Austria, go marry.") The very names of the three chief wars of the first half of the eighteenth century, the Wars of the Spanish, Polish and Austrian Successions, suggest that wars only occurred when matrimonial arrangements had got into an inextricable tangle.

There was no doubt something rather petty and sordid about this matrimonial diplomacy. A dynastic compact by which provinces and their inhabitants are transferred from one owner to another like estates with their livestock is revolting to the susceptibilities of our democratic age. But the eighteenth-century had its compensations. It took the shine out of patriotism; but, with the shine, it took the sting. A well-known passage in Sterne's *Sentimental Journey* relates how the author went to France quite forgetting that Great Britain and France were engaged in the Seven Years' War. After a little trouble with the French police, the services of a French nobleman, whom he had never met before, enabled him to resume his journey without any further unpleasantness. When, forty years later, on the rupture of the treaty of Amiens, Napoleon gave orders that all British civilians between the ages of eighteen and sixty who happened to be in France at the moment should be interned, his action was regarded as an example of Corsican savagery and as an illustration of Wellington's subsequent dictum that he was "not a gentleman," and indeed Napoleon offered excuses for his procedure; yet it was only what even the most humane and liberal government to-day would do as a matter of course and of common sense. War has now become "total war," and it has become so because parochial states have become nationalist democracies.

By total war we mean a war in which it is recognized that the combatants are not only the selected "chessmen" called soldiers and sailors but the whole populations of the countries concerned.

Does Toynbee regard ideology as an important element in determining the severity of international conflict? For this purpose, he regards militant Christianity and militant national democracy as performing much the same function. Clearly, however, he does not regard ideology as *essential* to international conflict. Which of our models of death-dealing behavior in Chapter 3 might fit the causation mechanism of the wars of "succession" — perhaps "status" in a very specifically defined sense?

Is what Toynbee refers to as "total" war something new? From this standpoint, was the Peloponnesian War more like World War II, or more like the War of the Austrian Succession?

What factors may contribute to make a war fought with a strong ideological motivation a very bloody one? Some of them are: the ability to dehumanize the opponents, the putting aside of cultural norms against killing, and a stronger sense of in-group identity. Even though it might do all of these things, is ideology *essential* to very bloody wars, or to "total" war? What other variables might be operative? In the Peloponnesian War, the rigid discipline and state upbringing imposed on Sparta's youth undoubtedly contributed to the severity of the war. In contemporary times, the advent of nuclear weapons has made total destruction very easy. What made World War II so bloody? In so far as the behavior of American troops was concerned, think again of S. L. A. Marshall's data.

Is the problem of maintaining "credible" guarantees, so that an

190

ally will not seek to build an independent fleet, of the same order as maintaining them so that an ally will not seek to build an atomic bomb? If the latter appears a more serious concern, even one where species survival may be at stake, what may be done to reduce the other risks that may flow from maintaining "credibility?" In fact, the whole "credibility" notion fundamentally means that dominant powers are locked in an increasingly intricate and increasingly deadly embrace, a negative symbiosis that must somehow be completely broken.

What is meant by "worst feasible case assumption?" One party assumes, without actual knowledge, that the other will do the worst or most threatening thing that it has reasonably within its capacity to do, such as building as many ICBM rockets as it has the industrial capacity to build. How might a party that makes such "worst feasible case" predictions be induced to make less harsh predictions?

Colonization. Did the program of colonial conquests by the European powers have motivations other than ideology, parallel to some of the reasons for Greek city-state colonization? The very early colonization by the Spanish had been largely motivated by gold, which could be shipped back home and used to stimulate the economy and buy luxuries for the aristocracy, as well as by the enlarged status that the newly acquired territories brought to the rulers. The very early English colonization was less a deliberate act of government than a safety-valve for dissident religious groups. Consider this analysis:

By the early eighteenth century, however, England was colonizing America in much the Greek city-state pattern—to establish favorable patterns of trade and gain tax revenues, perhaps to some extent to have an outlet for a growing population, while denying to the colonies an independent fleet or army and final political decision-making power, thus having a final control of the lands and the people upon them, with a consequent augmentation of power and status. When the colonies grew large enough, the status of the local elite demanded at least full political equality through representation, or political independence, and they obtained the latter (with some mass support for both the status of equality or independence and the control of British taxes), in a rather low-key conflict in which the total cost to the colonists was 4,400 dead. The ex-colonists then proceeded on a massive century-long process of contiguous colonization—economically and politically the most successful ever undertaken—accompanied by the subjugation of the small indigenous Indian populations. They solved the problem the Greeks and British had had by giving each of the newly colonized areas full political equality with the original areas, including a joint voice in the central authority to which all were subject on certain common questions.

191

In the eighteenth century, England was acquiring power over India, by a process of colonization that became a pattern for England and France particularly, and to a lesser extent for Germany, Holland, Belgium, and other states. Like the earlier Spanish colonization of Latin America, this pattern did not involve so much the transfer of home populations (there were some, as the French in Algeria and the British and Dutch in South Africa) as it involved the establishment of power and favorable trade relations. India could supply spices and cotton, Indochina and Indonesia rubber, South Africa gold and diamonds, and each of the new colonies could provide some outlet for home products. But as the nineteenth century wore on, the economic-advantage argument for colonial expansion wore thin. It was already becoming clear that most of the colonies would cost more to administer (at least for societies which, unlike the Spaniards, saw certain "Christian duties" in areas such as education and health care) than they could possibly yield in benefits, at least for many decades. Yet the dynamic of colonization, by the latter part of the century, had almost assumed a life of its own. It was integral to the *definition* of the role, the status, and the success of a British, French, or German head of state that he seek to acquire additional colonies. It was the mark of a "great state." (Can you think of any somewhat comparable status-races today?) At the time, the only apparent reason for the colonization of Africa and other areas (besides augmenting the status of the leaders vis-à-vis other people) was some ideological notion of bringing "Christian civilization to the heathen."

It is clear that later decisions of great importance were founded on the notion of status or "glory" associated with the control of colonies: for example, after World War II, the French decided to resume control over Indochina. French leaders feared that independence for Indochina would encourage demands for independence in the French colonies of sub-Saharan and North Africa, and felt the need to resume control over their overseas colonies as a partial counterweight to their humiliating defeat in World War II. France was, after all, one of the "Big Five," with veto power in the United Nations, and she had to dress for the occasion. The British, fortunately, were somewhat more rational. A Labor government that had ideological reasons for *not* keeping the colony gave independence to India in 1947. Most of the colonial possessions of both Britain and France were not, however, relinquished until the 1960s. In a sense, by that time, "status" demanded the *relinquishment* of colonial holdings, since it was becoming increasingly likely that retention might reduce the real resources and influence of the colonial power. Some of the liabilities of retention might be civil war in the colony, the hostility of ex-colonies that were now important trading partners with the mother country, and, increasingly, vocal internal opposition from political groups that regarded colonies as inconsistent with democratic ideology. From the colonies' side, civil war was encouraged by the desire of the indigenous elites to obtain the full power and status of independence, and by the mass grievances generated by economic exploitation. (In each of the major post-war colonial struggles — in Indochina, Malaya, Kenya, and Algeria — large landholdings by the citizens of the colonial power, and their local allies, produced considerable support for the rebellion.)

America's role as a colonial power has, of course, been a subject of hot debate. The United States got into the colonial race, in the classic sense of direct political control, late, and got out early. The Spanish-American War of 1898 was fought against a colonial power, Spain, to aid in the liberation of Cuba (where our initial occupation ended in 1902) and the Philippines (where we stayed on, but granted independence in 1947). We carried out, however, a series of extended military interventions in Central America and the Caribbean in the first three decades of this century, partly to safeguard American citizens and investment against political disorder, partly to gain new concessions (for example, the Panama Canal and Canal Zone), and partly to carry the gospel of political democracy to the Caribbean area. As Teddy Roosevelt decreed in a "corollary" to the Monroe Doctrine, we had a special interest there. Unfortunately, the naive Americans generally left behind scoundrels and despots, rather than democrats, and an immense fund of ill-will. The doctrinal basis for intervention was discarded in 1933, and a "good-neighbor" policy adopted, but sporadic interventions in the Caribbean region continued when United States strategic or financial interests seemed to be seriously threatened (Guatemala in 1954, the Cuban "Bay of Pigs" in 1961, and the Dominican Republic in 1965).

The United States also has a current series of overseas political dependents. These range from Puerto Rico, ceded by Spain after the Spanish-American War, and self-governing except in the foreign policy and military areas (her citizens have full United States citizenship with the economic advantage of paying no United States taxes); to the Canal Zone, acquired in 1903, with its "Yankee" population and direct United States "sovereign" control, set in the middle of Panama and operating the Canal. In the Pacific there are military stations like Midway (1867) and Wake Island (1898), which have no indigenous populations; Guam (1898) and American Samoa (1899–1904), Pacific islands with a combined population of around 100,000, having a measure of self-government (and in Guam, United States citizenship) under United States Interior Department tutelage. The tiny Pacific islands of Micronesia, comprising the Mariana, Caroline, and Marshall groups, and another 100,000 people, were successively under the control of Spain, Germany, and Japan, and in 1947 were made a "Strategic Trust Territory" under United States administration by the United Nations Security Council. They are administered by the Interior Department with little self-government.

In terms of the past history of colonial control, which of these relations with political dependents seems to raise the most significant problems? What changes might resolve these problems? Do we have enough data about these United States possessions to be able to make reasonable judgments? Consider the previous materials on land-tenure in relation to internal conflict.

All of the foregoing discussion, however, is of the problems of direct colonial control. Are there more subtle forms of "colonization" through trade and investment patterns? How would you describe the

Russian relationships to Czechoslovakia, Poland, or East Germany, or the Chinese relationship to Tibet? What of the United States relationship with countries—ranging from Canada to much of Latin America to Iran or Saudi Arabia—in which there are large investments by United States firms?

The relation of war to economic ties between countries. Can one infer from the account of the Peloponnesian War that patterns of trade or investment between states are likely to be destabilizing or war-promoting, or would we miss something in making such a judgment? What of United States technical assistance and engineering for a truck factory in Russia? Would patterns of Athenian trade with *Sparta* in goods which *each* desired or thought necessary have been destabilizing? Is Chinese importation of Canadian and Australian wheat likely to be destabilizing? Even if the foregoing examples are regarded as likely to be stability-*promoting,* what of United States trade or investment with Japan, France, Brazil, Israel, or Syria? The factors involved here are highly complex, some stabilizing and others the reverse. What do you think of the following tentative analysis:

Much more detailed historical and statistical study is needed, but in general it seems likely that a relationship in which one country genuinely benefits from the raw materials, goods, technology, or investment of another is a relationship that *reduces,* so long as the relationship continues, the risk that the benefitting country will initiate serious conflict with the other. To the extent that benefits are bilateral and flow in each direction (as in the Common Market), or to the extent that the benefitting country is a militarily much stronger one, the risk that the other country will initiate serious conflict by armed attack is also low, but it is probably no lower than it would be otherwise, and is not *reduced* by the trade relationship. The major problems arise out of two broad classes of situations:

One, where the country that has been conferring a benefit, without what constitutes (in its eyes) an adequate bilateral return, decides to end the benefit. Such an action might involve nationalizing a foreign-owned oil or extraction industry, thus threatening an established pattern of supply; or even taking over a foreign-owned manufacturing industry that sells locally, to the extent that this act threatens an established pattern of dividend remittance; or else terminating a government-sanctioned export relationship for sending food or raw materials to the benefitted country. Such action deprives the benefitted country of its benefits, which may be major or minor in relation to its economic vigor and perceived material needs; moreover, the severing of such a relationship may be seen by the benefitted country as a reduction of its power and status, and possibly as establishing a precedent which, if unpunished, may spread to other countries from which it receives similar benefits. Thus, the

194

benefitted country may apply economic, political, or even military sanctions to a country that, for example, nationalizes basic industries after a change in political direction or in government, or threatens action of this kind. There was probably some element of these motives in many small-scale United States interventions in Central America and the Caribbean, and sometimes elsewhere, over the late nineteenth and early twentieth centuries. This kind of situation was probably one reason for the more recent indirect military intervention in Guatemala (1954) and the attempted intervention in Cuba (1961). These motives do not, however, seem to have played a significant role in the overt intervention in the Dominican Republic or in Vietnam, and there does not presently seem to be any threat of it with Chile, where major nationalization is pending. It was perhaps a factor in the Russian interventions in Hungary (1956) and Czechoslovakia (1968); although in these two cases, as with the United States in the Dominican Republic, Cuba, and Guatemala, a more important perceived reason for armed intervention appears to have been the threatened withdrawal of a "strategic" benefit rather than of an economic one. The main motive for intervention was to prevent the threatened end of political alliance by a buffer-zone state, or a state whose position the dominant beneficiary regarded as otherwise sensitive in military terms. Perhaps the clearest case of economically motivated intervention in recent years was the British–French move against Egypt during the 1956 Mideast war. There, the Egyptian nationalization of the Suez Canal was perceived as a threat to the continued movement of a major part of the Mideast oil upon which the British and French economies were heavily dependent.

Two. An even more serious problem may arise, however, when one or more major powers are isolated from the "benefit system" and decide for reasons of economic necessity or status to impinge on existing benefit-relationships among other countries. Such impingement may range from ingratiation or "probing," to arrangements with benefit-conferring countries that can exist side-by-side with pre-existing benefit arrangements, to arrangements that threaten to reduce the expected benefits to the previous recipient, to arrangements that actually reduce such benefits. As the new relationship progresses up this scale, the previous dominant partner may feel itself threatened in economic or status terms to such an extent that it responds, with violence or the threat of violence, against the old partner or the impinging power. Some of the current developments in the Mideast may be following this pattern. United States sanctions against Cuba, including the missile-crisis confrontation with Russia, can also be partly explained by a fear that Cuba might become a successful "exporter" of revolution or major disorder to other areas of Latin America where the United States had vital beneficial arrangements, especially Venezuela with its oil and Panama with its canal.

However, following this model, it would seem that a situation in which most benefit relationships were mutual would largely solve the first of the two problems. The second problem could be solved by an arrangement in which all major powers were receiving major benefits from each of the other major powers or from their close allies. With this arrangement, possible retaliatory loss of *this* benefit would act as a restraint against substantial "raids" on the other country's benefit relationships elsewhere in the world. Such a system, which seems achievable, should significantly reduce the potential for international violent conflict.

On the Mideast problem, consider the following article and chart from *Time*,[7] and the further chart from *Newsweek*:[8]

THE POLITICAL POWER
OF MIDEAST OIL

In terms of international economics and politics, Middle Eastern oil is the world's balance wheel.

— John Emerson,
Chase Manhattan Bank Economist

Each time a new crisis flares in the Middle East, Western oilmen are beset by a thousand and one Arabian nightmares. That has never been more the case than now, when the unstable elements of conflict in the post-Nasser Arab world could bring trouble at any time. Will the Arabs turn off the oil taps? Might Russia grab control of the world's richest reserves? And how badly would an interruption hurt the U.S.?

Those nightmares are not likely to come true, if only because it is in the Arabs' — and the Russians' — interests to keep the oil flowing. The U.S. itself is relatively immune to oil blackmail because only 3% of its supplies come from the area. Middle Eastern oil is, however, vital to U.S. interests and strategy in a broader sense. The economic well-being of NATO countries and of Japan depends upon it.

Seven Sisters. The Middle East and North Africa have 70.4% of the earth's proven reserves, amounting to 371 billion barrels, and last year provided 39% of international needs. Europe gets 58% of its oil from the Middle East and has only 60 days' supplies on hand at any time. Japan relies on the Persian Gulf for 90% of its oil.

The U.S.'s interest in keeping that oil flowing is not only strategic. The Middle East reserves are controlled by seven companies, known to oilmen as "the Seven Sisters." Five of them are American-owned: Jersey Standard, Mobil, Texaco, Gulf and Standard of California. (The other two are British Petroleum and Shell.) U.S. companies produce 100% of Saudi Arabia's oil, 75% of Libya's, 50% of Kuwait's, 40% of Iran's and 25% of Iraq's. The companies' investments are calculated to be $2.2 billion in book value alone. A more realistic assessment of their potential worth over the next ten years amounts to $20 billion.

This stake is important to the U.S. balance of payments. The companies earned about $1.3 billion in 1968, reinvested $263 million in the region and repatriated the rest. At the same time, the producing countries used their oil

196

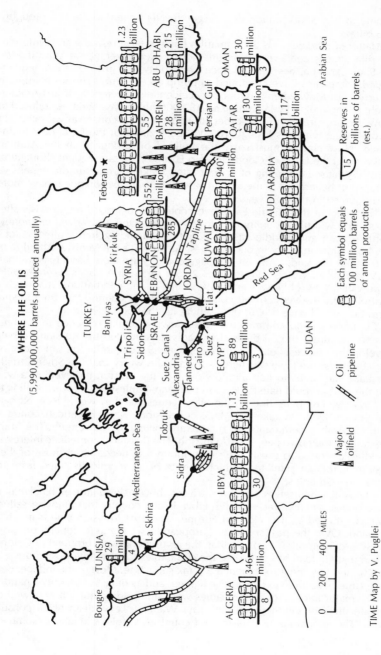

WHERE THE OIL IS
(5,990,000,000 barrels produced annually)

TURKEY

Teheran ★

Mediterranean Sea

Banlyas

Kirkuk

SYRIA

Tripoli

Sidon

LEBANON

ISRAEL

IRAQ

552 million

285

Eilat

JORDAN Tapline

Suez Canal

Alexandria

Cairo

Suez

planned

Persian Gulf

BAHREIN
28 million

4

QATAR
130 million

4

ABU DHABI
1.23 billion

215 million

OMAN
130 million

3

Arabian Sea

KUWAIT
940 million

SAUDI ARABIA
1.17 billion

Red Sea

55

EGYPT
89 million

3

SUDAN

Tobruk

Sidra

La Skhira

LIBYA
1.13 billion

30

TUNISIA
29 million

4

Bougie

ALGERIA
346 million

8

0   200   400 MILES

Each symbol equals
100 million barrels
of annual production

Major
oilfield

Oil
pipeline

15 Reserves in
billions of barrels
(est.)

TIME Map by V. Pugllei

Reprinted by permission from *Time*, The Weekly Newsmagazine, © Time, Inc., 1970.

197

income to buy $500 million in U.S. goods. Net benefit to the U.S.: roughly $1.5 billion.

Matter of markets.   U.S. companies have so far survived war, revolution, guerrilla attacks and every Arab attempt to exert leverage on Washington. The Suez Canal has been closed since the Six-Day War in 1967, but American-owned companies have continued to pump oil. The most serious disruption occurred last May, when a bulldozer accidentally severed the Trans-Arabian Pipeline (Tapline) in Syria, cutting off 480,000 bbl. a day. Syria has refused to allow repairs, presumably in order to embarrass the conservative regime in Saudi Arabia, which is losing $100,000 each day that the pipeline remains closed. Now tankers must carry the bulk of oil produced in the Arabian Gulf around the Cape of Good Hope to Europe. The consequent shortage of ships has caused a tripling of charter rates, making it much more expensive to transport heating oil to the U.S. In parts of Europe, fuel-oil prices have more than doubled in the past year.

The wells of the Middle East have continued to work through crisis after crisis — and will likely continue to do so — because the Arabs need oil money. North African and Middle Eastern countries, including Iran, collect a total of $4.8 billion annually in oil revenues. As Kuwait's Oil Minister Abdul Rahman Attiiqi has said, "Any oil stoppage could cause more harm to Arab than to American interests." Oil provides 76.5% of Saudi Arabia's revenue, 94% of Kuwait's, 79% of Libya's and 56% of Iraq's. The international markets are controlled by the Western oil companies, and any country that tried to shut them out would have a hard time selling its "hot oil" at a profit.

Communists and commerce.   The growing Soviet influence in the area has not yet upset the oil deals. The Iraqis have invited the Russians to help develop their newest field, for instance, but U.S. companies are still operating the country's older wells. There is always the worry that the Soviets might persuade the Arabs to halt the flow of oil to the West in the event of a war. But the Arabs would hate to do so in peacetime unless Russia were willing to pay massive compensation for the oil revenues that they would lose. Nor are the Soviets likely to take over U.S. concessions when American contracts with the Arab governments run out toward the end of the century. The Arabs are training their own people to do the job. The Russians' immediate interest in Middle East oil is to satisfy their own future fuel needs — and those of their Eastern European satellites — which cannot be economically filled from remote Siberian fields.

The Arabs themselves, however, are not above using a little oil blackmail to raise prices, as Libya recently did. Libya is one country that enjoys a seller's market, situated as it is close to Europe, where its low-sulfur oil is much in demand. Over the past six years, Europeans have come to depend on Libya for 30% of their oil. Playing on that, the revolutionary government of Colonel Muammar Gaddafi has pressured the companies to raise their posted price by 13.4% and pay the government a 5% tax surcharge. Most of the independent companies operating in Libya have agreed, and as of last week only a handful of the major international companies were still holding out. "It may well be a watershed for international oil," says Walter J. Levy, dean of oil consultants. "The temptation of Persian Gulf countries to follow at least to some ex-

tent the Libyan example and methods will be very strong, if not irresistible."
Estimated additional cost to Europe if the Libyan precedent spreads to all
producing countries: $1 billion a year.

Such an increase would also bring the price of Middle East oil closer to
that of oil produced in the U.S., where the domestic market is protected by import quotas. At the present rate of rise in demand, the U.S. will need to import
an estimated 50% of its oil by 1980. The only visible source for imports on
such a scale is the Middle East. By best estimates, Alaska's North Slope holds
no more than 10% as much as the reserves of the Arab countries and Iran, and

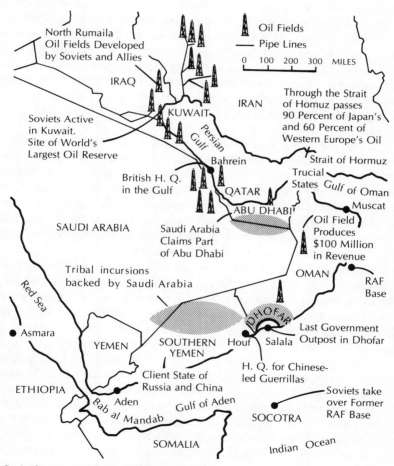

North Rumaila
Oil Fields Developed
by Soviets and Allies

🛢 Oil Fields
— Pipe Lines

0   100   200   300   MILES

IRAQ

IRAN

Through the Strait
of Homuz passes
90 Percent of Japan's
and 60 Percent of
Western Europe's Oil

Soviets Active
in Kuwait.
Site of World's
Largest Oil Reserve

KUWAIT

Persian Gulf

Bahrein

Strait of Hormuz

British H. Q.
in the Gulf

QATAR

ABU DHABI

Trucial
States Gulf of Oman

Muscat

SAUDI ARABIA

Saudi Arabia
Claims Part
of Abu Dhabi

Oil Field
Produces
$100 Million
in Revenue

Tribal incursions
backed by Saudi Arabia

OMAN

RAF
Base

Red Sea

DHOFAR

Asmara

YEMEN

SOUTHERN
YEMEN

Houf   Salala

Last Government
Outpost in Dhofar

H. Q. for Chinese-
led Guerrillas

ETHIOPIA

Client State of
Russia and China

Aden

Rab al Mandab

Gulf of Aden

SOCOTRA

Soviets take
over Former
RAF Base

SOMALIA

Indian Ocean

Reprinted courtesy of Joe Wagner; from *Newsweek*, January 18, 1971.

there is little hope that Indonesia's offshore fields will prove rich enough even to fill Japan's needs. Simply paying for large amounts of imports will precipitate a huge balance of payments drain unless American companies profit proportionately from the growing world demand for oil. For the foreseeable future, the oil-thirsty world will depend heavily on the bountiful reserves of the Middle East, for which the consuming countries will have to pay an increasingly steep price.

The Russians' "immediate interest in Middle East oil is to satisfy their own future fuel needs — and those of their Eastern European satellites — which cannot be economically filled from remote Siberian fields," according to the *Time* article. Might Russia have other kinds of interest as well? What of their construction of underground ordnance depots and a communications station on Socotra, shown on the *Newsweek* map, or the support of Yemeni guerrillas? Is the Chinese involvement in Southern Yemen (see map) a factor? Could the Russians be simultaneously trying to acquire strategic military bases vis-à-vis the United States and prestige as a "revolutionary leader" vis-à-vis China?

To the degree that economic reasons are a major motivating factor, however, are there any possible solutions that would lead to less competition and uncertainty? What if the Russian oil resources in Siberia are theoretically capable of being shipped to Japan more cheaply than Japan gets her present oil from the Mideast? Might some sort of exchange arrangement be made, by which Japan would assign to Russia the right to Japan's usual share of the Mideast production, while Japan would receive an equivalent amount of Siberian oil?

Within the variety of "alliance" or "client-state" or "benefit" relationships, it is not always the apparently dominant power that calls the tune. Would it make a difference if one or more other major powers were actively courting the lesser state, or threatening to do so? Consider again the appeal of the Corcyran ambassador to Athens. Is manipulation by the lesser state a problem in the Middle East?

Advantages and dangers of alliances. Are "alliances" likely to increase, or reduce, the dangers of war? Which would you say is *most* dangerous — an alliance, or a firm intention to defend, not formalized in an alliance? *If* one intends to come to the defense of a lesser state, is it best to clearly announce that intention in advance? Consider, in this connection, the Korean conflict, which may have had its genesis in a statement by the United States Secretary of State, Dean Acheson, that omitted South Korea from a list of countries that the United States

200

regarded itself as committed to defend. The invasion of South Korea by North Korea followed shortly after the statement. On the other hand, might a *formal* announcement, in some circumstances, be viewed as bellicose or status-threatening?

Which of *these* is most dangerous—an alliance, or a firm intention *not* to defend, come what may? Of course the latter is not *always* less dangerous. Part of the danger depends on what the other country is, whether the "defense" is against an internal insurgency that has some outside support, or a clear invasion across national boundaries; and whether, for example, the assurance is given to Thailand or to Japan, to Yugoslavia or to West Germany. If it would be intolerable to have Communist countries invade and conquer all countries beyond the United States borders, *why* would it be intolerable, and how widely should one spread the net of defensive assurances? There is great concern today about these difficult questions. While there are no easy answers, a number of factors seem to have had, at least in the past, an important bearing on American thinking: first, the United States has been especially concerned if the other country had a well-developed democratic political tradition and a modernized social and economic structure, so that its people would clearly be worse off under externally imposed Communist domination (for example, the NATO countries, Israel, and today Japan; also today, some of Latin America, particularly Venezuela and Mexico). Second, it has made a difference to the United States if the country was the source of vital economic benefits (for example, Venezuela, or Canada, or—by connection with our NATO allies or with the United States companies investing there— parts of the Mideast). Also, it mattered whether the country occupied an especially strategic position (the Caribbean, Central America). Beyond that, it was a question of whether there was a special "historic" relationship (the Philippines, Latin America) or simply whether the country was "on our side" or at least "not on their side" (these categories include just about all non-Marxist societies, and one or two of the Marxist ones).

The ideological, economic, and self-defense underpinnings of the first three categories seem unlikely to change greatly. It is the fourth and fifth categories—both South Korea and Vietnam originally fit in the latter category—that are undergoing intensive examination. Here, at least, the "insurgency" versus "invasion" question seems important to what has been called the "Nixon doctrine": that we will *not* come to the military defense of one of these countries (at least in Asia) if the government is so unpopular with its own people that it is threatened by a major insurgency. On the other hand, one may encourage reform measures that will improve the lot of the population and thereby render insurgency less likely. None of the countries in the first category has had a major insurgency threat, with the possible exception of Venezuela, where the threat ended after the government carried out a substantial land reform in 1958–64. None of the countries that have carried out a major non-Communist land reform has had a major insurgency after the reform. Consider, in relation to America's possible "defense" commitments, especially if they were to extend to insurgency situations, the "IRI" ratings on page 172.

Causation in Total War

Twice in the present century mankind has engaged in the most massive conflicts in all human history. World War I took eight and one-half million lives on the battlefield, and World War II fifteen million. In World War II, particularly, there were also massive numbers of casualties among civilian non-combatants. Using Richardson's data, over 60 percent of *all* human deaths from *all* lethal conflict during the period from 1820 to 1945 were attributable to these two wars. The entire economic and political life of the great industrial societies was mobilized for these conflicts, which some have referred to as "total war." These conflicts are close to us in time and similar to the kind of holocaust-conflict that we fear most. Therefore, by studying them more closely we might learn more about our current dangers and how to deal with them.

World War I.   Consider the following account of the precipitating events of World War I, prepared by Charles A. Taylor, a graduate student in Conflict Studies at the University of Washington.[9]

The assassination of Archduke Franz Ferdinand, heir-apparent to the Austro-Hungarian throne, by an obscure Bosnian named Galviro Princips on June 28, 1914, marked the beginning of the July Crisis, which culminated in the outbreak of the First World War in August of the same year. This is not to suggest that Europe marched to war because of Ferdinand's assassination alone; rather, this event was a spark, igniting a powder keg of international tensions that had accumulated since the 1870's. A brief discussion of this "powder keg" is necessary before examining the diplomatic maneuvers that took place during that fateful summer month, and such a discussion is facilitated by viewing the pre-war situation from the standpoints of the nations involved.

Austria-Hungary. The Dual Monarchy during the late nineteenth and early twentieth centuries is an example of power in decline trying to reassert itself. The decaying Ottoman Empire to the east and the Balkan Wars of 1912–13 had given rise to several small, independent states, none of which were adverse to further territorial aggrandizement at Austria's expense. Serbia, particularly, was a thorn in the side of the Dual Monarchy. The aged Emperor Francis Joseph was reluctant to deal firmly with the Serbs, but a new generation of Austrian leaders advocated a more vigorous policy in the Balkans.

Germany. The Austro-German alliance was the foundation of the Triple Alliance, the maintenance of which was one of the prime objectives of German diplomacy during this period. Germany could ill afford to stand idly by and watch her ally insulted or, worse yet, dismembered piecemeal by the smaller Balkan states. Germany was committed to the maintenance of Austria as a "Great Power," and was bound by both interest and treaty to support Austrian foreign policy. Additionally, Anglo-German and Russo-German military rivalry were at a peak in 1912–14 in the competitive construction of armaments and "improvement" of armies. In the background was Prussia's defeat of France and annexation of Alsace-Lorraine in the Franco-Prussian War (1870–71), which, ironically, led Bismarck and the leaders of newly united Germany to base their diplomatic policy on concern over French revenge. France, after all, had run amuck on the continent under Napoleon, and was regarded as a potentially dangerous foe. Germany's effort to isolate France diplomatically had failed when a Franco-Russian alliance was developed, adding concern over being surrounded to the German leaders' concerns over France.

France still smarted from the humiliation it had suffered at the hands of Germany during the Franco-Prussian War of 1870–71, which resulted in the loss of a valuable piece of real estate, the province of Alsace-Lorraine, to Germany. "Revanche" against Germany was always in the mind of any fashionably nationalistic French leader of this period, and the alliance with Russia was regarded as vital to both "revanche" and the balance of power in Europe, given the presence of militaristic Germany on the French border. This alliance in turn tied France to Russian ambitions in the Balkans, despite their potentially disastrous implications for European peace.

As the leading colonial power and traditional keeper of the European balance of power, *Great Britain* viewed expanding German naval and military power with apprehension. A warship-building race between the British and Germans had been going on for a decade before the war, and visions of loss of control of the seas and total German dominance on the Continent haunted British statesmen. Accordingly, the Triple Entente between Great Britain, France, and Russia came into existence in 1907. Great Britain also guaranteed the neutrality of Belgium and Holland.

Historically, *Russia's* diplomatic mission had been to obtain control of

203

the Straits (Dardanelles and Bosphorus) between the Black Sea and the Mediterranean with the intention of obtaining a warm water port, necessary for strategic reasons, and one of the requisite attributes of a truly European power. Both considerations made Russian diplomats suspicious of any other "Great Power" activity in the Balkans. Complicating this outlook was a sentiment known as "pan-Slavism," a feeling of "brotherhood among the Slavic peoples." The practical result of this feeling was that Russia encouraged, or at least did not actively discourage, Serbian incursions against Austria.

Serbia, strengthened by the results of the two Balkan Wars, caused no end of trouble for Austria and Germany. The nationalistic Serbs wished, with tacit Russian support, to liberate all Slavic peoples under Austrian suzerainty and unite them in a single national state, and organizations in Serbia and Bosnia waged a campaign of agitation (including violence) against Austria. As stated before, Austria would eventually be forced to deal with the Serbian problem, and Ferdinand's assassination provided the "new generation," who were inclined to take a hard line with Serbia, with a convenient opportunity.

The diplomatic crisis that occurred immediately after the assassination can be characterized as the "explosion of the powder keg." The Austrian government, convinced of the complicity of the Serbian government in the assassination plot, and convinced that such insults could no longer be endured, presented their case to German officials, notably the Kaiser and his Chancellor. By July 6, Austria had obtained German support of whatever measures the former might take against the Serbs. The measures consisted principally of an ultimatum issued to the Serbian government by Austria on July 23. This document was described by Sir Edward Grey (the British Foreign Secretary) as the "most formidable set of demands ever placed upon one sovereign state by another." Presumably, the Austrians reasoned, the Serbian reply to this ultimatum would be unsatisfactory, and a "local" war between Serbia and Austria would ensue, resulting in a crushing military defeat of Serbia. Austria's prestige as a "Great Power" would then be restored.

Events proceeded according to the Austrian timetable. Although the Serbian reply to the ultimatum was extremely conciliatory, it was judged to be unsatisfactory by the Austrians, and war was declared on Serbia on July 28, with the tacit approval of Germany. In the midst of the heightening international crisis (July 30), Russia began to mobilize, ostensibly in support of the Serbs, followed by German mobilization on the 31st. Incredible as it may seem, general war was at this point inevitable.

"Mobilization means war" was the slogan of the period, meaning that once the build-up for war was begun, it could not be followed by a stand-down, but only by an attack. Mobilization involved the calling up of large numbers of reserves, comprising the bulk of the armies, as well as a fundamental reorganization of the nations' economies. Stand-down, it was thought, would leave a nation vulnerable to attack. Russia, particularly, seemed caught in a dilemma: if war were imminent, it had to begin mobilization early because of the great distances that troops had to travel and the poor network of transportation. But once Russia *had* mobilized, it would be economically, politically, psychologically, and logistically impossible to stand-down — and perhaps have to *re*mobilize for a renewed threat. Once Russia began to mobilize, therefore, it seemed inevitable that it would do whatever followed "logically" from a state of full mobilization, namely, attack Germany or Austria.

The mobilization plans had been developed in great detail by the general staffs of all countries concerned, and the prevailing concern was that attack should follow mobilization as soon as possible. In the case of Germany, it was considered vital by the General Staff that an attack to the west should take place before Russian mobilization could be completed, and this is essentially what occurred, using the "Schlieffen Plan" that had been General Staff gospel for many years. The commencement of the attack on France on August 4 violated the neutrality of Belgium, thus involving Great Britain. So, by August 5, despite frantic diplomatic efforts to the contrary, the "war that nobody wanted" had begun. Virtually all parties confidently expected to have the "troops home by Christmas."

The causes of the conflict were clearly complex. Why does the above account describe the situation separately from the perspective of each nation involved? Are these perspectives consistent? That is, France is described as concerned by "militaristic Germany" on her border. Does the account of German perceptions indicate that they regarded themselves as "militaristic," in the sense of having any further designs on French territory? If not, and if the description is accurate (it would, I believe, be accepted by most contemporary historians), *why* were the perceptions inconsistent? This is an example of a situation in which "worst feasible case" analysis was operating. Of course it is much easier, 58 years after the event, to put oneself in each party's position and understand their differing perceptions of the facts. Consider, for a moment, whether Russia and the United States may have differing perceptions of current facts, for example, on the significance of a Nixon visit to China. And what of China's perceptions? Some of these differences in perception are just as dangerous now, of course, as in 1914. How might such differences be limited, or even eliminated? Is this a vitally important problem in reducing the chances for large-scale conflict among the United States, Russia, and China? What are some of the other problems?

What do the important motivations appear to have been, for the various powers concerned? What was the role of colonies? Of the "arms race"? Of fear of attack? Of perceptions of threats to the leaders' power or status? Note that Austria was *the* single power most responsible. What special factors were operating in her case? What is the possible significance of "power in decline"? Was the assassination a mere pretext, or somewhat more than that? (How might England, even today, react to the assassination of the Home Secretary in Belfast, by an Irish Republican Army extremist? How might we react to the assassination of the Vice President in Hong Kong by a Chinese Maoist?)

Note the general expectation that troops would be "home before Christmas." Again, these confident predictions of victory by each side were mutually inconsistent perceptions. What might have given them a more adequate picture of the probable consequences of their actions in July 1914? Would intelligence operations alone have been sufficient? What of the possible role of the media? Of public education?

After the end of the fighting in 1918, Germany had undergone a series of jolting experiences. The war had been lost, at great cost; the monarchy had ended, and had been replaced by the Weimar Republic, which proved weak and ineffective—even to maintain public order and enforce its own laws—through much of the post-war period. A blockade imposed by the victorious allies pending signing of the peace treaty caused great hardship. Instead of establishing an occupying force and economic aid to rebuild—as after World War II—the peace treaties cost Germany its overseas colonies, the eternally disputed province of Alsace-Lorraine, and other small bits of territory. Also, France was to occupy the rich Ruhr basin, and a heavy burden of reparations was to be paid. Later, in 1923, there was an unparalleled inflation, with the mark reaching 4.2 *trillion* to the dollar, which ruined much of the middle class. Beginning in 1929, the depression hit Germany hard. Unemployment had reached three and a quarter million by the end of 1930, and six million by January 1932. Political violence was common, and there was an increasing polarization away from the moderates, towards the Nazi and Communist extremes. Running on a platform that emphasized both a radical nationalism and extreme measures to restore employment and economic functioning, the Nazi vote skyrocketed from 2.6 percent of the total vote in May 1928 to 18.3 percent in September 1930 and 33.1 percent in November 1932.

World War II.   Now, consider Taylor's account of World War II.[10]

A motivation-oriented analysis of the origins of the Second World War is simplified by the fact that two relatively clear-cut aggressors can be identified: Germany and Japan.
Europe.   On January 28, 1933, Adolf Hitler took the oath as Chancellor of Germany. This event inaugurated the redressing of the humiliations that Germany had suffered at the hands of Great Britain, France, and the United

States at Versailles in 1918. Aggression actually began with the occupation of the Rhineland (March 1936), followed by the incorporation of Austria into the Reich (March 1938). The Munich agreement (September 1938) ceded the Sudetenland to Germany, and in March of 1938, Hitler forcibly occupied the remainder of Czechoslovakia.

War with the West came over the question of Poland, whose security was guaranteed by a mutual assistance pact with Great Britain, signed in August of 1939. Hitler (having signed a non-aggression pact with Stalin on August 23), assured of Soviet non-intervention, invaded Poland on September 1, 1939. In the face of this aggression, Britain and France declared war on Germany shortly thereafter.

Following the invasion and conquest of Poland there ensued a six-month period that is commonly termed *sitzkrieg*, or "phony war," during which the parties were officially at war, but without hostilities. In May 1940, however, the sitzkrieg was ended by the invasion and rapid conquest of France. A period of German consolidation (including the "Battle of Britain") ensued until April 1941, when Hitler again began offensives in the east. Yugoslavia and Greece were subdued in short order, and the last great offensive, the invasion of Russia, was initiated in June. The remainder of the war in Europe consisted of Allied attempts to dislodge the Germans from their vast, newly conquered empire.

Consider the following excerpts from *The Rise and Fall of the Third Reich* by William L. Shirer (pp. 418–19):

> "The aim of German policy," he [Hitler] said, "was to make secure and preserve the racial community and to enlarge it. It was therefore a question of space (Lebensraum)." The Germans, he laid it down, had "the right to a greater living space than other peoples . . . Germany's future was therefore wholly conditional upon solving the need for space."
>
> Where? Not in some far-off African or Asian colonies, but . . . "in immediate proximity to the Reich."

Do these statements answer the question of Hitler's motives? Was the attack to the west initiated merely to provide "cover" for the offensives in the east, where *Lebensraum* was abundantly available, or did Hitler really consider world conquest? The debate over this question still rages. Consider also what is regarded as Hitler's "last will and testament," in which he said, "The aim must still be to win territory in the East for the German people." (H. R. Trevor-Roper, *The Last Days of Hitler*, p. 125.)

Consider also descriptions by foreign correspondents of the public mood in Berlin immediately after the declaration of war by Britain and France from *Berlin Diary*, by William L. Shirer (p. 141): "No excitement, no hurrahs, no cheering . . . There is not even any hatred for the French and British . . ." This lack of response is in direct contrast to the enthusiasm that followed the outbreak of the First World War, and the same apathy was duplicated in other European countries.

The War in the Far East. Japanese intentions in the Far East began to emerge with the occupation of Manchuria in September 1931, an action

207

opposed by both the League of Nations and the civilians in the Japanese government with little success. Conflict began in earnest with the Japanese invasion of Northern China in July 1937. In response to this aggression, the United States insisted that Japan withdraw from China, and an embargo was placed on the sale of war materials to Japan. The militaristic faction of the Japanese government began to press for a showdown with the United States, which took the form of the surprise attack on Pearl Harbor on December 7, 1941.

Temporarily freed from the menace of United States naval power in the Pacific, Japan began its long series of Far Eastern conquests, including Malaya, the Philippines, Sarawak in December, and Singapore in mid-February, 1942. Again, the Allied actions in the Pacific consisted largely of attempts to dislodge the Japanese from their newly conquered empire.

Robert Butow provides an insight into Japanese motives in the following excerpt from *Tojo and the Coming of the War* (pages 133–34):

> Everything the United States and Great Britain did to assist China and to strengthen their own security was denounced in Japan in terms which ignored Japanese aggression in China. The powers were repeatedly accused of seeking to deny Japan her rightful place in the world. The continual irritation which this produced in Japan's relations with America and Britain after 1938 created the situation for which Hideki Tojo ultimately became responsible. If this cancer of animosity could not be healed by the medication of diplomacy, then it would have to be cut away by the surgery of war. In two short years, this thought became the underlying principle of Japan's foreign policy — the irrefutable logic of those who sought to diagnose the nation's illness so as to provide a cure. . . . She was fighting "simply for her conception of her Mission in Asia." She was fighting to prevent Asia from becoming a second Africa.

According to Butow, Japan felt that it should be the power that controlled the destiny of the Far East. If this notion remains true to any degree, it raises interesting questions about the current situation, because Japan has now achieved the position that it held before the war, namely that of "top dog" in the Far East. Will Japan be content to remain a highly industrialized, nonnuclear world power in the future? Or would she opt for a course of action that would make her the arms-producing member of an Asian coalition designed to hold mainland China in check? Some thinkers, notably Herman Kahn, see this as a possibility for Japan.

How does the concept of *Lebensraum* help explain Germany's behavior? Was it a grass-roots, popular demand for expanded territory and food production? Or was it basically Hitler's private, pseudo-Darwinian concept of "superior space for a superior race"? (To use minor statistical differences in the gene pool in various portions of Europe as a basis for describing a "race" was, of course, without biological foundation, let alone the attribution of "superiority" to that "race.") Gordon Wright, in *The Ordeal of Total War*,[11] comments that Hitler "obviously viewed the conquered east, as far as the Urals and a little beyond, as one vast living space for the Herrenvolk," and notes that Hitler spoke of a goal " 'in the long run to open up an area of settlement for some hundred million Germans in this territory.' " This process was to take several generations (the number exceeded the total population of Germany), with a goal of perhaps "ten or twenty million settlers in the first postwar decade." All of this appears most consistent with the idea of *Lebensraum* as a personal vision, rather than as an immediate material need. Certainly, Germany was one of Europe's most densely populated countries, with a substantial degree of dependence on imported foodstuffs. But Germany's pre-war dependence on agricultural imports was no greater than that of Great Britain, and not markedly different from that of Switzerland or the Low Countries. Also, there were adequate exports to counterbalance the needed imports.

Very few individual *families* of Germans, moreover, appear to have had a strong motivation to seek extensive new lands. Germany was not a nation of westward-expanding, land-seeking farmers like the United States in the latter half of the nineteenth century, but a modern industrial state whose population was steadily moving from the farm to the city. When Germany annexed western Poland in 1939, Wright notes that "[t]he Warthland, largely agrarian in character, was earmarked as the breadbasket of the expanded German Reich."[12] About a million Poles and Jews were forced out, and the remainder allowed "to remain for the time being, to provide a convenient labor force." But "[i]t was easier to expel the Jews than to find the right German colonists to replace them." Ultimately, about 200,000 "ethnic Germans" from eastern Europe were screened and settled as farmers in the annexed areas. Most Germans who moved there went as "officials or businessmen."

If *Lebensraum* were largely Hitler's personal dream, there was nonetheless a broadly felt need for the war to mobilize the German economy. Asa Briggs, writing in the *New Cambridge Modern History*, notes that Hitler's largely inherited strategy to abolish unemployment "led to substantial gains in total output and employment between 1933 and 1936. Unemployment fell to 1.6 million in 1936, approximately the pre-depression figure, and to less than 0.5 million two years later."[13] This was despite the fact that Hitler followed a largely "guns *and* butter" policy in the early stages of the war, and did not move to full wartime mobilization of the economy until 1942.

However, the Nazi ideology struck broader chords. Hitler's *Lebensraum* concept was, after all, based on the notion of the inherent "racial superiority" of the Germans. Jews and Slavic peoples were viewed as inferior "submen." This ideology probably galvanized many Germans, at least for a time, with a sense of specialness and superiority, of supreme genetic status among humans. This feeling may have helped to achieve some sense of solidarity and mobilization for a common purpose among the Germans, although the various accounts of lack of public enthusiasm at the conflict's start might suggest that the "obedience" model was more predominant than that of cooperation or ideology. (Compare also Kenneth Keniston's observation, quoted at page 106.) The jump from a smug sense of superiority at a Nazi rally to the systematic slaughter of millions of humans was a long one. Over five million Jews, and several million other civilians, mostly from the eastern countries, were murdered before the end of World War II.

It is clear that the personality of the man who led the Germans gave much of the bizarre and demonic cast to their conduct of the war. Many efforts to analyze Hitler's personality have been made, but the data is far too fragmentary for any certainty. Ironically, in view of his passion for some ideal of "Aryan purity," Hitler himself was born an Austrian citizen; his family name may have originated in Czechoslovakia, and the exact identity of his ancestors is much in doubt. His father was a minor Austrian customs official, apparently domineering and ill-tempered, who died when Hitler was thirteen. Hitler did poorly in school, quitting when he was sixteen to live at home, "indulging in dreams of becoming an architect or artist," as the historian Alan Bullock puts it, not looking for a job, and supported by his mother, who had little control over him. In 1907, at the age of eighteen, he set off for Vienna to make a career as an artist, but was not accepted for admission to the Academy. His mother was dying of cancer, but he stayed in Vienna, returning home only for the funeral. For the next five years he was buried in loneliness and obscurity, doing occasional odd jobs as an artist and living in poverty, but apparently still harboring vaguely grandiose ideas about his capacities. He served in World War I and was wounded, and it is possible that he may have suffered brain damage. Throughout his life, he neither smoked nor drank, and he may have been sexually impotent.

210

After the war, he began to pull various parts of the current intellectual life into his political viewpoint, developing the central themes of violent nationalism and "racial purity" that were to become the pillars of Nazi ideology. He burst, as we have pointed out, onto the scene of a Germany prostrate with defeat, in economic turmoil and torn by political violence. It would seem most accurate to say that Hitler offered to the German people order, full employment, and a sense of superiority, and in turn they followed him where he chose to lead.

Japan had not undergone any internal stresses nearly as severe as those that had occurred in Germany, nor were its leaders as bizarre or pathological as Hitler. Fewer than twenty percent of the war's 15,000,000 battle deaths occurred in the Pacific or China theaters, and civilian deaths there were far fewer than in Europe. Japan's final concept of the "greater Asian co-prosperity sphere" involved control, rather than displacement, of existing populations, and Japan committed no acts comparable to the Nazi slaughter of civilians. In the 1920s, Japan was a nation in the middle of the process of modernization, heavily reliant on trade and import patterns, and probably more vulnerable in certain sectors of its economy to changes in those trading patterns than was Germany. The Japanese countryside remained rather poor and unmodernized, holding half of the total population, half of whom in turn were tenant farmers. Raw silk was the second most important agricultural product, and about forty percent of all farming families were engaged in its production as a secondary pursuit. The textile industry, comprising silk and cotton products, employed about one quarter of Japan's industrial workers. In describing the crucial internal shift in power from the civilian politicians to the military, J. W. Davidson, writing in the New Cambridge Modern History, gives the following explanation:[14]

We have seen the importance of raw silk in Japan's exports, the dependence of about half the peasantry on its production and the overwhelming dominance of American demand. The American depression led immediately to a fall in raw silk prices of some 50 percent during 1930, thus striking at the Japanese economy as a whole and especially bringing poverty to the countryside. The impact of world depression was a major factor in discrediting the liberal policy and the political leaders of the 1920s and setting the stage for reaction at home and aggression abroad in the 1930s.

* * *

Japan's return to the gold standard had been closely followed by the onset of the world depression. The effect on the Japanese economy of falling prices and contracting markets was thus exacerbated by its recently increased exposure to world pressures. Nor could Japan obtain assistance from the United States or Britain, since they too were facing economic crises. The decline in incomes and employment was widely attributed to the defects of the government and its policies.

The growth of popular opposition greatly strengthened the hand of the military. The view that Japan's survival depended on the strengthening of her armed forces and the consolidation of her position in China, rather than upon her co-operation with the Western powers, now possessed mass support. High-ranking officers, both in Tokyo and in Manchuria, therefore prepared to take revolutionary action. A plot to overthrow the government in May 1931 had failed. But the seizure of Mukden on the night of 18–19 September marked the beginning of a period of military dominance in Japan.

The seizure of Mukden, in Manchuria, by Japanese troops was supposedly to protect the large Japanese investments in Manchuria, because of the internal dissension and general political weakness that had plagued China since the overthrow of the Manchu emperors in 1912 (the occasion for the Mukden incident was an alleged explosion on a key railroad line). All of Manchuria was then invaded and conquered, and the puppet state of Manchuko established.

All of the following factors would seem to have played a significant role in Japan's movement toward war:

a. The ideology and status-drive of the Japanese military leaders, who sought to extend Japan's dominance to additional Asian colonies (besides Korea, Taiwan, and Micronesia, which Japan already possessed).

b. A sense of competition with American and British power in China and the Pacific. (Was it American and British economic penetration, or political influence, that was taken as the greatest challenge?)

c. Severe economic problems that weakened the internal power of the Japanese civilian leadership vis-à-vis the military.

Does it seem likely that the Japanese people had any more grass-roots enthusiasm for their leaders' decision to make war than the German people had for Hitler's?

Germany and Japan appear to have had a number of general cultural features in common, during the 1930s, which made their populations highly responsive and nondissenting in accepting the leaders' decision. (One can, in a very rough way, compare the characteristics of "warlike" primitive societies listed on pages 160–61: certainly Germany and Japan both had highly stratified class systems, and in both, military glory and warrior virtues were highly extolled.) By contrast, the Italians were largely unwilling to follow where Mussolini wished to lead. The Italian army suffered fewer than 150,000 deaths in the war, less than five percent of the casualties suffered by their German allies; Italy promptly surrendered to the Allied invaders in 1943; and there were active anti-Fascist partisan groups among the populace who in fact killed the fleeing Mussolini (and his mistress). Fighting alongside the British and French in World War I, however, the Italians had suffered over 600,000 dead. Does this fact suggest that specific ideological justifications may be of considerable importance in determining to what extent a given population will accept and support a war? Why wasn't Hitler's ideological vision adequate to mobilize the Italians? Might there also have been significant cultural factors, apart from ideology, contributing to the differences between German and Italian responses? Consider the role of popular dissent in limiting or ending the engagement of three of the western democracies in four conflicts during this century: England in the Irish rebellion, France in Indochina and Algeria, and the United States in Vietnam. What features (within a society) appear to enhance the role of such dissent?

The Cuban missile crisis. The Cuban missile crisis of 1962 was the most serious confrontation among the great powers in the post–World War II period. Consider Taylor's account of the chief events of that crisis:[15]

The 1962 Cuban missile crisis can be considered the most serious international incident of the past decade, if not in world history. From October 16th to October 28th, the world was poised, or at least believed that it was poised, on the brink of thermonuclear war. Had a similar incident occurred in the pre-nuclear era, it would certainly have been classed as serious, but not to the extent of having as its consequence the destruction of a major portion of civilization. Accounts of the crisis should be considered more as journalism than history, since there are large gaps (notably the lack of an account of what occurred in the Kremlin during the crisis) in the information that is now available.

The actual events, if not the decision-making of the crisis, are well documented. On October 16th, President Kennedy was presented with evidence (photographs taken by a U-2 surveillance aircraft) that the Russians were well along in the process of installing medium- and intermediate-range ballistic missiles at various locations in Cuba. Kennedy immediately summoned his closest advisors, forming the "Executive Committee of the National Security Council" (Ex Comm), and charged it with the task of recommending alternative courses of action.

Ex Comm spent long hours debating various courses of action, ranging from acceptance of the Russian *fait accompli* to a full-scale invasion of Cuba. Finding acceptance unacceptable and an invasion too costly, Ex Comm finally recommended a compromise measure: a blockade of the island, coupled with a demand that the Russians remove the missiles immediately. It was essentially this course of action that Kennedy specified in his televised speech on the evening of the 22nd.

Two days later, when the first Russian ships approached the blockade and reversed course, the mounting tension was eased. Numerous exchanges between Kennedy and Khrushchev followed until the 28th, at which point Khrushchev agreed to the removal of the missiles.

During the crisis period, the United States was preparing for a full-scale invasion of Cuba by massing troops, ships, and aircraft in the vicinity of the island. Kennedy's reluctance to resort to this alternative is understandable; McNamara estimated that the invasion would require 250,000 men (including a 90,000 man landing force) and 2,000 air sorties, and that 25,000 United States casualties could be expected. The willingness of several national leaders (including the Joint Chiefs of Staff) to recommend the invasion as an immediate course of action, without trying the blockade as an alternative, is a matter of record. Their reasoning appears to have been that, *if* an invasion were going to be needed at all, it was important to launch it immediately, before the Cubans could prepare to repulse it.

Taylor seems correct in suggesting that we do not yet have a complete enough view of the facts of the crisis to provide a truly "historical" account. Based on the materials available, however, does it seem that the event was a great success for President Kennedy? Estimates are that perhaps 48 Russian intermediate-range missiles would have become operational in Cuba if the United States had not acted. Does this seem a sufficient reason over which to risk world war? Should Khrushchev have taken the risk of putting them there? Should Kennedy have reacted as he did? Might both leaders have been largely wrong in their courses of action?

In answering these broader questions, a number of more particular ones have to be answered, for which the data is presently incomplete. Consider, however, the bearing of the following lines of inquiry:

First, what was Khrushchev's motivation? Did he perceive the missiles as a way of safeguarding Cuba against a potential United States invasion, perhaps planning, later, to keep secret whether it was really Russia or Cuba that controlled the operational missiles? Did he see the Cuban missiles as a way to increase Russian prestige, measured in deliverable warheads, at a cost less than that of building additional ICBMs? Cuba was, at that time, actively supporting several guerrilla insurgencies in Latin America. Might Khrushchev have thought that it would increase Castro's status in Latin America, or strike fear into Latin leadership, if the missiles were placed in Cuba? (Much of Latin America was within range of the missiles, and it is a fact that the Organization of American States, including such independent-minded states as Mexico and Uruguay, and the leftist Goulart regime then in Brazil, unanimously supported Kennedy's position.)

Second, did the missiles significantly alter the actual balance of strategic power? It is possible that part of Khrushchev's motivation was to mount a response to the United States Polaris submarines, which represented a new, virtually invulnerable, strategic weapon, deliverable from positions off the Russian coast. Would it have been of *crucial* importance to know whether or not the Cuban missiles presented a first strike threat? ("First strike" means that they represented a capacity, alone or in combination with other weapons, to destroy enough of this country's strategic weapons in a surprise attack so that we would be unable to retaliate effectively. However, subsequent analyses make it seem highly unlikely that this was the case, even considering the vulnerability of the United States land-based missiles as though they were the *only* retaliatory force, and disregarding the separate strategic deterrent represented by Polaris and the B-52.) But was there any basis on which the number of missiles in Cuba in the future, once *some* had been permitted, might have been *limited?* Could this point, perhaps, have been negotiated, or else a limit flatly stated by the United States? The operation of deterrence is discussed in Chapter 7.

Third, what was Kennedy's motivation? Was he concerned chiefly with his personal status as a leader, badly damaged by the Bay of Pigs fiasco a year earlier, and by an unsuccessful summit meeting with Khrushchev shortly thereafter? Was he concerned or angry that the Russians had lied to him about the emplacement of the missiles? Did he believe that "weakness" on this issue might lead to Russian pressures elsewhere, perhaps in West Berlin? Did he fear the effect that the enhanced prestige or increased fear of Castro might have on some of the Latin nations? Was he concerned with his political vulnerability at home? (It was only eight years since Joseph McCarthy's attacks on alleged "pinkos" and "commies," and numerous politicians were expressing concern over the threat that these Russian missiles would represent. The crisis, moreover, arose during the month preceding an off-year national election: in two weeks, one third of the Senate and the entire House of Representatives would be up for re-election.) If Kennedy feared a domestic political shift that might threaten his domestic program, or constrain him in other areas of foreign policy, did he have no other alternative? The American public, according to the polls, strongly supported the position that Kennedy took. Might he have led successfully in another direction if he had refused to view the missiles as a threat? Or did Kennedy's own earlier characterizations of the Russians and of the danger from Cuba during 1961 and 1962 box him into the position he took (that is, threaten his domestic political position if he now changed his characterizations)? Could he have responded simply by "counter-threatening" that we would put 48 more missiles into Turkey? Or would this move have failed to meet all or most of his purposes?

In how many of the above matters is national interest, power, or prestige clearly separable from personal interest, power, or prestige of a President? Are there any means by which a clear separation of national interests and personal interests might be achieved?

Fourth, what of the legal basis for the United States action? Is it significant that the only doctrinal basis for objecting to the missiles, under international law, was in the provisions of the O.A.S. Charter concerning the efforts of foreign powers to achieve leverage over O.A.S. member states? Russia was not a party to any treaty that made its conduct improper. Cuba, while originally a member of the O.A.S., had been expelled the previous year, as part of the hemisphere measures to isolate and boycott it, and was therefore presumably no longer bound to observe the O.A.S. treaty provisions. On the other hand, the nations of the O.A.S. did unanimously support the United States' position in the crisis.

Fifth, were the consequences of the United States action fully thought through? What if the Russians could have brought in more missiles and warheads by air, instead of by ship? (This result was in fact considered by Ex Comm, but it appeared that the Russians were unable to fly non-stop at that time, requiring refueling at locations where nations friendly to the United States could refuse them the use of airport facilities. But what if this had not been the case? What should the United States have done then?) The incoming ships were, apparently, not regarded as the chief problem. The chief problem was that missiles already in Cuba might become operational. If this had happened, what alternatives might have existed? Would "surgical" air strikes have been preferable to an invasion? What if only an invasion could assure that we had dealt with *all* of the missiles? Does the mode of attack make any real difference? If we could have limited our action to "surgi-

216

cal" air strikes, would this course have been relatively risk-free? What of the Russian personnel then in Cuba? Was Russia's only option to respond in Cuba or not at all? What about Turkey, where *we* still had intermediate-range missiles? What about West Berlin?

Sixth, when the Russians suggested that we remove *our* missiles from Turkey as a quid pro quo for their removal of the missiles in Cuba, should Kennedy have accepted? (We later removed our missiles from Turkey, but not, so far as is known today, as part of any "deal" or "understanding.") Could Kennedy have accepted such a "trade" without encouraging the Russians to make a similar move whenever they wanted us to withdraw from a position already taken? Or is recip-rocal removal of the missiles in Turkey a clear and limited case of "What's sauce for the goose is sauce for the gander"? If Kennedy had accepted a formal exchange, which of his purposes, listed previously, would still have been served? Which of Khrushchev's possible pur-poses, also listed previously, would have been served, and which not?

What would you have done if you had been Kennedy? If you had been Khrushchev?

Given the present system of international relations and the war-making potential of the major powers, there is likely to be a significant risk of World War III at any time that a problem reaches the crisis stages, as it did in Cuba. Is it *then* too late, realistically, to look for broad, non-violent options? Must our concern thus be to order affairs so that a problem *never* reaches the crisis stage? If "crisis" really means "threat," a great deal turns on the perceptions held by the leaders of the major powers of what the opposite leaders' long-term goals and interests are. Are these perceptions likely to fully correspond to real-ity? How can they be made more realistic? This is not to say, how-ever, that even reality is likely to represent a situation of simon-pure amiability of aims. How can *this* aspect of reality be changed? Chapter VIII is largely concerned with these questions.

FOOTNOTES, CHAPTER 5

[1] Lewis A. Coser, "Violence and the Social Structure," *Science and Psychoanalysis,* VI (1963), pp. 30–42.

[2] Martin Oppenheimer, *The Urban Guerilla* (Chicago: Quadrangle Books, 1963), pp. 104–5.

[3] Thucydides, *The Complete Writings of Thucydides: the Peloponnesian War,* trans. Crawley (New York: Random House, 1951), p. 13.

[4] Thucydides, *The Complete Writings of Thucydides: the Peloponnesian War,* pp. 20–24.

[5] Thucydides, *The Complete Writings of Thucydides: the Peloponnesian War,* p. 24.

[6] Arnold J. Toynbee, *A Study of History,* Somervell abridgement (New York: Oxford University Press, 1946), pp. 283–85, 286.

[7]*Time,* October 19, 1970, pp. 81–82.

[8]*Newsweek,* January 18, 1971, p. 29.

[9]Charles A. Taylor, "Crisis and Conflict in the 20th Century" (University of Washington, January 1971), unpublished, pp. 11–15.

[10]Taylor, "Crisis and Conflict in the 20th Century," pp. 21–25.

[11]Gordon Wright, *The Ordeal of Total War* (New York: Harper and Row, 1968), p. 113.

[12]Wright, *The Ordeal of Total War,* p. 118.

[13]Asa Briggs, "The Shifting Balance of World Forces 1898–1945," *New Cambridge Modern History,* vol. XII (Cambridge University Press, 1968), p. 73.

[14]J. W. Davidson, *New Cambridge Modern History,* vol. XII (Cambridge University Press, 1968), pp. 361–71.

[15]Taylor, "Crisis and Conflict in the 20th Century," pp. 33–34.

6

Contemporary Conflict:

The U.S.A.

American society has enormous problems: poverty and malnutrition, ghettoes and poor housing, overpopulation and pollution. The "insolence of office" and unresponsiveness of public officials that Hamlet bemoaned four centuries ago is infinitely worse in our society of 200 million people. Vast reforms have occurred over the past forty years — social security, the progressive income tax, medical care, welfare and workman's compensation, minimum wage, the end of child labor, insurance of bank deposits, one-man one-vote, at least a formal end to segregation, effective unionization, FHA assistance for the small-home builder, reasonable prices for farmers, and widespread availability of college education — but even vaster reforms will be needed over the coming years. Problems remain that may well be called "long-time-line violence:" babies die in infancy and adults die before their time for lack of medical care, cigarette manufacturers make profits while killing tens of thousands a year, lives are shortened by air pollution, people die every day in unsafe cars, and the racial equality is far from a reality.

Radical reforms are needed. But is *violent* radicalism really aimed at *reform?* Is this "radicalism" a policy calculated to achieve these urgently important ends? Are the bombers and burners really intent on building a better society, or a better world? Or are they trapped in some personal nightmare, working out some private course of psychotherapy in ways that are fundamentally unrelated to the need for reform, and that may even push needed reforms decades into the future? In this chapter, we shall try to analyze the really violent "reformers" who have played a role in contemporary American society.

The Bombers, the SDS, and the
Student Revolutionaries

SDS.   Steven Kelman, who graduated from Harvard in June 1970, observed the transformation of Harvard's SDS (Students for a Democratic Society) whose slogan (1966) was "Build, not burn," to one whose slogan (1969) was "Build not, burn." Kelman was the founder of the Harvard YPSL (Young People's Socialist League), many of whose substantive goals are clearly within the radical tradition. But he broke sharply with SDS over the latter's increasingly disruptive tactics, and over the goal of revolution — which seemed to Kelman far more likely to alienate the mass support needed to achieve radical changes than it was likely actually to achieve change in the desired directions. In *Push Comes to Shove*,[1] Kelman paints one of the few first-hand portraits of the post-1967 variety of student extremist. The excerpts here are from his chapter, "SDS Prepares for Confrontation." Kelman begins the chapter by noting the major changes that had occurred in SDS since he was a freshman three years earlier. He speaks of activists who, by the end of the period, clearly thought in terms of a takeover of society and extermination of their enemies.

John Berlow was a Harvard sophomore, one of the students who was to be most severely punished for his part in expelling deans from University Hall in April. In December, I attended a lecture by a Progressive Labor party "trade union organizer" in Lowell Lecture Hall. After the sustained applause (but no question period) which followed his interminable remarks, I got up and slowly followed the crowd out. John Berlow was standing at one of the exits selling *Progressive Labor* magazine.
"Is this the issue which says that the Russian invasion of Czechoslovakia was caused by a tactical division between the Soviet and Czech revisionists on how best to restore capitalism?"
Berlow's square-jowled business executive face, the hair neatly combed and the skin still tanned from his most recent trip to his Florida home, became contorted as his muscles tightened his cheekbones and lips. "Kelman, you're going to die," he began, seriously. "When we take over, you're going to be killed."
"Who's going to kill me? You?"
The answer, after a pause, was a curt, cut-off syllable. "Yes." He meant it.

Another time, the following incident was related to Kelman:

"He has this friend in SDS, and you spoiled the kid's mescaline trip last night." John laughed.

"How come?"

"Shucks, he said he kept on hallucinating about how he was an executioner holding an axe over your head and killing you."

(Kelman, as a nonviolent radical in the old tradition, was vastly distasteful to the new SDS, in much the same way that the Democratic Socialists in Europe and America drew the fury of the militant Communist party of the 1930s and 1940s.)

Kelman continues by recounting the takeover of the Harvard SDS by the (Maoist) Progressive Labor Party faction. At the same time the ideology of the older non-PLP people, which came to be called the "New Left caucus" turned itself into something just as bad. Three years earlier, Kelman had argued with this group

. . . about whether it was right to allow people into the leadership of anti-Vietnam demonstrations who favored the Vietcong. Now militant support of the NLF is at the very core of SDS philosophy. Even ending the war, on any terms other than a Vietcong victory, is seen as unimportant or even pernicious.

A Vietcong victory, rather than peace negotiations, was strongly favored by SDS by late 1968; SDS refused to condemn the Russian invasion of Czechoslovakia; and by 1969 SDS had reached this position:

Resolution adopted at SDS national council meeting in April 1969 by the "right wing" of SDS, after the Maoist Progressive Labor party bolted the meeting, entitled "Fight U.S.–Soviet Collusion Against China":
The recent Soviet imperialist attacks on the Chinese border are part of the overall U.S.–Soviet plan to encircle China. They are attempting to defeat the Communist Party of China and the Chinese masses, who have fought against Soviet revisionism and counterrevolution . . .
All chapters are urged to carry on educational work and agitate around this issue. Slogans such as

> Russia, get out of China now!
> Fight US–Soviet collusion!
> US get out of Taiwan now!

should be popularized and demonstrations should be built to make visible our vigorous opposition to this new imperialist trick.
At its June 1969 convention the right wing of SDS, in expelling the Progressive Labor party from SDS, set up, *inter alia*, the following "principle" as a *condition for SDS membership*. According to their official statement, those who do not "support the Democratic Republic of [North] Vietnam, as well as the Democratic Republic of China [sic], the Peoples' Republic of Korea and Albania, and the Republic of Cuba" are *"no longer members of SDS."*

221

Kelman then points out that in the background of the development of SDS confrontation tactics in 1967–68 was the emergence at Harvard of an almost universal student opposition to the Vietnam War. No escalation of the war had occurred between spring 1967 and fall 1967, when this consensus emerged; Kelman suggests that the change in the draft regulations to end exemptions for graduate students — which would affect the college classes graduating in June 1968 and all subsequent classes — may have played a major role in turning students against the war. He adds,

But students should have realized that in many cases it was not our oft-praised idealism and sensitivity — those traits which we frequently and stupidly believe we are the first generation in world history to possess — which led us into mass action against the war. It was something close to self-interest. An enlightened self-interest, nothing to be ashamed of — but nothing to become a self-righteous self-proclaimed guardian of morality over either.

But such a self-righteousness, of the type that engulfs either the newly converted or the guilty conscienced, a new Cotton Matherhood of burning frenzy, suddenly enveloped Harvard in the months between September and November of my sophomore year. On other issues the good old Harvard "cool" remained. But to say one supported the war in Vietnam quickly became a rough equivalent of saying one supported Bull Connor's police dogs in Birmingham — and certainly much worse than saying one supported, say, Mao's invasion of India. . . .

Kelman notes that "the new SDS was born with two events that followed one right after another — the Confront the Warmakers Pentagon Mobilization in October [1968] and the sit-in against Dow Chemical Company the following week." He suggests that the SDS chose to move in this direction, rather than staying where it was and building mass student support (since its old position now reflected the strong anti-Vietnam views of the students) for three reasons: first, because many felt a psychological or social need for establishing a vanguard, minority, "rebel" status; second, a number of ex-liberals-now-turned-SDS-radicals (who joined as 1968 progressed) evinced extreme frustration and emotionalism over the Vietnam issue. Most of the *older* SDS members "conceive of their work as a very long and arduous process of changing American society as a whole, while the *new* influx became frustrated out of their minds when the war didn't end within three or four months of their politicization!"

* * *

The frustration of these students was the frustration of elitists who expected that their views would and should hold considerably more weight than those of a mere majority. Frustration with not getting results from the system is by far the most frequent reason given by kids for joining SDS. The standard line goes something like, "We wrote letters. We marched. We worked for McCarthy. But still the war went on." I have heard this argument repeated tens of times, and *never* heard anyone respond, "Yes, but did we ever convince a majority of the people that our views were right?"

Since the new influx of people came into SDS in the first place precisely because they were tired of the old route of democracy, the New Left could hardly satisfy them if it remained true to its old slogan of "Let the people decide."

Finally, the SDS leadership, mostly long-time radicals, found "the old sources of excitement were becoming routine and dull." They began tasting the forbidden fruits of Lenin, Mao, and Castro, and moving towards an ideology that combined elements of Herbert Marcuse's critique of civil liberties with Lenin's notions of imperialism. Kelman continues:

And, if for no other reason than that their followers demanded it — both the naturally attracted and the new influx — the SDS leadership built the New SDS.

But just as "not not" means "yes," so the "new new" Left means "Old Left." The term *New Left* had originally been developed in the early sixties for the student movement growing out of the ban-the-bomb and civil rights demonstrations to distinguish it from the Old Left, which was viewed as insufficiently loose and free in spirit, and above all hopelessly caught up in outmoded dogmatism and clichés. The new New Left was built out of what the leaders read from the worst of the Old Left, and it was to be as dogmatic and cliché-ridden as the Old Left ever was.

They were going to "disrupt the war machine" at the Pentagon. *The idea was to provoke a confrontation,* to radicalize people through contact with hot police flesh and cold police clubs. Everyone knew in advance that there was going to be violence, even if it wasn't directly scheduled on the program. One can hardly attempt to enter the Pentagon building in massive numbers with the purpose of stopping its operations and not expect violence. As always, of course, many soft-hearted (and perhaps overly soft-headed) kids went to the "peace march" expecting some sort of love-in.

* * *

The Dow sit-in threw me and many of my friends into a week-long state of depression. Not because a sit-in had taken place, for I think that sit-ins are a justified tactic of civil disobedience on occasion. But the goals and justification of the sit-in that one heard from New Leftists and their sympathizers under the next week of intensive political activity completed the picture of the New SDS. Added to the purposeful attempt at violent confrontation pioneered at the Pentagon march and the attack on the university as an institution pioneered by Jared Israel was now the attack on the concept of so-called bourgeois civil liberties (a term which was probably used for the first time on the

223

Harvard campus, without jesting, since the early 1930s Young Communists used it) and the contempt for the notion of majority rule.

* * *

Students tired quickly, even of frustration, and the level of resentment at Harvard on April 7, 1969, the day we returned from spring vacation and two days before the occupation of University Hall, was much lower than it was in the days before Dow. Many fewer students were drafted than had been originally predicted. The University Hall occupation may, in a sense, be viewed as an act of desperation rather than confidence.

Yet simply to view the Dow sit-in as the high point of a frustration whose fever pitch cooled afterward is a mistake. For within the New Left, Dow was a new beginning, not an end. The SDS ideological repertoire—including the specific arguments used against ROTC on campus a year later—is just a series of variations on the theme first written (or rather, rediscovered, from the ancient Stalinist text) at Dow.

And the ideological "development" which accompanied Dow was very important in another respect. SDS's growth has always been dependent on its ability to shock, its ability to become steadily more extreme. But an *ideology* can become only so extreme before it falls off the political spectrum entirely. As the ideology developed into pure slave-labor camp vintage Joe Stalin, and the literary level down to the depths of the slogans in the *Peking Review*, there was nowhere left for SDS to "develop" *ideologically*.

The only way one could become more extreme was by becoming more extreme *in practice*. And here it was a question of groping out into the darkness, of *daring* to act in ever more outrageous ways. Indeed, one of the leading SDS slogans now, taken from the *Little Red Book*, became, "Dare to struggle, dare to win." The concept of the dare is psychologically fascinating, for it expresses exactly the playing with fire, the fear and trembling, that New Leftists feel as they experiment with ever more extreme methods. And with the dare, as children practice the art, it is always that one tries it first. If he is successful, the others, losing their fears, follow along.

So, able to go no further with ideology, Harvard SDS learned from the Columbia building occupation and strike the notion of trying to shut down a whole university. Imagine, what an idea! A tingling, dazzling, almost sexually exciting idea! Take over a building and shut down the *whole* university. "Dare to struggle, dare to win." Harvard SDS prepared for confrontation as we all returned in September 1968 from summer vacation and the Democratic convention fiasco, because they had gone as far as they could go with ideology: now only action would shock. They prepared for confrontation before they had dreamed up the issues on which to stage the event. As soon as we came back, we saw sprayed with red spray paint (the spray gun is the psychedelic age's functional equivalent of the mimeograph machine for the radical) all over the walls and sidewalks of Cambridge, TWO, THREE, MANY COLUMBIAS!

And now, as I write, the latest dare that's been successfully tried is guns on campus. I was having pizza with my brother one night in May, during reading period, after everything had quieted down, and he informed me, matter-of-factly, "You know, in SDS now, all they're talking about with each other is guns." Before Cornell they would have never dared.

At Columbia in 1969, when SDS failed to shut the place down, their unsuccessful and brief sit-in featured rubber hoses, knives, and beaten-up students and professors. New Left brutality.

The dares go on. All this is becoming "accepted" on the campus. The moderates are quiet.

Kelman continues with a closer analysis of the character and background of the SDS supporters. He notes that there was a kernel of idealism in almost all the New Left members, a rejection of Babbittry and materialism, and a search for a new life. (The psychologist Kenneth Keniston has developed considerable interview material from pre-confrontation radicals on this factor, some of which is reproduced later in this chapter.) Kelman, writing from his post-confrontation perspective, asks,

Is there *something* rotten in the kernel, something that might lead one to expect that it would grow as it did?

And he replies:

The answer is yes, and to locate the rottenness we must first see that in any class society there are fundamentally two sorts of revolts against that society. The first is the revolt of those physically, socially, and economically at the lower end of the society, the revolt that demands more recognition and a better place for the lower classes. This revolt responds to the question "What's wrong with society?" with answers like "People are starving here," "Workers have no job security here," or "The rich get almost everything here." It is this revolt which has and continues (even in American so-called affluent society) to lie behind the mass movements of protest within a society, such as the civil rights or trade union movements.

The second revolt is a revolt of a section of the elite against the society. This revolt has different responses to the question "What's wrong with society?" more philosophical answers like "We have no purpose in life here," "People don't love one another here," "I am bored here," and "Everyone here is just a stupid beer-guzzling slob, who only wants me to conform to his narrow-minded standards." The elite revolt mourns the lack of culture, the overflow of cars, the ethic of keeping up with the Joneses, the intolerance against free drugs and sex, the uniformity of little boxes on the hillside, the straight clothes and short hair. And, among youth, "My parents are a drag/ have sold out/don't give a shit for me/are trying to keep me down." Or, "*I* don't want to fight in Vietnam."

Both revolts are justified, because in America both criticisms can be made. And, if successful social change is to take place, these two somewhat dis-

225

parate revolts must succeed in reaching at least some sort of working alliance. For neither Negroes and workers nor students and middle-class rebels form a majority by themselves. But the problems are so immense, for each revolt contains an element of contempt for the other.

The revolt of the lower classes is directed primarily at the upper classes, and it is clear that workers make little distinction between the upper class they are accustomed to and the upper class in its rebellious variety. They see the fancy clothes, the refusal to work hard, the domineering self-assurance, and who is to blame them for being just as turned off to the SDS commissars as they are to their bosses?

The early stages of the elite revolt are in fact directed precisely against those "toiling masses," of whom the New Leftists, trained in the SDS line, are later to sing the praises. . . .

So the rotten part of the kernel of the SDS revolt is that part of the content of the rebellion which is directed, not against society's elite so much as against *ordinary people*. The revolt can then come to seek not so much a new society free from elitism as a new elite, a rebel elite, holding sway. . . .

* * *

Who's in Harvard SDS? Followers of Freud would sketch out a psychological portrait of sublimated parental revolt and sexual frustration. (Bluntly put, the way one friend always does, "Kids in SDS are dissatisfied because they don't screw enough girls.") Followers of Kenneth Keniston, pace the Yale psychologist's sycophantic account in *The Young Radicals,* would sketch a different psychological portrait of youthful enthusiasm, revulsion against hypocrisy, sexual honesty, and loving adjustment to the parents who taught them the glorious ideals for which they are now so nobly struggling.

As more of a follower of Marx, I think it would be useful to apply a class analysis to the sole phenomenon to which SDS refuses to apply this method: themselves, of course. Family income: average for U.S., $8000 a year; average for Harvard, $17,000 a year; average for SDS, $23,000 a year. (Source: poll of family incomes taken in Soc Sci 125, an SDS-run course taken almost entirely by New Leftists.) Secondary school education: of the 150-odd Harvard students arrested after the occupation of University Hall, approximately 50 percent attended prep school, with the largest representation from the most exclusive ones like St. Paul's. Just over 40 percent of the Harvard student body as a whole comes from prep schools. (Source: my roommate Elliott Abrams, who performed a herculean labor of hate in looking up the high school backgrounds of each of the arrested. All sociologists should be grateful.)

In any fluid society social classes are constantly rising and falling. In the United States in the last thirty years the most conspicuously rising class has been intellectual-professionals. At the same time, one could hardly point to any major diminution of the wealth of the upper upper class. To answer the question, Who is in SDS? it is necessary to look at SDS members from both of these groups. For both bear marks of their respective class origins, and these influence their roles in SDS politics.

SDS at Harvard, and at most schools I think, could never have gotten started without the initial services of the hereditary radicals. (In many universities, although not Harvard, the New Left could still not keep going without this group.) They are radicals in the same way the Boston Irishman's son is a Democrat—by instinct. It should be noted that one of the most important reasons for the growth of the New Left in the sixties is the fact that the children of young adults of the thirties, a radical era, have now reached student age. The "silent generation" students of the fifties were children of young adults of the twenties, a conservative decade. Irving Howe estimates that during the thirties and forties a million Americans may have passed through membership in the Communist party. Many are still radicals, if only under the table—or, to put it more accurately, at the dinner table—today.

Around these talkative dinner tables the hereditary radical absorbed from early childhood certain notions about who the bad guys and who the good guys are. The father of Pete Orriss, co-founder of Harvard SDS in 1964, was active in the Doctors Committee to Aid the Spanish Republic in the 1930s. His younger sister, while a student in *ninth* grade, was the New York City high school coordinator for the 1966 spring antiwar Mobilization. According to Nat Stillman, an early Harvard SDS leader who joined and later left the group, well over half of the Harvard SDS executive committee in its early days was made up of people who identified with or were members of the old-line Communist party, U.S.A.

The hereditary radicals come to Harvard with their political commitments already well established. They major in social studies or government, and (today) join the New Left caucus of SDS. That by 1969 the New Left caucus as an organized group had a grand total of *twelve* members (compared to over fifty in the pro–Progressive Labor group) is a good indication that the hereditary radicals have been displaced as the dominant force within SDS. In fact this constitutes an important part of the tragedy of SDS. For they fell victims to the irrationalism and antiintellectualism which they themselves unleashed but which later got out of (their) control.

The hereditary radicals combined the confidence and optimism of members of a rising social group with the political beliefs they had inherited from their parents. Temperamentally they are on the same wavelength as the moderates. They just happen to have different political beliefs. They get good grades at Harvard and are very skilled at writing and speaking. (The atrocious leaflets produced by Harvard SDS are mostly written by PL, although the style of the hereditary radicals has begun to deteriorate under the influence of "competition" from the ranters.)

Above all, you can *talk* with the hereditary radicals. They are human beings, not mechanized robots like PL people. Mike Kazin plays pinball and has a lot of nonpolitical friends. (Of all the members of PL, the only one known to play pinball is government tutor Alan Gilbert.) He goes out with nonradical girls on occasion. He even spoke with a reporter from the *Wall Street Journal*. (For this he was denounced as a "counterrevolutionary" at an SDS purge meeting.) The politics of the hereditary radicals is horrible, but at least one feels that they have come to it through genuinely having been convinced of it.

For hereditary radicals, like hereditary Democrats and Republicans, are not in politics for extrapolitical reasons. They have strong political opinions, and they were always taught to act on the basis of their opinions. Members of a rising class, they confidently and self-assuredly believe that their views must be right. It's as easy as that—there's simply nothing "special" for them about being a radical.

Because their politics are simply goal-oriented, the hereditary radicals are also more hesitant about purgative flagellatory activities like building occupations. It is clear (as PL alleges, although with their own pinch of conspiracy theories, exaggerations, and lies) that the hereditary radicals were less anxious and more afraid to take over University Hall than was PL. Almost none of the leaders of the New Left caucus, up to and including SDS co-chairman Kazin, were arrested. The handful of Communist party members on campus were not even in the building. Mark Dyen put it bluntly to me after the strike, "One reason that PL has gained so much new support since April ninth is that they led the building take-over, and we dragged our feet." The hereditary radicals tried to conceal their fears in a hocus-pocus of SDS rhetoric about "making sure we've built a base" and "necessary revolutionary preconditions," but the real source of their hesitancy was easier to understand. Mark Dyen, Mike Kazin, and Miles Rapoport would get no feeling of personal liberation (perhaps only a sort of satisfaction at "a job well done," which finally bringing the Harvard bastion down certainly was) from taking over University Hall. But they might get jail and expulsion.

That was more than Mom and Dad had led them to bargain for and this was why they hesitated.

At the beginning the hereditary radicals were everything in Harvard SDS. When I was a freshman they still dominated the organization, and all the freshmen in SDS came from hereditary radical backgrounds. Not only did the hereditary radicals introduce the campus to New Left thought, but they were the first to venture further to taste the forbidden fruits of Lenin and Fidel, unleashing the idological one-upmanship which they were too intellectual to keep up with. They could not quite descend to the level of primitiveness required once the mentally ill began entering SDS and gathering around its fringes. "I wish I could give simple answers like PL does and say that the reason for racism in America is to give capitalists twenty-two billion dollars extra profits, or the reason for the war in Vietnam is so that corporations can move their plants to Vietnam and hire workers at a dollar a day," I overheard Mark Dyen say one day over dinner to some kid who was asking him how the New Left caucus differed from PL. (The twenty-two billion figure on racism is not just grabbed out of a hat. PL takes the difference between the average incomes of whites and blacks in America, one thousand dollars, and multiplies it by twenty-two [million] to get their "precise" figure.) "Unfortunately, these answers just aren't true." (Dyen's point was that the main difference between him and PL was the latter's "sloganistic and simple-minded intellectual analysis.")

Thus the hereditary radicals lost control of their own organization. The revolution consumed its own children. . . .

The hereditary radicals—the intellectual Left extremists at Harvard—suffered a sad fate at Harvard. For they at least were good people.

The same cannot be said for the other major social stratum which provides recruits for SDS and the backbone of the new cadres recruited into the organization between the time I arrived at Harvard and April 1969. These are WASP rebels. The sight of an aristocrat who has lost the will to live is esthetically degrading. These declining members of the American aristocracy are not at all similar to the standard aristocratic stereotypes. They are neither self-confident men at the top, uncaring of those below, nor the humane, social-service oriented democratic aristocrat.

* * *

It is in the guilty aristocrat that we see clearly politics not for politics' sake, but for self-expression, the possibility of recapturing a lost vitality that one feels too weak to create for oneself. As a freshman one of these aristocrats was beaten up at a freshman dance by some townie, in front of his date, and unable to offer the slightest resistance. In September of his freshman year he told some friends that before the year was over he would have to "fuck an Oriental girl." I hadn't seen this kid since I was a freshman until he emerged in PL during the strike.

Josephine Biddle Duke, Barnard College student, made the motivations of this group rather clear when she told a reporter for the *New York Times* that it was neither intellectual analysis nor reading Marx and Lenin that brought her to the New Left. Rather it was the feeling that one's "oppression" was being shared within the group. When workers in the early 1900s sang, "What force on earth is weaker than the feeble strength of one? But the union makes us strong!" they were expressing the reality of their situation. When heiress Josie Duke needs her SDS "comrades" to share her oppression, it is only a pitiful revelation of her own smallness.

The declining aristocrats in SDS are all, *to a man,* pro-PL. Not only is there not a single one who's been attracted by the weak reformism of the Young People's Socialist League, but there is not a single one of them in the New Left caucus, which is ideologically similar to PL but emotionally a self-confident reflection of an intellectually sophisticated upper middle class. PL's rantings are about on the intellectual level that such students, whom I always considered products of favoritism at the admissions office, can comprehend. And PL's promises of blood even before the revolution — through show trials "exposing" misleaders during the confrontation and physical attacks on New Left caucus meetings after the June 1969 SDS convention — promise a new vigor to the spineless.

During the Harvard strike, according to Dave Bruce, my roommate in my sophomore year, virtually everyone around the exclusive final clubs was wearing red armbands. . . .

* * *

These are the two social strata from which SDS recruits the bulk of its cadres and very active members. Its less active members are generally former moderates "frustrated" with democracy and similar in many ways to the hereditary radicals. They generally do little organizational work because a good many of their pent-up frustrations were dissipated through the traumatic decision to change the self-image they have of their role in society (from governor to guerrilla) and join SDS. And no categorization can give a real picture of all the individuals, with their hopes and hang-ups, who end up in SDS for their own very personal reasons.

Take the only PL member at Harvard who actually comes from a working-class background. He came to Harvard a Young Republican and originally planned to become a priest. He attempted to get elected to the YR executive committee but knew he was looked down on because of his Boston accent and loud clothes. Among the PL aristocrats, he could be revered: "Shit, man, a real worker. . . ."

* * *

American conservatism has abandoned any legitimate claim to speak for idealism. In a way it is unfortunate that there are so few idealistic conservatives around, so that left-of-center students could realize that one may respect someone's sincerity and idealism and still have very strong disagreements with his politics. On campus today, "he's sincere" and "he's idealistic" have become defenses in themselves of SDS behavior.

Students don't realize that there also exists the idealistic "revolutionary conservatism" of the youths who were the backbone of Mussolini's support before 1922 and who won the German universities for the Nazis. Like SDS, they accuse all their opponents of being people who put their self-interest above what is right. (A Nazi youth slogan was "Common good before personal advancement.") It was the Nazis who invented the phrase "the system" (*Das System*) to describe the hated Weimar democracy of compromise and soullessness. ("The system must die so that the people can live" was another Nazi slogan.)

People often forget that the Nazis were bitterly hostile to the traditional German Conservative party, which they branded as "reactionary" and "the class war party of capitalism.". . .

Today's New Leftist shares with the young Nazi the moral arrogance and contempt of "mere procedures" which block the way to getting what he knows is right. They share large parts of the critique of modern "bourgeois" society (a term both use, with contempt), especially of the negative effects of such a society: its stifling conventionality, its puritan respectability, its inability to inspire individuals to higher purposes. Their prescriptions may seem different but in practice turn out not to differ that much. Murdered Jews and kulaks were both presented as exploiters. And, as a speaker at a Berkeley teach-in argued some years ago, the Vietcong is all right because they only murder "unpopular people."

And the Nazis and the New Left pay each other the proper respects. Asked whether he didn't find it odd that he was a supporter of the John Birch Society when he entered Harvard and a member of the pro-PL caucus of SDS as a junior, Don Mahoney told a friend of mine, "I've always seen through liberalism." The SDS line was that George Wallace's supporters among blue collar workers were the easiest workers for SDS to reach since, unlike those who had voted for Humphrey, the Wallace supporters had "seen through the Democratic party and trade union misleaders."

230

Adolf Hitler said shortly after coming to power:

There is more that binds us to Bolshevism than separates us from it. There is, above all, genuine revolutionary feeling . . . I have always made allowance for this circumstance and given orders that former Communists are to be admitted to the Party at once. The petit bourgeois Social Democrat and the trade union boss will never make a Nazi, but the Communist always will. [Italics added.]

Kelman's final quotation is from the German author Fritz Stern, apropos of some of those who might be appalled by the results of their "revolution":

Moeller—and the other Germanic critics—did not want *that* Third Reich, and would not have acknowledged the reality of Hitler's Reich as the realization of their dream.

But, we must ask, could there have been any other "Third Reich"? Was there a safe stopping place in this wild leap from political reality? Can one abjure reason, glorify force, prophesy the age of the imperial dictator, can one condemn all existing institutions, without preparing the triumph of irresponsibility?

Kelman's study is the best yet available of the genesis of a confrontation-seeking SDS and of the personalities associated with it. But is it fully adequate to understand the white "revolutionary"? A number of passages, for example, deal with the extremely violent rhetoric and fantasies of some SDS members. But are rhetoric and fantasies proof of an actual capacity for *committing* violent acts, particularly acts of lethal revolutionary violence? Is it possible that, for some of those involved, the acts of lesser violence—the rhetoric, the angry outbursts, the hate-filled speeches, the provocatively arranged Pentagon march, or the sit-ins—may have diverted aggression from potentially more lethal channels? For some, this may have been true, but unfortunately what we know, or at least what we speculate on the basis of evidence on the nature of violence, indicates that many others who moved leftward with SDS have other and complex motivations that may well lead to lethal violence.

Some types of potential for violent actions, such as those stemming from childhood frustrations, or from stress or boredom, may at least theoretically be capable of catharsis or other forms of assuagement in which the impulse is satisfied by or diverted to some other less violent activity. But assuredly, there are *other* well-recognized sources for

231

violent actions that are likely to be stimulated by precisely the SDS activities that were going on at Harvard (and many other universities) in 1968. The New Left rhetoric, in particular, has moved towards the creation of an *ideology* that offers justification for lethal violence, and the creation of groups within which there is a strong sense of solidarity and *cooperation*. Some of the actions, also, could lead to forms of *imitation* in which fine distinctions disappeared and the actual activity escalated towards lethal consequences. The 1969–70 bombings of university and public buildings, for example—although the death of the Wisconsin graduate student was apparently unintended—create precedents in which extremely lethal consequences might follow with just marginally less concern over choice of targets, times, or warning techniques. Parallel possibilities of lethal consequences clearly lurk in the use of such "revolutionary" techniques as airplane hijacking and kidnapping of public officials. (Several political kidnappings in other countries, including one by the extremist QLF (Quebec Liberation Front) in Canada, have resulted in the death of the person kidnapped.)

Even in terms of "frustration" theory, if a basic part of many radicals' frustration were not so much a carry-over from childhood as a reaction to *current* problems (for example, a combination of the Vietnam war and the threat of the draft), and if the lower levels of violence do not lead to an immediate "solution" of the problem as the radical perceives it, at least those in the group who have a lower threshhold of tolerance for frustration may move toward more violent tactics in an effort to achieve their goals.

The apparent size of the movement, moreover—in terms of vocal if not active support—may cause the role of "revolutionary" to become a recognized one among the college and high-school population of the country. This phenomenon may lead to violent acts through *imitation* and also through the more formal mechanism of *obedience*. The "revolutionary" groups, in effect, become a kind of sub-society with their own internal structure, and leaders achieve sufficient legitimacy to be able to command obedience from groups of followers, even though the followers themselves feel no strong emotional or ideological involvement. If a command to do lethal violence, given by a figure perceived to have legitimate authority within that social group, follows after a gradual pattern of "escalation," moreover, Milgram's electric-shock experiments suggest a frighteningly high likelihood that the command will be obeyed.

232

In June 1969, SDS split into Progressive Labor Party and "National Office" factions after a bitter convention torn by both personal power strivings and an ideological split between "class war" and "colonial struggle" theories. At one point, the Black Panther delegate denounced the PLP faction as "racist." The Women's Liberation delegate in turn denounced the Black Panther delegate as a "male chauvinist." Through history, extremist groups have often undergone this kind of divisive internal struggle and fission. What processes may be at work behind this phenomenon?

Psychological analysis of young radicals.   Kenneth Keniston, a Yale psychologist who had done in-depth psychological investigation of an earlier generation of students in *The Uncommitted* (finished in 1964), carried out a psychological study of some of the leaders of "Vietnam Summer" from June to September of 1967, which was published as *Young Radicals* in 1968. "Vietnam Summer" was still a non-violent "radical" project. Keniston carried out his interviews with fourteen of its leaders, eleven men and three women. All of them were white, the average age was twenty-three, and all had at least begun college. Most came from upper-middle-class families. Some common features stand out in these families and in the early lives of these 1967-vintage "radical" leaders (some or many of whom, of course, may not have remained activists as more violent tactics evolved). Typically, the family had a strong mother who, where the radical-to-be was male, pushed the son to work hard in school and was frequently active in social causes. The father was an ambivalent figure, generally idealistic, but sometimes dominated by the mother and rather frequently unable to carry out his ideals in life. The families generally evinced a high degree of social concern, frequently were highly conscious of politics, and in at least three cases, conscious of older "radical" politics. Many of the families were involved in anti-McCarthy work during the 1950s witch-hunt era, and through this and other causes often earned enmity or aloofness from some of their neighbors. Values and desired behavior on the part of the children were usually promoted by reasoning rather than by physical punishment or deprivation of desired items. There was, in general, an early sense on the child's part of being "special." In adolescence, these radicals were particularly intense and particularly oriented to principle, and generally departed from what Keniston describes as the American pattern of handling the problems of adolescence through "submersion into the teen-age culture." Keniston believed that their actual engagement in "radical" political work, leading to the Vietnam Summer, involved much less a rebellion against parents or discontinuity with earlier background, than an attempt to apply principles already developed within the family. There was a mixture of motives, however, which Keniston delineates in this interview describing one young radical joining a 1967-type New Left group:[2]

Well, I was able to develop a couple of friends. . . . Secondarily, I could say it was because of the idea that, in terms of my religious training, when you are committed to something, you have to do it, even if you'd like to do something else, even if you're tired. When you're picketing, you have to keep going. That's what you believe and you have to do it. . . . And they were a really interesting group of people. They were people I could talk with. . . . One of them had a beard which made it a very interesting thing to belong to that group. And a couple of the girls had long hair and sort of looked as if they were beatniks [laughs] . . . and then, it wasn't difficult for me within a month or a month and a half to take some kind of leadership there. . . .

Since Keniston has not specifically identified the various persons he interviewed, it is impossible to tell how many of them may have been SDS members or others who went on to the more aggressive activities of 1967–1968 and subsequent years. The prior passages from Kelman's book, however, seem to suggest some parallels between the original SDS leadership and the "radicals" that Keniston describes as coming out of the old-radical tradition. The group that Kelman describes as "WASP" or "decadent aristocrats," who began moving into SDS subsequent to the summer of 1967 and formed the bulk of the Maoist-oriented PLP (Progressive Labor Party) faction, do not, however, appear to have been on the scene—at least the leadership scene—of Vietnam Summer. One may speculate on possible differences between these groups, such as discontinuity with parental values, or "rebellion." On the other hand, Kelman's account suggests that, once someone had joined, the imperatives of the organization and the jockeying for factional power determined an SDS leader's succession of moves at least as much as did his personal hostilities or degree of ideological commitment. Once someone, somewhere had done a thing—for example, seizing buildings at Columbia or carrying rifles at Cornell—a local SDS leader often felt compelled to imitate it as part of the avant-garde definition of revolutionary role. It seems that all through the late sixties the definition tended to include more and more violent tactics.

Because we cannot definitely trace Keniston's subjects into SDS or other post–1967 radical organizations, it is, of course, not possible to carry speculation as to proclivity of these subjects towards *lethal* violence any further.

Some of the psychological characteristics of more current violent radicals are described in "A Psychoanalyst Looks at Student Revolutionaries," by Herbert Hendin, which appeared in the *New York Times Magazine* in January 1971.[3] This article is based on depth interviews and psychological tests carried out at Columbia University with fifteen students believing in the need for violent revolution and actively working to radicalize others. Many of them advocated bombings and other extreme acts, although none had yet participated in them. They had, however, generally been involved in using physical intimidation, fighting with police, seizing buildings on campus, and "trashing" or destroying property. All fifteen were white, and from families that were middle-class or above. Among Hendin's findings were the following:

. . . Their actual lives were strikingly different from widespread conceptions about them, particularly the ideas that they are the products either of overpermissive families, or of healthy "superior" families with whom they are not in conflict.

* * *

These students generally had parents with little ability or desire to see their children as they are, or to confront their actual feelings. This kind of emotional abandonment is anything but "permissive."

* * *

Although most of the students interviewed did have parents with a left-wing or at least liberal background, their ideology proved to be less important than the fact that political discussions were the closest thing to personal exchanges that took place in the family — a circumstance that may have some bearing on the use of politics to express feelings that are personal. An atmosphere of polite estrangement seemed to prevail between these parents who got along well with each other on the surface but who were not deeply involved with each other.

All the students felt their parents had not been physically affectionate toward them or each other, and described their fathers as especially repressed and emotionally tight. . . .

* * *

Some of the students said they took part in their first serious radical action at college "to see how it felt." They discovered that it "felt" better than almost anything they had felt before, that the exhilaration and excitement of a

235

building-occupation or a confrontation with the police elevated them to a pitch of emotion they did not normally experience. They came to need the exhilaration of a violent political action to such an extent that far from choosing radical politics freely out of a wealth of possible choices, it became the only possible life for them.

The radical involvement, however, does more for these students than give them the thrill of becoming "action freaks." In the revolutionary culture many have found a "family" which understands their emotional needs better than their real families ever did. Since the radical movement discourages exclusive monogamous relationships, it does much to soften these students' anxiety over not being able to form deep attachments. The same young men who complain of passivity in their personal relations find that they can be forceful and aggressive in behalf of the radical cause. Many who suffer from a lack of direction find that the radical involvement brings them to life and focuses their energies. The prospect of each new violent protest provides an outlet for their anger and gives some relief to their depression.

Danger from outside—from college, police and Federal authorities—cements the closeness that comes from shared values and beliefs and tightens the bonds within the revolutionary "family."

* * *

Perhaps the greatest pressure exerted by the radical community is on students to prove their commitment to the cause through their willingness to commit violence or be arrested. . . .

* * *

Identification with the poor and the oppressed permits these radical students to react to poverty and oppression without having to face how personally impoverished, victimized and enraged they feel. Their acute sense of injustice derives from their personal, if often unrecognized, experience as victims. To insist that these students are products of overprivilege, the spoiled sons and daughters of the affluent, is to insist that the only hunger is for food and the only deprivation is material and economic.

* * *

Student revolutionaries are accused of not providing any alternative plan for a future society. But these students are hardly interested in their own future, let alone in the future of the rest of us. The future will "take care of itself" or "the future as an idea is vastly overrated" are typical of their comments. They predict they will die young either in the revolution or in some nuclear or ecological disaster that will end the world. The prediction of cataclysm for the world must be seen partly as a projection of their inner world. . . .

The emotional "abandonment" of which Hendin speaks was illustrated by accounts of parents who refused to express an opinion on important decisions or actions in their children's lives, or who avoided direct conflict by failing to recognize their son's or daughter's own special feelings and characteristics, saying their child was not really "himself" when he acted differently than their own tastes or opinions would suggest, rather than either accepting his action or expressing honest and concerned disagreement. Other such parents expected their children to keep their feelings to themselves and stay out of sight; and one particular set of parents cared so little that they left a little girl alone in the house for hours just after a tonsillectomy, where she became panic-stricken when she began to hemorrhage.

The semi-documentary-style film *Ice* was made at the beginning of 1969, by a director who considered himself a revolutionary, and deals with revolutionary activity — including kidnapping, assassination, and guerrilla forays — by a group of young men and women in an America of the near future. It focuses at length on the lifestyles and personalities of the revolutionaries. Nearly all are white; most appear to be in their twenties. Their activity as portrayed is strikingly without joy, zest, or spontaneity, and most of them seem emotionally "flat" people, who have great difficulty in relating to other human beings, and who find in the revolutionary group a kind of desperate belonging that ends or minimizes their isolation. "All Power to the People" is translated for them into almost literally sexual terms; failure is seen as resulting in castration or sexual abuse by the authorities. Their discussions are largely of revolutionary tactics; their ideology consists only of catch-phrases with no concrete platform of reform.

Discussing the preceding material, viewing *Ice*, and considering other materials bearing on the contemporary violent white radical, Irving Berlin, head of the Division of Child Psychiatry at the University of Washington, suggested to me the following tentative picture of the violent radical's behavior: typically, he comes from a home in which, regardless of general "political activism" or "social consciousness," there is little emotional contact with the child as a human being. Often this situation may be associated with what has been termed the "maternal depression" syndrome, in which the mother is emotionally incapable of establishing real human contact with her children, and which appears upon examination of preliminary data to be found as frequently in the middle-class suburbs as in the ghetto. The parents' withdrawal creates frustration and rage in the child, but the family is typically one in which violent behavior is not accepted, and there is no "acting out" or direct expression of violent impulses. The child approaches maturity with a desperate need for human contact and full of pent-up rage. A radical group may offer him both an intense sense of belonging and an opportunity, with others' support and a generalized ideological justification, to express his rage in action.

In terms of our psychological models, this personality sketch would suggest that the mechanisms motivating the 1970-vintage white radical toward violence are a mix of intense frustration with cooperation and ideology (see Chapter 3). As in the infantile-dependency model, however, the frustration is a basic one from early years, and gives rise to a rage, or to an ability readily to become filled with rage, that carries forward into later life. Is the brief interview quoted by Keniston on p. 234 inconsistent with such personality characteristics?

In offering "explanations" of behavior, we should not lose sight of the fact that there are many genuine grievances in this society, and that major reforms are needed in environmental quality, housing, and taxation, and in basic features of human communication, institutional operation, and participation in decision making. But what concerns us here is those who accept and urge *lethal* violence as a solution, and who do so, moreover—to the extent that they put their purpose in any communicable form—with the justification of a generalized ideology that does not even offer a specific program to cure the ills. In this connection, do you find it significant that the black radicals have consistently held themselves apart from the successive "Vietnam Summer" and "SDS" and *"Ice"* versions of white radicalism?

Followers of young radicals.   All of the previous materials have dealt primarily with a "core" or "cadre" or "leadership" group in white radicalism. If their efforts are ever to gain momentum, however, they must be able to count on at least a somewhat broader group of followers who will be motivated to join the revolutionary groups, who will accept the leaders' legitimacy, and who will obey orders. Concerning some characteristics of a contemporary radical follower, specifically in the most extremist white revolutionary groups, the following article appeared in *Newsweek* on October 12, 1970:[4]

"WE'LL BLOW UP THE WORLD" A 19-YEAR-OLD U.S. TERRORIST TELLS HIS STORY

Seeking entree to the clandestine world of the radical terrorist groups stirring such concern today, *Newsweek's* Los Angeles bureau chief, Karl Fleming, placed a classified ad . . . in a local underground newspaper. The ad drew a phone call from a youth who finally agreed to a rendezvous with Fleming on a stretch of beach near Venice, Calif.—which led to some remarkable conversations. The conditions of the encounter precluded any direct checking of the young revolutionary's statements (though a number of the details that went into his story did turn out to be independently verifiable). In all, he convinced a seasoned, normally skeptical correspondent that he was a chillingly authentic specimen of what he purported to be.

"We'll blow up the whole f—— world if it comes down to it. And if our people start getting hassled and busted, we'll shoot police cruisers full of holes and kill every pig on the street."

The hard words sounded incongruous coming from the diminutive, red-haired kid in blue jeans and mustard-colored windbreaker who had approached me across the sunny Venice beach, glancing furtively over his shoulder to make sure that "the pig" wasn't lurking nearby.

He said his name was Larry. Period. He had lustrous brown eyes and softly freckled cheeks, and he wore his hair short. The haircut, he says, is camouflage. He belongs to a 50-member, all-white, all-male revolutionary terrorist gang, he says, and the short hair keeps him and other members of his group from attracting the attention of "the pig."

Over the course of the next week, in a series of interviews that totaled perhaps 24 hours, "Larry" revealed himself to be politically naive and a mere foot soldier in his bitter, rebellious band—a spear carrier not privy to political strategy and top-priority secrets. Nevertheless, the information he had absorbed provided a rare glimpse of the operations and violent schemes of what appears to be a widespread if haphazardly organized network of underground guerrilla bands.

Larry's own group has no name—for security reasons. Its members range in age from 18 to 23 and one-third of them—like Larry himself—are Vietnam veterans. Using his Army training as a demolitions expert, Larry has, he says, taught other revolutionaries how to use explosives, has gone on weekend shooting maneuvers with his group and has helped pinpoint potential targets such as power plants and armaments factories. He won't talk about whether he has personally blown anything up. "You don't want to hear about that," he says.

But he does offer a rationale of sorts for his group's activities. "The main reason for blowing up what we have so far," he says, "is just to let the people know we are here." Similarly, he wanted to tell his story to me, he says, so that "the people" can be won over to the coming revolution. "The people have to be told that we're not really a bunch of Communist murderers in disguise," says Larry. "We want change now. And nothing is at our disposal but violence. We can't even demonstrate without getting clubbed and tear-gassed. Well, if we can't live in peace, then the rich can't live in peace. There will be all-out war within a year. And when the pig picks up arms this time, he won't get rocks and bottles back—he'll get rifle rounds."

Larry's concept of the brave new world that would follow the revolution amounts to little more than rudimentary anarchism. "Our idea is that a person ought to be able to do anything he wants to do—smoke dope or make love on the beach—as long as he doesn't hurt anybody else," he says. "There is a lot of talk going on among all the groups about what kind of government we would have. It wouldn't be one man. Maybe a group of 100. It would be something like a democracy, but more free than one. Private-enterprise capitalism would be out. People wouldn't have to 'rip off' [steal] anymore. They would have what they need."

"Nam."   Larry is 19 and a high-school dropout, the son of a Midwest steelworker. During his year in Vietnam he mastered lessons that would be valuable when he turned revolutionary. In "Nam," Larry learned, for example, how to extract a pound of C4 plastic explosive from a Claymore mine and ship it back to the U.S., and how to construct a bomb and place it against a building so that the charge will do the most damage. And his opportunity to rebel came soon enough. Always a malcontent, Larry finally refused to fight any more after he had killed three Viet Cong. He recalled his feelings during our conversations: "Man, they've got VC who'll stand in a field and shoot at jets with rifles. They must believe strong in something. I can't kill people like that. I had just as soon kill Americans."

He talked that way in Vietnam, too — and attracted the attention of a member of the White Panthers, a Stateside revolutionary group. The White Panther, Larry says, "asked me if I wanted to join a group when I got home and fight against the U.S. I said sure, I could dig it." The recruiter gave Larry some phone numbers in Arizona, California, Montana, Ohio, Kentucky and Tennessee. After getting his undesirable discharge, Larry says, he used the numbers to make contact with his Los Angeles group.

He was duly examined and accepted, though few applicants are. Blacks aren't: "Accepting discipline from a group like ours hurts their status with their own people, so it makes bad vibrations and causes hassles." Women aren't accepted either. "Chicks can't be depended on," Larry says. Even so, he says, women are now being trained in secret guerrilla camps in the California, Colorado and Montana mountains to shoot, to carry ammunition cross-country, to administer first aid, even to plant bombs.

Larry's organization meets weekly, each time in a different place. The meetings last two to three hours. Attendance three times a month is mandatory. Members split up into five-man squads and train in demolition, street fighting, booby trapping, bomb setting, sniping, night marching and foraging. If there is a particularly dangerous mission to do, the members cut cards or draw straws. No more than ten people go on a job, so as not to jeoparidze the whole organization.

Che.   More than half of the members are college-trained, he says. Many are politically sophisticated and conversant with revolutionary theory and history. But when Che Guevara, the Viet Cong or other revolutionaries are discussed at the meetings, the talk is of military tactics, not ideology. Larry believes that theoretical revolutionary discussion is confined to the higher leadership councils, and he is not admitted to them.

Indeed, as a low man on the revolutionaries' totem pole, Larry has been given only the scantiest information about his comrades in the band. He does not know the last names of any of them and he has been given the telephone numbers of only four. All the members do meet together, but only first names are used. "We don't have any established patterns," Larry says. "I don't know anybody important. If one man knew too much and got busted, he could finger every dude in the organization."

"Main Man." The members work at "straight" jobs, some as electricians, telephone repairmen, truck drivers and laborers. The "main man" is a waiter, Larry believes. But, typically, he isn't sure.

There is obviously a lot Larry doesn't know, including precisely how much communication and joint planning there is among the various underground groups. He knows that his group shared a 20-pound shipment of C4 explosive (from Vietnam) with a Washington state group, and that the Washington group shared ammunition it "ripped off" from an Army depot. But he doubts that there is any tightly knit conspiracy among the various revolutionary groups. Right now, he reports, there is some talk of a revolutionary "D Day" of sorts — a one-day campaign in which all the groups would join in a series of surprise attacks around the country on utilities, truck lines, war plants and police stations.

Larry says he has personally visited five revolutionary bomber groups. From conversations, he deduces the total number of such organizations in the U.S. to be as high as twenty. "Some of them are crazy and blow stuff up just to hear the noise," he says. "But some of them are really mellow, like the dudes who got the Shaker Heights [Ohio] police station. Man, that was a good demolition job."

It is a shared hatred of the police and the courts — as agents of established authority — that brought his organization's first members together. "Most of them have been f—— over by the pig and the courts," says Larry. "We've got people who are willing to walk into police stations with a satchel of explosives and detonate them just like that. Man, you could get all the members you wanted just by standing outside courtrooms and saying 'Sign up here for the revolution.'"

Dynamite. His organization, he says, has 30 weapons, including an M-1 rifle, a shotgun, a .357 Magnum, a .30–06 rifle and a Browning automatic. On weekends, the members take their weapons and travel in several vehicles to camps where they train within a five-hour drive of Los Angeles. On three weekend trips, Larry says he tutored other members in demolition and had target practice with the M-1. He says they have 100 cases — 2,500 sticks — of dynamite hidden away, but not at the camps. To get dynamite, he says, you have to steal it, or "dress up like a super-farmer and go into some little country town and buy it for blowing up stumps."

Before joining the California group several months ago, Larry says he visited a secret guerrilla camp so high in the Colorado mountains that it is obscured most of the year by clouds. His tale of the camp plays like a vignette from one of Jean Luc Godard's more imaginative revolutionary fantasies — but Larry insists it is all true.

He got in touch with the mountain guerrillas, he says, by using another telephone number given him in Vietnam. After reaching a contact in Flagstaff, Ariz., he says, he was told to travel to a certain intersection, where he was met by a guide who emerged from a clump of trees. They hiked six hours before reaching the camp, a strung-out array of sleeping bags and tents

241

pitched beneath pine trees. Larry estimates that there were fully 1,000 people in the camp—most of them, he says he was told, were college students there for summer training. The guerrillas, he says, practiced firing and demolition and even staged mock battles. Their rations included rabbit and venison cooked on skewers over open fires, fish and a few staples. Provisions were bought in several different towns, Larry says, to avoid arousing suspicion.

Camp. About 100 guerrillas stay all year, he reports, burying their firewood in snow banks, cooking surreptitiously—living sparely so as to escape detection. Whatever money they needed was brought in by student sympathizers. Most of the members of the permanent guerrilla group, Larry gathered, were wanted by the police.

He stayed, he says, only a day, although he was asked by the leader, "a Castro-looking dude smoking a cigar," to remain as a demolition teacher. But he couldn't stand the cold, and for that reason also passed up a similar camp in Montana and chose California instead. From talking to the mountain rebels, Larry says he concluded that there are as many as ten such camps at various spots around the country.

Tape. I told Larry that some people simply wouldn't believe him, so he grudgingly agreed to submit to a lie detector test if I wanted it. To try to corroborate and flesh out the story, I asked him to arrange for me to meet other members of his group. But fearing identification, they refused. However, I did get Larry to carry a tape recorder to last week's meeting, and to invite the unidentified leader to say anything he wished. Larry returned with this terse, harsh-voiced message on the tape:

"What we're doing, we're making things so f—— uncomfortable people can't brush us off like fleas. We want freedom and peace, not half-truths and bull——. Small group? Man, others are everywhere. Watch out, maybe your best friend is out to overthrow a government. Naw, man, we're not f—— followers of some Communist organization. Man, you want a message for the people: do what you believe in, but don't believe in something you're going to hate. Freedom and peace shall follow."

Next day, Larry telephoned to say the organization was now fearful that he had become a security risk and had ordered him into temporary exile. He said he was splitting—he didn't say to where.

Here, indeed, is a different kind of person from those portrayed by Keniston, and apparently different also from any of Kelman's SDS types. "Larry" is a high-school dropout, son of a blue-collar worker, without ideology, and willing to leave "politics" to his leaders. In his group, a third, he claims, are Vietnam veterans. He brings a special skill—demolition—for which he is given approval and recognition, and like any man with a "job" in a structured organization, he takes his orders.

A nineteen-year-old with an undesirable discharge has virtually no chance of finding any sort of satisfying work in our society, and he is

242

not eligible for any veterans' benefits that would aid him in furthering his education. It would appear that Larry was driven into the arms of a group that encouraged and respected him for his talents. In consenting to the interview, Larry may well have been demonstrating a need for further recognition.

Whether his activities may also reflect deeper mental illness, triggered possibly by combat experience in Vietnam, or whether he simply sought belonging, excitement, stimulation, or recognition, and was willing to take orders in return for getting it, one cannot speculate on the evidence available. What one can speculate, and it is a frightening speculation, is that if "Larry's" account of his activities is true, there could be hundreds more nineteen-year-old, dropout, veteran "Larry's" moving into the same kind of activity, ready to take orders from the would-be radical leaders who have split off in every direction from the fragmented SDS.

One grave difficulty in attempting to limit or prevent violence by people like "Larry" is that it is extremely difficult to understand what they want. It seems unlikely that any single program, like land reform for the peasants of Vietnam, will suffice to prevent the potential "followers" from following. The causes of rebellion here appear quite complex, often quite personal, and quite vague by comparison with those in societies like Russia, China, Mexico, or Vietnam. (The problems underlying black rebellion, which we shall examine in the next section, appear by contrast to be more tangible and concrete—and hence much easier to deal with, at least in the sense that one can articulate a program responsive to the problem.) Unfortunately, there does not have to be a widespread source of discontent, or many "Larry's," in order for the resulting disruption to be quite considerable for a complex, interdependent society such as ours. Possibly some changes, such as sensitivity training for police, improvements in the judicial system, or legalization of "pot," would be effective to dissuade some of the potential followers, since these issues may be important foci of their friction with society. But are these adjustments likely to be made in response to the kinds of pressures the violent white radicals have attempted to develop?

Long-term goals of young radicals. One striking thing about the white radical groups, related to the problem of finding out what even the leaders want, is the lack of clear articulation of any specific, reformist program; the society, we are told, is "imperialist" and "racist," and the entire structure must go. The following imaginary *Playboy* interview (early 1970) between a renowned author and a leader of the "Weatherpeople" SDS faction illustrates these attitudes.

Q. OK, assume I'm the President and the Congress and the state legislatures. And I say, you've got it. It's all yours. Do whatever you want.

A. The pigs go.

Q. You're going to fire all the police?

A. Yes.

Q. *All* the police, every last one?

A. Yes.

Q. Will you replace them with anybody else?

A. A pig is a pig. Our society doesn't need policemen.

Q. What about petty crime, and robbery, and burglary, and so on, will those stop like turning off a faucet?

A. They'll stop. This will be a people's society. No one will want for anything.

Q. What if some people are antisocial? What if some people are used to being petty criminals, and consider it their life style? And what if some people don't want to work at all?

A. One question at a time. Crime is a creation of capitalism, because people who are in need steal.

Q. Don't people steal in China, and Russia, and Cuba? And don't they have police there?

A. None of those is a perfect socialist society. They have eradicated most capitalism, but not all.

Q. Well, for one thing, I'm not sure what you'll do more or different than they have. But let that go for a moment. What if someone is in need of heroin, and steals to buy it—to "feed his habit"? Will you stop him, or will you give him heroin?

A. No one will need heroin in our society. Non-addictive substances, however, particularly pot, will be made legal.

Q. Well, OK. But on heroin, what do you do with the guy who already has the habit?

A. We treat him, help him get rid of it.

Q. What if he doesn't want to get rid of it? All experience so far with treatment programs shows it's very hard to get someone off if he doesn't really want to be off.

A. We'll treat him anyhow. We'll keep him off. And when he sees the kind of society we're building, he'll want to stay off.

Q. I suppose that has to do, in part, with the idea of making things better for the underdog, especially the black man, who today sometimes turns to heroin out of despair?

A. Right on. After we get rid of the pigs, we'll get rid of racism. In fact, getting rid of the pigs will be a big step towards ending racism.

Q. Now, I think it's a very good idea to get rid of all racism. But I wonder what you plan to do. There are quite a few blacks who are pretty screwed up from the pressures and so on, and the broken or violent homes. Most black crime has a black victim. Do you think that will stop overnight if you get rid of all law enforcement?

A. Pretty much. They'll know we're on their side.

Q. Now, what will you do for blacks. Will every black get a job?

A. If he wants one.

Q. And if he doesn't, if he's been on welfare for three generations?

A. We'll train him. He'll want a job in this society.

Q. What about black separatists, will they get a separate society?

A. I don't think they'll want one with what we're going to do. But if they still do, we'll give them some territory. For anybody who wants to go there.

Q. It'll be a separate nation?

A. Yes.

Q. With its own foreign policy, and army, and so on?

A. Foreign policy won't be a hassle anymore. The army goes, with the pigs.

Q. What if the black society wants a police force and army?

A. They won't. Anyhow, as I say, I doubt that anybody will even want a separate black society.

Q. Now you say the army will go too. Will you destroy all the weapons, A-bombs, and tanks, and so on, and muster everyone out?

A. Yes. If you don't want to make war, if you're not expansionist and involved all over the globe, you don't need an army.

Q. You trust the Russians and the Chinese not to take any advantage of our complete disarmament? What about Western Europe, what if the Russians decide to take over?

A. Fine. They're all imperialist societies. They taught us how to be imperialist.

Q. Do you think the Russians would do a good job of running them?

A. Better than they're doing now for themselves.

Q. Do you think the Russians did a good job in Czechoslovakia?

A. That was a counter-revolutionary clique. The Western press distorted it completely. The Russians were right. They were supporting the genuine socialist elements in the country.

Q. Did the French and Italian and Romanian communist parties also distort it? They were all opposed.

A. They were misled. The distortions were very clever.

Q. I want to return to this question of an army. What will you do if Mexico looks around and sees that we have no army, and after a while starts thinking, "Well, they took Texas and the Southwest away from us, let's get it back."

A. They're right. We did take it away. We should give it back.

Q. *All* of it?

A. Most of it. We'd negotiate.

Q. And if they insisted on all, seeing as how we had no army, and that you agreed with the principle?

A. If they wanted it that badly, they could have it all.

Q. What about the people who live there?
A. I suppose they could move back, or stay and be Mexican citizens, which-ever they wanted.
Q. What if the Mexicans wanted their skills, and insisted the border be closed and they all remain?
A. That's unrealistic. The Mexicans wouldn't want such a large group to stay against its will.
Q. Well, say just doctors and engineers, then?
A. We took the land, not those people. They should be able to come back.
Q. But if the Mexicans insisted?
A. Well, we'll do anything that's right, but I'm not saying we'd be complete pacifists. If somebody tried to screw us, we'd raise a people's army and fight back.
Q. So under some conditions, there might be an army?
A. Yes, although I think the conditions you've imagined are remote.
Q. And you think that it's remote the Russians would take advantage of us in any way, when our first disarmament occurred?
A. Yes.
Q. But, just assuming they did, could you get ready in time to respond? If, for example, they threatened us with their nuclear arsenal, wouldn't it take too long to build atomic weapons of our own after they were all destroyed?
A. Your question reflects a completely establishment mentality. I refuse to admit the possibility.
Q. They wouldn't take advantage?
A. No.
Q. Even though, you've already said, they're not a completely socialist state, and they need a police force and even a secret police?
A. No. They won't take advantage.
Q. What, by the way, will you do differently here? Will you take over all private property?
A. All productive property, and luxuries like jewelry or fur coats, of course. People can keep homes and things like that.
Q. Will you collectivize agriculture?
A. Yes.
Q. Even if farmers don't want it?
A. Once they understand, they'll want it.
Q. But isn't it true that the farmers in Russia and China *still* don't "under-stand," and that productivity has suffered enormously under collectivi-zation?
A. It's easier here, the farms are already big.
Q. Speaking of land, let me ask you what you plan to do with the problem of Indian lands.
A. Give them back. What was stolen should be returned.
Q. That would mean a very large part of the country, wouldn't it?
A. Quite a bit.
Q. Would that be the Indians' own private property?
A. Actually, there would be a process of negotiation. They don't need all

246

the land back. There aren't that many Indians. They could have part of it, and we would give them additional benefits in return for the other lands.

Q. Benefits such as what?

A. I don't know, the details would have to be thought through.

Q. I asked before about how your socialism would be more "perfect" than Russia's or China's. Would you have a free press?

A. Truth is truth. If they print it the way it is, that's OK.

Q. Would the papers and TV stations be privately owned, then?

A. No, the people would take them over.

Q. Who, committees locally elected or something like that?

A. Yes, probably.

Q. What if a local committee started criticising the regime over their TV station, or in the local newspaper?

A. If they were right, we'd shape up. Otherwise, they'd have to stop.

Q. What if they refused?

A. We'd make them.

Q. How? I thought you didn't have any police.

A. We would have administrative officials.

Q. What if they barred the doors, and told the officials to go to hell?

A. Then we'd raise a militia locally and storm the place.

Q. What if the local citizens agreed with their elected committee?

A. If the committee wasn't giving it to them straight, I doubt that would happen. If it did, we'd raise a force elsewhere. As I say, we're not pacifists.

Q. Incidentally, what if the Mafia continued to operate? Would you use local militias against them?

A. Yes, probably.

Q. Wouldn't they have to gather information and so on?

A. Yes.

Q. Wouldn't they just end up as police under another name?

A. No, it would be the people.

Q. *Some* people, not all?

A. Yes, but responsible to all.

Q. Anyhow, going back, there would be these limitations on freedom of the press? Could they express themselves on matters of opinion, where they differed from the government's position?

A. It all grows, man. It's all organic. "Positions" will come from the bottom up, not the top down, in our society.

Q. That sounds good, but I really wonder whether you could ever get 200 million people taking the same position on complex questions. You'd be bound to get a lot of people who wouldn't even think about it. And a lot of communities or groups would come out with varying viewpoints on, say, whether to end all police services, or disarm completely, or give Texas back to Mexico, or give up a lot of former Indian lands, or let Russia take over Western Europe. You're not going to get unanimous support on positions like those. What if you get massive dissent? In fact, do you *really* think a majority of Americans would voluntarily agree to a program such as the one you outline?

247

A. Man, you have been brain-washed. You don't understand how things will work once this rotten, shitty, imperialist-racist framework has crumbled.

Q. You don't think that the developed needs, and habits, and opinions of people, formed over their whole life span up to now, will be the chief factor? You think you can tear down institutions and change all that overnight? You think the effect of your activities won't be to make *most* people stubborn and mad, and make the chance of getting *any* reform much more difficult?

A. No. You can't reform the system. It's been tried. You have to start fresh.

Q. But weren't Social Security, and Medicare, and the progressive income tax with its larger bite of big incomes, and the extension of the Bill of Rights by the Supreme Court, and the guarantees of collective bargaining and minimum wage, and child labor laws, and insuring people's bank accounts, and the broad availability of a college education, and one-man one-vote, and the improvements in civil rights legislation (like open housing, although it still has a long way to go, and public accommodations, and voter registration, both of which have worked pretty well) — aren't those all important reforms within the system in the last forty years? Why can't there be another group just as significant in the next forty years? I think there can, and that you're just screwing up the chances of getting them by polarizing the society, and making everybody hold on to what they've got.

A. Man, I think you've stopped interviewing.

Q. Well, let me ask just two more questions. Assume what I said at the start isn't true, it isn't just handed over to you. Would you use violence to achieve your goals?

A. Yes.

Q. Would you kill people?

A. If we have to.

Q. Is it likely you would have to?

A. Yes. The pigs and racists and imperialists won't just lie down. We'll have to take it away from them.

Q. And you think most people will support you in this?

A. When they really understand the nature of the society we're fighting, yes.

Q. Well, I'm afraid *you* don't understand the process. Anyhow, thanks for the interview. It's been interesting, if rather hair-raising.

Trend away from violence. As of late 1971, only a small number of deaths appeared clearly traceable to the efforts of the white radical youth or student groups. One, the death of a graduate student in the bombing of the Army Mathematics Center at the University of Wisconsin (which also destroyed a large part of the Physics building in which the center was housed), appears to have been inadvertent. A warning was phoned to authorities, but the bomb detonated only a few minutes later, before the building could be cleared. Another death was that of a policeman shot in the holdup of a Boston bank; the alleged perpetrators were a group of white radicals, chiefly from Brandeis University. Several were ex-convicts who were studying under a special program at Brandeis. White radicals may also have been responsible for an explosion at a munitions plant in the state of Washington, which took three lives. In addition, several of the radicals have been killed by their own bomb-making materials. It appears that the three who were killed at the Greenwich Village town house in March 1970 were making "antipersonnel" bombs. (There was also at least one incident, in Seattle, where it appeared that a second bomb had been timed with the intention that it explode at an interval after the first explosion and kill police and rescue workers on the scene. Fortunately, it did not achieve its purpose.) There have also been some incidents, some involving deaths of police, where the source of the violence — white radical, black radical, or unaffiliated psychotic individual — is unknown.

Weatherpeople SDS leader Bernadine Dohrn, in a statement attributed to her at the end of 1970 (entitled "New Morning," after a recent Bob Dylan album), urged a movement away from violence, and an alternative direction in which "as revolutionaries we change and shape the cultural revolution" by organizing, calling demonstrations, and convincing people "that mass actions against the war and in support of rebellions do make a difference." She states that "people become revolutionaries in the schools, in the Army, in prisons, in communes, and on the streets," rather than "in an underground cell," and urges "the movement to go out into the air . . . sharing our numbers and wisdom together with young sisters and brothers." The *New York Times* describes the statement as "close to a recantation of the Weatherman commitment to violence as the only and vital instrument of revolutionary change."[5]

The explosion at a Greenwich Village town house in March, in which three young radicals were killed, Miss Dohrn wrote, "forever destroyed our belief that armed struggle is the only real revolutionary struggle." The town house, at 18 West 11th Street, was being used as "bomb factory," and Miss Dohrn said in the article that the three victims had been making "antipersonnel bombs."

"At the end, they believed and acted as if only those who die are proven revolutionaries," the statement bearing the name of Miss Dohrn said. "The group had spent so much time willing themselves to act that they had not dealt with the basic technological considerations of safety. This tendency to consider only bombings or picking up the gun as revolutionary, with the glorification of heavier the better, we've called the military error."

249

Bernadine Dohrn's statement used the term "Weatherpeople" rather than "Weathermen," apparently a shift brought about by charges of "male chauvinism" within that and other radical organizations. A *Christian Science Monitor* survey early in 1971 showed an even broader trend away from violence. Radicals were turning to local activities such as organizing food co-ops and other community projects or to "cultural trips" such as macrobiotic foods, yoga, or mysticism. These groups were described by one of those who was interviewed as "a merging of the hip and political communities." Those who joined a bombing group or PLP were described by friends as being on "Stalinist trips" that would reach few people. The bombing of the Wisconsin math center, which caused the death of a graduate student, was described by a former Weatherman as the work of "a nut," and was perceived as a shattering occurrence that isolated the radicals. Police and FBI reactions also created a sense of powerlessness and an atmosphere of "paranoid" distrust. Also,[6]

Part of the antibombing feeling is due to a wave of antileadership and antielitist sentiment sweeping the movement, largely due to the influence of the women's liberation movement, which is perhaps the most powerful force in many radical communities at the moment. The concept of "macho men" — i.e., men out to prove their manhood through daring exploits — is consistently attacked by the women's movement.

"Weatherman is a macho trip," says a delicate woman's movement activist in Berkeley (backed up by her boyfriend), as she swings her work-booted foot. "They're crazy. I don't feel safe anywhere; I could be bombed. It's elitist politics. They're into death — that's a real male trip."

Thus at the beginning of 1971, there appeared to be a swing back towards "Vietnam Summer" types of activity by the Weatherpeople, and towards local community work and non-violent lifestyles by many other radicals. Does the shift seem reassuringly permanent? If not, what factors might contribute to its permanency or impermanency?

Black Revolutionary Violence

Characteristics of black individual violence. In terms of arrest data, a staff report to the National Commission on the Causes and Prevention of Violence showed the following distribution and racial pattern for four major crimes:[7]

250

	HOMICIDE	ASSAULT	RAPE	ROBBERY
BLACK AGAINST BLACK	66%	66%	60%	38%
WHITE AGAINST WHITE	24%	24%	30%	13%
BLACK AGAINST WHITE	6%	8%	10%	47%
WHITE AGAINST BLACK	4%	2%	—	2%

Thus 72 percent of all homicides were committed by blacks; nine times out of ten, the victim was also black. Blacks also accounted for 74 percent of assaults, 70 percent of rapes, and 85 percent of robberies. Again the overwhelming majority of the victims — except of robbery — were also black.

Blacks, however, account for only 11 percent of the population. How do we account for the hard fact that blacks commit a greatly disproportionate number of crimes of violence, including homicides, as well as the fact that most of the victims are black? (Indeed, only one homicide in ten is interracial: black killing white *or* white killing black.) And what implications does this data have for the problems of lethal group violence within American society?

The homicide rate for black Americans considered separately is around 50 per 100,000, higher than the highest national rates shown in Chapter 1 for Colombia, Mexico, and Ethiopia. The overall homicide rate (white and non-white) is higher for large cities — the six largest cities have 10 percent of the United States population but account for 30 percent of all major violent crimes. Moreover, in about two-thirds to three-fourths of the cases in which the relationship is known, homicides and assaults occur between relatives, friends, or acquaintances, not between strangers. As the National Commission on the Causes and Prevention of Violence puts it in its final report, *To Establish Justice, To Ensure Domestic Tranquility,* issued in 1969:[8]

The ostensible motives of homicide and assault are often trivial, usually involving spontaneous altercations, family quarrels, jealous rages, and the like. The two crimes are similar; there is often no reason to believe that the person guilty of homicide sets out with any more intention to harm than the one who commits an aggravated assault.

Drinking is fairly likely to have occurred before the homicide.

The "typical" United States murderer is a young, relatively uneducated, unemployed or low-skilled black, living in a city, who quarrels after drinking with a black friend and escalates the violence to the point of killing him. At current rates, roughly one out of 800 white Americans may be expected to commit a homicide sometime in his lifetime. For blacks, the figure would be one out of fifty or sixty.

Ghetto life as contributing to violence. As the Commission carefully points out, "these difference in urban violent crime rates are not, in fact, racial; they are primarily a result of conditions of life in the ghetto slum." Referring to the previous report of the President's Commission on Crime, from which we quoted in Chapter 1, the Violence Commission continues:[9]

In its 1967 Report the Crime Commission described the linkage between violent crime and slum conditions in large cities as "one of the most fully documented facts about crime." Referring to numerous studies conducted over a period of years, the Commission found that violent crime, its offenders and its victims are found most often in urban areas characterized by:

low income
physical deterioration
dependency
racial and ethnic concentrations
broken homes
working mothers
low levels of education and vocational skills
high unemployment
high proportions of single males
overcrowding and substandard housing
low rates of home ownership or single family dwellings
mixed land use
high population density.

In one of the staff reports submitted to the Violence Commission, *Law and Order Reconsidered,* "a few of the facts of life in the ghetto" are given to suggest in even greater detail "the level of frustration that prevails there."[10]

Unemployment rates for Negroes are double those for whites. In the ghettoes in 1966 the unemployment rate was 9.3 percent overall and even higher for blacks. Moreover, in these urban poverty areas two and one-half times the number unemployed were *under*employed: part-time workers looking for full-time jobs, full-time workers earning less than $3,000 per year, or dropouts from the labor force. Among nonwhite teenagers—a group well represented both in riots and in radical black militant activities—the unemployment rate in 1967 in poverty neighborhoods was approximately 30 percent.

Blacks own and operate less than one percent of the nearly 5 million private businesses in the country—typically small, marginal retail and service firms. Twenty-odd banks out of a national total of 14,000 are black-owned; 7 automobile dealerships out of 30,000; fewer than 8,000 construction contractors out of a total of 500,000. In Washington, D.C., blacks comprise two-thirds of the population but own less than 7 percent of the business. Ninety-eight percent of all black income is spent outside the black community.

In the metropolitan northeast, Negro students start school with slightly lower scores than whites on standard achievement tests, by sixth grade they are 1.6 grades behind the white students, and by 12th grade, they are 3.3 grades behind. Many Negroes — between one-third and one-half among male students — fail to finish high school, the Negro drop-out rate being more than three times the white rate.

In 1965 a black woman was four times as likely to die in childbirth as a white woman; the black child was three times as likely to die in infancy as the white child. White people on the average lived 7 years longer than black people.

In 1966 the national illegitimacy rate among non-white women was 26 percent; in many large city ghettoes it is over 50 percent: in Harlem 80 percent of the firstborn are illegitimate. In 1966 over 50 percent of the known narcotics addicts were Negroes. Rates of juvenile delinquency, violent crime, venereal disease, and dependency on public assistance are many times higher in disadvantaged Negro areas than in other parts of large cities.

Clearly this preliminary material suggests that black Americans in urban ghettoes suffer from handicaps in almost every aspect of their lives. To visualize more concretely some aspects of living in a ghetto, consider the following *Newsweek* dispatch from the *Seattle Post-Intelligencer* (September 27, 1970).[11]

GHETTOS RISING HIGH

Eight years ago, Mayor Richard Daley beamed over a happy gathering, gestured toward the newly completed Cabrini-Green housing development on Chicago's Northwest Side and said: "Let's do more and more of these fine things for the city."

With "fine things" like Cabrini-Green, Chicago needs no disasters. For the project's 23 high-rise buildings, crammed with 15,000 human beings, represent everything that is wrong with big city public housing today.

Crime comes off the streets and into the corridors in such projects; so do all the frustrations of the black poor. In every urban area in the country, the results have been the same: instead of eradicating city slums, the high rises have created new ones — more crowded, chaotic, hopeless and furious.

The kids set the tone. The first thing a visitor to Cabrini-Green sees is a group of tough young dudes lining the walkways to one of the buildings. They are members of the Cobra Stones. Their leader, the police note, wears a white hat; their hit men wear red hats; the goon squad has brown hats. They favor sleeveless shirts and stand scowling and arrogant with their arms slightly bent so the muscles show.

Inside, the concrete stairways are littered with trash, the green walls embedded with grime. Using the elevator is an adventure. It creaks and jerks; its doors close with force enough to break a child's arm. Muggers use the steel cages as traps for their victims.

And everywhere, at all hours, there is noise: the din of screaming, laughing, crying children, the smash of broken bottles and windows, the blare of radios, the keening of police sirens, the exasperated voices of people who live too close to other people.

"It made you feel like everybody lives in one big common room," says a woman who recently managed to move to a better neighborhood. "It made you feel naked and stripped." And she adds wonderingly: "The first thing I noticed when I moved away was the quiet. When I walked down the streets, I could hear my heels click. Imagine, I could hear my heels clicking."

Youth abounds. Seventy percent of the inhabitants are under 18 and half the families are fatherless. The project is almost entirely black, and the kids are young enough to feel angry and old enough to feel hopeless. The combination is volatile: knives are commonplace; many youths pack guns.

"There's even a Browning automatic rifle somewhere in there," says Lt. Raymond Skawski of the 18th District Police Station. "We know it's there, but do you think anyone will tell us where it is?"

Skawski notes that nearly all the trouble is made in the high-rise buildings of Cabrini-Green. The earlier-built, lower buildings are reasonably law-abiding. "In the row houses, we have very little trouble," he says. "But in the high rises there's just too many kids."

There are other problems, too. A family of four must have an income of less than $6,000 to be admitted. If the income exceeds $6,900, the family must leave. Thus, the solid citizen is hustled out almost as soon as he begins to make good, and with him goes the nucleus of responsible tenant leadership.

The crowding is not merely in the apartments. Cabrini-Green is a ghetto island in a neighborhood of mixed ethnic groups, and the people feel surrounded by hostility, if not actually imprisoned.

"Everything and everybody is contained in this little area," says an inhabitant. "It's like the city says, 'you stay here and we'll bring everything in.' So you go to the grocery and wait in line, you go to the hardware store and wait in line. A young person doesn't get an idea of what it's like on the outside."

Now, of course, the unholy conglomeration of politicians, housing bureaucrats and architects who foisted multi-story dwelling places on the public is the first to admit that the original concept has been discredited, that the high rise does not alleviate but aggravates slum conditions.

In San Francisco, housing authorities assign only the eldery to high rises. Even the U.S. Department of Housing and Urban Development has gotten the message. Recently, it issued guidelines urging the construction of low-density, low-scale units.

But the harm has already been done and must be lived with, though in many cities, Boston and New York, for example, slum dwellers cling to their century-old tenements rather than risk the muggers, rapists and random violence of the projects. In St. Louis, the mammoth Pruitt-Igoe Homes are now almost deserted after a stormy decade and a half during which teen-age gangs fought one another over extortion-rights to whole floors.

It may be too late, even for the smaller children, the ones who play on the stairways because the bigger kids have marked off most of the scant playground area as their own turf. One of these smaller ones, a bright-eyed 5-year-old, caught sight of a visitor recently, took aim with his toy revolver and, gritting his teeth, pulled the trigger.

These Commission reports and the above newspaper piece suggest that a whole range of the psychological models for aggressive behavior may be applicable simultaneously and pointedly to the situation of many black Americans. There is an intense desire for status (note the clearcut role symbols used by the "Cobra Stones"); there is intense frustration, environmental stress, acquisitiveness, imitation (frequent violent acts are seen as the child grows up), and a situation facilitating identification of "us" and "them," cooperating in-group and enemy out-group. All of this is often combined with a disintegrated family structure that may not be able to transmit strong cultural sanctions against violence.

Black group violence.   To what extent are the factors that lead to violence in the form of homicides of black against black translatable into violent group behavior of blacks against whites? The National Advisory Commission on Civil Disorders (the Kerner Commission), which reported on the extensive ghetto rioting of 1967, is probably the best-known of the various Presidential commissions that have been working on the problems of violence. In all, some 200,000 people participated in violent disturbances in black communities over the years 1964–68. There were 191 dead, mostly blacks. Before turning to the Commission's report, it might give historical perspective to recall that there has been other group violence in the United States in the past. Three interracial riots in East St. Louis, Chicago, and Tulsa in 1917–21 took the lives of 108 blacks and 49 whites. The reason for these riots was chiefly white fear of increased black competition for jobs and social mobility. The New York draft riots of 1861, chiefly by Irish and other immigrant workingmen, were in opposition to Civil War conscription, and although estimates vary, some 1000 died, many of them black. At various times in the past extensive group violence has also taken place over such issues as farm foreclosures and the right of labor to strike.

255

In summary, the Commission presents the following "Profile of a Rioter":[12]

The typical rioter in the summer of 1967 was a Negro, unmarried male between the ages of 15 and 24 in many ways very different from the stereotypes. He was not a migrant. He was born in the state and was a life-long resident of the city in which the riot took place. Economically his position was about the same as his Negro neighbors who did not actively participate in the riot.

Although he had not, usually, graduated from high school, he was somewhat better educated than the average inner-city Negro, having at least attended high school for a time.

Nevertheless, he was more likely to be working in a menial or low status job as an unskilled laborer. If he was employed, he was not working full time and his employment was frequently interrupted by periods of unemployment.

He feels strongly that he deserves a better job and that he is barred from achieving it, not because of lack of training, ability, or ambition, but because of discrimination by employers.

He rejects the white bigot's stereotype of the Negro as ignorant and shiftless. He takes great pride in his race and believes that in some respects Negroes are superior to whites. He is extremely hostile to whites, but his hostility is more apt to be a product of social and economic class than of race; he is almost equally hostile toward middle-class Negroes.

He is substantially better informed about politics than Negroes who were not involved in the riots. He is more likely to be actively engaged in civil rights efforts, but is extremely distrustful of the political system and of political leaders.

This is far from answering the question at the beginning of this subsection, of course, since it is a profile of a quite large group that engaged in behavior such as looting and burning, not of the much smaller sub-group that carried violence against the police and other persons. At least two of the factors cited seem worth special comment: first, the rioter was typically not a migrant. This may suggest that the migrant is more likely than the black born in the northern ghetto to appreciate his present status and material well-being as superior to his previous position in the South. Hence, in terms of what we have referred to previously as "relative deprivation," the migrant feels less frustrated than the locally raised black by what he doesn't have. Second, and also noteworthy, is the hostility toward middle-class blacks, which has been documented by a number of observers. Rather than suggesting that there is no racial hostility in the background of the riots, this indicates that there were *two* characteristics defining the rioters' accepted group: to be black *and* to be non-middle class. Thus, race remained an essential part of the definition of the "in-group," but not of the "out-group." (With their Marxist ideological underpinnings, the insurrections in Algeria and pre-1954 Indochina also reflected something like this—the "in-group" was all non-middle-class Algerians, or Vietnamese; while well-to-do Algerians and Vietnamese were largely distrusted and lumped with the French.) In terms of our original question, is the notion of frustration being "directed towards persons in a less favorable and protected position who are unable to mobilize adequate retribution," discussed on page 77, a possible explanation for the high frequency of black violence against other blacks?

The Kerner Commission also did a comparative survey, based on some 1,200 post-riot interviews, of the importance of various categories of grievance, summarized in the table on page 258.[13]

The three highest categories of grievances, which are the three that the Commission listed as "first level of intensity," are the following:

a. Police practices (includes physical and verbal abuse, inadequate channels for complaints, discrimination in employment and promotion, general lack of respect, abuse while in custody, and failure to respond to calls).

b. Unemployment and underemployment (includes lack of full-time jobs, union discrimination, discrimination in hiring by local and state government and in placement by state employment service).

c. Inadequate housing (includes poor housing code enforcement, discrimination in sales and rentals, and overcrowding).

How should these weighted grievances affect our perceptions of the primary models for aggressive group behavior by blacks? Certainly the leading position given to "police practices" suggests that a sense of powerlessness may be of great importance—this is a reaction which may be described, in various settings, in terms of "frustration," "status," or "infantile dependency." However, the two bread-basket concerns—employment and housing—taken together outweigh concern over police practices by a substantial margin. These are areas where the effects of denial may be "acquisitiveness," "frustration," and perhaps also "stress," in the case of housing.

Interestingly, general "white attitudes" appear well down on the list, with less than one-seventh the weight given "police practices." This suggests that the immediately perceived abuse of power, including physical force and the threat of force, is felt far more intensely by the blacks than any abstract "racism" in the society, or in supposed attitudes of whites with whom they are not in close contact.

257

WEIGHTED COMPARISON OF GRIEVANCE CATEGORIES*

	1ST PLACE (4 POINTS)		2ND PLACE (3 POINTS)		3RD PLACE (2 POINTS)		4TH PLACE (1 POINT)		TOTAL	
	CITIES	POINTS	CITIES	POINTS	CITIES	POINTS	CITIES	POINTS	CITIES	POINTS
Police Practices	8	31½	4	12	0	0	2	2	14	45½
Unemployment & Under-Employment	3	11	7	21	4	7	3	3	17	42
Inadequate Housing	5	18½	2	6	5	9½	2	2	14	36
Inadequate Education	2	8	2	6	2	4	3	3	9	21
Poor Recreation Facilities	3	11	1	2½	4	7½	0	0	8	21
Political Structure and Grievance Mechanism	2	8	1	3	1	2	1	1	5	14
White Attitudes	0	0	1	3	1	1½	2	2	4	6½
Administration of Justice	0	0	0	0	2	3½	1	1	3	4½
Federal Programs	0	0	1	2½	0	0	0	0	1	2½
Municipal Services	0	0	0	0	1	2	0	0	1	2
Consumer and Credit Practices	0	0	0	0	0	0	2	2	2	2
Welfare	0	0	0	0	0	0	0	0	0	0

* The total of points for each category is the product of the number of cities times the number of points indicated at the top of each double column except where two grievances were judged equally serious. In these cases the total points for the two rankings involved were divided equally (e.g., in case two were judged equally suitable for the first priority, the total points for first and second were divided, and each received 3½ points).

Is it fair to say that, with the exception of the relatively low-weighted "white attitudes," *all* of the listed grievances are susceptible to specific and fairly readily defined solutions? What would these solutions consist of? Have some of them already been initiated, subsequent to the March 1968 Kerner Commission report? What has been accomplished in your community?

Black militant ideology. The Violence Commission staff report entitled *Law and Order Reconsidered* discusses the causes of radical black militancy. In addition to the intense material and economic frustration of ghetto life and the failure, as perceived by some blacks, of the pace of reform under the nonviolent civil rights movement, two further factors encouraging violence are suggested.[14]

The ideological cause. By the mid-1960's, then, many militant black leaders had become convinced that the aims and methods of the civil rights movement were no longer viable. The failures of the white majority to meet black expectations, the fact of the urban riots, and the increasing American involvement in Vietnam all served to catalyze a fundamental transformation in militant black perceptions of the place of the Negro in American society. This transformation resulted in what can be called an "anticolonial ideology," which is aptly expressed by a spokesman of the Black Panther Party as follows:

We start with the basic definition: that black people in America are a colonized people in every sense of the term and that white America is an organized imperialist force holding black people in colonial bondage.

Unique when expressed by Malcolm X in 1964, the anticolonial perspective now provides many militant blacks with a structured world view—and, in the case of the radicals, with a rationalization for violence. Many articulate black militant spokesmen now see the final hope of black Americans in identification with the revolutionary struggles of the Third World. Even moderate leaders focus attention on the discrepancy between the massive commitment of American resources abroad and the lack of a decisive commitment to cure the social ills stemming from racism at home. Martin Luther King wondered, for example, why "we were taking the black young men who had been crippled by our poverty and sending them 8,000 miles away to guarantee liberties in Southeast Asia which they had not found in Southwest Georgia or East Harlem."

Black militants in America have in the past looked to Africa for recognition of common origins and culture, and the influence has been reciprocal. W. E. B. DuBois, one of the founders of the NAACP in 1909–10, saw that the "problem of the color line" was international in scope, and was a guiding force behind the movement for Pan-African unity. Marcus Garvey, founder in 1914 of the Universal Negro Improvement Association, and other American and West Indian black nationalists have stimulated the development of Afri-

259

can nationalism and informed the intellectual development of some of its leaders.

Today the successful revolt against colonialism in Africa and other non-white regions has created a heightened sense of the international character of racial conflict and has provided the impetus for the growth of an anti-colonial ideology among American black militants. The revolt against colonialism has altered the structure of political power in the world, demonstrating to black militants in America that peoples supposed to be culturally and technologically "backward" can emerge victorious in struggles with ostensibly superior powers. "Two-thirds of the human population today," wrote Malcom X, "is telling the one-third minority white men, 'Get out.' And the white man is leaving." With the disintegration of white rule in Africa and the rise of autonomous black nations, political autonomy for Negroes in America — ranging from traditional democratic concepts of community control to notions of geographic separatism — has received a new impetus — and a new ideological component.

The success of the movements for political independence in the colonial countries required a recognition that the plight of the "native" was a political problem, and that political action was the most effective vehicle of major social change. Early nationalist movements in Africa, therefore, sought ideologically to turn nearly every aspect of life into a political issue. This was true, for example, of the area of culture, whose political importance lay in the fact that "natives," as people without history or culture, were also seen as people without political claims of their own, and therefore as people to be dealt with from above — benevolently or otherwise.

Political ideology also worked its transforming magic on violence. Through the same process of "politicization," instances of black resistance in history were ideologically redefined as precursors of contemporary political struggles. Native crime was redefined as "pre-revolutionary" activity. Instances of rebellion were sought in the past and their significance amplified.

This process extended to the creation of a whole new world view. History was viewed as an arena of struggle between colonial power and native population, with heavy emphasis on the intrinsically violent character of colonial domination and its supposedly irrevocable hostility to the interests of non-whites. Colonialism was seen as dependent on the routinization of violence, both physical and psychological, against the native. Consequently, revolutionary violence against the colonial regime was not only necessary, but justifiable, on both political and psychological grounds. Colonialism, wrote Franz Fanon, "is violence in its natural state, and it will only yield when confronted with greater violence." Further, he said, "at the level of individuals, violence is a cleansing force. It frees the native from his inferiority complex, and from his despair and inaction; it makes him fearless and restores self-respect."

Under the influence of radical militant propagandists such as Stokely Carmichael, similar ideological developments have taken place among some blacks in America. The anti-colonial ideology has enabled black radicals to see urban riots as the harbingers of revolution and to see in urban violence the means of destroying white domination and achieving black dignity. If, as the Panthers would have it, "White America is an organized imperialist force holding black people in colonial bondage" then it follows that violence against the police and other agents or symbols of authority is not crime but heroism, not merely an unlawful act but a revolutionary gesture against an illegitimate government.

This poisonous ideology has found fertile soil in the black ghettoes of America. Its roots do not yet, perhaps, go very deep, and the commitment to organized violence is found only among a relatively small group of black radicals. Most Negro leaders continue to believe that change can come in this country through legitimate, orderly political processes, and, indeed, that this is the only way it will come. But the anti-colonial ideology has the potential for further growth, and it will grow to the extent that the white majority can successfully be cast by radical propagandists in the role of oppressors of the black majority.

* * *

The psychological cause.   All men are born with drives and needs which conflict with those of other human beings. In all societies, parents, caretakers and authority figures of one kind or another are charged with the responsibility of meeting the child's basic needs and helping the young convert their drive energy into skills and patterns of behavior which will help them cope with the demands of an adult society. This is the process of "socialization." Without satisfactory socialization, these energies may result in a variety of troublesome forms of personal behavior, including self-destructive action and unwarranted conflict and violence against people and property.

When, however, the young are adequately developed and socialized and are able to cope as adults, they enjoy a sense of adequacy and security. Being able to cope and as a result receiving the respect and acceptance of significant peers is the primary way an individual meets basic and man-made needs. When members of a society experience satisfactory patterns of socialization, a high level of peace and stability can exist in families and the society without the use of physical force to control individuals or groups.

The basic pattern of socialization running through the black man's history in America has been the destructive, unsatisfactory relationship of dependency and subordination vis-à-vis the white man. In slavery the master functioned as a father, ruler and god. The condition of total power in the master and total powerlessness in the slave, with the master providing and regulating the slave's most basic needs, resulted in an intense emotional bond between the black slave and the white master. Over time the values of the white master and of the slavery system were often internalized by the slaves and transmitted from generation to generation under the continuing influence of the slavery system. The myth of Negro inferiority and white supremacy was widely and deeply ingrained into black man and white man alike.

Under segregation and in the ghetto the same pattern prevailed, although in a constantly weakening form. The clear implication of segregation was still that whites were superior and Negroes inferior, that the white man was the father and the Negro, the "boy." But other social forces were now unleashed: even under the segregation system black dependency on white power was

261

sharply decreased in comparison with slavery, and in the teeming racial ghettoes of the Northern cities the old relationship of dependency became attenuated in the extreme.

The widening "crack" in the pattern of forced dependency was the beginning of the development of a positive black group identity. Many blacks, as preachers, teachers, physicians, lawyers and other professional service people, began to develop skills which gave them a sense of adequacy and the capacity to cope. In the South in particular, successful business communities developed. Black youngsters were able to identify with people like themselves in positions of leadership and respect. Obviously the level of self-respect was limited by the implications of a segregated system, but nonetheless it was of tremendous value in enhancing black self-esteem. More among the black masses were better able to earn enough money to take care of their families and as a result were able to develop a sense of personal adequacy. Involvement in two world wars and achievement in entertainment, athletics and other areas, together with the myriad effects of migration to Northern cities, began to change the black American's image of himself. A more positive sense of self began to replace the previous negative self-contempt.

Black adequacy and competence is now built on more than white approval. A significant number of black parents no longer teach their children to accept white authority right or wrong. On the other hand, many whites, now economically more secure and better educated, no longer need or approve of the scapegoating of blacks. The white majority is increasingly transcending the limits of the old racial myths of America. In short, the tie that bound—the old socialization pattern of black social, economic and psychological dependence on a dominating, often oppressive white community— is now breaking decisively for the first time in American history.

With the destruction of the old socialization pattern and the breaking of the dependency bond have come expected responses, some constructive, some destructive. The painful social process is in some ways analogous to the difficult period of adolescence in the individual when the achievement of adult independence often seems to the youth to require a destructive rejection, not merely a quiet putting away, of childish things. Many militant blacks who are now seeking a positive cultural identity and a new pattern of black socialization also experience a "black rage" against whites who seem to block this development by their unwillingness to "get off the back" of the striving black man. In the case of the black radicals, this rage is expressed in aggressive violence against the newly vulnerable symbols of white authority such as the police.

The breaking of the dependency bond, acceptance of blackness as a positive value, and a sense of outrage is an energizing, explosive set of psychological developments for the rising generation of militant blacks. The black American often experiences intense and ambivalent feelings as a result and is confronted with numerous questions and conflicts. Should he attempt to become a part of the mainstream of his society—now changing but once so abusive and rejecting—or is he obliged to retaliate or reject it? Does manhood require retaliation, rejection or even violence? Can he trust what he sees as

262

a white America which has never before demonstrated itself trustworthy with regard to recognizing and protecting the human rights of black Americans?

The new feeling among blacks sometimes results in a loss of self-control after "trigger incidents" (reflecting the old pattern of white superiority and black helplessness) with attendant burning of property and other acts of violence. With a temporary breakdown in personal control, some blacks loot and plunder the "symbolic enemy." This reaction is not one that is found only among a small "riff-raff" who are sometimes thought to be responsible for urban riots. Studies of participation in the 1967 riots have found that (1) a substantial minority, ranging from 10 to 20 percent, participated in the riots; (2) one-half to three-quarters of the arrestees were employed in semi-skilled or skilled occupations, three-fourths were employed, and three-tenths to six-tenths were born outside the South; and (3) individuals between the ages of 15 and 34 and especially those between the ages of 15 and 24 are most likely to participate in riots.

In the one-to-one black-and-white relationship where mutual respect exists and where interaction occurs on a personal rather than symbolic level, constructive interaction between the races is less difficult, perhaps more so than ever before. It is in his abstract role as the symbolic enemy that the white man is anathema to some radical black militants. Disturbingly, this symbolic perception of whites has filtered down to youngsters, sometimes as young as three or four years of age. Just as young members of the Klan and other children of the "white ghetto" are taught that it is permissible to abuse blacks, some young blacks are now being taught that it is permissible to abuse whites — in particular, white policemen (or "pigs" in radical argot).

How do the two causes labelled "ideological" and "psychological" in the above analysis correspond to our previously described models for aggressive behavior?

Does the first of the two causes seem more likely to apply to younger blacks? Better-educated young blacks? Better-educated young blacks who are seeking a leadership role in their group? How about the second of the two causes?

How many of the explanations for violence by blacks living in the ghetto apply to the situation of blacks serving time in maximum-security prisons, guarded mostly by whites, as at San Quentin? (While Attica was far bloodier than San Quentin, all the Attica killing was done by the authorities, not by the prisoners.) Which causal mechanisms are likely to be more important, and which less important, in prison violence? What factors in the situation are most likely to determine, in ghetto riots and in prison riots, the degree of violence of the authorities' response? At least up till now, the latter would seem to include the extent of personal frustration (long waiting, abrasive or insulting behavior by the rioters) experienced by the responding forces; ideological responses to actual or rumored killings by the rioters; fear; and the extent to which actual behavior is left to imitation or response to *ad hoc* commands by lower-echelon officials, rather than being firmly integrated into a command chain that insists on precise, minimum application of violence — including use of non-lethal weapons wherever possible — and that is present to monitor compliance.

With the foregoing materials, we now have a reasonably good basis for thinking about one important document of black radicalism, the "Black Panther Party Platform and Program." The following ten points are detailed as "What We Want" by this document:

1. We want freedom. We want power to determine the destiny of our Black Community.

2. We want full employment for our people.

3. We want an end to the robbery by the CAPITALIST of our Black Community.

4. We want decent housing, fit for shelter of human beings.

5. We want education for our people that exposes the true nature of this decadent American society. We want education that teaches us our true history and our role in the present-day society.

6. We want all black men to be exempt from military service.

7. We want an immediate end to POLICE BRUTALITY and MURDER of black people.

8. We want freedom for all black men held in federal, state, county and city prisons and jails.

9. We want all black people when brought to trial to be tried in court by a jury of their peer group or people from their black communities, as defined by the Constitution of the United States.

10. We want land, bread, housing, education, clothing, justice and peace. And as our major political objective, a United Nations-supervised plebiscite to be held throughout the black colony in which only black colonial subjects will be allowed to participate, for the purpose of determining the will of black people as to their national destiny.

Additional detail is stated in ten corresponding "What We Believe" points, including a cash equivalent for "forty acres and two mules" to be paid to the black communities (under point 3), the possibility of turning housing in the black communities into cooperatives (point 4), and organizing black groups for self-defense against "racist police oppression and brutality" (point 7). Finally, although somewhat ambiguously, the Black Panthers demand a "separate and equal station" (language, curiously, that is close to the Supreme Court's "separate but equal doctrine" of *Plessy* v. *Ferguson*, which was the justification

264

for segregated schools, and the overturning of which in *Brown* v. *Board of Education* in 1954 began the modern civil-rights movement).

How does the foregoing document compare with the black grievances described and weighted in the Kerner Report? Are many of the items similar? Which items are prominent in one but not in the other? Would it be fair to say that, in the main, this document takes the chief grievances described by the Kerner Commission and places them in an ideological framework? Now, black radicals seem to be moving, quoting Panther Bobby Seale, "away from violence and toward service." Again, will this shift endure?

Black Violence and White Violence: Questions and Comparisons. Based on the materials covered, what do you think of the following table as an attempt to suggest the typical content and priority of concerns that move radical leaders and radical followers, black and white:

	LEADERS	FOLLOWERS
Black:	community self-determination; drastic change in political mechanisms, including separation of black community; Fanonist "colonial" ideology; leaders' seeking high personal status; employment, housing, education.	police practices and reasonable status; jobs, housing, education, recreation, political structure, and grievance mechanisms.
White:	group belonging; Vietnam, women's liberation, foreign relations, racism, other sweeping "altruistic" reform issues; Maoist-Marcusian ideology; leaders' seeking of high personal status (with some exceptions); some factions with "life-style" concern, others with little or none.	group belonging, role-recognition and reasonable status; lifestyle ("Larry syndrome": free sex, free pot); Cambodia, grape boycott, conspiracy trials, and other *ad hoc* "altruistic" reform issues; Vietnam, university administration, other part-"personal concern" and part-"abstract reform" issues.

Comparison of black and white leaders. Note that this summary suggests that ideological concerns play a much more significant role for the leaders than for the followers and that the leaders have a much greater drive to achieve high status. But the *program* of white radical leaders is rooted in relatively generalized issues of social reform, and that of white followers in corresponding specific reforms derived from the broad program (except for "life style," where some of the leaders, especially the PLP variety, may be extremely "square" and puritanical, at least in personal behavior patterns). In contrast, the *program* of black radical leaders comprises, in essence, a broadened version of specific reform goals sought by the black community. Moreover, the black leaders seek reforms that are largely in direct response to the causes that have given rise to their own rage and aggression. What the white leaders seek is largely irrelevant to the specific causes of *their* rage and aggression, rooted deep in their childhood experiences, for which there is *no* relevant reform. Little wonder then, if this summary is anywhere close to the mark, that the black and white radicals generally each go their own way.

Are there other characteristics of the leadership that distinguish the two groups? Both black and white radical leaders appear to be better-educated than the average white or black in society; virtually all the top white leadership has a college (or higher) degree or else has dropped out of college. Huey Newton and Bobby Seale were both law students, although Eldridge Cleaver only has a high school diploma (received in San Quentin); most of the other top black radical leaders have had at least some college training. However, the top white leadership seems to come from substantially more affluent backgrounds than the blacks or even than most other whites. (Kelman notes that SDS members at Harvard had fathers with average incomes of $23,000 versus $17,000 for the Harvard average, according to a survey in one class.) Many of the top black leaders came from very large, poor families, often migrating in their youth from the southern or border states. At least a large segment of the white leadership moved from strongly developed nonviolent reformist concerns to their present positions—a process typified by the story of Diane Oughton, the heiress who moved from good works in rural Guatemala to the brownstone in Greenwich Village where she died making what Bernadine Dohrn describes as "antipersonnel bombs." It seems that a much smaller fraction of the present black radical leadership is rooted in previous nonviolent civil rights activity. A much more detailed study and comparison might be useful.

The overall differences in perception and program of white and black radical leaders will, almost certainly, continue to result in substantial differences in tactics and targets. If violence is used, who is most likely to bomb a police station? A recruiting station or ROTC building? Why? If a political kidnapping were carried out, who is most likely to demand Angela Davis' release as ransom? Who most likely to view Daniel Berrigan as the top "political prisoner"? (However, there is considerable expression of admiration and concern for black radical prisoners in the white radical and general "underground press.") Who is most likely to blow up an ammunition depot and kill a couple of production workers? Who most likely to burn down a grocery store or a real-estate office? The differences in past and possible future tactics are not absolute, of course, but the differing tendencies and prime targets would seem to be fairly well established.

Tactics for moving radicals away from violence. Which group of radicals could most readily be moved away from violence by the adoption of reform measures? The blacks, fairly clearly, because theirs is a specific set of basic concerns to which concrete responses can be made (assuming that there is likely to be little weight behind a separatist movement if the detailed grievances described in the Kerner Report are largely satisfied). Even at the best, however, such responses would take a very substantial re-allocation of resources and a period of years to accomplish. Thus, even if group violence by blacks largely disappeared, there would be a further period of time needed for the enormous individual violence (recall the high homicide rate) growing out of years of social disintegration and neglect to decline. (Would the speed of this decline depend on the extent to which such violence grows out of, for example, current economic frustrations compared with the extent to which it develops from the imitation of models of violent behavior perceived in childhood?)

Which group of radicals could most permanently be moved from violence by initially changing their *leaders'* minds about the efficacy or appropriateness of violence to achieve their goals? Possibly the whites (note the Dohrn statement on page 249). In the first place, ideology—at least short of an ideology of violence for some purpose learned at mother's knee—seems more flexibly adaptable from a violent to a non-violent response than deep personal frustration. Most of the white radical leadership appears not to have grown up with poverty, overcrowding, or models of violent behavior to imitate; most of the black radical leadership has. Also, there seems no inherent reason why a group, to offer a sense of intense "belonging," must have vio-

267

lence as its tactic. There should be a real effort to identify other intense collective experiences—for example in certain kinds of community organizing—that might offer a practical psychological alternative.

On the other hand, to the extent that white radicals are convicted and sentenced to prison, or have such threats hanging over their heads if they return to this country, especially for reasons such as minor property damage or "conspiracy," it is possible they *will* feel deep personal frustration and a sense that there is little more to lose by committing what Bernadine Dohrn now calls the "military error." For violent political activities, however, the threat of punishment may well deter—see the discussion of "frustration" and "displacement" on page 75, and note that Kelman comments that many Harvard demonstrators did not want to go so far that they would risk losing such future *desiderata* as security clearances or admission to the Bar with "good moral character." Thus the threat of punishment cannot be wholly sacrificed by a society that wishes to limit disruption and to channel reformist energy into existing routes for redressing grievances. The solution to this apparent dilemma, perhaps, is to be extremely careful to bring criminal actions only when a clearly serious violation is charged (for example, conspiracy to kidnap, as contrasted with conspiracy to cross state lines to incite a riot that results only in minor property damage and little or no physical injury). Combined with this new attitude toward punishment, there must be a clear opening up of alternative channels that promise to address themselves to the kinds of reforms that the best of these radicals seek, in the many areas where these reforms seem vital: more Nader's Raiders, more Congressional self-reform, more reordering of government spending priorities, more humane approaches to criminal-law reform, more efforts for an international détente, more monitoring of pollution, more of the reforms urgently needed for the black and the poor, and more career opportunities for young reformers who wish to make these basic concerns their lifework.

Is it fair to say that there has been substantial progress in at least several of the above categories over the past two years? How might, say, the scope and pace of domestic reform from 1933 to 1968 compare with the presently perceived needs? Is it significant that the federal budget has grown from $3.5 billion in 1930 to a non-military budget of around $150 billion in 1970?

There is a reference on page 267 to an ideology, sanctioning vio-

268

lence for certain purposes, that might be "learned at mother's knee." Where might one find examples of that kind of rooted ideology? Does their existence suggest that new violence-sanctioning viewpoints or value-systems, maintained for a couple of decades or more, may begin to take on a new and more sinister life of their own?

To the extent that some of the current radical leadership is self-selected to have a strong drive for status and power, one might also expect that a certain segment of that leadership, both white and black, would yield neither to reform nor to reasoned persuasion, but would insist on maintaining a "revolutionary" role. They would pursue the "military error" and — if the risks of pursuing it in the society-at-large with a dwindling group of co-activists became too great — might displace their aggression onto the erstwhile revolutionary factions, whom they could blame for having "sold out" the movement. Such internecine warfare within radical fringe groups, illustrated in the brief account of the SDS split in the first sections of this chapter, has been frequent throughout history.

Poor white grievances. Consider the impact of those of the "radical" leaders who are basically elitist in the sense described by Kelman and others. These leaders are likely to be condescending to, and often hostile to, the low-income white, the "hardhat" or the "redneck," or the guy with a crew-cut drinking beer and watching TV. Their attitudes and tactics towards the low-income white are likely to continue and reinforce attitudes that often lock poor white and poor black alike into the embrace of mutual misery and mutual hatred. Instead of forging an effective political coalition of poor people seeking reform, such "radical" leadership and rhetoric only intensifies the plight of the blacks and delivers the poor-white vote into the hands of those who are generally most likely to ignore the plight of *all* the poor, white and black, urban and rural, northern and southern. This arrogant, elitist, and counterproductive aspect of a good deal of the radical white leadership ignores the very real political possibilities of getting those reforms that *are* urgently needed. A Violence Commission staff report on *Assassination and Political Violence* describes the reactions and concerns of poor whites:[15]

We selected for study two current American vigilante-type movements, neither a stranger to violence, and both responding to a perception of a black threat; (1) The North Carolina Ku Klux Klan — a product of the rural poor whites in the South, called by Peter Young, consultant to this Task Force, the

269

White Ghetto; and (2) The North Ward Citizens' Council of Newark, an example of a so-called backlash group.

* * *

[Peter Young's analysis then follows:]

The gaping wounds of American black people can no longer be denied, but it is still possible for a little while longer yet to maintain the fiction that this is an isolated case and that the ordinary white American is doing very well indeed in this paradise of free enterprise and democracy. But truth will out— in fact, it already has. (The white ghetto exists just as surely as the black.). . .

The average Tar Heel Kluxer (as I have known him) was born into grinding poverty, poorly educated in substandard schools, economically exploited and officially harassed.

Most white Americans (and many black people) have some difficulty in believing that in this year 1968, in this prosperous America, that *white* citizens exist by the millions in an environment which is so lacking in elemental respects as to be fertile breeding ground for hatred which is finally expressed in a murderous racism.

Permit me, then, to quote at some length from the report of *another* Presidential Commission, the National Advisory Commission on Rural Poverty:

"Rural poverty is so widespread, and so acute, as to be a national disgrace, and its consequences have swept into our cities, violently. . . . They (the programs) were developed without anticipating the vast changes in technology, and the consequences of this technology to rural people . . . Most rural programs still do not take the speed and consequences of technological change into account . . . In contrast to the urban poor, the rural poor, notably the white, are not well organized, and have few spokesmen for bringing the nation's attention to their problems . . . The more vocal and better organized urban poor gain most of the benefits of current antipoverty programs . . . the Nation's major social welfare and labor legislation largely bypassed rural Americans . . . we have been oblivious of the rural poor . . . Rural poverty in the United States has no geographic boundaries. It is acute in the South, but it is present and serious in the East, the West and the North. Rural poverty is not limited to Negroes . . . whites outnumber nonwhites among the rural poor by a wide margin . . . Hunger, even among children, does exist among the rural poor . . . The rural poor have gone, and now go, to poor schools . . . Unemployment and underemployment are major problems in rural America . . . Most of the rural South is one vast poverty area . . . The community in rural poverty areas has all but disappeared as an effective institution."

Those who profess surprise that an organization such as "The Klan" should emerge from the environment described above are naive. What do they expect?

* * *

I am not in the business of comparing misery, of saying that Group A in the southern country side is more miserable (or less) than Group B in the

270

northern metropolis. I am simply saying that for *both* Group A and Group B — and perhaps Groups C through G as well — the level of unrelieved misery has long since passed the tolerance threshold, and we are therefore — surprise! surprise! — confronted by an explosive level of alienation that is marked by frequent incidents of violence.

. . . For the low-income Southern white — whose grievances are numerous, legitimate and painfully real — it comes therefore as an unbearable shock to hear repeated expressions of governmental concern for the problems of *black* people. Never mind that these expressions are almost invariably hypocritical, designed simply for vote-getting purposes. The point is that the low-income Southern white — that bigot, that redneck, that racist, that hate-monger — doesn't even get the hypocritical expressions of concern from the government which is also *his*. It is exactly at this point that the average white ghetto citizen displaces his hatred from government officials (where it belongs) to his black neighbors, who also are victims of the very same shell game. This shell game is *profitable* for some; the driving of a deep wedge between ordinary white and black citizens is precisely what perpetuates the power of a tiny minority, the country club elite. Quite often, the Klansman, as indigenous leader in the white ghetto, has a better understanding of this than do his followers. Example: the young preacher at the Klan rally at Four Oaks, N.C., shouted to the multitudes — "When they say HEW, they mean *nigger* health, they mean *nigger* education, they mean *nigger* welfare! You and I are just going to have to suffer it out by ourselves, the best way we can, like we always done." But is this Klan preacher, at rock bottom, furious with "niggers" or "they"? To ask such a question is to answer it. And it is similarly no accident that the *overt* expressions of hostility in the Wallace campaign are always directed at "pseudo-intellectuals, pointy-headed guideline writers," etc.

* * *

But at some level of his being, the white ghetto citizen knows he is living a lie. Dimly, he recalls his many human contacts with black people all along the twisted trail of his life. He *is* on fire with hatred, as the result of a difficult life in an impoverished environment; this diffused hatred is suddenly focused on "the nigger," as if the latter were a lightning rod for all the ailments of the world. Yet in the very act of picking up his gun and acting out his hatred, the white ghetto citizen protests that it is not "niggers" whom he *really* hates. And to a considerable extent, he is right. What we call "racism" is more the expression than the cause of the highly contagious, collective frustration which afflicts the white ghetto these days in epidemic proportions.

You see, there is a magnificent Gravy Train which continues even now to roll across the American landscape. But unfortunately, it does not make all the required stops.

The Report then describes the New Jersey group:

The North Ward Citizens' Council in Newark, N.J., has been labeled a white vigilante group and has been identified with the so-called "white back-

271

lash." With the help of Peter Young, we taped a campaign speech and an interview with Mr. Anthony Imperiale, head of the North Ward Citizens' Committee, who was running for city councilman-at-large. His campaign speeches were demonstrably successful; he won his seat by a greater majority than any other candidate. Thus, the campaign speech and the interview, both of which are summarized in the appendix, merit the reader's special attention.

From the speech and interview we can conclude that the persons to whom Mr. Imperiale apparently appeals are not sick persons. They are, however, learning to resent what appears to them to be the position of favoritism taken by the government toward the urban Negro. They are beginning, like the Klansmen, to see the government as hostile rather than responsive to the needs of their community. They are quick to spot and resent the hypocrisy of the white legislator who requires the integration of the public school to which they must send their children because they cannot afford the private school to which the legislator sends his children.

Klan resurgence in North Carolina and white backlash vigilantism in Northern cities is a warning signal that the American racial crisis is not going to be solved at the expense of the low-income white. We have already heard from the Negro precincts that the crisis cannot be solved at their expense. This crisis can only be solved, not at someone else's expense, but at ours.

A schematic comparison of conditions in white and black ghettos is offered in the report:

Similarities

1. No liquid capital for investment.
2. Low level of skills—people becoming "obsolete."
3. Feelings of powerlessness, rage, alienation, etc.
4. Fierce compensatory pride.
5. Heavily armed and arming.
6. Violence as a life style—has been expressed internally, but now is beginning to be externalized.
7. Infrastructure of indigenous, secret organizations operating outside the legal, constitutional framework.
8. Significant political activity outside two-party system.

Differences

1. White ghetto: No intellectual leadership or indigenous professional services.

Black ghetto: Increasingly adequate intellectual leadership—black cultural explosion.

2. White ghetto: Family structure still intact, but under increasing strain.

Black ghetto: Family structure splintered—no father figure, matriarchy.

3. White ghetto: Vices largely private and unorganized, with possible exception of "moonshine" liquor.

Black ghetto: Racket-ridden community—heroin, prostitution, numbers, etc.

4. White ghetto: Few, if any, *constructive* governmental programs—much abuse, threats, etc.

Black ghetto: Many poorly conceived, mismanaged governmental and private programs—innumerable expressions of concern. Hopes aroused, then dashed.

5. White ghetto: Constant harassment from most *state and federal* law enforcement agencies but not ordinarily local police.

Black ghetto: Constant harassment from *local* police.

6. White ghetto: Advanced paranoid delusions that United States is about to be taken (or already has been taken) by Communist-Jewish-black conspiracy.

Black ghetto: Mild paranoid delusions among militants that official policy of *overt* genocide is just over the horizon.

Based on this and the preceding material, how many of the psychological "models" for extreme violence would appear applicable to such poor *white* groups? Does the "frustration" model seem especially applicable here? What are the mechanisms by which this violence, or at least an extreme political and social hostility, might be displaced onto blacks? Is it likely that strongly worded criticism of the expressed values, life style, or "racism" of these poor whites by affluent, educated whites will improve the situation or make it worse? If the latter is more likely, what *can* be done to make it better, and perhaps even to begin to forge a common political alliance for needed reforms?

Fighting revolution with money. What does the Report mean when it suggests that "the American racial crisis . . . can only be solved, not at someone else's expense, but at ours"? If "ours" means the educated, middle- or upper-middle-class white who is most likely to read the Commission's words, and if "expense" is taken at its face value, the suggestion means that substantially higher taxes must be paid, if the enormous sums are to be found with which to effect the needed reforms for *both* blacks and whites. Also, at least part of the solution lies in the reordering of our spending priorities. Could this reordering be achieved by reductions in defense spending, made possible by a "winding down" of the arms race? But can this measure alone provide the huge sums needed?

In the United States the average income tax burden of a married couple with two children, on earnings of $20,000, is 21.9 percent. In Canada it is 27.4 percent, in West Germany 28.5 percent, in Great Britain 35.4 percent, and in Sweden and Denmark over 40 percent. Such discrepancies, in general, hold over the whole range of incomes from $15,000 to $50,000 per year. The United States income tax would have to increase by 20–25 percent to put us on a par with even the *lowest* of these other national income tax structures. This, in a sense, is the most truly "radical" suggestion: to say that middle-class Americans must raise their overall taxes to levels more comparable with the taxes of other industrialized societies. Otherwise, there is no real hope of providing the necessary millions of units of new housing, the jobs, the education, the well-trained and well-paid police, the adequate nutrition, the recreational facilities—the release from at least these basic material causes of frustration, put-downs, overcrowding and dependency. Without these reforms, the whole society will live with the continuous spectre of violent crime, riot, and still more persistent, patterned, and extreme forms of group violence.

FOOTNOTES, CHAPTER 6

[1] Steven Kelman, *Push Comes to Shove* (Boston: Houghton Mifflin Company, 1970), pp. 106–61.

[2] Kenneth Keniston, *Young Radicals* (New York: Harcourt, Brace and World, Inc.), pp. 4–5, 14. 144–146, 254–256.

[3] Dr. Herbert Hendin, "A Psychoanalyst Looks at Student Revolutionaries," *New York Times Magazine*, January 17, 1971, pp. 18–30.

[4] Karl Fleming, "We'll Blow up the World," *Newsweek*, vol. 76 (October 12, 1970), pp. 49–50.

[5] "Views Attributed to Miss Dohrn Indicate a Shift from Violence," *New York Times*, December 25, 1970, p. 18.

[6] Trudy Rubin, "Young Radicals Finding Violence a Dead End," *Christian Science Monitor*, January 15, 1971, p. 1 (Western Edition).

[7] Also reported in *U.S. News and World Report*, September 21, 1970, p. 39.

[8] National Commission on the Causes and Prevention of Violence, *To Establish Justice, to Ensure Domestic Tranquility*, p. 27.

[9] National Commission of the Causes and Prevention of Violence, *To Establish Justice*, p. 30.

[10] National Commission on the Causes and Prevention of Violence, *Law and Order Reconsidered*, pp. 104–5.

[11] "Ghettos Rising High," *Seattle Post-Intelligencer*, September 27, 1970, p. 28.

[12] National Commission on the Causes and Prevention of Violence, *To Establish Justice*, pp. 128–29.

[13] National Commission on the Causes and Prevention of Violence, *To Establish Justice*, p. 149.

[14] National Commission on the Causes and Prevention of Violence, *Law and Order Reconsidered*, pp. 101–4, 109–12.

[15] National Commission on the Causes and Prevention of Violence, *Law and Order*, pp. 281–82, 284–90.

7

Technology of Conflict:

**The genie is out
of the bottle**

In Chapter 2, Konrad Lorenz speaks of the development of weapons as a crucial stage in the genesis of lethal conflict among men. Since that stage we have travelled light-years from the flung stone, the club, the knife, or even the flintlock pistol, and we seem to be travelling faster all the time. Since World War II, the nations of the world have spent well over a *trillion* dollars on the maintenance of armies and the development and procurement of weapons. What are these weapons? What are their avowed uses, and, above all, what are the dangers that they pose?

A Note on Modern
Weaponry

The technological seesaw. What may be called "modern" weaponry (apart from weapons of mass destruction, which will be discussed later) is not an absolute and clear-cut category. Increasingly powerful weapons and new methods of using and transporting them developed as the nineteenth century progressed. Steadily more powerful cannons and mortars were developed; by World War I, the German "Big Bertha" could send a projectile forty-seven miles. In a sense, this was really an early, short-range "ballistic missile," using a high-explosive projectile rather than a nuclear warhead.

The machine gun was a development of great importance, particularly in maintaining defensive positions against attacking troops, but curiously enough, it was largely discounted by military "experts" who viewed its operations in the Russo-Japanese War of 1905 and found it to be only moderately effective. This assessment helped shape the tactics of mass attack in the trench warfare of World War I, against which the machine gun took an appalling toll. What the "experts" had failed to see was that the 1905 machine gun was a large, unwieldy affair standing high above the ground and easily exposed to fire; also that the Japanese were willing to take enormous losses to reach and overrun their objectives, despite the fire of the machine gun.

The tank, a primitive weapon at the start of World War I, was fully operational by the end, and of considerable significance in neutralizing machine gun-defended positions. In World War II, the tank itself was to a significant extent neutralized by the bazooka, and later by the recoilless rifle. Heavier armor and increased mobility and firepower have recently partially restored the balance in favor of the tank; and even more effective means of offense, especially the helicopter, with its high mobility, have been developed still more recently.

This series of developments reflects one aspect of the technological seesaw and its relation to the comparative effectiveness of attacking and defending forces. At first, attacking ground troops could be stalled by the machine gun (defense), which was partially neutralized by the tank (offense), in turn offset by the bazooka and recoilless rifle (defense), but in turn offset by better tanks and by the high mobility achieved with helicopters (offense). A significant next step in defense, certainly, would be the development of a reasonably accurate weapon

276

for use against helicopters that was compact enough (including ammunition or missile) to be carried and served by one or two men. The United States already has such a weapon, called "Redeye." It has been remarked that, if such a weapon came into use in Vietnam, in the hands of the Vietcong and North Vietnamese, it might significantly alter the military balance.

But overall, this panoply of new weapons has led to a sharp change from the massed infantry attacks of former days; infantry now operate in spread-out patrols or skirmish lines, frequently use the protection of armored personnel carriers, and on defense stay behind cover or in a foxhole. Their chief function is often to make the men on the other side stay put and keep their heads down, while they are located and attacked from remote distances by artillery or bombarded by aircraft.

Total war becomes possible. Great changes have taken place in weaponry in the environments of water and air, as well. Naval vessels acquired steel armor beginning in the 1860s, and steam propulsion replaced sails; wireless communication came in shortly before World War I. With this combination of civilian technologies applied to military purposes, fiercer naval engagements were possible, but even more important was the revolution in logistics. With speedy transportation and communication possible over great reaches of water, vast supplies and armies could be transported across oceans, and the United States could make a significant contribution to a major European land war. By World War II, millions of men and vast quantities of supplies could be moved quickly thousands of miles. United States supplies could cross the Atlantic to Murmansk and help save Russia from the Germans. Fast, long-distance transportation and communication had made war on a truly global scale a possibility. In World War II, the possibility became a reality.

Arrayed against the new surface ships was the technological development of the torpedo-firing submarine. A great battle of technologies was fought, as first the submarine, then the surface vessels and "killer subs" that were developed to defend against it, got the upper hand. On the attacking submarine's side were the increases in speed and maneuverability, in the speed and depth of dive, in the range and accuracy of the torpedo, and in the lack of operating noise. On the defender's side was greater speed and maneuverability on the surface than that of the submarine below, combined with the introduction and subsequent refinement of the depth charge and the introduction and steady improvement of sonar with which to detect and locate the enemy below. (Sonar was used also by the submarine, to "stalk" its prey and to locate and evade the attackers.) The balance shifted back in favor of the submarine, however, with the introduction of nuclear power in 1954. Today a submarine can remain submerged almost indefinitely and run much farther than its predecessors, in almost total silence.

The airplane first flew in 1903; by the end of World War I it could perform a variety of functions in reconaissance and, to a limited extent, attack enemy troops. But by World War II, the role of the airplane in warfare had enlarged enormously. Bombing techniques had been tested by the Germans in Spain and the Italians in Ethiopia in the late 1930s, and they received their first full employment in the Battle of Britain in 1940, when large-scale raids by aircraft were carried out for the first time. In one way, the medium and long-range bomber was distinguished from all the other modern weapons discussed above: *it was uniquely adapted to direct attacks on the industrial and civilian heartland of the enemy.* Millions of civilians died in the conventional bombing raids of World War II — as many Germans in single attacks on Hamburg and Dresden as Japanese in the atomic bombings of Hiroshima and Nagasaki. For the first time in the modern era, "total" war, fought against both the frontline troops and the industrial heartland, became possible. A good army no longer protected a civilian population from the full horrors of war. (Distance still did, however, for neither the Germans nor Japanese had bombers of the range needed to attack the United States.) Since World War II, jet aircraft have been introduced, and bombers with inter-continental ranges and supersonic speeds. Bomb loads, the use of painful weapons such as napalm and "cluster-bombs," and armaments for aerial combat have increased greatly, as have features such as altitude and range (the F-111, for example, can skim at tree-top height using special guidance radar, or fly at 50,000 feet). Computerized devices can now drop bombs with stunning accuracy on pre-selected targets. Also in the air now are the ballistic missiles descended from the V-1 "buzz bombs" and V-2 rockets developed by the Germans in the closing days of World War II. Defense against air attack has improved, as well; radar was introduced early in World War II, and is now used to guide sophisticated ground-to-air missiles against attacking aircraft. But the aircraft, in their turn, carry a bewildering array of electronic and other gear to jam or confuse the radar and to evade or destroy the missile.

The closest thing to an attack on the United States proper was, of

278

course, Pearl Harbor, which was made possible by the wedding of technological changes in naval and air warfare. The aircraft carrier extended the effective range of small aircraft enormously, and made tactical air support of amphibious landings on faraway shores possible. Both the United States and Japanese maneuvered with these leviathans in the Pacific war theater.

The risks of advanced "conventional" weaponry. Current United States naval doctrine holds carriers to be of major importance. The great variable appears to be their vulnerability to attack from submarines or other sources (even porpoises, trained to place contact mines on the hull, as at least one author of fiction would have it). The battleship—the mainstay of naval power at the start of World War II—was made obsolescent by the fact that such a huge machine could be destroyed by a single submarine or divebomber that had penetrated its defenses. The carrier may prove as vulnerable, but has the advantage of being able to use its planes for anti-aircraft and anti-submarine defense.

One frightening aspect to the vulnerability of naval power may be its political implications. The sinking of ships, with its dramatic toll in lives, was the focal event that propelled the United States into three wars (the battleship *Maine* in the Spanish-American War, the passenger liner *Lusitania* in World War I, and the warships at Pearl Harbor in World War II). The alleged attack by North Vietnamese torpedo boats on United States destroyers in the Tonkin Gulf in August 1964 (which did not even lead to casualties) occasioned the first United States bombing of North Vietnam and the "Tonkin Gulf Resolution," by which the Senate gave President Johnson an apparent *carte blanche* for his later escalation of the conflict. On the other hand, conflict was averted in two other recent incidents—the inadvertent Israeli strafing of a United States spy ship during the 1967 Mideast War, and the North Korean seizure of the *Pueblo*, also a spy ship, in 1968—but one may wonder what the result would have been had it been the Egyptians who attacked the United States ship (as we first thought it might have been) or if the North Koreans had sunk, rather than captured, the *Pueblo*. And what sort of escalation might have resulted if the Chinese had given three or four submarines to the North Vietnamese, and the latter had succeeded in using them to destroy a United States carrier? Great fears over the potential vulnerability of our naval forces are now developing in response to Russia's recent increase in naval construction and development. The *political* implications and risks

279

of the use of modern naval technology are constantly with us, as are the political transformations wrought by the new weapons technologies of land and air, even without regard to nuclear capacity. For land warfare, the transformations consist in a limitation on large land armies as such, and the increasing importance of a ground force that reflects heavy investment in capital equipment and in complex technical skills for its personnel (and, alternately, the usefulness of the highly mobile and dispersed ground forces of guerrilla war, operating often almost invisibly with local civilian support). For air warfare, the transformations are seen in the constant possibility that overwhelming destruction may be rained on populations from the sky, perhaps with friend and foe, soldier and civilian, alike indifferently destroyed.

Nuclear Weapons and "Deterrence"

Many of the weapons thus far described are capable of causing, and have already caused, tens of millions of deaths in large-scale war. But certain weapons associated with the most modern technologies are generally singled out as a special category, sometimes called "weapons of mass destruction," since their use on population centers would be almost inherently unselective (for example, they could not be restricted to factories or marshaling yards) and would kill large numbers of noncombatants. The precursor of this category of weapons was the poison gas used in World War I, although these early gasses were only used against combat troops, and actually caused "only" an estimated 100,000 out of the eight and one half million deaths suffered by the combatants (it was also quite an unpredictable weapon, since a change in wind could blow a gas cloud back on the lines of the army that was employing it). But the truly enormous qualitative change in weaponry is usually considered to be the development of atomic (fission) bombs in 1945, and their use against the Japanese cities of Hiroshima and Nagasaki in August 1945. As these single weapons, each carried by a single aircraft, and each with the approximate explosive power of 20,000 tons of TNT (20 kilotons) exploded, each city was destroyed, and in each bombing, some 100,000 people perished. Later, hydrogen fusion or "thermonuclear" bombs were developed, with explosive power measured in tens of megatons (*millions* of tons) rather than tens of kilotons. By 1968, the hydrogen (thermonuclear) bomb had existed for fifteen years, and Lincoln Bloomfield, director of the Arms Control Project of the Massachusetts Institute of Technology's Center for International Studies, wrote: "Added together, the estimated worldwide stockpile of about 50,000 megatons (that is, fifty *billion* tons) of nuclear weapons comes to about 15 tons of TNT equivalent for every man, woman and child on earth."[1]

In the next excerpt, David Inglis points out that a "typical" one-megaton bomb "can cause severe blast damage, sufficient to knock down brick apartment houses," for a radius of five kilometers. This describes a circle with a diameter of 10 kilometers, of 6¼ miles. Consider this fact in relation to *your* city. For a vivid picture of what it would be like to be a survivor of such a blast, the British film *The War Game* is highly recommended. It should not, however, be seen "cold," but only in a context in which the viewers are prepared to discuss (immediately after viewing) their fears and concerns, and to look for constructive alternatives to such a holocaust.

With the development of the H-bomb, it is possible, for the first time in human history, to conduct a war that would wipe all mankind from the face of the earth—and that, at the very least, could be expected to result, in a single day, in casualties greater than those resulting from all conflict since man appeared on the planet. Clearly, this change in the technological variable has made the systematic study and absolute elimination of large-scale lethal conflict one of mankind's most pressing needs.

The nature and effects of nuclear weapons. The following materials deal in depth with the development of nuclear and thermonuclear weapons, and the unprecedented problems that they pose. David Inglis, a senior physicist at the Argonne National Laboratory in Chicago, and a former chairman of the Federation of American Scientists, did this excellent background piece, "The Outlook for Nuclear Explosives," in *Unless Peace Comes,* a forecast of new weapons published under the editorship of Nigel Calder in 1968.[2]

A sound judgment of the likely future of nuclear weapons must be based on an appreciation of the basic processes involved in present nuclear weapons. The existence of bulk matter, of chemical reactions, of life, of a universe sparsely studded with enormous furnaces known as stars, and of nuclear weapons, depends on the availability of certain kinds of particles pushing or pulling on one another with particular kinds of forces. The particles and forces are limited in kind.

The atom has its encircling electrons bound to its heavy central nucleus by electric forces. Readjustments of the energy of this electric attraction provide the power of the oil burned in a stove, or of a chemical explosive such as dynamite or TNT. Such burning gives off a relatively modest amount of energy per atom involved, perhaps one or two "electron-volts" for each atom. The central nucleus is held together by forces so much stronger than electric forces that, when rearrangements occur among the protons and neutrons of which the nucleus is composed, the energies involved are measured in millions of electron-volts.

The forces of nature seem to make possible the building of only about a hundred kinds of chemical elements — enough to make chemical and life processes sufficiently varied and still not too confusing. The trick is a very interesting one. There are two quite different kinds of forces between the particles within the nucleus. These neutrons and protons attract each other with very strong "nuclear" forces, but the protons push each other apart by electric forces. The cohesive nuclear forces dominate in very small nuclei but increase more slowly than the disruptive electric forces as nuclei grow in size. Nuclei with more than about one hundred protons (and a slightly greater number of neutrons) do not exist, because if they were formed, the electric force would quickly split them apart.

The result of these immutable laws of nature is that, when dealing with the light nuclei containing only a few particles, we can gain useful energy from the forces of attraction by fusion of nuclei to make a bigger nucleus. At the other end of the list of nuclei, among the very heavy ones containing many protons and neutrons, we can gain useful energy if we can disturb a nucleus in such a way as to cause the electric repulsion to cause *fission*, to "split" the nucleus into smaller nuclei. Among the heavy elements, uranium-235 and plutonium-239 have nuclei that, when "prodded" by neutrons, will undergo fission. In the process, the fragments of a nucleus release a couple of other neutrons, which then hit other nuclei and cause further splitting — the famous chain reaction.

In between the very light and the very heavy nuclei there is a long middle part of the list where the cohesive and disruptive tendencies just about cancel one another; the nuclei are very stable and nothing can happen that involves large amounts of energy. The entire list of available nuclei is well known, and if we except radioactive decay, which is of limited usefulness, fusion and fission are the only ways of obtaining such large amounts of nuclear energy from the materials and forces that can be manipulated on earth.

EXISTING NUCLEAR WEAPONS

Fission came first, in the original A-bomb. Whether an explosive chain reaction will work in a mass of uranium-235 or plutonium-239 depends on several numbers characterizing the behavior of nuclei. Many of the Western scientists who devised the first A-bombs during World War II rather hoped that nature had determined these numbers in such a way as to make the bomb impossible. It turned out otherwise, and the very first bombs were a thousand times as powerful as the biggest chemical-explosive bomb that had ever been made, the twenty-ton "blockbuster." The power was equivalent to that of 20,000 tons of TNT—twenty kilotons, as one says. Such cold numbers mean little until translated into terms of the depth of human tragedy caused at Hiroshima and Nagasaki.

The fusion process is the basis of the much more powerful H-bomb, typically of megaton force—equivalent to a million tons or more of TNT. It is achieved not by neutrons but by banging nuclei of light atoms together so violently that they fuse. A very energetic impact is required to overcome the electric force between two nuclei that tends to keep them apart. The atoms have to be set in very violent motion; in other words the material has to be raised to a very high temperature. That is why the fusion reaction is often called a "thermonuclear" reaction. In practice, a uranium-235 A-bomb serves as the "trigger" to create the very high temperature and detonate the fusible material of the H-bomb.

The greatest practical difference between the A-bomb and the H-bomb is that the power of the A-bomb is limited by its having what is known as a critical mass, while for the H-bomb there is no such limit. An arbitrarily large mass of the appropriate light elements of an H-bomb can be assembled without danger of premature detonation. A large mass of plutonium, on the other hand, will explode spontaneously. The critical mass at which the chain reaction will begin depends on the supply of neutrons and their fate. A neutron born in the middle of a sphere of plutonium may or may not hit a plutonium nucleus, depending on how big the sphere is. It is like a bullet fired in a forest: it may miss the trees and escape into a field beyond unless the forest is quite large. For plutonium metal of normal density and with certain materials around it, there is a particular size that will let so few neutrons escape that the chain reaction will start. Above this size, the nuclear explosion would occur spontaneously, for there are always a few neutrons around to get it started. For a slightly smaller size, nothing drastic happens. But if the smaller size is compressed (like having the trees in the forest closer together), it may become supercritical and intercept enough neutrons to explode. The sudden compression or sudden assembly of separate pieces is accomplished by the use of chemical explosives.

There is also the economic difference that the main bulk of the light elements used in an H-bomb is much cheaper than the specially prepared uranium or plutonium used in an A-bomb. As Americans put it, the H-bomb gives "more bang for a buck." It appears as the "big economy pack" in the price list for nuclear explosives that may be made available by the U.S. Atomic Energy Commission for large-scale underground "nuclear engineering." The prices (which follow a straight line on a logarithmic graph) are typically:

KILOTONS	PRICE
10	$350,000
200	500,000
2000	600,000

The last big increase thus costs relatively little. The starting price is presumably the approximate cost of the A-bomb trigger, after the cost of getting into production has been written off.

A-bombs and H-bombs also differ in the proportion of radioactivity they produce. From a bomb burst high in the air, the chief radioactivity is that of the fission products, the radioactive fragments into which the uranium or plutonium nuclei split, in the A-bomb or in the fission trigger of the H-bomb. The H-bomb may throw much of its fission garbage higher into the upper stratosphere, where it may remain long enough to lose much of its radioactivity. The most potent fission products decay in a few hours or days, but some—strontium-90, for example—continue little diminished in power for many years. The fusion reaction in the H-bomb produces mainly the light radioactive substance tritium, a gas (a form of hydrogen) that mixes in the atmosphere and does not settle back to the ground. The abundant neutrons released in the fusion reaction also react with nitrogen in the air to produce carbon-14, with long-lived radioactivity.

A "clean" bomb is one that produces considerably less than the normal amount of radioactivity in proportion to its explosive power. If we forget the less important tritium, a large H-bomb may be said to be relatively "clean" if it releases only the fission products of its A-bomb trigger—perhaps less than the radioactivity produced by the Hiroshima bomb. But we must still be wary of overconfidence in the word "clean"; it is a relative term.

"Dirty" on the other hand, may mean very dirty indeed. Beyond the simple A-bomb and the less simple H-bomb there is a further combination that may be called the fission-fusion-fission bomb, or the jacketed H-bomb. This is a cheap and dirty big bomb that takes advantage of the fact that, although the common form of uranium-238 does not undergo fission with the relatively slow neutrons available in an A-bomb, it will do so in response to the more energetic neutrons made in the fusion process in an H-bomb. Thus this cheap material may be wrapped around an H-bomb to use up the escaping neutrons. It adds enormously both to the power of the explosion and to the radioactive contamination. In addition to its cheapness, the jacketed H-bomb appears to have other military advantages, for it was adopted and probably figures importantly in arsenals. Its main advantage may be compactness, arising from the fact that fission creates much more energy per atom that fusion does, even though a uranium atom is only about the same size as the light atom lithium involved in fusion. Another consideration is that a jacket, or "tamper," of heavy material is needed in any case to prevent the insides from blowing themselves apart before the chain reaction has had time to develop, and the heavy jacket may as well be something that makes still more energy.

* * *

The cold facts concerning the destructive power of present bombs are well known, but too frequently forgotten. Although the range of nuclear weapons that have been tested extends from under one kiloton to fifty-seven megatons, the most important part of the range for distant strategic attack extends from one-third to ten megatons. The early models of American submarine-based missiles carry one-third-megaton warheads, later models nearer one

284

megaton, with enough accuracy for anticity attack. Most American land-based intercontinental missiles carry about three megatons with greater accuracy so that they can be used against missile sites. Some of the largest missiles, including Soviet missiles, which are fewer and heavier than American missiles, carry more, and some long-range bombers, which are not yet obsolete, carry two ten-megaton bombs.

A one-megaton bomb can cause severe blast damage, sufficient to knock down brick apartment houses, to a distance of five kilometers over an area of seventy square kilometers. The radius for such damage for a ten-megaton explosion is about eleven kilometers, and the area 400 square kilometers — six times as great. This illustrates a "law of diminishing returns" for the size of bombs: ten times the power obliterates only six times the area. The wasted energy of the larger bomb goes into pulverizing the central part beyond complete destruction, though it may be "useful" against underground missile sites, or for caving in blast shelters if these ever became part of the civil defence program.

Blast damage is not the only, and perhaps not even the most important, kind of damage from a large nuclear burst. The radiation from the bomb not only causes radiation sickness and horrible skin burns such as were experienced at Hiroshima and Nagasaki but it also causes fires to break out at quite large distances. The distance to which the sudden burst of heat radiation sets fire to buildings and trees depends on the weather and the dryness of the foliage, but it is something like three times the radius of severe blast damage, or nine times the area, and thus covers an area of well over 3000 square kilometers for a ten-megaton bomb.

No fire department can cope with thousands of fires at once, and in such a situation they spread madly. In some of the incendiary-bomb raids in World War II there developed "fire storms" engulfing large areas. In a fire storm the combined heat of many individual fires makes a strong wind toward the center of the burning city, which fans the flames. When many fires are started at once by the single flash of an H-bomb, the number of casualties per square kilometer by burning or suffocation in the resulting fire storm would probably be almost as high as in the central blast area, for only from the edge of the fire storm would people be able to struggle to safety. Because of the fire storm, one ten-megaton bomb (or about six one-megaton bombs) should suffice to destroy a megalopolis of 3000 square kilometers. There are already so many bombs in the arsenals of the nuclear giants that several times this destructive power can be targeted on each megalopolis, with plenty left over for destroying the smaller cities several times over, too.

FUTURE NUCLEAR WEAPONS

So much for the general principles available and their implementation in existing bombs. Nuclear weapons of the future will continue to be based on fission or fusion as the source of their energy. It is true that other ways of converting matter into energy are known to physicists, the most spectacular being the mutual annihilation of matter and "antimatter." Particles called antiprotons, antineutrons, and antielectrons (positrons) can be made in minute quantities and at great expense in high-energy experimental machines, and when one of these encounters its corresponding normal particle they both disappear, releasing a burst of energy. But the engineering problems of making and storing antimatter in militarily interesting quantities are so absurdly great that the possibility can be safely discounted for the foreseeable future.

It is likely, too, that existing explosives—uranium and plutonium for fission and lithium and heavy hydrogen for fusion—will continue to dominate in weapons. It is in principle possible that man-made elements heavier than plutonium might be used with the slight advantage of having smaller critical mass, but this is not a practical possibility, because it need not mean a much smaller weapon when the detonating device is included, because those heavier elements decay rapidly and thus cannot be stockpiled, and because their production and isolation in more than microscopic quantities is prohibitively expensive. For these reasons the postulated "californium bullet," for example, is no more than confusing fantasy.

Within the limitation of fission and fusion of the usual materials as the only energy sources, variations can be sought that may or may not have military significance. These include greater efficiency in using the nuclear explosives, and the development of very large or very "dirty" bombs, and very compact or relatively "clean" bombs.

The efficiency of existing bombs falls far short of one hundred per cent because the bomb blows itself apart so quickly that many nuclei do not have time to react. Much of the past effort to improve the bomb has been in this direction. The nature of recent testing suggests that the efficiency factor has been pushed about as far as is practicable; the situation is similar to that in automobiles—the current models are new in style but it is hard to discern any real improvement in terms of mileage per gallon.

For some purposes there will be a tendency toward more fusion and less fission, but for the biggest explosions the "dirty" bomb with much fission will probably be with us for a long time. There is no limit to how powerful an H-bomb may be made, nor to how dirty a "dirty" bomb may be made. It is possible that the arsenals of the future will include warheads much more powerful than present bombs. To put this possibility in perspective, one must, however, appreciate that a single large bomb is powerful enough practically to obliterate a large metropolitan area. There is thus no incentive to provide more powerful warheads than those in service, for the sake of destroying cities, or, more precisely, for being prepared to destroy them as part of the nuclear deterrent. But it is conceivable that incentives could be found for destroying still larger areas, such as whole forest regions, so as to ruin a land and deny sustenance to survivors of an all-city attack. During the last period of atmospheric testing the Soviet leaders talked of a one-hundred-megaton bomb, but actually did not go quite that far (fifty-seven megatons was the biggest they tested). The bigger bomb would have been feasible on either side, had this sort of incentive been felt. Such a bomb in appropriate weather would kindle forest fires over a radius of about 150 kilometers. It might also be useful in crushing blast shelters. If such a bomb is not made in the future, this will probably be either because restraining steps have been taken toward disarmament or because of the "law of diminishing returns"; six ten-megaton bombs would ignite as great an area as one dirty one-hundred-megaton bomb, with less world-wide radioactive fallout to react on the attacker.

It is technically possible to go very much further still, in deliberately making a very dirty bomb with the purpose of radioactive destruction of life on an entire hemisphere (northern or southern). In particular, the element cobalt when activated by a burst of neutrons from an H-bomb becomes a singularly powerful radioactive emitter of gamma radiation. The cobalt jacket would be wrapped around a big H-bomb, and there is no definite limit to the possible size of such a "cobalt bomb." Nevil Shute's novel On the Beach, set in Australia, carried a powerful message concerning the threat of nuclear war, but with a gentle euthanasia substituted for the horror of more likely forms of nuclear war and with some artistic license in the way the radioactivity destroyed all life on earth. The two main inaccuracies are that the attacking nation would have had no incentive to enter into a suicide pact with its enemies and that the nature of the atmospheric circulation would have confined the destruction to the northern hemisphere, at least for a longer time. Unless we can imagine an extremely hostile situation between the northern hemisphere as a whole and the southern hemisphere as a whole, we have little reason to worry that any nation will prepare a hemisphere bomb of this sort.

The strange name "doomsday machine" was introduced into nuclear strategy discussions to refer to a hypothetical instrument to obliterate life on the earth at the push of a single button, a sort of reductio ad absurdum of the nuclear arms race. Such an infernal machine is not technically absurd. There is little doubt that it could be constructed—for example by means of a few widely dispersed cobalt bombs. It is of no use to anybody not bent on suicide, unless it be for blackmail by someone who can put on a convincing act of courting suicide, and it is not a serious candidate for future arsenals.

* * *

Less improbable, perhaps, [than the successful substitution of a chemical or electromagnetic "trigger" for the A-bomb presently used as the H-bomb "trigger"] is the eventual design of efficient H-bombs using a plutonium trigger if, indeed, present H-bomb triggers are essentially uranium 235, as is suggested by Sir John Cockroft in the previous chapter. Then, with the rapid development of power reactors in many countries, which are potential sources of military-grade plutonium it would become much easier for those countries to acquire H-bombs.

* * *

In the category of "tactical" nuclear weapons, intended to be used as firepower for ground armies, some fantastic claims have been made about new possibilities, particularly concerning the "neutron bomb" that might slowly kill soldiers by neutron irradiation without doing as much property damage as is normal with nuclear weapons. Here the dream of a really cheap fission-free fusion bomb has been hailed as making possible greatly increased firepower on the battlefield. Aside from the technical implausibility, this enthusiasm seems to be based on a lack of appreciation of the destructive power of even "small" nuclear weapons. They may be "only" about as powerful as the Hiroshima bomb and on down to a tenth or even a hundredth of that power. They have been made compact enough to be shot from large cannon (or presumably to be carried on the backs of saboteurs), but they will probably not be made much smaller. If ever used in more than extremely modest numbers they will make battling armies obsolete and defence of territory equivalent to its devastation. Field commanders are subject to the temptation to use nuclear blasts for special purposes such as creating transportation bottlenecks, but if once they were used in war conditions, escalation would be almost automatic up to the big nuclear weapons that hold the greater interest and terror. To avoid this, if there must be conventional wars at all, it is vitally important that they be restrained to stay below the well-defined line between conventional and nuclear weapons.

About the likely course of the future development of new kinds of nuclear bombs and warheads, as distinct from delivery vehicles, we can say in summary, then, that there seems to be no room for great new surprises, if we shun technical and strategic absurdities. Nuclear weapons of a given power may become slightly more compact, but not much more. The range of power per bomb can be extended, but it cannot be very much extended usefully because present bombs are already so terribly powerful. It is not impossible, though it is unlikely, that the requirement for a fission trigger of an H-bomb can be eliminated to make H-bombs cheaper, but they are already remarkably cheap relative to their destructive power, so that the increased cheapness, if it should materialize, would be important only in hastening proliferation of nuclear weapons among countries not yet possessing them.

MUST THE BOMBS MULTIPLY?

One might be tempted to conclude from this that there is nothing to worry about, that the worst of nuclear weapons have probably been developed, and that we've become accustomed to living with them. The conclusion is far from justified. The world situation that we have been so lucky to live through these last few years is an awfully unsafe one in which no sane race of beings would choose to live if it could help it. Our having been lucky does not mean that we are safe, even though most of us have permitted ourselves to become unaware of the nuclear threat under which we live.

* * *

Up to now, most of the missiles of each of the nuclear giants, the United States and the Soviet Union, have been aimed at the other giant, and the main danger, that of an outbreak of nuclear war between them, has been deterred by the respect each has for the power of the other. This is the apparently stable balance in which we have developed too much confidence. The prospect has been that a war would bring damage almost entirely to the giants and perhaps some of their immediate allies, with some serious local fallout spilling over

288

the borders and with long-range fallout remaining not really very serious for most other countries. Here the most serious threat to the distant countries would be economic dislocation, unless it be some unanticipated world-wide plague. Bad as the prospect has been, it has been one that many of the countries of the world could reasonably view with greater complacency than could the nuclear giants who would bear the brunt of the attacks.

But in the absence of arms control, the moderately good side of even this bad situation cannot last. Even though the *kinds* of nuclear explosives may change very little, the increasing *number* of weapons can make the situation much worse in at least two ways, each of which makes the other more serious. The first is that the weight of explosives used in a prospective war between the nuclear giants will become so enormous that there will be "no place to hide" — that all countries will be disastrously damaged by the fallout. The second is that there will be so many nations equipped with nuclear weapons that the outbreak of nuclear war between some pair of them, possibly triggering one between the nuclear giants, will become very likely.

[The proliferation problem is considered in the next section.]

As matters have recently stood, there appeared to be signs that the total power of the nuclear weapons in the arsenals of the nuclear giants was leveling off, as though each side was becoming content with its possibility of inflicting terrible damage on the other and found it unnecessary to expend resources on a further build-up if the other side did not. The fact that the two opposing arsenals were not equal appeared to be considered relatively unimportant because the smaller was so enormous in its destructive power as to provide adequate deterrence.

Recently a new element has been introduced into the balance — the possibility of providing a partial defence against oncoming ballistic missiles. Although the idea of self-defence sounds innocuous, and an impenetrable defence could provide an entirely different basis for world stability, a merely partially effective defence can curiously be a very upsetting element in this otherwise fairly stable balance. There is no prospect of a completely impervious defence, but the possibility of a partly effective defensive system, based on the "antiballistic missile," or ABM, is at hand for both of the nuclear giants. Both the Soviet Union and, more recently, the United States, have started ABM deployment on a relatively small scale, probably for political more than military reasons. It is to be hoped that the scale will remain small, for a serious offence-defence race — as a new dimension of the arms race — would drastically increase international tension and the nuclear threat.

If, starting with stabilized numbers of intercontinental missiles, one side installs a substantial ABM system, the second side can respond by building more missiles to penetrate the defence and the first side is no safer than before. The interception by ABMs is estimated to be sufficiently inefficient for the cost to the second side of building the additional intercontinental missiles to be less than the cost of the ABM system to the first side. On a cost-effectiveness basis, there is thus no rational reason for the first side to start this step

289

in the competition in the first place. However, military demands are seldom long delayed by cost-effectiveness arguments, and the usual experience is that what can be built will be built. The hope of arms control is to break this trend at some point, but, lacking such artificial restraint, the likelihood is that the initiative in starting ABM deployment will be answered both by more intercontinental missiles and by some ABMs on the second side, to which the first side will respond with more ABMs to try to stop the missiles and more missiles to get past the ABMs, and so forth. Thus, in place of an arms race practically stopped, the ABM can, and probably will, carry a new arms race to entirely new dimensions.

The important point is that this process adds enormously to the numbers of nuclear weapons that would be used in a war between the nuclear giants and implies an amount of fallout that would spare no nation on earth, or at least none in the northern hemisphere.

The ABM possibility is thus a destabilizing factor, an effect arising partly from the uncertainty of performance of the ABMs. The problems of delivering and intercepting nuclear warheads are discussed at greater length in the next chapter. Suffice it to say here that future developments will probably involve several stages of countermeasures, the anti-anti-anti-ballistic missile, or methods to foil penetration aids and then ways to foil these methods, and that the ABMs themselves will have nuclear warheads.

For the types of ABMs that explode in the atmosphere and fairly near the targets they are trying to protect, the explosive power will be limited by the need to avoid damage by the ABM itself to the city being protected. Such close-in ABM bursts are being planned because of the necessity of distinguishing between an intercontinental-missile warhead and its accompanying swarm of light-metal "decoys" by the way they slow down in the atmosphere. Being limited in power, such an ABM must come fairly close to the warhead to destroy it, perhaps within a few hundred meters or so (the size of the fireball). But there will also be ABMs that explode outside the atmosphere far from the defended area. They can be made very powerful, and the X-rays that they emit can be intense enough to damage an oncoming intercontinental missile at a distance of perhaps several miles. The desire to put up such an instantaneous X-ray shield to intercept as much of the swarm of unidentified decoys, including somewhere the warhead itself, as may be aimed at a large metropolitan area provides the incentive for using powerful warheads in the ABMs. Their power will be limited by the instantaneous radiation damage on the ground and people below, from the gamma rays (that make skin burns and leukemia as at Hiroshima), and from heat that starts fires. At heights of hundreds of kilometers, even these limitations permit bursts of tens of megatons, perhaps more powerful than the oncoming intercontinental missiles against which they are deployed. Even though they are exploded above the atmosphere, about half of their radioactive products descend into the atmosphere and contribute to fallout.

Such an ABM "shield" is only an instantaneous flash, so at least one ABM is needed for each oncoming intercontinental missile (since they won't attack in squad formation). An intercontinental attack may be concentrated on a region, so the defence might desire as many of these ABMs in *each* region to

290

be defended as there are intercontinental missiles in the opponent's arsenal. Thus the potential military demands become enormous indeed in this defence-offence race. It seems likely that the cheapness and compactness of a "dirty" bomb will lead to its use in the above-the-atmosphere ABMs. It is conceivable that one day the size of the world's arsenal will be limited only by the available amount of fissionable material, although the limitation is more likely to remain, for the time being, in the cost of the delivery vehicles.

Without an ABM race, the hope remains that such enormous quantities will never be prepared for delivery, in keeping with the tendency for numbers of missiles to taper off toward a constant level. But if the world embarks on stage after stage of a great competition, the demand for actual weapons will be unlimited and the prospect will be of a large part of the available explosive stuff being used in an all-out nuclear war.

Some proponents of ABMs favor them partly in the hope that their deployment would lead to their further improvement, so that they might eventually be able to intercept most of a massive attack. Enigmatically, this would probably only make the situation worse for the noncombatants and no better for the combatants. Without ABMs, an all-out war between the nuclear giants might be over in hours, one or both sides having been beaten into collapse or submission by use of considerably less than total stockpiles. With very efficient ABMs, let us say ninety-nine percent efficient or more as an extreme hypothesis, the war might take years as initial arsenals were first exhausted and then improvised means of delivery were substituted to use more and more of the explosive material that had not been made into weapons in advance. The nuclear giants might be destroyed as before, but in this case would drag the rest of the world down with them by means of fallout.

In summary, increase in number is a more menacing aspect of the future of nuclear weapons than development in kind, though both types of change will make the future more difficult to handle and intensify the threat to civilization. Familiarity has bred contempt, while the world and its statesmen have become inured to "living with the bomb" and fatigued with patient negotiations that have done little more than hide a lack of decision. Yet we have actually lived through only a very few years, too few to be significant as a precedent, of the small end of a nuclear arms race that will become even more overwhelming if rational steps are not soon taken to terminate it and to deflect the efforts of mankind into more constructive channels.

The present extent of nuclear weaponry.   Where are we today? From 1945 to the present, five nations — the United States, Russia, Great Britain, France, and China — successively acquired first A-bombs, then H-bombs. The early A-bombs dropped on Hiroshima and Nagasaki each equalled the explosive power of 20,000 tons of TNT. The largest H-bomb tested to date, by the Russians, is estimated to have had an explosive force equal to 57,000,000 tons of TNT. A large number of warheads exist that are in the 5,000,000-tons-and-up (five megatons and more) size range. As Bloomfield stated, the total arsenals today exceed the explosive power of 50 *billion* tons of TNT, and there is general agreement that the figure is at least this large. The big warheads can be delivered by long-range ballistic missiles (ICBMs), submarine-launched missiles (SLBMs), heavy bombers such as the B-52, and other means. The following table, published in *Newsweek* on November 16, 1970,[3] shows approximate United States

HOW THE NUCLEAR GIANTS SQUARE OFF

UNITED STATES TARGET CAPABILITY		All or most of U.S.S.R.	Parts of U.S.S.R.	Other Warsaw Pact Countries	SOVIET UNION TARGET CAPABILITY		All or most of U.S.A.	Parts of U.S.A.	Other NATO Countries
Weapons	Number				Weapons	Number			
ICBM's	1,054	X		X	ICBM's	1,400+	X		X
Bombers	1,640	X		X	Bombers	250	X		X
Polaris missiles	656	X		X	Polaris-type missiles	208		X	X
Carrier aircraft	600		X	X	Other submarine missiles	420			X
Medium-range missiles	64		X	X	Medium-range missiles	700			X
Tactical fighters	400		X	X	Medium-range aircraft	700			X

Balance of terror: While SALT proceeds, so does the arms race.   Robert Ritter

Copyright Newsweek, Inc., November 16, 1970.

and Russian capacities as of that time. (For figures cast in terms of separately targetable strategic warheads associated with the three long-range delivery systems — ICBMs, submarine missiles, and heavy bombers — see p. 298.)

As for the smaller nuclear weapons, Inglis notes that "the range of nuclear weapons that have been tested extends from under one kiloton,"[3] and later that "[t]hey have been made compact enough to be shot from large cannon (or presumably to be carried on the backs of saboteurs)."[4] What are the implications of these weapons developments? May the existence of these very small "tactical" weapons lead to a temptation to use "just" them, especially when retreating in the face of a heavy ground attack? With what potential consequences?

A Congressional committee has recently noted that a bomb could be carried in a suitcase — for example, by a saboteur or agent taken ashore in a small boat; they added that a bomb with the power of the Hiroshima bomb could be built into a space the size of a high-fi console, or less. How important is this problem with regard to the potentialities for United States-Soviet conflict, or with respect to the five powers that presently possess nuclear weapons? How important does it beome in conjunction with the problem of proliferation of nuclear weapons into the hands of other powers (discussed in the next section)?

The strategy of deterrence. The concepts of strategy associated with mutual possession of nuclear weapons have grown exceedingly complex. Hundreds, perhaps thousands, of men are engaged in thinking through — sometimes with the use of computers and elaborate simulated "games" — the varieties of possibilities inherent in preventing, or carrying on, if prevention fails, atomic wars of various kinds, for various assumed purposes. None of these plans, however, can be based on any past precedent or historical experience, and the assumption that any leader will make "rational" or "predictable" decisions, once the power of the atom has been unleashed, seems a thin thread indeed from which to suspend the fate of mankind.

However, some basic features of United States-Soviet relationships against the background of nuclear weapons seem tolerably clear. The central strategy is one called "deterrence," the notion that the United States must have enough nuclear weapons so that, even if the Russians were to launch a surprise "first-strike" attack, the United States could retaliate by inflicting an unacceptable level of damage on the Russian population and industrial base. Thus, it is reasoned, the Russians will have no possible incentive to launch a first-strike, and since we have no desire to strike first, there will be no nuclear war. Presumably, the Russians reason in the same way, and the two nations thereby achieve what has been referred to as "the delicate balance of terror."

It *is* true, of course, that no nuclear war has occurred, and it may be that this is so because deterrence has "worked." There are, on the other hand, a number of difficulties with this strategy. One basic difficulty, certainly, is that it is founded on the assumption that, if the United States did *not* have enough nuclear weapons to inflict heavy damage, the Russians *would* be seriously tempted to strike first. Of course, the Russians did not strike against the Chinese in the mid-60s, when the Chinese clearly appeared to pose a potential long-term threat to the Russians (a nation of 700 million, denouncing Russia in the most vehement terms, claiming that one million square miles of Russia actually belonged to China, and sharing with Russia the longest border in the world).

The Chinese did not yet possess the capability to deliver a single nuclear weapon, let alone hundreds or thousands of nuclear weapons, against Russia, although they were rapidly moving towards such a capability. Yet the Russians did not launch a preemptive attack. In part, it may be that deterrence becomes a self-fulfilling prophecy—once one acts as though deterrence must be the basis for relationships between two particular countries (and perhaps in the Stalin era, when we first acted as though this were so, there was a strong basis for the action), it is likely to *become* the basis for the relationship, and for the way in which both parties think about it—even if the original cause for behaving that way no longer exists.

A second basic difficulty with the theory is that it is a coherent framework for "scaring oneself to death," a fundamentally paranoid world view. Nobel Peace Prize winner Philip Noel-Baker, writing in the same volume as David Inglis (*Unless Peace Comes*), paints the following picture of the pre-World War I arms race in a section entitled "We Have Been Here Before":[4]

The modern arms race may be said to have begun with the Franco-Prussian War in 1870. In that war, to the astonishment of the military experts, the Prussian conscripts totally and swiftly defeated the long-term professional army of Napoleon III. Napoleon had boasted that his troops were ready for battle down to the last gaiter button. But the discipline, the skill, and the courage of the Prussian conscripts were not inferior to those of the French professionals; while the steel guns with which Krupp had furnished them were notably superior to the iron guns of Schneider.

When that war was over, many governments decided that they must adopt conscription and re-equip their forces with modern arms. Thus the number of men in the national forces of the countries of the world greatly increased; the market for all kinds of military equipment expanded. In the last four decades before World War I, no industry in the world grew so fast as the production of arms, and no other investment held such a glittering prospect of quick and large returns.

Serious efforts to prevent arms races and secure international order can be traced back to the shock of the Franco-Prussian War, which gave some hints of what modern war would be like. But when the nations gathered at

The Hague in 1899, on the initiative of the Czar of Russia, they were diverted from the serious discussion of general disarmament to what is now called "arms control." They produced some "laws of war," intended to preserve a gentlemanly atmosphere in battle. These "laws," prohibiting the use of gas, fire, air bombardment, and merciless attacks by submarines on merchant shipping, did not outlast World War I.

Nevertheless, in the years before 1914 many national leaders tried to resist the pressure for armament expansion. The chief cause of dissension between Germany and Britain was the battleship building programs reinforced by misinformation about the scale of the programs. At the eleventh hour, Britain offered a "naval holiday," but it was refused and everyone agreed that war was inevitable. Here we can identify von Tirpitz as the militarist who won the day despite the opposition of the German Chancellor and other leaders. But that does not exonerate the other militarists, on both sides. For years they had sustained frenzied and untruthful propaganda in support of battleship construction, starting with British construction directed against France in 1893. The competition was given a new twist by a British innovation, the Dreadnought, which rendered obsolete the previously existing battle fleets of both Britain and Germany. Ironically, the battleships played very little part in the war when it came, and there was only one inconclusive engagement between the main fleets.

Noel-Baker probably overstates the inevitability of war resulting from the battleship-building race. But it was certainly a serious contributor to the tension and mistrust between Britain and Germany, and helped enormously to create an atmosphere in which war was highly likely and accommodation extremely difficult. Yet vague ideas of "deterrence" were certainly bound up with the battleship-building program. Even today, concerns about a new "naval construction gap" between ourselves and the Russians were increasingly being voiced in 1971–72.

In the same way, the "deliverable-warhead race" or the "missile race" (recall the cry of "missile gap" that was a powerful issue in John F. Kennedy's 1960 Presidential campaign?) creates a frame of mind in which fear, tension, and suspicion predominate in American assessments of Russian power and Russian motivations. The Russians, in their turn, tend to view us through the same suspicion-tinted glasses. The meaning of "worst" in "worst feasible case" analysis between the United States and Russia today makes the significance of the "Dreadnought" pale in comparison.

"Deterrence" theory leads to questions and conclusions like these:

We: "The Russians are building new SS-9 rockets that can carry a ten-megaton weapon. There is no reason to build such a powerful rocket unless they wish to have the capacity to attack our ICBM missiles in their concrete silos. Such an attack, coming by surprise, might destroy so many of our missiles that the Russians could then say to us "Surrender, or we will launch a further attack, this time directed at your cities, since we know you no longer have the capacity to make a retaliatory response." Our deterrent capacity would be destroyed, and we would have to surrender. Surely the Russians would not spend the money to acquire a capacity of this kind, a first-strike capacity, unless they intended to use it, once it was fully developed. Therefore, we must counter their SS-9s: we must build ABMs, with which we can knock down many of the rockets, so that our destructive capacity remains sufficient to deter them even if a large number of individual rocket installations are destroyed."

They: "The Americans are acquiring a capacity to knock down our incoming rockets. It is true that these ABMs, at present, are only deployed around offensive missile complexes; but what if sometime in the coming years they take advantage of their fully developed ABM technology and numerous existing ABMs to quickly deploy ABMs around their cities?

"Then they might well be in a position where they could launch a first-strike against us, knowing that we could not effectively retaliate against their population centers, because their ABMs would knock down our attacking rockets. Their desire to be able to make ever more terrible threats seems to be confirmed, moreover, by the fact that they are increasing the already enormous number of their offensive weapons by converting them to "MIRVs" (multiple independently targeted re-entry vehicles). Therefore, to assure our safety against such a strategy, we must build enough additional rockets so that we are certain of being able to overwhelm any additional ABM defense they might put in operation, by getting many rockets through that defense even though others are knocked down. In this way, we will preserve our present deterrent capacity."

We: "The Russians are building yet more rockets. They must be truly intent on being able to destroy our retaliatory capability in a sudden first strike. We must therefore build more ABMs to defend our missile sites, and hasten the deployment of MIRV on both submarine and land-based missiles.

"Also, the Chinese are acquiring a small nuclear-rocket capability. Perhaps we should take advantage of our ABM technology at least to deploy ABMs around Washington, D.C., so that our decision-making center would have some protection against the kind of limited nuclear blackmail that the Chinese might have the capacity to carry out."

They: "The Americans are building still more ABMs and MIRVs. Also, they are already talking about placing ABMs around their most important population center. Perhaps if their leaders know they will be saved, they will have much less compunction about suffering even very large losses elsewhere. This talk about fear of Chinese rockets seems nonsensical, and is probably just a cover. We must build still more rockets to remain secure in our ability to deter. And we must consider retargeting several scores of additional missiles on Washington, D.C., to overwhelm any possible defense, so that their ABM does not give them a sense of safety and unlimited power. Also, we perhaps should place ABMs around our own capital, lest their far right-wing generals be tempted to an insane act."

We: "The Russians continue to build more rockets. Their terrible intentions become ever clearer. Lest the neo-Stalinists and hard-line military within their government be tempted to some insane act, we had better increase both ABM and MIRV. Also, we should consider further measures, such as mounting some of our ICBMs, for safety, on railroad cars that shuttle back and forth in a random pattern that cannot be used as a fixed target, and equipping our bombers with short or medium-range missiles instead of conventional H-bombs."

Etc., etc.

Much of this dialogue has already occurred, and the process of developing ABM and MIRV is advancing (the United States is already deploying MIRV, and a limited ABM defense covering six ICBM complexes has been approved). Many of the potential consequences are discussed in Inglis' article.

In the last chapter of the book, we shall discuss in some detail various means by which it might be possible to break out of this mutually fear-enhancing system of perception, action, and reaction.

It is sometimes asked whether deterrence is fully "credible" in this sense: once an attack has been launched, "deterrence" has failed. Knowing that the destruction of one's own country is inevitable in a few minutes, or has already occurred, what would be the reason to launch a return attack on the enemy territory and population? It would be "the dead taking revenge from the grave." Therefore, the reasoning goes, would such a return attack ever, in fact, be launched? One American political scientist advanced the notion that the United States should *not* respond to a Russian first strike, on the grounds that

Russia would be the only country with the resources necessary to rebuild the decimated United States society. Hopefully, there is a Russian equivalent of this American thinker.

However, it seems to me that this is *not* one of the weaknesses of the "deterrence" notion—it would almost certainly work as it is supposed to, horrible though the results would be. Rational calculation about the "purpose to be served" would be unlikely in the extreme, with the wife and children, the friends, the country, and all the life prospects of the decision makers lying dead and in ruins. Role conception, ideology, and a fierce hatred born out of the utter frustration

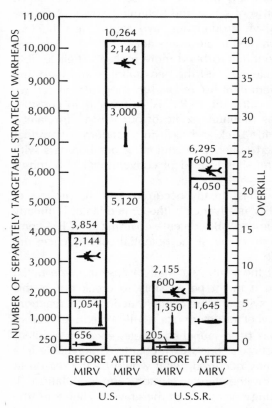

Strategic balance between the U.S. and the U.S.S.R. is shown at left in terms of the numbers of separately targetable strategic nuclear warheads already deployed and the numbers projected for 1975 if present plans to deploy multiple independently targeted reentry vehicles (MIRV's) go into effect. The symbols indicate the means of delivery; the numbers give the actual total of deliverable warheads in each category. The scale at right suggests the enormous "overkill" capacity possessed by each side in either circumstance; it is calibrated in units of 250—a highly conservative estimate of the number of nuclear warheads required to devastate the 50 largest cities on each side. The chart includes only strategic (that is, intercontinental) nuclear warheads, not tactical or intermediate-range nuclear weapons.

From "The Limitation of Strategic Arms," by G. W. Rathjens and G. E. Kistiakowsky. Copyright © 1970, by Scientific American Inc. All rights reserved.

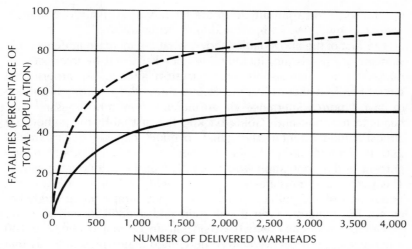

Futility of seeking to mitigate the consequences of a full-scale nuclear exchange between the two superpowers by negotiating modest reductions in strategic-force levels or by resorting to moderately effective "damage-limiting" measures is illustrated in this graph, in which the expected fatalities in the U.S.S.R. are plotted as a function of the number of U.S. megaton-range warheads delivered. The solid curve indicates the immediate, easily calculable fatalities; the shading represents the face that the total fatalities would probably be much larger. In either case, because of the very large number of deployed weapons, the effects of small changes in the total of delivered weapons would be negligible. The expected effects of a Russian attack against the U.S. would be similar.

From "The Limitation of Strategic Arms," by G. W. Rathjens and G. B. Kistiakowshy. Copyright 1970, by Scientific American Inc. All rights reserved.

of every ongoing activity and personal relationship in the decision maker's life would, almost certainly, lead to a return attack for a "purpose" long served in human societies under such circumstances: revenge. One does not picture the bank guard, lying mortally wounded after a robbery, foregoing the chance to get off a last shot at the fleeing robber because he knows his own life is already ended. One does not picture the father, left alone for five minutes with his daughter's confessed rapist-murderer, foregoing violence because he knows his daughter is already dead and cannot be brought back to life.

Increasing risks of the arms race. For further perspective on the technical background and results of deterrence-oriented weapons development, consider the two foregoing tables from "The Limitation of Strategic Arms," an article in the January 1970 issue of *Scientific American* by G. W. Rathjens and G. B. Kistiakowsky.[5]

The first of the above tables shows what the increase in deliverable strategic warheads (not including warheads carried by intermediate-range missiles, fighter-bombers or tactical aircraft, or carrier-based aircraft) will be after MIRV; the second shows the absurdity of striving to have "more" deterrence via an increase from four thousand warheads to ten thousand. Going back to the first table, the authors are almost certainly right in saying that "overkill" capacity begins around 250 deliverable warheads, if at that point an estimated twenty to forty percent of the population would be killed, as the second table shows. This percentage translates into *forty to eighty million people* out of a population of 200 million; beyond that, any further threat surely becomes meaningless. Even if one estimated overkill to start at 1,000 deliverable warheads (which would kill an estimated eighty to 140 million people in each country) the United States presently has that capacity even if only *one out of four* of her strategic weapons got through. All that the building of additional warheads accomplishes, for either side, is the creation of an atmosphere of fear and suspicion in which use of the weapons at some time appears to be made *more* likely than it would be if no further weapons were built.

Perhaps the most basic problem with deterrence is that it may, conceivably, work for ten or twenty-five years, or more, but is most unlikely to work over the long term. *What mankind must have, in the face of these weapons of annihilation, is a method of peacekeeping that will work for centuries, for millennia, not just for years or decades.* Lincoln Bloomfield, in *Disarmament and Arms Control*, notes the following grim estimates:[6]

A team of researchers from the RAND Corporation undertook in 1964 an unusual exercise in predicting the future, using a so-called Delphi Method of polling experts as to what certain future developments might be anticipated, and when. One key question had to do with the predicted probability of another major war. On the basis of the median answers, experts believed there was a 10 percent likelihood of its happening within ten years and a 25 percent probability in 25 years. Even more striking were the predicted ways in which such a major war might break out. Eleven percent believed that it might happen by inadvertence, that is, by accident. Only 7 percent predicted a premeditated surprise attack at a time when there was no major crisis. Once a limited war started, 37 percent foresaw the probability of escalation. And — most sobering, given the nature of our world — 45 percent believed war would come, if it came, through escalation of an ongoing political crisis.

300

Even more sobering, perhaps, is the historian Arthur Schlesinger's account of the same subject in *1,000 Days*. President Kennedy, early in his term of office, said that he believed the chances of a nuclear holocaust occurring sometime in the sixties to be about fifty–fifty. Certainly it came very close to happening during the Cuban missile crisis. One such crisis per decade, even one every two or three decades, is an intolerable risk for the human race. The unhappy suggestion has been made that humanity, under the present strategic thinking, is like a tightrope walker who is asked to perform — without ever falling off — not just for minutes or hours, but on through the centuries.

There are, moreover, advocates of strategic theories whose long-run implications are even more disturbing than those of deterrence. Consider the following *New York Times* editorial, which appeared on November 1, 1970, the day before resumption of the current United States-Russian strategic arms limitation talks.[7]

NEW NUCLEAR SPIRAL

Strategic theories that only recently were thought discredited and that would require a tremendous further missile build-up seem to be reviving in Washington. The stimulus comes from a high-level nuclear study, coupled with pessimism over the strategic arms limitation talks (SALT) with Russia, which resume in Helsinki tomorrow.

A review of the nation's war plans by a National Security Council panel evidently has challenged the concept of deterrence which has guided American nuclear strategy for most of the past decade. The study suggests that a force capable of responding to a Russian "first strike" by retaliating against Soviet cities may no longer be a sufficient deterrent; it sees need for a defensive "counterforce" capable of destroying Soviet intercontinental missiles in their silos.

The catch is that a counterforce capability for defense could also be used offensively in a first strike against the Soviet Union. Any attempt by the United States to achieve such a capability would be less likely to restore American superiority than to set off another action-reaction spiral in the missile race.

The counterforce issue was first raised publicly in President Nixon's State of the World message last February. "Should a President," it asked, "in the event of a nuclear attack, be left with the single option of ordering the mass destruction of enemy civilians, in the face of the certainty that it would be followed by the mass slaughter of Americans?"

The implication of this question is that the United States should build a new invulnerable missile force — one that could destroy any ICBMs Russia held in reserve if it attempted a first strike at American land-based missiles and bombers. Presumably a plan of that scope would require highly accurate

MIRV multiple warheads installed in a new underwater long-range missile system (ULMS) — huge new submarines capable of firing ICBMs.

* * *

The fallacies in this scenario are many. A Soviet first strike against American land-based missiles and bombers, even in the unlikely event that it could succeed, would be deterred by invulnerable Polaris and Poseidon submarines. Similarly, an American counterforce capability, assuming it could be built, would be unable to destroy Russia's missile submarines.

The fundamental flaw in the whole argument lies in the theory that deterrence requires capability to destroy a high percentage of Soviet industry and population in a retaliatory attack on hundreds of Soviet population centers. The reality is that the possibility of losing even a dozen cities would deter a Soviet first-strike attempt — or an American one.

Secretary Laird has asserted that the United States will have to make a start on ULMS in twelve months, if a SALT agreement is not in sight by then. Even now plans for the new defense budget reportedly call for a substantial increase in funds for ULMS development. Yet there is no evidence that anti-submarine warfare techniques are in sight that could neutralize Polaris subs in this decade or even the next.

The United States has not been standing still while Soviet missile deployment catches up and passes ours. Rather, both sides have been pushing ahead with their chosen means of missile expansion: Russia with its giant SS-9 ICBMs and the United States with MIRV and the Safeguard ABM. There is vast overkill on both sides, but the new spiral in the arms race goes on — perhaps because both nations seek to bargain from strength in the SALT talks.

Instead of halting the missile race, SALT may very well stimulate it further, now that agreement appears unlikely within the next year. Only an immediate moratorium on MIRV testing and the deployment of MIRV, ABM and SS-9 missiles can preserve the present nuclear balance and the unique opportunity it presents to achieve a lasting freeze.

Future developments in nuclear weapons. We have discussed where we are today, which is sobering enough. But where will we be, ten or twenty years from now, if present technical developments continue? As far as the United States and Soviet Union are concerned, planning is already going forward on new "generations" of military hardware. Some of this hardware is probably basically stabilizing — given the present strategic postulates — and already operative. The developments now operative include early-warning "spy" satellites, which increase confidence that a surprise attack would be forewarned (see the discussion of these satellites, pages 364–65), and "BMEWS," the ballistic missile early warning system of the United States, which would give sufficient warning of an approaching missile attack over

302

the North Pole region to allow us to launch our ICBMs toward their targets before the attacking missiles could strike.

Given the BMEWS, the argument for the ABM becomes, "but you don't want our *only* option to be that of launching an attack against the Russians before their missiles hit." Strategically speaking, of course, one answer to this is that *if* an attack were ever launched, it would consist of enough missiles to overwhelm the protective shield of ABMs. But if deterrence theory "works" at all, an attack *never* would be launched, because the Russians know that BMEWS would warn of it and allow our missiles to be launched a few minutes before the silos were hit. A better way of increasing our options than ABM, it has been suggested, would be to build into our ICBMs a mechanism that could allow them to be diverted or disarmed after launch, but this proposal is countered by the possibility that the Russians could also trigger such a "disarm" mechanism. An even more cogent answer to ABM, perhaps, is that we *already have* the option of relying on our Polaris submarine and strategic bomber force: no attack presently conceivable could simultaneously threaten all three strategic systems. Hence we would not "have" to launch the ICBMs immediately.

The Soviets also have developed a "FOBS" (fractional orbital bombardment system), which is a missile that can be put into orbit and then called down to a target. This system could attack via the South Pole, and thus evade BMEWS detection. However, FOBS is expensive and relatively inaccurate, and could probably be detected by United States "spy" satellites in any event.

Submarines do not presently have a sufficient combination of accuracy and size in their missiles to pose a first-strike threat. If the Russians had such a submarine force, however, it could probably evade present forms of detection. There might be little or no time left to launch ICBMs, in the face of such an attack, and the present arguments for ABM, MIRV and other developments would presumably intensify several-fold. (Such arguments would still, however, ignore the protection given by Polaris and by the strategic bomber force, which would certainly be put on some form of airborne alert if such a Russian threat developed.) *Turn this situation around, then, and consider the probable Russian reaction to the "ULMS" development described by the New York Times editorial.*

Beyond the "thin" Safeguard ABM system being developed to protect missiles in their silos, a whole series of possible "defensive" missile systems are under study. These systems, for location on land and sea and in the air, begin with various versions of Sentinel, which approaches a so-called "thick" ABM defense to protect populated areas or cities. They include anti-ballistic missiles designed to be carried on submarines or aircraft, or placed on "Texas tower"-type ocean platforms; some ICBMs used in a dual or alternate ABM role; satellite-based interceptors that would knock down ICBMs by direct collision; land or ocean-based anti-satellite missiles; and defensive missiles that would protect against submarine-launched ballistic missiles (SLBMs) instead of against the long-range ICBMs.

Needless to say, the Russian response to these developments would almost certainly be to build more missiles as well as to undertake parallel developments of their own; and our response to their developments would, similarly, entail building more missiles. What seems likely is that, after expenditure of $100–$200 billion apiece on these developments over the 1970s, each side would find itself by the end of the decade with twenty to thirty thousand deliverable strategic warheads — roughly one for every seven to ten thousand of the other's population, *amounting to perhaps 500–750 separate warheads allocable to a city the size of Chicago or Leningrad* — and less security than it has now. (After MIRV, the United States will already be able to allocate some 250 warheads to Leningrad, on a pro rata basis. At present, about *100* warheads could be targeted on Leningrad, and the same number of Soviet warheads on a city the size of New York. Of course, if one decided to concentrate on certain targets, rather than allocating warheads to population on a pro rata basis, the number allocated to Leningrad or New York even now could be two or three hundred.)

Defense planners were developing these visions of future technologies in the heyday of the Johnson administration. The implications of these systems are frightening enough, but perhaps not as disturbing as the economic and institutional pressures that lead to decision making in favor of such weapons developments. Presumably, rational engineers and executives, operating within the framework of what President Eisenhower dubbed "the military-industrial complex," find themselves eagerly pushing to design and build exotic weapons systems that are clearly unnecessary; indeed, that are security-decreasing or strategically destabilizing. How might these economic and institutional pressures be effectively counterbalanced?

Another kind of future development, qualitative rather than quanti-

304

tative, is suggested by the following excerpt from a C. L. Sulzberger column in the *New York Times* of November 15, 1970[8] (Sulzberger is probably the most politically conservative of the Times' columnists):

> . . . Limited commitments to conventional defense are seen as increasingly outmoded, and yet total warfare is a dreadful absurdity that cannot be contemplated except as the ultimate deterrent only a superpower can afford to have and no one can afford to use.

* * *

> Research now proceeds in purely fission warheads whose explosive potential can be reckoned in tons, not kilotons, and is comparable to large conventional bombs. Their short-lived radiation effects could destroy an enemy's troops without causing unacceptable damage in cities or other areas.

* * *

> The argument is that democratic societies can no longer limit themselves to weapons known to be outmoded but must find new arms whose power is not wholly unrestricted, even to the extent of the so-called tactical A-bombs in today's arsenals. There appears to be no other middle road between supineness and suicide.

What are the problems posed by such possible technical developments and their attendant reasoning? Would the use of "only" a one-fiftieth kiloton nuclear artillery shell be equivalent to the use of twenty tons of high-explosive shells in all relevant ways? Consider again Inglis' discussion of present tactical nuclear weapons (pages 282–84).

Decision making and nuclear weapons. A major problem with nuclear weapons, apart from the weapons themselves, is that of the processes by which the decision to use or not to use them will be made. Consider the following viewpoint.[9]

> . . . Anatol Rapoport has argued that the main actors in the drama of human conflicts are no longer individuals but systems, superorganisms in which human beings play roughly the same role that the cell plays in the body. He calls these organisms *Stati Belligerens* — war-waging states. The most developed of these are Russia and the United States. These states are vast bureaucratic complexes with their own information receptors, data-processing centers, decision rules, communication networks, memory systems and effectors. To these mechanical leviathans, private human passions are totally irrelevant.

Is the operation of the "military-industrial complex" one respect in which these views have substance? What of the process by which a President would decide which Russian targets to respond against if

305

there were a Russian nuclear attack on a particular group of United States military targets? Would this decision be made, most likely, through on-the-spot choice, or would the President simply activate part of an existing computer program?

But is the description of *"Stati Belligerens"* perhaps sharply overstated? Consider the roles played by individual leaders in the initiation of World War II and in the resolution of the Cuban missile crisis, described in Chapter 5. Consider also the function of "Ex Comm" in the Cuban missile crisis. Are there ways in which leaders can increase their personal freedom of action, and decrease their dependence on particular institutional or bureaucratic mechanisms? Consider the significance of multiple information-gathering agencies: the CIA, military intelligence (several independently operating organizations), Congressional fact-finding through committee staffs, and the working press. The foregoing description of an all-powerful state would be more likely to be true in a society that had only one centralized information-gathering agency. Consider also the significance of multiple centers of policy-analysis and recommendation—the State Department, the National Security Council (Henry Kissinger's group), the Senate Foreign Relations Committee, the *New York Times*—as compared to the case of complete centralization. Might it be most accurate, in response to the description of the *"Stati Belligerens,"* to say that there are, at least in the United States, institutional structures for many purposes (especially for those functions that are most closely related to war-making decisions) that are redundant, mutually competitive, and mutually balancing? This balance and competition then tends to *preserve* the final decision-making options of the leadership. However, there are certain areas (especially those more remote from war-making, like the construction of weapons systems, as well as those for ultimately implementing a decision, like the probably detailed "response" plan for retaliation against each of the possible size-levels and target-combinations of an enemy nuclear attack) where the balancing or competing institutions have tended to be weak or nonexistent. The basis strategy of "balance" or "competition" suggests ways of reducing the problems posed by the "military-industrial complex." For example, there might be established an independent or competing means for evaluating proposed weapons and the need for them. Or, what of establishing a private company whose *sole* function would be proving to the government that it *didn't* need weapons, and taking as its profit a small percentage of the money saved?

306

Of course, even if all these balances were operative in the United States, the presence or absence of balancing institutions for all of these processes — intelligence, policy-making, weapons-building — in *other* societies looms as a most significant question.

Proliferation of Nuclear Weapons

But the very worst kind of development that can be foreseen, bad as the others are, is the proliferation of nuclear weapons into the hands of additional countries. In "The Perils of Nuclear Proliferation," another article in *Unless Peace Comes*, the late Sir John Cockroft, a Nobel prizewinner in physics and former director of Britain's Atomic Energy Research Establishment at Harwell, writes of the prospects for additional countries developing A-bombs made of either plutonium or uranium-235 (which is also the substance used as the "trigger" for an H-bomb). Uranium-235 can only be produced, at present, by a relatively expensive diffusion plant or centrifuge plant, but plutonium for the A-bomb can be acquired a good deal more easily, as Cockroft describes.[10]

PLUTONIUM FROM POWER REACTORS

Plutonium is an essential by-product of nuclear reactors, whatever the purpose for which the latter are built. The element is formed by the absorption of neutrons in the abundant isotope uranium-238. The plutonium production from low-power research reactors is usually negligible. With the rapid growth in electricity generation from large nuclear reactors, several countries, in addition to the five already possessing nuclear weapons, are acquiring a significant potential for plutonium production.

* * *

The potential annual production of plutonium by different countries can be estimated from data on the reactors of member nations published by the International Atomic Energy Agency; these estimates are given in the table below. The table shows the approximate potential plutonium production from power reactors in operation at the end of 1966 in countries not yet possessing nuclear weapons, and the additional potential production from power reactors known to be under construction at that time and due to start up in

307

the period 1968–71. From the table it appears that, by 1971, each of seven nations not already possessing nuclear weapons will have the potential to produce more than 100 kilograms of plutonium per year: Canada, the Federal Republic of Germany, India, Italy, Japan, Spain, and Sweden.

ESTIMATED PLUTONIUM IN KILOGRAMS PER YEAR

COUNTRY	FROM REACTORS IN OPERATION IN 1967	FROM POWER REACTORS UNDER CONSTRUCTION
Belgium	2	—
Canada	150	500
Czechoslovakia	—	75
Germany (Federal Republic)	75	160
India	10	180
Israel	5	—
Italy	160	—
Japan	80	220
Netherlands	—	10
Pakistan	—	60
Spain	—	120
Sweden	5	120
Switzerland	—	70

No figure for the mass of plutonium needed to make a bomb has been officially released, but the French physicist Bertrand Goldschmidt has published seven kilograms as a minimum figure.

It is well known that to be useful for military purposes the plutonium must not contain too high a proportion of plutonium-240. This isotope is formed in a reactor by neutron capture in plutonium-239. In other words, if newly formed plutonium-239 is left for a long time in a reactor it will tend to be degraded, as far as military application is concerned. For the production of military-grade plutonium the fuel elements must be extracted from the reactor before their useful life for power production has expired. This inevitably requires that the uranium throughput in the reactor is increased.

One hundred million dollars will buy reactor capacity adequate for the production of plutonium for several bombs a year, and if that is linked with economic power production, the net cost of the plutonium will be arbitrarily small, dependent on the value assigned to the electricity. An assured supply of uranium not subject to international safeguards against military use is required.

The plutonium has to be separated from the uranium in the reactor fuel rods, in a chemical separation plant of some complexity. These plants exist in the United States, the Soviet Union, Britain, and France—and also at Trombay in India and at Mol in Belgium, the latter being the Eurochemic plant, a joint project of thirteen European countries. The Indian plant is reported to have cost about $8 million and the Eurochemic plant about $36 million.

THE PRICE OF NUCLEAR FORCES

The possession of military-grade plutonium is, however, only a first step in the bomb-making process. The plutonium has to be assembled with an isotopic or other source of neutrons to initiate the chain reaction, and surrounded with high-explosive charges fired by very sophisticated electronic equipment and with built-in safeguards to prevent accidental explosions. The whole assembly will then have to be tested, and if the country concerned has adhered to the partial test-ban treaty, this can only be carried out underground, at not negligible additional expense. All of this is very costly, judging by the experience of the existing "nuclear powers," and the minimum expenditure, including a substantial outlay on a nuclear weapons establishment, might well be at least $300 million. Even greater sums are involved if uranium-235 is also to be manufactured and H-bombs are to be assembled and tested. The cost of the French diffusion plant was of the order of $1 billion.

Nuclear bombs are, of course, of no use without means of delivery. The British V-bombers built for this purpose are said to have cost about $1,400,000 [sic: $1,400,000,000] and are becoming obsolescent. Britain is therefore having to build a small fleet of Polaris submarines, at a comparable cost. The French are going through the same sequence of building obsolescent bombers and new missile-carrying submarines at a similar level of prices. Nations acquiring nuclear bombs for the first time would probably follow the example of France and use bombers, in spite of the high degree of vulnerability to antiaircraft weapons.

The cost of a nuclear weapons program is primarily in the capital cost of providing the facilities for their development, production, and delivery: the cost of the weapons establishment, the cost of the plutonium separation plant, and the cost of the bombers or other delivery systems. In addition to these there will be the operating cost of the establishments for research and weapons development; the cost of the proving tests; the operating cost of the air force or rocket force. Compared with all these additional costs the cost of making plutonium itself is rather trivial, especially if it is linked with the production of economically useful electricity. The Institute of Strategic Studies, London, has estimated that the cost to Britain of the nuclear strategic forces was of the order of £100 million ($280 million) per year, in 1966–1967.

Any nation aiming at more than a token show of nuclear strength probably has to be prepared to spend at a comparable rate. It might be possible, at much less cost, to stage the test of a primitive bomb, in an attempt to create an illusion of nuclear armament, but to try to bluff about nuclear weapons while lacking a militarily significant delivery system could be an extremely dangerous policy.

Some indication of the cost of producing additional nuclear weapons once they have been developed is given by the U.S. Atomic Energy Commission's estimate of the cost of nuclear explosives that could be provided for a "Plowshare" program — that is, in the suggested use of nuclear weapons for peaceful engineering works.

There have been suggestions about possible "cut-price" nuclear weapons systems, and in particular about radiological weapons. Nuclear bombs inevitably produce radioactive fission products, and bombs of more than one megaton could produce lethal radioactive contamination over an area of hundreds of square kilometers. By analogy, radiological weapons would carry not nuclear explosive but concentrated radioactive material for dispersal over a target area, to render it uninhabitable for a short or long period. The only comparatively cheap source of highly radioactive material is the waste fission products from a nuclear reactor.

There would seem to be no military advantage in dispersing radioactive fission products derived from such a source rather than by dropping nuclear bombs. The problems of shielding the radiation of the fission products in aircraft, or in rockets before launching, would be formidable. They can therefore be neglected as potential weapons.

PROLIFERATION AND NONPROLIFERATION

Unfortunately there are many countries in the world that could afford to develop nuclear weapons and minimal delivery systems, particularly if they became convinced that national security depended upon doing so and if they believed that they could economize in other military expenditure. Although competent scientific manpower is required and the relevant engineering is not trivial (especially for the production of uranium-235), there are no "secrets" inaccessible to an industrial nation prepared to carry out the necessary research and development.

To speculate about which nations might seek to acquire nuclear weapons during the next few decades is somewhat invidious and must depend on many political and economic assumptions. Alignments of nations in alliances and in conflicts plainly exert restraining or provocative influences. From a global viewpoint, the chief cause for anxiety is the likelihood of a chain reaction in which the acquisition of nuclear weapons by one new country would provoke other nations to follow suit. For example, if three nations made nuclear weapons for the first time in the 1970s, ten might do so in the 1980s and thirty in the 1990s.

The chance of nuclear war breaking out, and possibly engulfing a large part of the world, must inevitably increase with the number of nations possessing nuclear weapons. The risk is aggravated by the suspicion that smaller countries acquiring nuclear weapons would be unlikely to develop the sophisticated command and control systems of the kind possessed by the United

States, the Soviet Union, and Britain. These systems are strongly biased against the possible delivery and detonation of the bombs as a result of false information, unauthorized action, or an engineering fault. The lack of such systems would greatly increase the risk of nuclear war by accident. Another important factor is the likelihood that some nations acquiring nuclear weapons would have a less responsible form of government, or be susceptible to revolutions that might bring reckless men to power. In that connection the use of nuclear weapons in civil war cannot be entirely excluded.

We have several examples of powers that are mutually hostile at present, for example Israel and Egypt and, to a lesser extent, Pakistan and India. The tensions that have been generated in the past would be enormously increased if they had the possibility of dropping only a few nuclear bombs on one another.

There are also strong economic arguments against the development of nuclear weapons by underdeveloped countries while their standards of living are so low. They need the whole of their scientific and technological effort for the development of their economy rather than devoting a large proportion to nuclear weapons programs.

Looking ahead even further, Bloomfield, in *Disarmament and Arms Control,* notes that:[11]

It takes only 5 to 10 kilograms of plutonium to make an A-bomb. To make 5,000 to 7,000 bombs a year, one needs 25,000 to 70,000 kilograms of plutonium. That is what civil reactors in some 40 countries will [collectively] be producing annually by 1980. A one percent diversion could yield 50 to 70 bombs a year. This means that unless the plutonium output is placed under inter-national safeguards, at least one-third of the countries of the world could possess their own nuclear arsenals in less than 15 years. Nuclear power may well make the desert bloom. But a large desalinization plant capable of delivering 100,000 megawatts of power could also produce, during a single day of operation, enough plutonium for 16 fission bombs.

John Cockroft names seven countries that might have a substantial capability for producing a plutonium bomb by 1971. Bloomfield names seven that had the technological capacity in 1968 or were then close to having it, and nine more who would have the capacity within "the years immediately ahead." James Dougherty, an American arms-control expert, writing in the July 1964 issue of *Current History,* listed eleven countries that had the capacity "to produce some Hiroshima-type bombs within this decade, if they should prove determined to do so."[12] The three lists may be compared:

311

COCKROFT	BLOOMFIELD	DOUGHERTY
Canada	Canada	Canada
Germany	Germany	Germany
India	India	India
Italy	Italy	Italy
Japan	Japan	Japan
Spain	—	—
Sweden	Sweden	Sweden
—	Australia	—
—	Belgium	Belgium
—	Brazil	—
—	Czechoslovakia	Czechoslovakia
—	East Germany	East Germany
—	Israel	Israel
—	The Netherlands	—
—	Poland	—
—	Switzerland	Switzerland
—	United Arab Republic	—

Six countries are on all the lists, and five more are on two of the lists. Even some countries not named on any of the three lists probably should be regarded as candidates for the "nuclear club" by 1980— South Africa is an example. And, as Bloomfield points out, by the 1980s the "club" may be open to forty countries or more.

In addition to the basic possibilities for proliferation, the miniaturization of nuclear weapons makes it increasingly possible to manufacture and use them without the development of complex delivery systems—particularly if a country is deliberately willing to run some significant risk of unauthorized or accidental triggering in order to acquire the supposed prestige of being a "nuclear power." For example, agents might carry a suitcase-size bomb into a potential enemy city, and there await instructions that might come at a time of crisis or warfare between the two powers. Bloomfield notes that one of the elements that "could upset the delicate balance of terror" is "a continued refinement of nuclear weaponry which would make it both cheaper and more transportable, and perhaps even put it within reach of malefactors down to the level of the underworld."[13]

A series of multilateral treaties may have bought some time for mankind to deal with the proliferation problem. They are discussed on page 360. There has also been a series of important bilateral agreements, under which countries that have received nuclear fuel for use in power reactors have agreed to a system of international inspection and accountability to prevent the diversion of reactor by-products to nuclear weapon construction. Not all reactors are subject to these safeguards, however, and there is the further possibility that a state possessing a reactor will obtain *additional* uranium from internal deposits or from another source (such as South Africa or China) for which it does not have to account. The reactor fuel, uranium-238, is not itself a bomb-making material like uranium-235, but produces weapons-grade plutonium-239 in the reactor. Uranium-238 exists in deposits in numerous countries besides those that have already built the bomb: The Congo, Canada, South Africa, Rumania, Australia, Burma, Ceylon, India, Japan, Portugal, Germany, Malagasy Republic, Chile, and a dozen more.

Biological and Other Mass-Destruction Weapons

Nuclear weapons are not, unfortunately, the only existing weapons of mass destruction. Perhaps just as important and dangerous, although much less publicized, are the weapons of "CBW," or "chemical-biological warfare."

A summary of present biological weapons. The biological weapons, especially, pose enormous dangers for human survival over the coming decades. A table from a recent United Nations report, *Chemical and Bacteriological (Biological) Weapons and the Effects of Their Possible Use,* prepared in mid-1969, shows some of the chief biological weapons and their potential effects (see pages 314–15).[14]

"Infectivity," of course, is an index of how much of the biological agent must be inhaled or ingested, on the average, for a human being to come down with the disease.

"Transmissibility" is the degree to which the disease can be passed from person to person. High transmissibility may not be a major virtue to the potential user of the weapon, especially if his own territory is adjacent to the country that he has attacked, and if he is uncertain about the effectiveness or possibility of mass vaccination of his own population. If the user wants "zero" transmissibility, he may turn to the biological toxins — such as the virulent food-poisoning chemical pro-

SOME BIOLOGICAL AGENTS THAT MAY BE USED TO ATTACK MAN

DISEASE	INFECTIVITY	TRANSMISSI-BILITY	INCUBATION PERIOD	DURATION OF ILLNESS	MORTALITY	ANTIBIOTIC THERAPY	VACCINATION
Viral							
Chikungunya fever	Probably high	None	2–6 d	2 weeks – a few months	Very low (<1%)	None	None
Dengue fever	High	None	5–8 d	a few days to weeks	Very low (1%)	None	None
Eastern equine encephalitis	High	None	5–15 d	1–3 weeks	High (>60%)	None	Under development
Tick-borne encephalitis	High	None	1–2 weeks	1 week to a few months	Variable up to 30%	None	Under development
Venezuelan equine encephalitis	High	None	2–5 days	3–10 days	Low (<1%)	None	Under development
Influenza	High	High	1–3 days	3–10 days	Usually low, except for complicated cases	None	Available
Yellow fever	High	None	3–6 days	1–2 weeks	High (up to 40%)	None	Available
Smallpox	High	High	7–16 days	12–24 days	Variable but usually high (up to 30%)	None	Available
Rickettsial							
Q-fever	High	none or negligible	10–21 days (sometimes shorter)	1–3 weeks	Low (usually <1%)	Effective	Under development
Psittacosis	High	Moderately high	4–15 days	1 –several weeks	Moderately high	Effective	None
Rocky Mountain spotted fever	High	None	3–10 days	2 weeks to several months	Usually high (up to 80%)	Effective	Under development
Epidemic typhus	High	None	6–15 days	A few weeks to months	Variable but usually high (up to 70%)	Effective	Available
Bacterial							
Anthrax (pulmonary)	Moderately high	Negligible	1–5 days	3–5 days	Almost invariably fatal	Effective if given very early	Available
Brucellosis	High	None	1–3 weeks	Several weeks to months	Low (<25%)	Moderately effective	Under development
Cholera	Low	High	1–5 days	One to several weeks	Usually high (up to 80%)	Moderately effective	Available
Glanders	High	None	2–14 days	4–6 weeks	Almost invariably fatal	Little effective	None
Melioidosis	High	None	1–5 days	4–20 days	Almost 100% fatal	Moderately effective	None

Plague (pneumonic)	High	High	2–5 days	1–2 days	Almost 100% fatal	Moderately effective if given early	Available
Tularaemia	High	Negligible	1–10 days	Two to several weeks	Usually low some-times high (up to 60%)	Effective	Available
Typhoid fever	Moderately high	Moderately high	1–3 weeks	A few to several weeks	Moderately high up to (10%)	Moderately effective	Available
Dysentery	High	High	1–3 days	A few days to weeks	Low to mod-erately high depending on strain	Effective	None
Fungal Coccidioidomycosis	High	None	1–3 weeks	A few weeks to months	Low	None	None

duced by the botulinum organism. The toxin is a chemical, rather than a self-reproducing organism, but botulism produces 60–70 percent fatalities and is highly resistant to therapy.

The attacker may seek a very high rate of "Mortality," or he may actually prefer prolonged weakness and disability, followed by recovery for most of the victims.

"Antibiotic therapy" and "Vaccination" are significant items to the extent that the attacker wants to know the probability of fatal results or prolonged illness in the enemy population. They are also very important if the organism is one that may be transmitted back to his own population, with disastrous results if they have not been effectively vaccinated or cannot, at least, be given highly efficient antibiotics. Some of the vaccines listed as "available," moreover, may not be fully effective or may be difficult to produce in quantity. To this extent, non-transmissibility may be a necessary feature of the biological weapon for the potential attacker.

In late 1969, the United States renounced all use (first use *and* retalitory use) of biological and biological-toxin weapons, as well as first use of lethal chemical weapons. The process of destroying stockpiles of biological weapons commenced in the spring of 1971, after study and approval of environmental safeguards. This was a major step, but much remains to be done.

The United Nations report from which the table of biological weapons is taken was requested by the Eighteen Nation Committee on Disarmament, and by the General Assembly. It was prepared by fourteen leading experts, from the East and the West, including specialists from the United States and the U.S.S.R., who reached *unanimous* conclusions. Secretary General U Thant, in a preface, recalls part of his own previous statement on chemical and biological weapons, and notes some of the conclusions of the present report.[15]

. . . In some respects, they may be even more dangerous than nuclear weapons because they do not require the enormous expenditure of financial and scientific resources that are required for nuclear weapons. Almost all countries, including small ones and developing ones, may have access to these weapons, which can be manufactured quite cheaply, quickly and secretly in small laboratories or factories. This fact in itself makes the problem of control and inspection much more difficult. . . .

* * *

I am particularly impressed by the conclusion of the consultant experts wherein they state:

The general conclusion of the report can thus be summed up in a few lines. Were these weapons ever to be used on a large scale in war, no one could predict how enduring the effects would be, and how they would affect the structure of society and the environment in which we live. This overriding danger would apply as much to the country which initiated the use of these weapons as to the one which had been attacked, regardless of what protective measures it might have taken in parallel with its development of an offensive capability. A particular danger also derives from the fact that any country could develop or acquire, in one way or another, a capability in this type of warfare, despite the fact that this could prove costly. The danger of the proliferation of this class of weapons applies as much to the developing as it does to developed countries.

The momentum of the arms race would clearly decrease if the production of these weapons were effectively and unconditionally banned. Their use, which could cause an enormous loss of human life, has already been condemned and prohibited by international agreements, in particular the Geneva Protocol of 1925, and, more recently, in resolutions of the General Assembly of the United Nations. The prospects for general and complete disarmament under effective international control, and hence for peace throughout the world, would brighten significantly if the development, production and stockpiling of chemical and bacteriological (biological) agents intended for purposes of war were to end and if they were eliminated from all military arsenals.

If this were to happen, there would be a general lessening of international fear and tension. It is the hope of the authors that this report will contribute to public awareness of the profoundly dangerous results if these weapons were ever used, and that an aroused public will demand and receive assurances that Governments are working for the earliest effective elimination of chemical and bacteriological (biological) weapons.

The characteristics of biological weapons. The report itself is by far the most authoritative review of any of the weapons of mass destruction. The credentials of the writers, and their careful understatement, make it a hair-raising document. Here are excerpts:

Potential toxicity. Although more toxic than most well-known industrial chemicals, chemical warfare agents are far less potent on a weight-for-weight basis than are bacteriological (biological) agents. The dose of a chemical agent required to produce untoward effects in man is measured in milligrammes,[1] except for toxins which may be in the microgramme range.[2] The corresponding dose for bacteriological (biological) agents is in the picogramme range.[3]

*   *   *

[1] One milligramme equals 1/1,000 of a gramme [original numbering retained for all footnotes].

[2] One microgramme equals 1/1,000 of a milligramme.

[3] One picogramme equals 1/1,000,000 of a microgramme.

317

Because they infect living organisms, some bacteriological (biological) agents can be carried by travellers, migratory birds or animals to localities far from the area originally attacked.

The possibility of this kind of spread does not apply to chemical agents. But control of contamination by persistent chemical agents could be very difficult. Should large quantities of chemical agents penetrate the soil and reach underground waters, or should they contaminate reservoirs, they might spread hundreds of kilometres from the area of attack, affecting people remote from the zone of military operations. Although we know of no comparable substance likely to be used as a chemical warfare agent, the spread of DDT over the globe illustrates, in an extreme form, how man-made chemicals can spread. This chemical insecticide is now found in the tissues of creatures in all parts of the world, even in places in which it has never been used. For example, as a result of its transfer through food chains, it is found even in the tissues of the penguins which live in Antarctica.

* * *

CONCEPTS OF THE USE
OF CHEMICAL AND
BACTERIOLOGICAL
(BIOLOGICAL) WEAPONS
IN WAR

There is no military experience of the use of bacteriological (biological) agents as weapons of war, and the feasibility of using them as such has often been questioned. One issue which has frequently been raised concerns the validity of extrapolations made from laboratory experience to military situations in the field. Some recent investigations under field conditions throw light on this point.

In one field trial, zinc cadmium sulfide (a harmless powder) was disseminated in particles two microns[4] in diameter from a ship travelling 16 kilometres off shore. About 200 kilogrammes were disseminated while the ship travelled a distance of 260 kilometres parallel to the coastline. The resulting aerosol travelled at least 750 kilometres and covered an area of over 75,000 square kilometres.

This observation provides an indication of the size of area which might be covered by a wind-borne aerosol, but it does not tell whether the bacteriological (biological) agents which might be spread in an aerosol would still retain the ability to produce disease. All bacteriological (biological) agents lose their virulence or die progressively while travelling in an aerosol, and the distance of effective travel of the cloud would depend on the rate of decay of the particular agent in the particular atmospheric conditions prevailing.

Some idea of the relative size of areas which can be covered by bacteriological (biological) and chemical aerosols can be gained from this same experiment. Had the particles that were carried been a bacterial or viral agent,

[4]One micron equals 1/1,000,000 of a metre.

318

they would not have caused casualties over as large an area as the one covered, because of decay of the agent while in the aerosol state. However, depending on the organism and its degree of hardiness, areas of from 5,000 to 20,000 km² could have been effectively attacked, infecting a high proportion of unprotected people in the area. If the same means are applied to a hypothetical chemical attack using the most toxic chemical nerve agent, then about 0.8 kg of agent would have been released per km². The downwind hazard from this, in which some casualties might be expected, would not have extended more than one kilometre, and probably less, unless meteorological conditions were extremely favourable (see chapter III). The area covered by such a chemical attack might thus have been from 50 to 150 km², as compared with the 5,000 to 20,000 km² for the bacteriological (biological) attack.

For purposes of sabotage or covert (secret, as in sabotage actions behind enemy lines) operations, small aerosol generators for bacteriological (biological) agents could be built, for example, into fountain pens or cigarette lighters. It is also possible to conceive of the distribution of bacteriological (biological) agents by hand to poison either water supplies or ventilation systems [emphasis added], especially in a situation of breakdown of sanitary facilities due, say, to military mobilization or to a nuclear attack. In addition to producing casualties, such an attack could produce severe panic. If half a kilo of a culture of Salmonella[1] had been added to a reservoir containing 5 million litres of water and complete mixing had occurred, severe illness or disability would be suffered by anyone drinking 1 decilitre (about 3 ounces) of untreated water.

*   *   *

Medical Protection

Chemical attacks.   No general prophylactic treatment exists which could protect against chemical attacks. Antidotes (atropine and oximes) to nerve agents are of value if administered within half an hour before or within a very short time after exposure. Atropine is itself toxic, however, and might incapacitate unexposed individuals given large doses. Skin can be protected from the vapours of blister agents by various ointments, but they are not effective against liquid contamination.

Bacteriological (biological) attacks.   Vaccination is one of the most useful means of protecting people from natural infective disease and the only useful means available for prophylaxis against bacteriological (biological) attacks. The protective value of vaccines against smallpox, yellow fever, diphtheria and other diseases is fully established, although the protection they afford can be overcome if an immunized individual is exposed to a large dose of the infectious agent concerned. It is probable, however, that even those existing vaccines which are effective in preventing natural infectious diseases might afford only limited protection against respiratory infection by an agent disseminated into the air in large amounts by a bacteriological (biological)

---

[1] *Salmonella*: a group of bacteria, many species of which produce severe intestinal infections, including gastroenteritis, food poisoning (ptomaine), paratyphoid fever and typhoid fever.

319

weapon. Moreover, whole populations could not be vaccinated against all possible diseases. The development, production and administration of so many vaccines would be enormously expensive, and some vaccines might produce undesirable or dangerous reactions in the recipients.

This picture is not significantly altered by certain new developments in the field of vaccination: e.g., the use of living bacterial vaccines against tularaemia, brucellosis and plague; or aerosol vaccination, which is particularly relevant to vaccination of large numbers of people. There have been recent advances in the control of virus diseases, but at present none of these is practicable for the protection of large populations against bacteriological (biological) warfare.

Prophylaxis against some diseases can also be provided by the administration of specific antisera from the blood of people or animals previously inoculated with micro-organisms, or products derived from them, to increase the antibody-levels (immunity) in their blood. Tetanus antitoxin is used in this manner, and until more effective methods replaced them, such antisera were used for many diseases. It would, however, be impossible to prepare specific antisera against all possible bacteriological (biological) agents and to make them available for large populations.

* * *

Detection and Warning

* * *

Bacteriological (biological) attacks. Unlike chemical weapons, bacteriological (biological) weapons cannot readily be distinguished from the biological "background" of the environment by specific chemical or physical reactions, and are dangerous in much lower aerosol concentrations than chemical agents. The problem of early detection and warning is thus even more difficult than for chemical weapons. A partial solution to the problem has been achieved with certain nonspecific but very sensitive physical devices, such as particle counters and protein detectors (protein is a typical constituent of micro-organisms). Presumptive evidence of a bacteriological (biological) attack might be obtained if there is an unusual deviation from the normal pattern of material in the air recorded by the instruments. The elevation of such a deviation, however, would necessitate intensive and prolonged study of the normal pattern in a given location.

* * *

Once a bacteriological (biological) attack had been suspected or detected, it would be necessary to identify the specific agents involved so that proper protective measures could be taken and chemoprophylaxis and treatment planned. Identification would also help to predict the incubation period and hence the time available for remedial measures to be taken. At present the only means of identifying specific microorganisms is by normal laboratory procedures. Many routine laboratory methods of identification require as long as two to five days, but some recent developments have reduced this time ap-

320

preciably. It is possible to collect the particles from large volumes of air and concentrate them in a small amount of fluid. Bacteria can then be trapped on special filters and transferred to nutrient media, where sufficient growth may take place to permit identification of some kinds of bacteria within fifteen hours. Another method, the fluorescent antibody technique, can be highly specific and is applicable to bacteria and some viruses. In some cases, it allows of specific identification within a few hours. But despite all these recent developments, laboratory identification of biological agents is still a complicated and unsatisfactory process.

* * *

. . . It is estimated that the most toxic nerve gases may cause death at a dosage of about 10 mg min/m³.[2] Less toxic ones are lethal at dosages of up to 400 mg min/m³.

* * *

Botulinum toxin is one of the most powerful natural poisons known and could be used as a chemical warfare agent. There are at least six distinct types, of which four are known to be toxic to man. Formed by the bacterium *Clostridium botulinum,* the toxin is on occasion accidentally transmitted by contaminated food. The bacteria do not grow or reproduce in the body, and poisoning is due entirely to the toxin ingested. It is possible that it could be introduced into the body by inhalation.

Botulism is a highly fatal poisoning characterized by general weakness, headache, dizziness, double vision, dilation of the pupils, paralysis of the muscles concerned in swallowing and difficulty of speech. Respiratory paralysis is the usual cause of death. After consumption of contaminated food, symptoms usually appear within twelve to seventy-two hours. All persons are susceptible to botulinum poisoning. The few who recover from the disease develop an active immunity of uncertain duration and degree. Active immunization with botulinum toxoid has been shown to have some protective value, but antitoxin therapy is of limited value, particularly where large doses of the toxin have been consumed. Treatment is mainly supportive.

* * *

Effects of a nerve gas attack on a town.   The population density in a modern city may be 5,000 people per square kilometre. A heavy surprise attack with non-volatile nerve gas by bombs exploding on impact in a wholly unprepared town would, especially at rush hours, cause heavy losses. Half of the population might become casualties, half of them fatal, if about one ton of agent were disseminated per square kilometre.

If such a city were prepared for attack, and if the preparations included a civil defence organization with adequately equipped shelters and protective masks for the population, the losses might be reduced to one half of those which would be anticipated in conditions of total surprise.

[2] A dosage of one mg min/m³ consists of an exposure for one minute to gas at a concentration of one milligramme per cubic metre.

321

Although it would be very difficult to achieve, if there were a high level of preparedness, comprising adequate warning and effective civil defence procedures, it is conceivable that most of the population would be sheltered at the time of the attack and that very few would be in the streets.

Given a town with a total population of 80,000, a surprise attack with nerve gas could thus cause 40,000 casualties, half of them fatal, whereas under ideal circumstances for the defence, fatalities might number no more than 2,000. It is inconceivable, however, that the ideal would ever be attained.

* * *

Bacteriological (biological) agents could be used with the intention of killing people or of incapacitating them either for a short or a long period. The agents, however, cannot be rigidly defined as either lethal or incapacitating, inasmuch as their effects are dependent upon many factors relating not only to themselves but to the individuals they attack.

A number of natural diseases of man and domestic animals are caused by mixed infections (e.g., swine influenza, hog cholera). The possible use of two or more different organisms in combination in bacteriological (biological) warfare needs to be treated seriously because the resulting diseases might be aggravated or prolonged. In some instances, however, two agents might interfere with one another and reduce the severity of the illness they might cause separately.

* * *

Anthrax.   Under natural conditions, anthrax is a disease of animals, the main source of infection for man being cattle and sheep. Its vernacular synonym "wool sorter's disease" indicates one way men used to contract the disease. Depending on the mechanism of transmission, a cutaneous (skin) form (contact infection), an intestinal form (alimentary infection) or pulmonary form (airborne infection) may develop. The lung or respiratory form is most severe, and unless early treatment with antibiotics is resorted to, death ensues within two or three days in nearly every case.

Antibiotic prophylaxis is possible but would have to be prolonged for weeks, inasmuch as it has been shown that monkeys exposed to anthrax aerosol die if antibiotic treatment is discontinued after ten days. In certain countries, several types of vaccines are employed, but their effectiveness has not been fully evaluated.

The anthrax bacillus forms very resistant spores, which live for many years in contaminated areas and constitute the most dangerous risk the disease presents. From epidemiological observations, the inhalation infectious dose for man is estimated at 20,000 spores. Experiments on animals show that anthrax can be combined with influenza infection or with some noxious chemical agent and that the susceptibility of the animal to airborne anthrax infection is then markedly enhanced.

With suitable expertise and equipment large masses of anthrax bacilli can be easily grown, and heavy concentrations of resistant anthrax spore aero-

322

sols can be made. Such aerosols could result in a high proportion of deaths in a heavily exposed population. Immunization could not be expected to protect a heavy aerosol attack. The soil would remain contaminated for a very long time and so threaten livestock farming.

* * *

Plague. Under natural conditions, small rodents, from which the disease is transmitted by fleas, are the main source of human infection with plague. This is how "bubonic" plague develops. If the plague microbes are inhaled, pneumonic plague develops after a three-to-five-day incubation period. The patient suffers from severe general symptoms and, if untreated, normally dies within two to three days. A patient with pneumonic plague is extremely contagious to contacts.

Preventive vaccination is moderately effective against bubonic, but not pneumonic, plague. If administered early, streptomycin treatment may be successful.

In a study of experimental pulmonary plague in monkeys, it was found that an average dose of only 100 bacteria caused fatal disease in half the animals tested. Animal experiments have also shown that particles of one micron diameter (125,000th of an inch), containing single microbial cells, can cause primary pneumonia, with a rapid and fatal outcome. If the aerosol is formed by larger particles (5–10 microns diameter), microbial cells are deposited in the nose and other regions of the upper respiratory tract, and primary foci of the disease develop in the corresponding lymphatic nodes. A fatal generalized infection may then follow.

A large mass of plague bacteria could be grown and probably lyophilized (freeze-dried) and kept in storage. The agent is highly infectious by the aerosol route, and most populations are completely susceptible. An effective vaccine against this type of disease is not known. Infection might also be transmitted to urban and/or field rodents, and natural foci of plague may be created.

* * *

Venezuelan equine encephalitis virus (VEE). In nature, VEE is an infection of animals (equines, rodents, birds) transmitted to man through mosquitos which have fed on infected animals.

The disease has sudden onset, with headache, chills and fever, nausea and vomiting, muscle and bone pains, with encephalitis occurring in a very small proportion of cases. The mortality rate is very low, and recovery is usually rapid after a week, with residual weakness often persisting for three weeks. No specific therapy is available. The vaccine is still in the experimental stage.

Numerous laboratory infections in humans have been reported, most of them airborne. In laboratory experiments, monkeys were infected with aerosolized virus at relatively low concentrations (about 1,000 guinea pig infectious doses).

Inasmuch as the virus can be produced in large amounts in tissue culture or embryonated eggs and airborne infection readily occurs in laboratory workers, concentrated aerosols could be expected to incapacitate a very high per-

323

centage of the population exposed. In some areas, persistent endemic infection in wild animals would be established.

* * *

Other than for sabotage, the use of aerosol clouds of an agent is the most likely form of attack in bacteriological (biological) warfare. For example, material can be produced containing infective micro-organisms at a concentration of 10,000 million per gram. Let us suppose that an aircraft were to spray such material so as to produce an aerosol line source 100 kilometres in length across a 10 kilometre per hour wind. Then, assuming that 10 percent of organisms survived aerosolization, and that subsequent environmental stresses caused them to die at a rate of 5 percent per minute, about 5,000 square kilometres would be covered at a concentration such that 50 percent of the unprotected people in the area would have inhaled a dose sufficient to infect them, assuming that the infective dose is about 100 micro-organisms per person. This particular calculation is valid for agents such as those which cause tularaemia or plague, as well as for some viruses. The decay rate of the causative agents of Q-fever, anthrax and some other infections is much lower, and the expected effect would be still greater.

The effects of bacteriological (biological) attacks obviously would vary according to circumstances. Military personnel equipped with adequate protective measures, well trained in their use and provided with good medical services could, if warned of an attack, be able to protect themselves to a considerable degree. But effective early warning and detection systems do not yet exist. On the other hand, attacks on civil populations are likely to be covert and by surprise, and, at present, no civilian populations are protected. Unprotected military or civilian personnel would be at complete risk, and panic and irrational behaviour would complicate the effects of the attack. The heavy burden that would be imposed on the medical services of the attacked region would compound disorganization, and there would be a major risk of the total disruption of all administrative services.

In view of the extensive antipersonnel effects associated with agents of the kind with which this report is concerned, it is useful to view them against the area of effect of a one-megaton nuclear explosion, which, as is well recognized, would be sufficient to destroy utterly a town with a population of one million. It should, of course, be emphasized that direct comparisons of the effects of different classes of weapons are, at best, hypothetical exercises. From the military point of view, effectiveness of a weapon cannot be measured just in terms of areas of devastation or numbers of casualties. The final criterion will always be whether a specific military objective can be achieved better with one than another set of weapons. The basic hypotheses chosen for the comparison are rather artificial; and, in particular, environmental factors are ignored. But despite this limitation, table 5 gives data that help to place chemical, bacteriological (biological) and nuclear weapons in some perspective as to size of target area, number of casualties inflicted and cost estimates for development and production of each type of weapon. The figures speak for themselves.

324

TABLE 5. COMPARATIVE ESTIMATES OF DISABLING EFFECTS OF HYPOTHETICAL ATTACKS ON TOTALLY UNPROTECTED POPULATIONS USING A NUCLEAR CHEMICAL OR BACTERIOLOGICAL (BIOLOGICAL) WEAPON THAT COULD BE CARRIED BY A SINGLE STRATEGIC BOMBER

CRITERION FOR ESTIMATE	NUCLEAR (ONE MEGATON)	TYPE OF WEAPON CHEMICAL (15 TONS OF NERVE AGENT)	BACTERIOLOGICAL (BIOLOGICAL) (10 TONS)
Area affected	Up to 300 km²	Up to 60 km²	Up to 100,000 km²
Time delay before onset of effect	Seconds	Minutes	Days
Damage to structures	Destruction over an area of 100 km²	None	None
Other effects	Radioactive contamination in an area of of 2,500 km² for 3–6 months	Contamination by persistence of agent from a few days to weeks	Possible epidemic or establishment of new endemic foci of disease
Possibility of later normal use of affected area after attack	3–6 months after attack	Limited during period of contamination	After end of incubation period or subsidence of epidemic
Maximum effect on man	90 percent deaths	50 percent deaths	50 percent morbidity; 25 percent deaths if no medical intervention
Multiyear investment in substantial research and development production capability*	$5,000–10,000 million	$1,000–5,000 million	$1,000–5,000 million

*It is assumed that indicated cumulative investments in research and development and production plants have been made to achieve a substantial independent capability. Individual weapons could be fabricated without making this total investment.

3. Effects on Animals

The way bacteriological (biological) weapons might be used against stocks of domestic animals would probably be the same as that used in attacks against man.

* * *

Covert bacteriological (biological) attack during peacetime directed against domestic animals could give rise to serious political and economic repercussions if large numbers of stock were affected. For example, African swine fever occurs endemically on the African continent as a subclinical disease of warthogs. In 1957 it was accidentally brought from Angola to Portugal, and then in 1960 to Spain. Despite strict and extensive veterinary measures that were enforced, losses in pig breeds were estimated to amount within a single year to more than $9,000,000.

Isolated attacks against stocks of domestic animals during wartime would have only a nuisance value. However, if a highly infectious agent (e.g., foot-and-mouth disease) were used, even a local attack could have very widespread effects because of spread by the normal commercial movement of animals, particularly in highly developed countries. Extensive attacks with travelling clouds could, however, lead to a disastrous state of affairs. The history of myxamatosis (a rabbit disease) in Europe provides a parallel. Not only did it drastically reduce the rabbit population in France, into which it was first introduced; it immediately spread to other countries of Europe, including the United Kingdom. The risk of the uncontrolled spread of infection to a number of countries is an important consideration in the use of some bacteriological (biological) weapons.

The possibilities of protecting domestic animal stocks against bacteriological (biological) attacks are so remote that they are not worth discussing.

4. Effects on Plants

Living micro-organisms could also be used to generate diseases in crops which are economically important either as food or as raw material (e.g., cotton and rubber). Significant food crops in this respect include potatoes, sugarbeet, garden vegetables, soya beans, sorghum, rice, corn, wheat and other cereals and fruits.

* * *

If the induced disease was easily transmissible from man to man, and if it was one against which the population had not been effectively immunized, it is possible to imagine what could happen by recalling, say, the periodical appearance of new varieties of influenza virus, e.g., the 1957 influenza pandemic. In Czechoslovakia (population about 14 million), 1,500,000 influenza patients were actually reported; the probable total number was 2,500,000. About 50 per cent of the sick were people in employment, and their average period away from work was six days. Complications necessitating further treatment developed in 5–6 per thousand of the cases, and about 0.2 per

326

thousand died. Those who are old enough to remember the 1918 influenza pandemic, which swept over most of the world, will judge the 1957 outbreaks as a mild affair.

* * *

The experiences from fairly recent smallpox epidemics can also be used to illustrate the social effects of an accidentally introduced, highly dangerous airborne infection. In New York (1947) one patient started an epidemic, in which twelve persons became ill and two died. Within a month more than 5 million persons were revaccinated. Similarly in Moscow, in January 1960, a smallpox epidemic of forty-six cases (of whom three died) developed, caused by a single patient. At that time 5,500 vaccination teams were set up and vaccinated 6,372,376 persons within a week. Several hundreds of other health workers searched a large area of the country for contacts (9,000 persons were kept under medical supervision, and of these 662 had to be hospitalized as smallpox suspects).

* * *

Bacteriological (biological) weapons could be directed against man's sources of food through the spread of persistent plant diseases or of infectious animal diseases. There is also the possibility that new epidemic diseases could be introduced, or old ones reintroduced, which could result in deaths on the scale which characterized the mediaeval plagues.

* * *

Endemics or enzootics of diseases (i.e., infections spreading at a low rate, but indefinitely, in a human or animal population) could conceivably follow a large-scale attack, or might be started by a small-scale sabotage attack, for which purpose the range of possible agents would be much wider and might even include such chronic infections as malaria.

* * *

The microbiological expertise necessary to grow agents of bacteriological (biological) warfare exists to a large extent in many countries, inasmuch as the requirements are similar to those of a vaccine industry and, to a lesser extent, a fermentation industry. Apart from the combination of the highly developed technologies of these two industries, there remains only a need for some specialized knowledge, expertise and equipment to permit the safe handling of large quantities of bacteriological (biological) agents. Consequently, existing facilities in the fermentation, pharmaceutical and vaccine industries could be adapted for the production of bacteriological (biological) agents. But the technological complexities of producing bacteriological (biological) agents in dry power form are very much greater than for wet spray systems. Moreover, it would be desirable to provide an effective vaccine with which to protect production staff. The technical difficulties would increase with the scale and complexity of the weapon systems that were being developed. But the fact remains that any industrially advanced country could acquire whatever capability it set out to achieve in this field.

The difficulty and cost of providing for the transport and storage of bacteriological (biological) weapons are considerable, since special storage conditions, e.g., refrigeration, and stringent safety and security precautions are essential. In addition, testing to determine the potential effectiveness of the material produced would require considerable and costly testing facilities both in the laboratory and in the field.

Despite the fact that the development and acquisition of a sophisticated armoury of chemical and bacteriological (biological) weapon system would prove very costly in resources and would be dependent on a sound industrial base and a body of well-trained scientists, *any developing country could, in fact, acquire, in one way or another, a limited capability in this type of warfare — either a rudimentary capability which it developed itself or a more sophisticated one which it acquired from another country. Hence, the danger of the proliferation of this class of weapons applies as much to developing as it does to developed countries.* [Emphasis added.]

* * *

Existing armaments which (with some modification) could be used to deliver agents in order to generate local outbreaks of disease could also contaminate large areas with pathogens. For example, a single aircraft could cover with a bacteriological (biological) agent an area of up to 100,000 square kilometres, although the area of effective dosage might be much smaller due to loss of the infectivity of the airborne agent.

Although in the development and production costs of chemical and bacteriological (biological) agents might well be high, the cost of the complete weapon system (see chapter I) would be even greater. The cost of developing, procuring and operating a squadron of modern bombers far outweighs the cost of the bombs it could carry. *However, for some purposes, an existing weapon system or a far less sophisticated means of disseminating might be used.* [Emphasis added.]

* * *

It is almost impossible to conceive of the complexity of the arrangements which would be necessary to control the consequences of a large-scale bacteriological (biological) attack. . . .

Whatever might be done to try to save human beings, nothing significant could be done to protect crops, livestock, fodder and food-stuffs from a chemical and bacteriological (biological) weapons attack. Persistent chemical agents could constitute a particular danger to livestock.

Water in open reservoirs could be polluted as a result of deliberate attack, or perhaps accidentally, with chemical or bacteriological (biological) weapons. The water supply of large towns could become unusable, and rivers, lakes and streams might be temporarily contaminated.

Enormous damage could be done to the economy of a country whose agricultural crops were attacked with herbicides. For example, only 10–20 grammes per hectare of 2,4-D could render a cotton crop completely unproductive (see annex V). Fruit trees, grape vines and many other plants could also be destroyed. Mixtures of 2,4-D, of 2,4-5-T and picloram are particularly potent. The chemical known as paraquat can destroy virtually all annual plants, including leguminous plants, rice, wheat and other cereals. Arsenic compounds dessicate the leaves of many crops and make them unusable as food. There are no means known at present of regenerating some of the plants which are affected by herbicides. Experience has shown, however, that in the case of some species either natural or artificial seeding can easily produce normal growth in the next growing season. But the destruction of fruit trees, vines and other plants, if achieved, could not be overcome for many years. For most practical purposes, it would be impossible to prevent the destruction of cultivated plants on which herbicides have been used, and, depending on a country's circumstances, widespread famine might follow.

* * *

THE RELEVANCE OF CHEMICAL
AND BACTERIOLOGICAL
(BIOLOGICAL) WEAPONS TO
MILITARY AND CIVIL SECURITY

* * *

As previous chapters have also shown, neither the effectiveness nor the effects of chemical and bacteriological (biological) weapons can be predicted with assurance. Whatever military reasons might be advanced for the use of these weapons, and whatever their nature, whether incapacitating or lethal, there would be significant risk of escalation, not only in the use of the same type of weapon but of other categories of weapons systems, once their use had been initiated. Thus, chemical and bacteriological (biological) warfare could open the door to hostilities which could become less controlled, and less controllable, than any war in the past. Uncontrollable hostilities cannot be reconciled with the concept of military security.

Since some chemical and bacteriological (biological) weapons constitute a major threat to civilian populations and their food and water supplies, their use cannot be reconciled with general national and international security. Further, because of the scale and intensity of the potential effects of their use, they are considered as weapons of mass destruction. Their very existence thus contributes to international tension without compensating military advantages. They generate a sense of insecurity not only in countries which might be potentially belligerent but in those which are not. Neutral countries could be involved through the use of chemical and bacteriological (biological) weapons, especially those whose territories bordered on countries involved in conflict in the course of which chemical and bacteriological (biological) casualties had been suffered by garrisons and civilians close to frontiers. The effects of certain bacteriological (biological) weapons used on a large scale might be particularly difficult to confine to the territory of a small country. Large-scale chemical and bacteriological (biological) agents and chemical agents might be used for acts of sabotage. Such events might occur as isolated acts, even carried out in defiance of the wishes of national leaders and mili-

329

tary commanders. The continued existence and manufacture of chemical weapons anywhere may make such occurrences more likely.

Obviously, any extensive use of chemical weapons would be known to the country attacked. The source of the attack would probably also be known. *On the other hand, it would be extremely difficult to detect isolated acts of sabotage in which bacteriological (biological) weapons were used, especially if the causative organism were already present in the attacked country. Because of the suspicions they would generate, acts of sabotage could thus provoke a conflict involving the widespread use of chemical and bacteriological (biological) weapons.* [Emphasis added.]

* * *

Proliferation of biological weapons. Why do you think certain passages of the report are italicized? What is the thread common to the italicized excerpts?

How do the problems of "miniaturization" and "proliferation" in the biological-weapons field compare with those in the nuclear field? Are they worse? If so, how much worse? Do you suppose that all of the countries in the three lists on p. 312 are capable of developing biological weapons? Might *already* have biological weapons? How many additional countries might be capable of developing such weapons? The report indicates the usual need for expensive delivery systems and various safeguards for biological weapons. But it also suggests that a limited capability might be achieved with much less expense for certain purposes.

In relation to the proliferation question, consider the following story, carried in the Seattle *Times* on November 20, 1970:[16]

ARMY CHECKS REPORT OF PLAN TO STEAL BIO-LOGICAL WEAPONS

An informant has notified the United States Customs Bureau that the revolutionary Weatherman organization is planning to steal biological weapons from Fort Detrick, Md., and contaminate a major city's water supply, the Army said yesterday.

An Army spokesman said it has not been determined if the informant's reports are reliable, but that the amounts of biological materials available at Fort Detrick are insufficient to carry out such a plan.

Fort Detrick is the Army's biological-weapons research center.

The informant reported that the Weatherman members planned to obtain the biological materials by blackmailing a homosexual lieutenant at Fort Detrick, the Army said, confirming an account in Jack Anderson's syndicated column.

The Weatherman plan, according to the informant, was not to kill anyone but rather "to incapacitate a population by infection for seven to 10 days." The plan's aim is to cause havoc, he said, and increase possibilities of revolution.

The name of the target city was not disclosed, nor were the identities of the informant, his contact or the Fort Detrick lieutenant, the Army spokesman said.

The final passage excerpted from the United Nations report speaks of possibilities of sabotage, as do several earlier passages. Are there circumstances under which acts of sabotage might be likely to happen? Would the material used necessarily be lethal? (Consider the Weatherman story—why might they prefer non-lethal organisms? "Non-lethal," however, referring to biological weapons, cannot be an absolute distinction. A disease that makes most people severely ill is bound to kill some.) Would the attack necessarily be directed at human beings, or might it be directed at crops or animals? (What resemblances does the possible technique of using bacteriological methods to clandestinely reduce an opponent's food crop over a period of years bear to what we called "long-time-line" oppression in Chapter 1? What are the differences?) If crop sabotage were suspected, or even clearly documented, what would be the options for response? Might the need to protect one's own population or agriculture make it difficult to carry out a clandestine attack, or would this depend on the speed with which the attack might threaten to spread back to the attacker's own territory?

Some horrifying scenarios of secret attacks can be developed. Imagine, for example, that the time is ten years from now. South Africa has ruthlessly repressed a rebellion in the mandated Southwest Africa territory. Now South Africa sees the United States and Russia "ganging up" to support a United Nations-sanctioned black African attack, and feels severely threatened. Then a severe political crisis simultaneously affects a pair of great powers—the United States and Russia, or the United States and China. South Africa thereupon dispatches two submarines to release an aerosol cloud of anthrax spores off the West Coast of United States, hoping that we will blame this attack on the other power involved in the crisis, and that a nuclear war will start. Such a war will ultimately leave the Southern Hemisphere countries the only surviving societies (because of the relatively separate wind-circulation systems of the Northern and Southern hemispheres), with South Africa their acknowledged leader.

What can be done to prevent something like this from happening *sometime* over the next twenty or thirty years? Or the next hundred? Would we leave it to a computer—programmed, of course, by human beings—to decide who the "most likely" source of a clandestine or sabotage attack was, as of any given day, and retaliate accordingly? There must be better ways. Some of them will be considered in Chapter 8.

In 1925, a treaty was entered into that prohibited the use in war of "asphyxiating, poisonous or other gases, and of all analogous liquids, materials or devices," and also extended the prohibition "to the use of bacteriological methods of warfare." The United States signed this treaty, but never ratified it; among the major powers, Japan and the United States are the only ones not agreeing to be formally bound (Russia and Communist China have both accepted the treaty). However, the United States declared in World War II, through President Roosevelt, that it would not be the first to use such weapons. In late 1969 President Nixon announced that the United States renounced *all* use of biological warfare (both first use and retaliatory use) and would proceed to destroy all stockpiles; he furthermore confirmed that the United States renounced first use of chemical warfare. He also asked the Senate to ratify the 1925 treaty, and at the same time the Eighteen Nation Disarmament Committee began considering a broader form of the 1925 treaty. (What shortcomings can you see in the treaty language? Is the prohibition of *use* alone sufficient?)

Other possible weapons.   A number of other frightening weapons-development possibilities were discussed in a seminar presentation in which the author joined Frank Herbert, the distinguished environmentalist and author of *Dune*, late in 1970. Herbert suggested that "We live on a Waarfarin world," ecologically and with our new weapons technology. "Waarfarin" is the rat poison developed to get around the fact that rats will stay away from ordinarily poisoned grain after observing one of their members eat it and die; Waarfarin requires a number of trips to the grain-pile before it works, so the rats fail to associate the effect, a particular death, with the cause, the eating of the grain. Likewise, we are building up a weapons technology that threatens us with ultimate obliteration, Herbert said, but we are getting there by sufficiently slow stages that few seem to notice.

The seminar discussion went on to cite, besides the nuclear, chemical, and biological weapons, such future possibilities as 7–9 cycle "sonic" weapons, used as a fear-inducer; powerful laser weapons; setting off earthquakes in an enemy's territory by triggering geological stresses; tampering with weather, as by clandestinely removing larger-than-average rainfall from clouds before they pass over an adjacent enemy's territory downwind (quite similar to clandestine biological warfare against crops and livestock); genetic weapons, such as a water additive that slowly alters proportion of male-to-female births in an enemy population, or that amplifies sex-drive, or counteracts population control measures. "Cloning" (a process in which a *skin*-cell nucleus is implanted in a de-nucleated ovum, and a complete individual is produced with *exactly* the biological characteristics of the organism that supplied the skin cell; cloning, already successful with frogs, is now being tried with mice, and will probably be possible for humans sometime in the 1980s) could be used, for example, to serially produce a race of "super-soldiers" from a single individual; selected environments could be destroyed with giant solar reflectors in space, or chemicals could be used to destroy the protective layer of ozone high in the atmosphere over an enemy's territory; if some items of education can be transmitted chemically (as suggested by recent experiments making mice terrified of the dark), an attacker could secretly introduce chemicals to create fear, or chemicals which will "trigger" a desired response on a given signal; chemicals might also be used to suppress intelligence; etc., etc.

Although the list is horrifying, it should not be taken to mean that science and technology are necessarily "bad." Quite the contrary, predictions for the coming decade strongly suggest that much the same accumulation of knowledge and theory that can result in the horrible weapons described can be used to cure cancer, prevent heart disease, improve the health of infants, eliminate birth defects, dramatically increase food production, produce cheap power without burning fossil fuels, help clean up the environment, and increase human capacities. Thus, the simple and total repression of science and technology seems to be neither a politically feasible nor a desirable solution. What solutions might help to separate out and repress "bad" science, while preserving and encouraging "good" science? We shall consider some of the alternatives in the last chapter.

333

FOOTNOTES, CHAPTER 7

[1] Lincoln P. Bloomfield, *Disarmament and Arms Control*, Headline Series, No. 187 (New York Foreign Policy Association, 1968), 17.

[2] David Inglis, "The Outlook for Nuclear Explosives," in *Unless Peace Comes*, ed. Nigel Calder (New York, The Viking Press, Inc., 1968), pp. 43–53, 56–63.

[3] *Newsweek*, vol. 76, no. 20 (November 16, 1970), p. 53.

[4] Philip Noel-Baker, "We Have Been Here Before," in *Unless Peace Comes*, ed. Nigel Calder (New York, The Viking Press, Inc., 1968), pp. 219–220.

[5] G. W. Rathjens and G. B. Kistiakowsky, "The Limitation of Strategic Arms," *Scientific American*, Vol. 222, No. 1 (January 1970), pp. 20, 24.

[6] Lincoln P. Bloomfield, *Disarmament and Arms Control*, Headline Series, No. 187 (New York Foreign Policy Association, 1968), p. 22.

[7] *New York Times*, November 1, 1970.

[8] *New York Times*, November 15, 1970.

[9] From a question asked by John Raser in "A Conversation with Herbert Marcuse," *Psychology Today*, Feb. 1971.

[10] Sir John Cockroft, "The Perils of Nuclear Proliferation," in *Unless Peace Comes*, ed. Nigel Calder (New York, The Viking Press, Inc., 1968), pp. 32–38.

[11] Lincoln P. Bloomfield, *Disarmament and Arms Control*, p. 44.

[12] James Dougherty, "Nuclear Weapons Control," *Current History*, Vol. 46, No. 47 (July 1964), p. 31.

[13] Lincoln P. Bloomfield, *Disarmament and Arms Control*, p. 24.

[14] United Nations Report, *Chemical and Bacteriological (Biological) Weapons and the Effects of Their Possible Use*, reprinted by Ballantine Books, New York, 1970, pp. 164–65.

[15] United Nations Report, *Chemical and Bacteriological (Biological) Weapons and the Effects of Their Possible Use*, pp. xix, xxiv–v, 12, 14, 20–22, 36–37, 41, 44–45, 55–56, 61–62, 69–74, 77–83, 85, 90–91, 125, 130, 141–53.

[16] *Washington Post*, November 20, 1970.

8

The Alternatives:

Understanding and ending lethal conflict

We have now covered a variety of phenomena of lethal violence, ranging in size from murder to World War II, and in settings from prehistoric times to present-day Vietnam. The evidence thus far available clearly does not allow a comprehensive theory of what causes men to kill other men in all circumstances and in all settings. However, the evidence does support certain working hypotheses that I believe hold out considerable hope for understanding many of these phenomena and for mapping out further lines of research, through which we can hope to understand *most* of them. Even more important, basic approaches for actually preventing and curing the disease of lethal conflict can now be outlined.

Some Working Hypotheses on the
Causes of Lethal Violence

I shall set out these working hypotheses in the order of the size of the conflict, ranging roughly from the smallest "quarrel," in Richardson's terms, to the largest.

Murder. The smallest quarrel also appears to be the most impulsive. Cross-cultural study is needed, but I strongly suspect that the great majority of murders in most other countries — particularly those whose homicide rate is near or above that of the United States — will be found to be impulsive, as they usually are in the United States, rather than planned or premeditated.

The availability of guns is an important factor; it *does* appear that the United States homicide rate might be as much as halved if guns were not readily available. The Chicago study shows 12.2 deaths per 100 reported gun attacks, versus 2.4 deaths per 100 reported knife attacks, and other data suggests that the only perceptible difference between "aggravated assault" cases and most homicide cases is that the victim dies. Thus, the weapon used — what we might well call the "Lorenzian variable" — appears to be of great importance in determining whether or not a homicide death will occur.

As to what motivates the impulsive attack of the killer in the first place, I think that it is generally clear that normally the murderer has a background of "relative deprivation" with respect to such things as material wants, parental affection, and status; also perhaps the murderer has been exposed to extensive models for violence, particularly in his own immediate experience (the relation of individual violence to media violence is rather secondary and tenuous, on the available evidence). Furthermore, it is likely that there have been frequent breakdowns of the processes by which a family socializes a child to be nonviolent. I believe this breakdown is facilitated when the values of the family (or of the whole culture) are actually ambiguous about violence, such as when they are on a "macho trip." Thus, a high homicide rate such as Mexico's (or that of a black ghetto) may typically involve a man who has achieved little material well-being or status, who has seen and perhaps been personally subjected to violence, and who has been taught from the cradle that there is a sharp personality differentiation between women and men, the latter being characterized

336

by aggressive self-assertiveness. He commits an impulsive killing that simultaneously vents his inward rage on a convenient, temporarily irritating, and relatively unthreatening object (that is, not "merchants, landlords, [or] wealthy persons") and validates his status of full manhood in his own eyes, and perhaps in the eyes of others around him.

The small proportion of *planned* murders appears to be traceable to a variety of special situations, ranging from a foreseen guard-shooting in a bank robbery, to the husband who covets his wife's wealth, to the clinically paranoid individuals with bizarre fears or delusions. The variety seems too great to allow even a working hypothesis to cover any large part of this ground, given the present state of our knowledge.

Riot. The lethal consequences of riots may run from one or two dead up to tens of thousands dead, as in India during partition, or Bogata in 1948. The killing of 200,000 suspected "Communists" in the villages of Indonesia in 1965 bears many resemblances, also, to large-scale riot (with the authorities in that case on the side of the rioters). Typically, the lethal riot appears to be an impulsive rather than a premeditated killing, likely to be carried out by socio-economic groups that are gravely deprived of material goods or status. At least temporarily, there is also a sense of common purpose within the group (defined as persons of *our* religion, *our* language, *our* race, or whatever may define the "we-they" polarization) and a sense of a temporary social norm, of varying degrees of strength, that killing opponents of the group is legitimate. The immediate occasion of the riot is often trivial, and bears hardly more relationship to the participants' underlying motivations than does the behavior of the murder victim to the murderer's motives.

Unfortunately, we are no more able at present to predict riots than to predict murders. But poverty and despair mark out the principal fault lines where we can expect either riots or murders to occur (typically *plus* group cooperation in one; *plus* childhood experience in the other). Deprivation is where we should concentrate our powers of observation, to see if more precise predictions can be made.

Insurrection. Here we move to a kind of lethal activity that exhibits some persisting structure. In insurrections there are leaders who remain leaders from day to day and are recognized as such by others in the activity. There are followers. However, these followers cannot be counted on simply to become followers upon command and to

337

obey orders thereafter. They have to be *self-selected* as followers against all the weighty pressures of an established society that commands them not to be followers of such a movement, and that makes dire threats of punishment if they should become followers. Again, I think that the chief motive impelling the followers is much the same intense relative deprivation of material well-being and status that we see in the violent rioter or the impulsive murderer. But here, for the first time, the threat of retribution is overcome, and the violence *is* directed at the "merchants, landlords, wealthy persons" or others (see p. 77) who are regarded as responsible for the deprivation. In this sense, the violence that sometimes accompanied the union movement appears to have been closer to insurrection than to riot, except that it was "limited insurrection," directed at the private police and "goons" and "scabs" of the factory owner, rather than at the entire social system.

Even many insurrections do not directly aim at the deaths of members of the ruling groups, but rather are cast in terms of "We seek your power, and if you oppose us by sending men somewhat like ourselves to defend your power, we will either kill them or persuade them to join us." Other insurrections, however, encourage the killing of ruling group members, such as the landlords or money-lenders who are found to be at hand. Thus, an insurrection harnesses the same energies found in a riot to a deliberate idea of removing the underlying causes of deprivation.

But what of the leaders? Our best data on revolutionary leaders come from the current studies in the United States, and there may be enormous cross-cultural differences. In general, however, Marx appears to have been correct in predicting that the leadership for revolution would come out of the upper classes. This seems logical in a number of ways. Such people have the education and leisure to develop a revolutionary program, persuade others of its merits, and establish a cadre of followers. They can afford "start-up" equipment such as weapons, apartments, rented houses, and mimeo machines (when they achieve some initial success or notoriety, they may be able to get "outside funding"). And they are probably less likely to be intimidated and overwhelmed by the presence of the existing order-keeping structure.

It would seem that at least three ingredients are involved in the process by which certain members of groups not ordinarily thought of as "deprived" assume revolutionary leadership. These ingredients

338

may be present in substantially varying quantities and mixtures, depending on such factors as the number of people "badly off" in the society, the obviousness of the rulers' "evil" in relation to cultural or religious norms, and even on the accidents of the way in which each insurrectionary group happens to be formed. The first ingredient of insurrectionary leadership is the individual's personal background, including such elements as parental indifference, or perhaps physical shortcomings, which create deep personal frustration and rage; the second ingredient is the availability and persuasiveness of ideological frameworks with which to criticize the perceived injustices and provide a program for reform (today generally Marxist, Leninist, Maoist, or some derivative); and the third is the particular individual's drive for status and power, which may be related to the first factor, but may also derive from family values, cultural norms, or personal biological variations.

Thus, an upper or upper-middle class young man (or woman) with deeply personal frustrations and a strong desire for status provides an ideology and a framework of action for a larger group of followers, whose sense of deprivation is typically of a more generally felt and tangible kind.

If an insurrection becomes established and gains administrative control of territory, it may acquire many of its fighting men by conscription roughly similar to that used by existing governments. Thus, fewer of its followers may join and work for the rebellion out of murder- or riot-related motivations. However, if the insurrection is built on a broadly perceived set of grievances, chances are good that at least a strong admixture of the rioters' typical inward motivation will exist in many of those who are "drafted."

We have not said much of the "establishment" side of civil conflicts, and will save that for the discussion of war.

War.   Here personal motivation on the part of the rank-and-file soldier typically ranges from very moderate to nil, except in special instances such as an invasion or a defensive war where he is fighting for his home territory (as the Russian was in World War II). Otherwise, the individual soldier usually has little to gain from the fighting, in relation to matters of material deprivation or status that affect his own life —although some few may be motivated by the artificial status created by medals or other combat-related rewards. Rarely, an ideology may inflame large parts of an army, especially one consisting of self-selected enlistees (for example, the first Crusades and perhaps the

339

armies of Napoleon). But generally, even if the leaders urge some matter of economic or strategic "necessity" or of "honor" in support of the war, the individual soldier in a modern war would only rarely perceive an immediate connection, sufficient to move him to kill, between these aims and *his* personal well-being or status.

The killing in modern war is typically done because those who have legitimate authority and superior status give an order that it be done. Increasingly, the killing is done through relatively impersonal means, in contrast to the rifle of the insurrectionary (although the booby-trap is arguably quite impersonal). Most of the killing in modern war is done not even by the machine gun, but by the bomber or fighter or artillery-piece, whose crews find that the target is usually a structure or place, or at most a few tiny dots far below. A nuclear-tipped missile is clearly still more impersonal.

At the apex of this command-and-obedience structure is a leader, typically even further removed from the actual killing than the revolutionary leader (although the latter, too, may not actually participate; it depends much on the leader's individual personality, on whether he is a Ho or a Che).

There would, however, seem to be many parallels in the personalities of revolutionary and "legitimate" leaders. Certainly, most legitimate leaders of large countries must have a strong drive for power and status in order to achieve their position. Most legitimate leaders have an ideological commitment, in this case a commitment to preserve, and perhaps to reform, rather than one to destroy the institutions of the society. In terms of personality structure, it would be useful to have much more data, but as a working hypothesis it seems likely that those leaders who are most likely to start large wars are ones who have suffered from some severe personal handicap or emotional deprivation.

Except in the case of invasion of the national territory or civil war, the leader's reason for fighting is typically perceived in terms that are closely linked to his own status. This does not mean that his reasons for fighting are purely personal, however. In addition to the leader's *personal* status drive, which is likely to be strong, there may be an assumed ideology that attaches to the nation's definition of leadership and that tells him, in effect, that in defending his status he will also be defending his nation's power and continuity, *and that this is right.* This ideology will also be expressed by competing sub-groups

340

within the country, so that the defense of status vis-à-vis another nation and the defense of internal political status may well be coterminous. Thus, the combination of the leader's personal status strivings and the inherited ideology attached to the leadership role lead him to order large-scale lethal violence even when the vast majority of the individuals in the population have no inward sense of motivation to engage in such violence. For example, a leader may order violence to protect trade, investment, raw materials, alliances, citizens abroad, strategic bases or positions; or to avenge "insults," deny strategic bases to another country, or settle minor border disputes.

In invasions, the case is somewhat different: invasion is a readily perceivable threat to the material well-being and existing status of the individual members of the society. Such a threat may also be perceived in the case of some attempted insurrections, where there is not a broad or deep base of grievances within the total society, especially if the insurrectionary's aims are perceived as a general threat to existing jobs, possessions, and status. Here, as in the invasion, the population may mobilize not only in response to orders, but also with an inward motivation to defend what is already theirs from a perceived threat. If such popular mobilization occurs, insurrection is likely to fail disastrously. It is one reason why an attempted "black revolution" based on some neo-Marxist or Maoist ideology would almost certainly end in great tragedy for American blacks. (Support for a foreign war involving no direct threat to the home territory may also sometimes be cast by government or media in terms calculated to arouse responses appropriate to a more direct threat—the "domino theory" is an example—but at least for a population that has not undergone an invasion within living memory, it seems doubtful that such exhortations affect actual battlefield behavior, or carry much beyond affecting political behavior.)

Essentially, these seem the key elements in the genesis of modern wars: first, the leader's perception of an external threat to his own power or status; second, the degree to which this perception is supported or overridden by the ideology that he views himself as safeguarding or by the nature of the leadership role that he see himself as fulfilling in that society; and third, the extent to which subleaders within the society may reinforce his response to the perceived external threat by creating a plausible internal threat to his power or status if he does not react in a particular way.

A Note on Five Basic Approaches
to Prevention and Cure

Nearly four fifths of all the deaths from lethal violence since 1820 appear to have resulted from large-scale conflicts involving over 30,000 deaths apiece. Even more sobering, such conflicts may, in the future, end all life on earth. Certainly, in attempting to resolve, prevent, or eliminate lethal human conflict, the first priority is the ending of such *large-scale* revolutions and wars. The three most likely means of doing so appear to involve the following steps: limiting or eliminating entirely the weaponry of large-scale conflict; redressing the grievances that may lead large populations to frustration and rage; and altering those perceptions and judgments of opposing national leaders likely to lead them to engage in large-scale conflict.

assumes wars are caused by grievances

In attempting to resolve, prevent, or eliminate lethal human conflict, we can perhaps identify five or more separate approaches, or paradigms.

1. The "control paradigm." This is the situation in which one country or group of countries *orders or coerces* an end to lethal conflict, or to certain categories of lethal conflict, being carried on by others. The United Nations Security Council is empowered to end lethal conflict by order or coercion and did so, for example, by the former means, in the June 1967 Mideast war. (In the Congo dispute of 1961, actual force was used.)

2. The "agreement paradigm." Here, instead of forcing others to conform to a no-conflict mandate, two or more parties themselves *agree* to end certain kinds or causes of conflict among themselves, or to undertake measures likely to reduce conflict among themselves. Such are the post-war arms-control agreements on subjects like nuclear testing and nuclear proliferation.

3. The "initiative paradigm." Here there is neither coercion nor agreement; one party simply takes a *unilateral step* calculated to change psychological and political perceptions within other countries, and thus to make conflict less likely. A recent important example of this approach is President Nixon's renunciation of biological warfare and his order for the destruction of America's biological warfare stockpiles.

4. The "amelioration paradigm." Basically, this is another version of "initiative," calculated to reduce *internal* tensions and conflict. Programs of democratic land reform are examples of such initiatives.

342

Sometimes such measures are also part of a context of dealings between nations, and thus may include one of the other paradigms, such as coercion or agreement, for example, the agreed-on application of American aid funds to the Taiwanese or Bolivian land reform.

5. Finally, there is what we may call the "utopian paradigm." This approach, less well defined than the others, seeks to deal with *basic* structures of the society as they affect lethal conflict, and more broadly, as they affect human want, pain, and unhappiness of all kinds. These very long-term measures may employ a mixture of the "control," "agreement," and "initiative" approaches, involving the broadest application of technological, psychological, and other kinds of knowledge. Programs may include such elements as the satisfaction of human material wants, the recasting of families (which may today produce rage-filled children) and the restructuring of political life (which may today produce status-hungry leaders).

The Control Paradigm

"Peace Probe."   Late in 1970, I wrote a short science-fiction story called "Peace Probe." The protagonist was a member of a United States "probe team" caught in the middle of a political crisis in Argentina in 1998. As the plot unfolded, it became clear that the "probe team" commanded enormous powers, even to the extent of being able to call down the obliteration of Buenos Aires by thermonuclear missiles. They were thus enormously feared by the Argentines, but back in the United States, they were national heroes, substantially of the astronaut variety. Little children dreamed of growing up and getting their Ph.D.s in "Psycho-Security Affairs" and then joining the "Probe Corps."

At the end of the story, we learn the historical background of the Peace Probe. A terrible war, World War III, had killed a billion people during 1978–79. Although badly damaged, the United States had emerged as the most powerful nation. At the end of the conflict, the first United States action had been to issue the "Unilateral Declaration," and to establish the "Unilateral Declaration Agency" to enforce it, as a branch of the American government. The "Unilateral Declaration" had set forth these basic principles:

343

First, all foreign arms and armaments designated by the President of the United States are prohibited and must be surrendered, including all nuclear weapons and biological agents. The President may change or add to the prohibited list from time to time, as he sees fit.

Second, all warfare between nations is prohibited. People are free to have whatever form of government they wish within existing international borders, but no nation is to cross those borders with force of arms or interfere coercively with the internal processes of another nation.

Third, an agency is established by the United States to police these requirements. The agency will be free to send its personnel into any country, and will carry out a program of "psycho-probing" leaders, scientists, military men, and whoever else they wish. The probing will be done with drugs, hypnosis, or other techniques that "do not cause avoidable harm to the subject." Questions may be asked concerning any activities prohibited by the Declaration: "Do you have any hidden biological weapons?" "Are you planning to make war?" and so on. The information thus uncovered may be used only for the purposes of the Declaration, and not to prosecute people under local criminal laws or to impose other kinds of local liability.

Fourth, any violation of the principles laid down, as well as any attempt to interfere with the probe agency in the performance of its work, will be punished with strong measures by the United States, up to and including the destruction of whole cities of the offending power. However, if the power cooperates in successfully tracking down the peace violators in their midst (as Argentina does in the story), no punitive action will take place.

Basically, then, the story is a scenario for a futuristic "Pax Americana." Focusing upon the dangers raised by the contemporary technology, it is the picture of one dominant power imposing worldwide peace on a frankly coercive basis. In order to establish a really credible threat that impending violations—for example, the secret production of biological weapons, which is what the story plot turns on—will be discovered, the program includes the use of sophisticated techniques for getting people to tell involuntarily what their plans and intentions are.

What is wrong with the "Peace Probe" approach, if anything? If you don't like it, can you articulate your reasons?

A possible "Pax Russo-Americana."   One obstacle to a "peace

344

Probe," at least today, is that there is no single dominant power that could impose such a peace. We wish to avoid World War III, not to predicate a "solution" on its results (compared to which "Peace Probe" might well be mild). Might *two* or more powers agree to set up a coercive agency on the "Peace Probe" model? For example, could there be a "Pax Russo-Americana" imposed on the rest of the world? How many of the following problems would be present in such a situation:

First, the coercive prohibition of conflict would not extend to the relations of the coercing parties themselves. They would continue to hold weapons, and might be locked into the same mutual "deterrence" posture as today, with the same risks.

Second, there would be no provision for dealing with internal conflict in each coercing party. What if irresponsible elements seized or acquired mass-destruction weapons?

Third, the coercing countries might lose a major incentive to help the less developed world.

Fourth, and even worse, the coercing countries might in time begin to abuse their power to exploit other countries economically, or to impose their political controls on them. Even today, a very plausible argument can be made that we do this to countries such as Panama or the Dominican Republic, and the Russians do it quite flagrantly in Eastern Europe.

Fifth, coercive prohibition of conflict only treats a symptom; it does not come to grips with many of the underlying causes that lead to large-scale violence.

Sixth, the exercise of such power is morally corrosive. Once the principle of "probing" is accepted, the initial limitations of the probing might erode. The ultimate result might then be a continuous monitoring of everybody for everything, and "1984" would have arrived.

How many of the preceding arguments can also be addressed to a unilateral "Peace Probe" situation? Can some of them be met by changes in the procedures? For example, a provision might be added to the "Declaration" to allow internal "probing" within the United States, under a constitutional amendment and rules laid down by Congress, to discover the unauthorized manufacture of mass-destruction weapons or plans for their acquisition. (And, in the case of bilateral action, there could be reciprocal "probing" of Russian and American nationals.) The problems of the underlying causes, which could not be solved with Peace Probe methods, could, however, be

345

dealt with by *other*, longer-term measures. But the immediate need is to reduce or remove the terrible threat posed by the mere existence of weapons of mass destruction in the wrong hands and by the scheming of power-hungry men. These latter, in a sense, are two major "causes" of conflict that could be isolated and dealt with by coercive control.

If the third, fourth, and sixth points remain as obstacles to both unilateral action and, more realistically, a "Pax Russo-Americana," are they powerful enough or *likely* enough to outweigh the benefits? Or is *this* a question that cannot be answered until one has explored in depth the variety and adequacy of *alternative means* of avoiding large-scale conflict? That is, perhaps a "Pax Russo-Americana" is better than World War III, but it may well be the least desirable among *several* alternatives for reducing sharply the likelihood of World War III.

Turning to violent crime, what if there were a Constitutional amendment that would provide for mandatory "psycho-probing" and loss of the privilege against self-incrimination, but *only* for major crimes of *violence* (that is, it would *not* apply to drug offenses, larceny, burglary, sexual conduct, or other non-violent behavior)? Such a measure — the argument for such a proposal might run — would only apply to criminal behavior of the worst type, respecting which there was a clear community consensus. Assume also that the proposed amendment would be "prospective" in its operation; that is, it would apply exclusively to crimes of violence committed after the date of the amendment's adoption, and not to "past history." What arguments could be made for and against such a proposal?

The Security Council. The "Peace Probe" idea is only a rather extreme form of an existing general mode of conflict prevention through imposed control or coercion. The most prominent example is the United Nations Charter, which contains the following provisions:

Article 39

The Security Council shall determine the existence of any threat to the peace, breach of the peace, or act of aggression and shall make recommendations, or decide what measures shall be taken in accordance with Articles 41 and 42, to maintain or restore international peace and security.

Article 41

The Security Council may decide what measures not involving the use of armed force are to be employed to give effect to its decisions, and it may call

346

upon the Members of the United Nations to apply such measures. These may include complete or partial interruption of economic relations and of rail, sea, air, postal, telegraphic, radio, and other means of communication, and the severance of diplomatic relations.

Article 42

Should the Security Council consider that measures provided for in Article 41 would be inadequate or have proved to be inadequate, it may take such action by air, sea, or land forces as may be necessary to maintain or restore international peace and security. Such action may include demonstrations, blockade, and other operations by air, sea, or land forces of Members of the United Nations.

Article 43

1. All Members of the United Nations, in order to contribute to the maintenance of international peace and security, undertake to make available to the Security Council, on its call and in accordance with a special agreement or agreements, armed forces, assistance, and facilities, including rights of passage, necessary for the purpose of maintaining international peace and security.

2. Such agreement or agreements shall govern the numbers and types of forces, their degree of readiness and general location, and the nature of the facilities and assistance to be provided. . . .

These provisions go beyond Article 2 of the Charter, which provides that "All *Members* shall refrain in their international relations from the threat or use of force against the territorial integrity or political independence of any state" (italics added). Articles 39–43 lay down principles and sanctions applicable to any nation that is engaged in aggression or other prohibited conduct, *whether it is a UN member or not.* That is, even if a nation has not agreed to accept the Charter and is not a member state, the Security Council will still regard it as bound by these rules of behavior, and, if necessary, will coerce it into compliance when it violates these rules. This was done, most notably, when North Korea, a non-member, invaded South Korea, also a non-member, in June 1950. Since the Russians were boycotting the Security Council sessions at the time and no veto was exercised, the Security Council called on United Nations members to help repel the North Korean aggression. A number of countries joined in the United Nations force, under the command of General Douglas MacArthur, and not only repelled the invasion, but at one point occupied most of North Korea as well. At that point, the Chinese entered the war, and the battle lines ended up near to the original 38th Parallel division between North and South Korea.

In general, however, the Security Council's power has not been effectively exercised. For one reason, Russia, the United States, Britain, France, and China each has a veto, which it can exercise to defeat any Security Council action, even if all the other powers vote for that action. For another, none of the anticipated agreements for making armed forces available to the Security Council on a long-term basis (see Article 43) were ever negotiated. Instead, on the few occasions when some sort of peace-keeping force has been established, it has been necessary for particular countries to make special, ad hoc agreements to supply troops for the specific purpose, and usually for a limited time. Additionally, funding has usually posed a problem in these operations.

In addition to the principle that the United Nations Charter prohibitions of aggression are binding on non-members, the principle has also been established that if the Security Council finds that prohibited aggression has occurred, the same coercion may be applied against member states, even if they claim that their aggression is justified by other Charter provisions. One provision that may frequently be invoked, for example, is the following:

Article 51

Nothing in the present Charter shall impair the inherent right of individual or collective self-defense if an armed attack occurs against a Member of the United Nations, until the Security Council has taken measures necessary to maintain international peace and security. Measures taken by Members in the exercise of this right of self-defense shall be immediately reported to the Security Council and shall not in any way affect the authority and responsibility of the Security Council under the present Charter to take at any time such action as it deems necessary in order to maintain or restore international peace and security.

But the principle just stated makes it quite clear that the Security Council is to have the final word, despite the objections of a member that it is acting in "self-defense." The Security Council asserted this authority, for example, in insisting on a cease-fire in the Middle East in the June 1967 war.

Article 41 provides that the Security Council may not only act coercively against a Charter violation, but may *require* all members to observe the sanctions (instead of simply calling on the assistance of volunteers). This provision was invoked for the first time against the white-minority government of Rhodesia in 1967, after the latter attempted to declare independence from Great Britain. The sanctions were only a cut-off of trade, however, and had little clear-cut impact. In March 1970 a resolution was introduced in the Security Council to censure Britain for not using force against the rebels. In the case of censure, the party to the dispute (Britain) has no Security Council vote—it would be otherwise with decisions to use or not use *sanctions*—and the censure was avoided only by the United States casting its first veto.

Generally, however, the United Nations has acted *with the agreement* of the parties affected. In such circumstances it has often been able to intercede in disputes with mediation, conciliation, fact-finding, and "buffer forces" to keep the warring parties apart (as in Kashmir and Cyprus), where they wish to be kept apart and not to have provocations or "incidents" between their forces flare into renewed fighting. These United Nations functions have been very valuable, and belong more properly under the "agreement paradigm," discussed later, than under coercive peace-keeping.

Regional control, single-nation control, and world government. Coercive peace-keeping has also been resorted to by regional organizations. When civil war threatened in the Dominican Republic in 1965, for example, the Organization of American States gave a broad interpretation to its Charter and related treaties to allow an OAS force to restore order in the Dominican capital, Santo Domingo. The validity of this action, vis-à-vis the prohibitions against the use of force in the United Nations Charter, turns on the following legal arguments: Article 52 of the Charter does allow "regional arrangements" to deal with matters of international peace and security that "are appropriate for regional action," provided that the actions are consistent with the United Nations Charter. But Article 53 provides that "no enforcement action shall be taken under regional arrangements" without Security Council authorization. Russia and others argued that the Dominican intervention was "enforcement action" and therefore illegal unless prior Security Council approval was obtained. The United States and others argued that "enforcement action" existed only if a regional organization had *ordered* members to supply troops for the action, instead of merely inviting them to supply troops (which was the case in the Dominican action). The United States further argued that the Security Council could ratify such action later, and need not approve it beforehand, and also suggested that ratification in some situations might be inferred from the Security Council's later failure to *dis*approve the action. While the United States arguments may seem somewhat tenuous, even to the non-lawyer, there are nonetheless some good reasons for accepting them, *if* the control paradigm is to be given major effect. It was originally expected that the Security Council would act on substantially all threats to the peace that might require use of armed force, and that the regional organizations would play a strictly secondary role. However, the Security Council has been largely paralyzed by the veto, and in situations like the Dominican Republic, it was clear that if *any* external force was to restore order, it would have to be a regional or national one. Thus the practical argument for expanding the role of regional agencies.

"Coercion" short of armed force has been used by both the United Nations and certain regional organizations. Notable examples are the United Nations-approved economic boycott of trade with the white-separatist government of Rhodesia, referred to previously, and the OAS-approved economic boycott of Cuba. These economic sanctions may have caused some discomfort to the people of the "punished" nations, but there is little sign that this discomfort was translated into pressure on the leaders to change their policies. Indeed, there appear to be various psychological processes which may help the leaders to stimulate a greater sense of solidarity and support among the population against the source of external coercion, as in North Vietnam during the United States bombing. (But, if the question is ever simply one of which *alternative* kind of coercion to use, the availability of non-lethal means must be scrutinized — for example, riot control via tear gas or the "soma" of Huxley's *Brave New World*, rather than guns.)

Coercive peace-keeping may also be employed by a *single* nation upon the territory of another. In the Dominican situation, the United States began a military intervention before the OAS had acted, later defending this action as calculated to "preserve the jurisdiction" of the OAS to act before the situation had gotten out of hand. If any intervention was to take place, it was probably better that it be regional than national, since the OAS presence helped shift the focus of the United States effort. The United States had begun by supporting the Dominican right-wing faction against the left-wing faction, but with OAS involvement ended by simply preserving a buffer between the

two sides and restoring municipal services. Russia intervened coercively in Hungary in 1956 and in Czechoslovakia in 1968 (in the
latter case with some "regional" support from the Warsaw Pact nations, but not in circumstances where any need to "restore the peace"
could plausibly be demonstrated). In general, it would appear that
the smaller the group of nations that is needed to legitimize a particular
use of the control paradigm, the greater the chances that coercion will
be employed simply in the service of the political or economic interests of a single power, and not in the overall interest of world order.

The strongest arguments for expansion of the coercion or control
technique as a means of eliminating large-scale conflict have generally
been cast in terms of world government. Basically, the concept has
been developed from the idea of a Security Council force, as set forth
in Article 43, towards an expanded concept of a single world organization holding a monopoly of force, or at least *more* force than any
individual member. Is this simply the "Peace Probe" suggestion under
another guise? Or does the possession of the force by the entire world
community change the situation in important ways? Consider again
the questions raised about the "Pax Russo-Americana" on p. 345.
How many of these points are adequately answered by the "World
Government" model? (What would you say to a United Nations-
sponsored "peace probe"?) Does such a model raise other potential
problems? What of the problems inherent in centralized governance
of a planet with three and a half billion human beings and a vast array
of economies, cultures, and values? Or can the centralization of
military power be separated from the centralization of general government? Does the problem of "moral corrosion" still apply to such
power as exercised by a world authority? What of the following argument: "The control paradigm, after all, merely reflects the way in
which nations keep peace within their borders. There is no reason
why an international police force should be any more morally cor-
roding than, for example, Sweden's or Great Britain's possession of
a police force." But *is* coercion or force really the chief basis for "keeping the peace" and maintaining respect for law? Do government officials themselves obey the internal laws of their nation because of the
threat of coercion or force? Today legal philosophers have generally
discarded the notion that "law is based on the command of the
sovereign" for the notion that law is more fundamentally based on a
consensus of the community that is being governed. How might we

seek to achieve a consensus of the *world* community that would give effect to *world* law, including the precept that "war shall not be waged"?

The Agreement Paradigm

While nations are far from a consensus on world government, they have reached consensus on a number of major points relating to the potential for lethal conflict. This consensus has been reflected in a series of post-war agreements on armaments and related questions.

Game theory for nations. The reason why these agreements were reached, basically, was that each nation—centrally, in each case, the United States and Russia—felt that its interests would be better served by agreeing than by not agreeing. The prerequisites for successful international negotiations leading to agreements are, of course, far more subtle and complex than this bald statement suggests. Consider the following analysis by Jerome Frank, in *Sanity & Survival.*[1]

Consider the story of the prisoners' dilemma: a district attorney holds two suspects whom he does not have enough evidence to convict. So he goes to each and says that if he confesses and his partner does not, he will get off with a one-year sentence for turning state's evidence, but if he refuses to confess and his partner confesses, he will get the maximum penalty of ten years for his stubbornness; if both confess, each will get a five-year sentence, but if neither confesses, they will be convicted on a lesser charge and each will get two years. Each prisoner thinks to himself: "If I do not confess, I stand to get a two-year sentence (if I can trust my partner also not to confess) or a ten-year sentence if he confesses; but if I confess, the worst that can happen to me is a five-year sentence (if my partner confesses) and I may get off with one year if he does not; so it is to my advantage to confess, especially since my partner is going through the same calculation and will therefore probably confess." Both confess and get five years, whereas if they had trusted each other, they would have been given only two.

Nations would face an analogous problem with a test ban agreement that lacked a foolproof inspection system, so that cheating would be possible. Let us assume that two nations, Neptunia and Plutonia, have signed such an agreement: "'If Plutonia does not cheat,' the Neptunian strategist reasons, 'then clearly it is in Neptunia's interest to cheat; for then we shall be ahead of Plutonia in our research on nuclear weapons. If, on the other hand, Plutonia does cheat, this is all the more reason why we should also cheat; for otherwise we let them get ahead. Consequently, regardless of whether Plutonia cheats or not, it is in our interest to cheat. We must therefore cheat in order to serve our national interest.'

352

"The Plutonian strategist, being in exactly the same position, reasons in exactly the same way and comes to the same conclusioń. Consequently, both countries cheat and in doing so are both worse off than if they had not cheated, since otherwise there was no point to the agreement (which presumably conferred benefits on both countries)."

The issue at stake in such games determines the size of the "payoffs" for the various possible outcomes, thereby influencing the relative strength of the players' motives to cooperate or defect. Regardless of the issue, however, the best outcome for both players will be reached if they trust each other. In Prisoners' Dilemma even the best outcome involves some loss for both, but in disarmament negotiations the cooperative solution would yield great rewards for all parties concerned.

The crucial feature of Prisoners' Dilemma is that it requires mutual trust while strongly tempting the players to try to doublecross each other: to reach the best outcome for both, each must trust the other in the very real sense of giving the other an opportunity to hurt him if he so chooses, but the game puts a premium on successful deceit. The best strategy for each contestant would be to convince his opponent that he will cooperate—so that the opponent will make a cooperative choice—and then defect. In the examples, Prisoner A would fare best if he could convince B that he (A) would never confess so that B would not do so; A could then confess and get a very light sentence at B's expense. In the international version, Plutonia would gain the greatest advantage if it could convince Neptunia that it would not cheat (so that Neptunia would not) and then cheat. Each contestant is torn between the contradictory goals of winning the other's trust and cheating him, and between his desire to trust the opponent and his fear of betrayal.

Prisoners' Dilemma lends itself readily to experimental manipulations— the payoffs can be quantified and the game computerized so that a lot of data can easily be obtained and analyzed. The game's dimensions can all be systematically varied—the payoff schedules, the number of trials permitted, the amount and type of communication permitted the players between and during trials, the extent to which players can "threaten" each other, as well as the players' personal qualities and relations to each other. Prisoners' Dilemma is a happy hunting ground for experimentally-minded social psychologists, and they have been eagerly exploiting it.

Unfortunately, as seems inevitable in a new field, the first crop of results are for the most part trivial or obvious, and their interpretation proves to be more difficult than the researchers had been led to expect. Subjects may be responding to motives arising from the context of the experiment of which the experimenter is not aware and which he cannot control. The "game" they are actually playing may not be the one the experimenter had in mind—they may be trying to do what they think he wants, for example, rather than defeat the opponent. While the conditions of these games are remote from those of international negotiations, some relevant sample findings are still worth presenting as examples of the promise held by experiments with prisoners' dilemma games. One group of findings concerns the role of communication in establishing mutual trust; the other the effect of introducing threats.

Communication and trust. An experiment explored the relationship be-

353

tween trust, trustworthiness, and amount of communication between the players. Each player could choose one of two alternatives, and the payoffs were arranged to tempt each to make the non-cooperative choice, leading to lower payoffs for both than if they had cooperated; to enhance this temptation, each was told to try to win as much as possible for himself without regard to how his opponent fared. The second player was actually an accomplice who made a cooperative choice on the first trial (there were five) and then followed the subject, cooperating or defecting depending on what he had done on the previous trial.

Subjects were divided into several groups, and the amount of communication between them was systematically varied—some neither sent nor received written communications before each trial, some only received them, some only sent them, none did both. The communications contained four levels of information: intentions, expectations as to how the other should respond, what the penalty for defecting would be, and how the other could absolve himself in the next trial if he defected. Of the many measures made, the most interesting for our purposes were perceived trust and trustworthiness — "trust" was defined as the subject's expectation that his opponent would cooperate, as determined by his answer to a question to this effect before each trial, "trustworthiness" as making a cooperative choice. Both were greater, the more complete the communication sent or received: 80 percent of those who sent or received notes containing all four items of information expressed trust and made cooperative choices as compared to only 11 percent of those not allowed to communicate at all; of those who sent or received incomplete communications, the percentage who trusted and cooperated ranged between 30 and 60. This finding lends experimental support to two features of the GRIT proposal: nations should clearly announce their intentions in advance and invite the adversary to cooperate.

Of subsidiary interest is the finding that only 20 percent of the subjects were double-crossers who defected after perceiving that the opponent trusted them, and only a quarter of these had sent a message indicating that they were going to cooperate—committing themselves apparently helped to keep them trustworthy.

Communication and threat. All negotiations include threats in some form, expressed or implied, and these often consist merely of one party's threat to prevent the other from achieving certain ends it desires, a type of threat that lends itself well to experimental study, since it is mild enough to be readily reproduced in the laboratory. The prototype for most such studies is a variable-sum game in which players pretend to operate rival trucking firms, and their earnings depend on being first to get their own trucks to a destination on a short road over which only one can pass at a time; either could use a longer road, which permits him to reach his goal independently of the other player's actions but which costs him money because of the time lost. In some variations one or both players control a gate that could deny the other's access to the short road—and this is the threat. The players have a common interest in working out an arrangement for taking turns on the short road, since this would yield the highest total gain for both, but their interests conflict because the one who uses it first or more often (depending on the variation of the game being studied) profits more.

Three different instructions were used: cooperative—try to win as much for yourself as possible, but you want your opponent to come out ahead also; individualistic—try to do the best for yourself regardless of what happens to him; and competitive—try to come out as far ahead of him as you can. Since variations in instructions, kinds of communication permitted, or power of the players relative to each other, feelings of like or dislike, and schedules of costs and payoffs all have been found to affect players' choices, no general conclusions can safely be drawn from the findings. A few on the effects of communication and threat may be cited, however, as examples of the type of question that can be explored with this technique.

The more competitive the players' orientation, the less likely they were to avail themselves of opportunities to communicate. Communication helped improve both participants' outcomes only when they were required to communicate a fair proposal before each trial, one they would accept if it were offered them by the adversary. If their first trials had ended in deadlock and mutual loss, the tutoring was unnecessary—experience was, as usual, a good teacher.

With respect to the capacity to threaten, a repeated finding was that when both participants had control of a gate—when both had weapons, as it were—they did worse than when neither had a gate.

Apparently, when a player uses a gate, he implies by this use of threat that he feels himself in some sense superior to his opponent—perhaps more courageous, perhaps of higher status—so that it is his opponent's duty to defer to him. To allow onself to be intimidated would therefore implicitly grant the other's right to demand submission—a humiliating posture—and the most effective way of rectifying this blow to self-esteem is to intimidate the threatener. These psychological motivations may contribute to the examples in Chapter 8 of counter-threat on the international scene.

The results in a modification of the trucking game, in which each subject could signal his intentions before each trial and also indicate what he thought the other would do, were shown to be strongly affected by whether the player intended to cooperate, to strive for precisely half the winnings, or to dominate. Cooperative pairs did much better than competitive pairs—hardly a startling finding—but in pairs in which one started with a cooperative and the other with a competitive attitude, both players fared badly in the long run. The cooperative partner's behavior apparently encouraged the competitive one to keep on pushing, until the former got angry and started to fight back, by which time it was too late. If the initially cooperative player immediately made a counter-threat, the players were much more likely to arrive at a cooperative agreement eventually. The moral seems to be, Don't let your opponent think he can take advantage of you,* a finding that casts doubt on the

---

* This can also be viewed as an example of the effect of disappointed expectations, like the finding that a friendly note following a hostile one elicits more friendliness than after a friendly one. There are many real-life analogies— for example, the interrogation technique of suddenly showing consideration for a prisoner after treating him roughly, or the negotiating maneuver of unexpectedly making a concession after being adamant.

effectiveness of turning the other cheek. To test this strategy further, the experimenters led subjects to think that their opponent refused to budge from a conciliatory strategy, even to the extent of accepting an electric shock each time his adversary blocked him. Since the "pacifist" was simulated by a computer, one cannot be sure how convincing he was, but a pacifist strategy did not in itself cause any player to change from a dominating to a cooperative strategy. In some runs, the "pacifist" explained the reason for his behavior, stressing his conciliatory intent, making fair demands, and emphasizing his refusal to use the shock and his intention to force the other to shock him if he were going to continue to be unfair. A small crumb of comfort for pacifists is that of the subjects who changed from dominating to cooperating, all were in the group receiving this communication—unfortunately, however, it reinforced other subjects in their dominating strategy because they saw the pacifist's tactics as efforts to trick them or make them feel guilty.

As far as they go, these experiments confirm the general experience that the more bargainers communicate their intentions and expectations, the better (provided, of course, that the communications are genuinely intended to achieve the best outcome for both parties), and that threats are apt to impede negotiations. The best results for both parties were obtained when neither used threats, but if one player did make a threat, a prompt, firm counterthreat was more likely than a conciliatory initial response to facilitate an ultimately successful outcome. At least in one experimental situation, pacifist strategies do not work.

IMPLICATIONS FOR INTERNATIONAL NEGOTIATIONS

Empirical and experimental studies of negotiations confirm the obvious fact that regardless of the issues, a successful outcome is impeded by the absence of mutual trust and lack of full and accurate communication. Their contribution lies in highlighting specific sources of difficulty that should concern all negotiators, and they also offer certain leads as to how negotiations could be improved.

In almost all international negotiations it is reasonable to assume some potential basis for mutual trust—even in war there are often tacit bargains between the combatants. The Prisoner's Dilemma depends on trust to the extent that both players must trust the person who sets the rules: if the prisoners did not trust the district attorney, there would be no dilemma, and each would simply refuse to confess and would take his chances. One important way of improving the chances for the successful outcome of negotiations, regardless of substantive issues, would thus be to pinpoint and combat sources of mutual mistrust. Participants in all negotiations could well make special efforts to get into the open the psychological sources of mutual misunderstanding and mistrust that operate out of awareness, including conflicting habits of thought and ways of proceeding, and above all, the universal difficulty in really hearing what the other fellow is saying — Adlai Stevenson's quip, "I sometimes think that what America needs more than anything else is a hearing aid," applies to all countries. If only it were enforceable, a splendid ground rule for all negotiations would be that there would be no bargaining until the parties could express each other's positions to their mutual satisfaction. Unfortunately, as demonstrated by the experiments on understanding the adversary's position, this is much more difficult than it seems, and I urge the reader to try it in his next disagreement with a friend or colleague — it is amazing how one's own thoughts keep intruding. Even if it is unattainable, however, merely striving for this goal would improve the atmosphere of all negotiations. As all psychotherapists know, the best way to get someone's favorable attention is to listen to him, not talk to him. To feel that a person is trying his best to understand you, especially someone you believe to be hostile or indifferent, creates a very favorable impression of his good sense, intelligence, and good will, and you are then in a much more receptive frame of mind for his ideas.

From the organizational standpoint, the goal would be to set up conditions that foster in the negotiators a cooperative rather than a competitive stance. The aim would be to reduce the barriers between the groups by making each feel, at every step of the way, that they are working on a joint enterprise. Instead of negotiators being selected by each group separately, for example, they could be chosen jointly from a panel of names put up by each; this "criss-cross" panel would weaken the "traitor trap," because the negotiators would consider themselves representatives of both groups, who would have implicitly committed themselves in advance to accept the outcome of the bargaining. This procedure is hardly feasible at the moment in international political negotiations, but it could perhaps be used to improve cultural, economic, and scientific negotiations.

At every step of the way it might also be possible to involve both groups in selecting problems to be discussed and devising alternative solutions, thereby taking advantage of people's greater readiness to accept innovations when they feel they have participated in their planning. An experiment testing the feasibility of such a procedure contrasted fixed with fluid negotiations: using the general group-conflict experimental plan, each of the competing groups first developed a set of alternative solutions to the problem rather than a single one. Group representatives in fixed negotiations were told to try to get their group's alternatives adopted, while in the fluid ones they were instructed to work with the other group's representatives to develop the best single ranking of both sets; according to independent judges, the list of alternatives arrived at jointly contained the best from each group, and included some new, creative ones not in either group's original list. That such procedures are of more than. theoretical importance is suggested by the finding that they improve outcomes of management-labor negotiations.

Perhaps the place to start would be in schools of international relations, political science, and law, where budding diplomats could participate in the kinds of experiments reviewed here. There would be powerful learning experiences in discovering at first hand that you really have not understood your adversary's proposal, despite your conviction that you have, or that group pressures hamstring you in reaching an agreement, or how differences in amount and type of communication can affect mutual trust.

An important lesson to be learned from this review is that major psychological obstacles to successful international negotiations lie in the negotiating parties' attitudes. Procedural improvements can be of some help, but real progress depends on convincing nations that they have become genuinely interdependent. International negotiations, especially those involving armaments, have become prisoners' dilemmas in which all nations have more to gain by cooperating than by competing, and in which, in fact, persistence in competitive attitudes can bring all to disaster.

Day by day the advances in science, mass communication, and mass transportation are increasing this interdependence. The psychological problem is how to make all people aware that whether they like it or not, the earth is becoming a single community.

Game theory for the United States and Russia. The "Prisoner's Dilemma" is an example of game theory, an analytical tool that is sometimes quite useful in considering international negotiating situations. At the most basic level, the application of game theory to the situation of the United States and Russia is not highly complicated. Both parties possess terrible destructive power, and use of it against each other would cause awful destruction. If, for example, you add up everything that is important to each nation — people, factories, cultural institutions, quality of life — and arbitrarily assign the number "100" to the sum of all these present values, then a major war between the two countries might be expected, let us say, to result in a probable reduction of 80 units for each side, so that each would end with $100 - 80 = 20$. The effect of such a war on each side might be described (in the coldest and most abstract way, but for a purpose) as "−80." Even if war does not occur, each nation might consider the present costs of the arms race and other military preparations: resources are diverted from urgent domestic needs and consumer production; men must serve in the army; the quality of life suffers through militarization, fear, and suspicion. If, through disarmament, these costs could be made unnecessary, the value to each party might be equal, let us say, to an addition of 25 units. Thus, under these circumstances, each might end up with $100 + 25 = 125$. The effect of disarmament and conversion to peaceful pursuits might be described as "+25."

Why doesn't one side simply disarm, then? Because if *only* it disarms, it fears the other side will *then* attack (or at least will push so hard that it will have to re-arm, at greater cost than keeping the original armament). Wholly defenseless, it might suffer a loss of 90 units,

358

while the other side under such circumstances might gain as much as 50 units (or alternatively the disarmed nation might have to re-arm, at a cost of at least 10 units, versus the hoped-for gain of 25, and all this while the other side might gain 10). Thus, the real effect of attempting to disarm, when the other side did not, would be a loss of at least 10 units, and perhaps as many as 90.

One way of picturing all of this is to show the results for each party if various pairs of "strategies" are followed:

U.S.	RUSSIA	GAIN OR LOSS (U.S./RUSSIA)
War	/War	−80/−80
Status Quo	/Status Quo (mutually "pushing," mutually "deterring")	0/0
Disarmament/Status Quo (that is, "pushing," but short of war)		−10/+10
Disarmament/War		−90/+50
Status Quo	/Disarmament	+10/−10
War	/Disarmament	+50/−90
Disarmament/Disarmament		+25/+25

Thus the cooperative strategy of "Disarmament/Disarmament" is the only one which assures a gain to both parties. On the other hand, it is possible that one or the other will hope for the situation in which it can "win" a crushing victory and 50 points (where no account is taken of the psychological burden placed on the "victors"). But a country that preserves the status quo in the hope of such a "gain" not only foregoes the clear possibility of gaining 25 through cooperating on disarmament, but runs the risk that the "status quo" will eventually lead to "War/War," with horrendous losses for both sides. Even on this bloodless analysis, a cooperative strategy of disarmament clearly seems to be the best.

The history of arms agreements. How much agreement on armaments *has* been achieved, and why hasn't there been more? Prior to World War II, the beginnings of a network of permanent treaties on subjects of conflict appeared. In the early years of the century, agreement was reached on certain laws of land and naval warfare, on prohibiting attacks on undefended civilian centers, on use of certain particularly painful weapons, on providing for decent treatment of prisoners of war, and on other subjects. In general, the matters covered did not relate to the balance of forces, but rather to the use of those forces in a "civilized" way. After World War I, the United States, Great Britain, and Japan agreed in 1921 to limit naval armaments by maintaining a 5–5–3 ratio of battleships among the three powers, respectively. Of all of these agreements, the only one that endured tolerably well through World War II was that concerning prisoners of war (with some major exceptions for the Japanese). Massive bombings of cities by both the Axis and the Allies, and new weapons, such as napalm, made a shambles of most of the restrictions on killing civilians and on using painful weapons.

The 1925 treaty on chemical and biological weapons may be the longest-lived major treaty on warfare that has not been broken in substantial ways. This may have less to do with the treaty, of course, than with the fears of unpredictable retaliation, or perhaps (for the biological agents especially) with a sense of universal opposition to this means of warfare, or simply with the uncertainty of controlling the agents once they were let loose. The United States and Japan were the only two major powers *not* parties to the treaty, but they did not use such weapons against each other, either. Although the treaty prohibited the use of such weapons by the *signatories* against one another, it did not prohibit their use by *non*-signatory states, nor did it prevent the development and stockpiling of such weapons, short of their actual employment. Efforts to bring about a broadening of the treaty to cover development and stockpiling are now being pursued through the 18-nation Geneva Disarmament Conference, which meets under United Nations auspices. (What is the function of such an extension? What possible problems do you see in implementing such an extension?)

In the post-World War II period, there are generally considered to be four major treaties on armaments and related matters. They are, with their dates of Senate ratification (Senate ratification requires a two-thirds majority of those present), the Antarctic Treaty (1960), the Partial Nuclear Test-Ban Treaty (1963), the Treaty on Outer Space (1967), and the Nuclear Non-Proliferation Treaty (1969).

The Antarctic treaty provides that the continent of Antarctica shall not be militarized, and prohibits any nation from asserting sovereignty over any part of the area. The dynamic behind this treaty was largely the perception that, otherwise, there was going to be a "race" to claim parts of Antarctica, and perhaps to emplace weapons there. These actions would have caused frictions, would have been expensive, and might have had unpredictable consequences, all for little or no gain in real "security." Thus, the parties saw a common interest in reaching agreement, and were able to do so.

The partial test-ban ends all testing of nuclear and thermonuclear weapons in the air, in outer space, and underwater by the parties to the treaty. It is "partial" because it does not cover *underground* explosions, for the reason that such explosions were difficult to detect (unlike the other kinds prohibited) with instruments usable at a distance. This difficulty of detection meant that any "suspicious" seismic events, or at least some number of them annually, would have had to be subject to on-site inspections. The Russians wished to limit the number of such inspections to a figure lower than that which we would accept as safe. Since we were unwilling to trust the Russians not to cheat, underground tests were excluded from the treaty.

There were several dynamics behind this treaty. The United States and Russia felt they would make only insignificant improvements in warheads with continued above-ground testing (underground testing and computer-simulation could meet most of the marginal needs that remained). But if other nations felt free to test above ground, it would be somewhat easier for nuclear weapons to proliferate — underground testing of a country's first nuclear device would be more difficult, at least, and more expensive. Moreover, there was an early "pollution scare" that fallout products like strontium 90 would gradually poison the environment, increasing mutations and deaths from cancer. This fear was a direct source of political pressure on the United States government from its own citizens, and of indirect pressure on both governments from other concerned nations, like Japan and India, whose friendship they wanted. On balance, both the United States and Russia had more to gain from stopping above-ground tests than from continuing (although there were some "voices of doom," such as Dr. Edward Teller's, when the United States signed the treaty). The treaty did not, however, purport to bind non-signers, and France and China remained outside the signatory group. Moreover, each signatory state could withdraw "if it decides that extraordinary events, related to the subject matter of this treaty, have jeopardized the supreme interests of its country." Presumably, "extraordinary events" might include an untrustworthy neighbor developing its own nuclear weapons. In any case, the treaty has been observed so far by the more than 100 countries that have signed it, and no country has yet withdrawn.

The outer space treaty is rather similar to that concerning Antarctica. No nation may place weapons of mass destruction in orbit around the earth, in outer space, on the moon, or on the planets. Nor may any country claim sovereign rights in space. Again, the rationale for the treaty was a mutual fear of a race to claim rights or implant weapons — a race that would be dangerous, costly, unpredictable, and futile. Over a long period of time, this may prove to be one of the most important treaties ever signed, and a century from now it might well be looked back upon as the most crucial and farsighted act of the Johnson administration.

The non-proliferation treaty prohibits signatories possessing nuclear weapons from assisting other nations to acquire a nuclear capability, and prohibits those signatories who do *not* have nuclear weapons from seeking to develop, test, or acquire them. Clearly it is a treaty in the interest of the nuclear powers (although, again, France and China have not signed). The advantages to the non-nuclear powers are that it may prevent an expensive and extremely dangerous race with their neighbors to acquire nuclear weapons, and that mutual non-proliferation leaves a much safer world than one in which ten, twenty, or thirty nations possess nuclear weapons. Unfortunately many of the key countries, such as India, Japan, and Israel, have not yet ratified the treaty. Moreover, if one or two such countries remain aloof from the treaty and in fact develop nuclear weapons, other countries are likely to use the "supreme interest" clause, similar to that in the partial test-ban treaty, to withdraw and develop their own nuclear weapons. There are also indications that some countries will not remain content with the treaty if the nuclear "haves" blithely continue to *increase* their armaments, widening the power and prestige gap between themselves and the nuclear "have-nots." (Is this problem analyzable in terms of what we have said previously about leaders and status?) This treaty stands as an important step toward preventing proliferation, but it seems far from definitive.

In addition to the negotiation of a broadened biological-weapons treaty, the Committee of the (18-nation) Conference on Disarmament agreed in mid-1970 on a treaty that would prohibit affixing mass-destruction weapons to the seabed. This is a start towards a general limitation of weapons in the ocean. The treaty was signed by the United States, Russia, and Britain (not France or China) in February 1971, preparatory to final ratification by their respective constitutional processes. Meanwhile, the United States and Russia are continuing their own bilateral discussions, called "SALT" (Strategic Arms Limitation Talks), attempting to limit the deployment of ABM and MIRV systems. As this was written, the Russians had reportedly offered to limit ABM deployment to the Moscow area, in return for our limitation of ABM to the Washington area. (Is this good or bad? What might such deployment do to the attitudes of leaders? To the actual safety of leaders? Might the two effects be quite different — that is, to make the leaders more "carefree" subjectively, but *less* safe objectively, if a war should occur? If so, why?) About the multiple warhead missiles, however, one of the most respected members of the scientific community was writing in late 1970, "By now the development of MIRV has probably gone too far (especially in this country) to stop it and maintain a ban on it except by the use of unacceptable inspection methods."[2]

The inspection problem in disarmament. The question of inspection has been a major problem in reaching agreement on armaments. Underground nuclear tests could not be detected, so agreement to limit them was not attempted, lest there be cheating. Once they have been tested and deployment has begun, MIRV installations cannot be detected without inspection at close quarters — probably of the actual warhead on the rocket. Since this kind of inspection would give away "secrets" or violate a sense of national "integrity," it seems unlikely that the parties would trust each other enough to allow it. Inspection is a major problem, if any existing weapons stockpiles are to be eliminated by agreement, since it would require very close observation to be sure how many weapons a party destroyed, and it would be virtually impossible — short of "Peace Probe" techniques — to be positive of how many weapons he had kept. Until inspection or other techniques become more sophisticated, it thus seems that any broad nuclear arms elimination agreement in the near future would be in the following form: "I will *destroy* two hundred one-megaton warheads and one hundred Minutemen-II-type rockets, inviting you to inspect in advance the materials to be destroyed and to be present at their destruction." Such an agreement would not be meaningful in the form, "I will *retain* only five hundred megatons of warheads, and only three hundred Minutemen-II-type rockets."

How can the inspection problem be resolved to facilitate additional agreements, restricting new arms developments and eliminating substantial amounts of existing armaments? There is, of course, always the possibility of improving the existing inspection methods. For example, better seismic detectors may eventually allow the addition of underground nuclear tests to the prohibited category, without concern over the problems of on-site inspection. If either side violates the ban, the violation will be detected on the other's super-seismographs, and therefore neither party is likely to violate the ban (for, if it does, the other party will, presumably, resume underground testing itself. Thus the violator will simply have undone an agreement that he presumably thought beneficial in the first place). Or entirely new kinds of inspection may be introduced. One new kind of inspection of great importance is satellite surveillance, and even a list of those United States and Russian satellites that are not avowedly military runs past 500 launchings in the last two years. The surveillance satellites on each side have high-power cameras, sufficient to detect the make of a car from more than a hundred miles up. Many of them have sophisticated eavesdropping or electronic equipment, and some have infrared detectors that can sense a rocket blasting off. Today, they are almost certainly adequate to bring news of a major military buildup or a multiple rocket launching. Tomorrow, they may approach the point of being able to "bug" everything but an insulated super-security room. Moreover, a satellite can be synchronized with the earth's rotation so that it can hover over and send back data from a single area. (Potentially, there are some nearly "Peace Probe"-type problems with this kind of surveillance, and these should be the subject of conscious public decision.)

In fact, the deployment of these "spy satellites" represents another, and quite important, United States-Russian agreement, in this case one that was probably tacit rather than express. When Eisenhower proposed "open skies" in 1955, allowing reconnaissance planes of each side to fly over the other country to ensure against surprise attack and increase mutual confidence, the Russians rejected the proposal. When we sent our U-2 reconnaissance planes over Russia nonetheless, the Russians shot one down and a bitter dialogue ensued. However, when first the Russians and then the United States began to launch satellites that passed over the other's territory in the late 1950s, neither side objected (it was we who *first* failed to object, which in a sense can be regarded as an "initiative strategy" like those described in the next section). At that time, international law only recognized clear sovereignty up to the height where the atmosphere would sustain flight by winged aircraft. One or two hundred miles up was a legal limbo, where the parties might have decided to go either way in asserting their "rights." They might have claimed sovereignty in *all* the supervening space over their territory, now that non-winged "flight" was possible, made loud complaints about the "overflight" of another's satellites, and started a multi-billion dollar crash program to shoot them down. Instead, a studious silence was maintained by all nations. This uncomplained-of behavior, over many months, began to harden into what most international lawyers would call a new "rule of international law," tacitly accepted, that no nation had sovereignty beyond the atmosphere and that satellite overflights therefore did not violate its territory (this now seems confirmed by the outer space treaty).

In addition to the mutual advantage gained from espionage by satellite, each side probably perceives a certain safety factor in having secret espionage agents on the ground, equipped with increasingly sophisticated equipment. Notably, the penalties for convicted spies in recent years have been relatively light, and the parties have shown great alacrity in exchanging convicted spies long before their prison terms were up.

But even with all of these informal inspection techniques, it may be doubtful whether agreement could be reached on really major measures of nuclear disarmament unless additional formal inspections were agreed upon (for example, several international teams that could arrive unannounced at command centers or "suspicious sites" to question, measure, and investigate). And few countries seem likely to agree to this degree of inspection. Inspections would be seen as violating "privacy" or "integrity," or as a way of "stealing secrets" or "gathering data" about the disposition of remaining forces, in preparation for an attack. What steps might *enhance* willingness to allow more inspection? Or is it hopeless? Would it seem likely that at least some major areas of mutual agreement—for example, an enlarged biological-weapons treaty covering manufacture and stockpiling— would be possible without either the United States or Russia insisting on inspection? Even though there would not be total assurance against violation, such a treaty might still accomplish several major purposes, including a reinforcement of national decisions against ever using such weapons, and an enhancement of mutual trust. Would such a treaty, by itself, be an adequate protection against the menace of biological weapons over a 50- or 100-year period? If not, how can we deal with the long-term threat, other than by "Peace Probe" techniques?

Other agreements to prevent conflict. In addition to agreements on arms and related matters, there have of course been important agreements on other aspects of the prevention or resolution of large-scale conflict. The United Nations was created out of broad agreement among nations, and provides a forum for continuous discussion and contact at a human level, even between representatives of the worst "enemies." It also offers a forum at which nations that badly misbehave (according to standards that they and others purport to accept), or that blatantly lie, are likely to be haled before a world audience and embarrassed. At the same time, it offers the possibility of working out many disagreements "in the hall," quietly and away from the glare of publicity that would accompany a formal conference. Apart from mutual agreement on the general mechanisms of the organization, specific agreement among Security Council members has also been required on each specific issue where the United Nations has provided peacekeeping forces, truce teams, or fact finders as part of an alternative to violent conflict (Indonesia in 1947, Kashmir in 1948, the Mideast in 1956,* the Congo in 1960, Cyprus in 1964).

Recall Jerome Frank's discussion of the importance of the atmosphere of negotiations, and of the techniques used in negotiations, in relation to the probability of successful agreement on *any* subject. Consider this in relation to such diverse problems as communication between ghetto blacks and police, or communication between the United States and Russia during the Cuban missile crisis. Consider in this light the problems of reaching agreement between students and university administrators in a "confrontation" situation, or the problems of reaching four-way agreement among the parties at the Paris peace talks. In which of these situations does "worst feasible case" analysis of the intentions of the other side prevail? Is it possible to improve the atmosphere of many contemporary negotiations so drastically that agreements that now appear impossible become possible?

Agreement on the mechanisms to be used may frequently be possible where agreement on the substantive issues is not. *Such mechanisms may then go far towards facilitating later agreement on specific substantive issues.* Consider, for example, the potential usefulness of agreement on the following:

Agreement to supply, as one of the "facilities" under Article 43 of the United Nations Charter, skilled manpower and financing for a permanent United Nations fact-finding and observer corps, which

*Pursuant to General Assembly, rather than Security Council, action.

366

could be instantly dispatched to any trouble spot to observe and report back objectively to the world community on the facts surrounding the particular conflict.

Agreement within this hemisphere to establish a parallel institution for the OAS.

Establishment within the United Nations of a permanent body for mediation or conciliation of disputes. What if, moreover, such a "mediator" was not simply passive? It could be further agreed that the mediator could make his own non-binding recommendations to the parties for settlement terms, thus avoiding the simple polarization of position found in numerous negotiations (these recommendations, however, could remain non-public unless the parties agreed otherwise). Also, the mediator would have his own staff of international civil servants, whom *he* could use to gather evidence, interview witnesses or experts, and generally question the basis for the parties' own arguments.

There are, of course, many other possible subjects of agreement that do not directly involve armaments. Consider, as examples, the potential significance and impact of the following:

An agreement to establish and finance a United Nations Youth Service Corps. Ten thousand young applicants would be selected by the United Nations, and would fulfill their own country's military service obligations by serving in the Corps.

A treaty prohibiting all signatories from interfering with the movement of their own citizens into and out of the country, bound for any destination.

A treaty granting dual or overlapping rights of citizenship to certain categories of persons — for example, Nobel Prize winners — or establishing "world" citizenship for them, with free right of movement.

The Initiative Paradigm:
"True GRIT"

Unilateral initiative strategy. What is the role of *unilateral* initiatives in working toward the goal of a peaceful world? Some of the most important thinking of the past decade has focused on measures such as those described in 1966 by Charles Osgood, a psychologist, communicator, and disarmament strategist, in *Perspectives in Foreign Policy*.[3]

CALCULATED
DE-ESCALATION AS
A STRATEGY

About seven years ago, at the height of tensions in the nuclear confrontation between the United States and the Soviet Union, several proposals for the control and gradual reduction of tensions in international relations appeared. One of these was a policy paper of mine bearing the most inprobable title, *Graduated and Reciprocated Initiatives in Tension-reduction*. I soon discovered that no one, including myself, could remember the title, even though it stated the essence of the policy proposal clearly and succinctly. Later I discovered that the initials spelled out G-R-I-T — which was an appropriate acronym, because *grit* is exactly what its execution requires.

Running the escalator in reverse. GRIT is a strategy of calculated de-escalation of international tensions. It is the application of *interpersonal* communication and learning principles to *international* relations — where the communication is more by deeds than by words and where what is learned is mutual understanding, trust, and respect. The fullest development of this approach, as a policy, has been presented in a paperback of mine called *An Alternative to War or Surrender* (University of Illinois Press, 1962).

This strategy can be thought of as running Herman Kahn's escalator in reverse. Steps in military escalation are *unilaterally initiated;* we do not negotiate with the North Vietnamese about increasing the tempo of our bombing or moving it closer to Hanoi and the Chinese border — we just do it. But each step we take threatens the opponent into *reciprocating* with aggressive steps of his own. Steps are *graduated* — to the extent that the escalation is calculated and controlled, that risk-taking is counter-balanced by prudence, and that the political objectives are limited. But military escalation is deliberately *tension-increasing*. Now, let us reverse just one of these features — change tension-production to tension-reduction — and see what we discover as a strategy.

We would have a situation in which nation A would devise patterns of small steps, well within its limits of security, intended to reduce tensions and carefully designed so as to induce reciprocation from nation B. When reciprocation is obtained, the margin for risk-taking is widened and somewhat larger steps can be taken. The direct effect of this process is damping of the escalation in mutual tensions and lessened chances of expanded war; the psychological side-effect is increased mutual confidence and trust. Both nations are gradually learning how to behave in a nuclear age.

The carrot and the stick. The rules we want each opponent to learn are these: (1) if he tries to change the status quo by force, we will firmly resist and restore the status quo; (2) if he tries to change the status quo by means that reduce tensions, we will reward him by steps having similar intent; (3)

if he tries to take advantage of initiatives we make in his favor, we will shift immediately to firm and punishing resistance; (4) if, on the other hand, he reciprocates to our initiative with steps of his own having similar intent, we will reward him with somewhat larger steps designed to reduce tensions. This is what I mean by *calculated* de-escalation. My colleagues in psychology would recognize this strategy as the familiar process of deliberately "shaping" behavior, here being suggested for use on an international scale. Needless to say, we have to follow the same rules if we expect others to learn them, and this is precisely what we have *not* been doing in Vietnam.

Is it possible simultaneously to maintain our national security and yet to behave in such a way as to induce reciprocation from a hostile opponent? In the book already referred to, I tried to spell out in some detail how this could be done; here I can merely state the criteria without elaboration. *To maintain security:* (a) we retain during the process our capacity to inflict unacceptable nuclear retaliation should we be attacked at that level; (b) during the process we retain capacities for conventional military resistance adjusted to the level of tension existing; (c) we graduate our tension-reducing initiatives according to the degree of reciprocation obtained from any opponent; (d) we diversify our initiatives both as to nature and as to geographic locus of application; and (e) the nature, locus, and time of announcement of our initiatives are unpredictable by the opponent. *To induce reciprocation:* (a) we persistently communicate our sincere intent to reduce and control international tensions; (b) our initiatives are publicly announced at some reasonable interval prior to their execution and identified with the general policy; (c) each announcement includes explicit invitation to reciprocation, but with form not necessarily specified; (d) announced initiatives are executed on schedule regardless of any prior commitment by the opponent to reciprocate; and (e) planned patterns of initiatives are continued over a considerable period of time, regardless of reciprocations given or even of tension-increasing events elsewhere.

It should be noted carefully that this strategy does include the "stick" as well as the "carrot." We retain a minimal but sufficient nuclear deterrent as well as appropriately graded conventional forces, so that we can effectively resist military escalations by others. But we *think* of these capabilities not simply as a deterrent but rather as a security base enabling us to take the persistent, calculated steps necessary to move toward a less dangerous world. If any opponent misinterprets our initiatives as a sign that we are "going soft," and makes an aggressive probe to test his interpretation — as the Soviets did in Cuba — then we shift promptly to the "stick"; we resist firmly, and punishingly if necessary, yet calculatedly, using precisely that level of force required to restore the status quo. As a matter of fact, such probes provide the most effective kinds of learning experience — for both sides. This was the lesson I think the Soviet Union learned from the Cuban missile crisis.

Can escalation and de-escalation strategies be "mixed"?   Just as military men speak of the best "mix" of weapon systems, in order to be prepared for all contingencies, so may political theorists think about the best "mix" of strategies to obtain objectives of foreign policy. As a matter of fact, this seems to be precisely what we have been trying to do in Vietnam. With one hand we have been escalating our military effort, both in the air and on the ground; with the other hand we have been holding out an olive branch tagged with "unconditional negotiations" and "economic aid." And we have been busily talking out of both sides of our mouths in the attempt to make this posture credible. But note, first, that our launching of air attacks on North Vietnam territory represented an attempt to change the status quo rather than restore it (clearly analogous to the Soviet attempt to implant nuclear delivery systems on Cuba); and note, second, that our attempts at de-escalation have all been in the form of words, not deeds. We are discovering the hard way that this "mix" of strategies will not work.

There is a fundamental incompatibility between escalation and de-escalation strategies. To obtain the reciprocations upon which GRIT must operate, the opponent must accept as bona fide the *intent* to reduce tensions — which is a bit difficult when bombs are raining about his head. GRIT also requires that our own government be able to take the initiative in designing and executing moves of a tension-reducing nature — which is a bit difficult in the face of charges of being "chicken." In the absence of accurate communication and shared understandings — to which, Herman Kahn points out, de-escalation is more sensitive than escalation — tension-reducing initiatives are likely to be so hedged about with conditions for home consumption that they are almost certain to be rejected. Prophecies about the intransigence of the opponent are thus fulfilled, and we find ourselves pushed still further up the escalation ladder, which still further blocks accurate communication of intent and disrupts shared understandings, except those of mutual fear and anger.

Escalation and de-escalation in relation to negotiation.   As I was writing the first draft of this section of the book on the first day of the new year, American diplomats were flying about the world — Ambassador Harriman to Poland and Yugoslavia, Ambassador Goldberg to Rome and Paris, former White House adviser, McGeorge Bundy, to Canada — all expressing our earnest desire for a negotiated settlement. There was a lull in the air bombardment of North Vietnam — although exactly the same planes were making steady sorties along the Ho Chi Minh trail in Laos and Cambodia. I had no doubts about the earnestness of our government's desire for peace, but I had grave doubts about the success of these endeavors. I made the pessimistic prediction then that these endeavors would fail — except for creating the impression at home that, as Secretary of State Dean Rusk has repeatedly put it, *they* are the ones who do not want peace. I am sorry this prediction was borne out, but it does underscore a fact about international life: if there is one thing that is true about an escalator, it is that you can't make it go up and down at the same time.

Escalation and de-escalation thus bear an intimate relation to the process of negotiation. It seems perfectly clear that a political policy of tension escalation, calculated or otherwise, can only hamper or even render impossible successful negotiations. It creates an atmosphere of resentment and distrust in which honest dealings cannot be expected. Worse, we can hardly expect those who have been bombed into negotiating to honor any agreements reached — they have every psychological justification for subsequent defection, as the Germans displayed so clearly after World War I. Calculated de-escalation, on the other hand, is explicitly designed to create and maintain an atmosphere of mutual trust within which agreements of increasing significance become possible. There is thus an intimate facilitative relation between non-negotiated steps of a tension-reducing nature and formal negotiations; there is a fundamentally antagonistic relation between military escalation and negotiation. To talk about bombing people into a negotiated settlement is deeply irrational — into surrender, yes, but not into honest negotiation.

De-escalation vis-à-vis the Soviet Union. Is all this an idealist's pipe-dream when set against the cold facts of a harsh, real world? Not at all. We have been quietly following this kind of policy vis-à-vis the Soviet Union for nearly three years, ever since the Cuban missile crisis. We did not eliminate any of our overseas bases when Khrushchev demanded it as a bargain for Cuba, but later we denuclearized bases in both Italy and Turkey on our own initiative. Since then there have been reciprocative moves in many areas, in reducing the production of fissionable materials, in cutting back military budgets, in cultural exchanges, and so forth. Note that these have not been negotiated agreements, requiring prior commitments from both sides, but rather reciprocal initiatives, requiring only post commitment for their continuation. The Soviets have even created their own name for it — *the policy of mutual example!*

Have the predicted psychological side-effects — reduced tensions and increased mutual trust — occurred? Each reader can be his own judge as to whether or not the Russian Bogey has been cut down somewhat in size over the past three years, even though the Soviet Union remains the major threat to our security by virtue of its nuclear capability. We apparently felt enough trust to send Ambassador-at-large Averill Harriman to Moscow in a fruitless attempt to gain their mediation in a negotiated settlement in Vietnam during the summer of 1965. I would argue that the Soviet Union would not have maintained its posture of relative neutrality with respect to Vietnam (in actions, if not in words) for so long a period had we not been successful in modifying the harshness of our image in their eyes. Our national image is now shifting in the opposite direction, however.

Can a powerful nation successfully apply GRIT? The immediate answer to this question is that it is much easier for a powerful nation to apply GRIT than a weak nation. Yet, interestingly enough, this is one of the strategies of international relations that can also be applied effectively by a small nation toward a great one. I am reminded of the way Finland, a previously conquered country with its back right up against the mighty Soviet Union, has been able to preserve not only its independence but its dignity. It should be illuminating to study in detail how relations between Finland and the Soviet Union developed following their military conflict.

But this strategy can be applied easier by a powerful nation. It has many bulges in the existing status quo in its favor, and each bulge — be it in terms of military allocations or in terms of economic allocations — represents an opportunity for calculated steps in the right direction. Does any step which redresses the status quo in someone else's favor necessarily mean a loss for

371

us? Fortunately, this is not the case: the greater the well-being and security of others, Communists included, the greater in the long run will be our own well-being and security.

But acceptance of such a controlled tension-reducing policy as GRIT requires denial of certain assumptions we usually make about our world. One is that our invulnerable nuclear retaliatory capability is nothing more than a deterrent. The fact is that the same nuclear power that deters, by virtue of its deterrent value, also provides the possessor with a margin of security within which to take limited risks. The deep issue of policy today is how we use this margin for risk-taking — in ways that narrow it or widen it.

Another assumption is that the only way to maintain credibility, that we would use our nuclear weapons if sufficiently provoked, is by presenting an image of implacable hostility toward opponents. The psychological fact is that a powerful nation like the United States can create credibility without provocation — by predictably encouraging acceptable means of changing the status quo and *equally predictably* discouraging unacceptable means. This is the proper use of the carrot and the stick.

A third assumption is that the only way to change the status quo in the direction of tension-reduction is by prior commitments on both sides, usually via negotiations. This is not necessary. We can substitute *post* commitment (via reciprocation) for prior commitment (via negotiation) as the necessary condition for continuing steps designed to control and reduce tensions between ourselves and others. We have done this successfully with the Soviet Union. GRIT enables a nation to take the initiative in changing the status quo, but without provocation and within reasonable limits of national security.

Muffed opportunity in Cuba. If our recent relations with Russia provide an example of successful application of GRIT, then our recent relations with Cuba are an example of failure to apply it where we had a golden opportunity. By all criteria, the Cuban revolution against the dictator Batista was a popular uprising. The ordinary people were oppressed, ill-fed, ill-housed, and poorly educated; even those Americans whose interests received favored treatment from Batista found it hard to stomach his regime. Despite what he later claimed, there is no evidence that Castro himself was a Communist at that time, nor did the communist underground take an active part in the revolution until a successful conclusion was in sight. We had an opportunity to make Cuba a viable demonstration of our readiness to support popular revolutions, but we muffed it.

When Castro decided to nationalize American interests in sugar, fruit, and oil — and (as I understand it) requested a long-term loan to repay the companies involved, either at the valuation they now claimed, if they would pay back taxes, or at the valuation used for tax purposes under Batista — our government would have none of it. Led by *Life* and *Time*, a large segment of the mass media shifted abruptly from talking about progress and promise to talking about execution and dictatorship. In just a few months, the Castro image was changed from bearded hero to bearded villain. I believe history will ultimately record that we literally drove the Cuban revolution into the arms of the Soviet Union and thence to Communism.

372

Be that as it may, we now have Castro parading around in our own back-yard like an angry little cock. Astonishing and heretical as it may sound, I would argue that we *still* could wean Cuba away from Communism, in fact if not in name, by persistent application of the kind of calculated de-escalation embodied in GRIT. The real needs of the Cuban people are for normalcy in their relations with the rest of the Western Hemisphere, particularly the United States. In a number of speeches — within the limits of his own kind of pride and amidst bursts of belligerent oratory — Castro *has* made gestures toward rap-prochement, the most recent being the arrangements for dissident Cubans to migrate to the United States. As I have argued elsewhere (*The Nation*, January 5, 1963), Castro would probably reciprocate to a carefully designed pattern of graduated moves on our part — to get agricultural machinery, medical sup-plies, an expanded market for his sugar, and so on. If such an endeavor failed, we might suffer a little hurt pride; if it succeeded, we might gain a much more secure and friendly hemisphere.

De-escalation in perspective. Calculated de-escalation as a strategy serves to damp the likelihood of nuclear war. It provides a controlled means by which the inequities in the status quos between "have" and "have-not" countries can be gradually redressed. One of the important characteristics of GRIT is that it does not require a high level of mutual trust for its initiation; given a sufficient amount of self-interest on both sides, a continuing pattern of reciprocative acts of a tension-reducing nature can literally *create* mutual trust where little of it existed before, which, of course, is also the case in inter-personal relations. Calculated de-escalation creates an atmosphere within which steps toward disarmament of increasing significance can be negotiated. Most people earnestly desire a more peaceful world — although they often have only the vaguest conception of what such a world would be like. They also desire the permanent elimination of weapons of mass destruction, in-cluding nuclear arsenals. It is my firm conviction that, given the existing sys-tem of competing nation-states, only some form of calculated tension de-escalation can create the security under which a progressive sequence of negotiated agreements leading to these ends could be undertaken.

Those most closely identified with the development of a sophisti-cated "initiatives" approach are Osgood and Robert Pickus, Presi-dent of the World Without War Council of the United States. "Wah-wookus" (with which I have been actively associated) is, in my view, the closest thing in this country to an organization that is really effec-tive in peace education at the community level. The most recent Coun-cil writings suggest the following seven-point context, within which initiatives can be measured and chosen:

1. and 2. Disarmament/Law–Law/Disarmament.

This recognizes that these two objectives cannot be separated. One cannot be placed ahead of the other. Universal, complete and enforceable disarmament cannot be maintained without law, just as law remains meaningless internationally without disarmament.

3. A strengthened sense of world community.

This recognizes that a disarmed world based on consent instead of imposed by violence requires a developed sense of unity and mutual responsibility among men.

4. Provision of nonviolent channels and well-conceived programs for needed changes and development in the quality of human life.

This recognizes that most men do not want law and stability if that requires keeping things as they are. Most of humanity lives under conditions of deprivation or exploitation, and they want change. In Asia, Africa and Latin America, economic, political and social change can come with or without mass violence, but it will come. For this change to come without chaos, nonviolent trends toward material well-being, education and freedom must be encouraged.

5. Achievement of understanding on how to move other nations to join us in pursuit of a disarmed world under law.

This recognizes that those seeking to commit this nation to leadership in achieving a just and stable peace must also find ways to change those attitudes and policies of other nations that block the road to a world without war. The single-minded focus on the Communist enemy that for so long gave cohesion to U.S. policy has given way to new realization of a rapidly changing world. This is a world in which almost half of the nations recognized by the United States are new nations which have achieved independence in this generation.

A primary concern of these new nations is to establish their national unity. Their desire to project a new identity adds problems to the obstacles posed by older nationalisms. In this explosive scene, it is more important than ever to assess realistically the power and purpose of key elements in the Communist world. Such an assessment rejects both the view of Communism as a demonic, unchanging, monolithic force, and also the unwarranted optimism which ignores the threat to democratic values and world peace posed by some current attitudes and policies of Communist nations.

6. Continuing peace research, particularly experimentation with nonviolent techniques for conducting and processing conflict.

This recognizes that values must be defended and that needed changes sometimes must be forced. Thus, those who turn away from mass violence must create and use other means by which conflict can be processed and change achieved, in the Communist world, in the developing nations, and in the West.

374

7. Widespread understanding of why men *should* turn away from war, and governmental actions consonant with that understanding.

This recognizes that progress in achieving the other six objectives is unlikely unless men and nations are impelled to work for them. This acceptance of obligation comes when men touch those root values which assert the brotherhood of all men, or when they encounter the knowledge or authority sustaining the commandment "Thou shalt not kill." Whether stated in religious or ethical terms, this widespread understanding represents an overreaching essential for a world without war.

In *To End War,* Robert Pickus and Robert Woito offer this perspective on an initiatives strategy:[4]

AMERICAN INITIATIVES

A policy of American initiatives is based on the belief that a dominantly military U.S. foreign policy cannot produce growth toward a world without war or develop successful opposition to the spread of totalitarian political systems. A favorable judgment of the feasibility of any of the initiatives proposed above does not require an optimistic assessment of the realities of power and policy in the Soviet Union or China. One can, for example, be profoundly pessimistic about present policy in Peking and yet come to the conclusion that initiative proposals for U.S.–China policy involve less risk and greater possibility for change in a hopeful direction than does continued isolation and potential military confrontation. The heart of the initiative approach lies in the very different question it seeks to answer: instead of, "How can our military power best influence their political and military policy," a peace initiative approach asks "What non-military acts can we take that give promise of producing the change in their attitude and policies that must come if we are to reach agreement on disarmament and world law?"

The initiative approach works with the processes of change. It rejects acquiesence to an opponent's will as it refuses to seek his destruction. It seeks instead to change him. A peace initiatives policy is distinguished by its goals—world disarmament and world law—from the more familiar military initiatives that constitute an arms race. But its method is a very similar one. It does not wait for agreement. It pursues its purpose by unilateral actions. A peace initiatives policy recognizes that any final settlement must be based on common consent, but asserts that there are situations (Vietnam is clearly one) in which only independent action taken without prior agreement can create a situation in which agreement becomes possible. A peace initiatives policy seeks to form vectors of influence on and within an opposing political system that could move that system toward agreement on world disarmament and world law.

375

Under what conditions can we expect initiatives to *produce* changed be-havior?

This can happen:

a. *When the initiative acts change the environment within which the leaders of opposing political systems act.*

The principle here is the same one that urges a continuation of the arms race: men respond to their environments. An initiative policy seeks to create an environment which increases internal pressure on Russian and Chinese leaders while focusing external forces and world opinion on the need for change in these leaders' military policies (as well as in our own).

b. *When the initiative acts change the balance of political forces within the opposing systems' leadership.*

Proponents and opponents of ABM deployment, of "thick" and "thin" systems and all the other elements in our ABM or MIRV controversies, surely exist in the Soviet Union. "Dove" and "Hawk" camps exist in every nation. U.S. initiatives could vitally affect the outcome of internal arguments over the feasibility of negotiating a general and complete disarmament agreement.

c. *When the initiative acts bring pressure to reciprocate on and within the opposing system.*

The American failure to bring significant pressure to bear on Hanoi and the NLF to end the war in Vietnam is a case in point. Could genuine peace initiatives do what military pressure has failed to do? What would be the impact, for example, of a unilateral American cease-fire (save under at-tack) combined with political initiatives that opened the way for the NLF to pursue their political objectives by means other than violence?

Most of the people of Vietnam are fighting neither Communist aggression nor American imperialism. They are fighting for their lives. Hanoi and the NLF have felt no pressure from them to end the killing because the U.S. has been successfully identified in the minds of many (in Vietnam and around the world) as the force that makes the killing go on. American initiatives to end the killing and to identify the forces that prefer victory to peace could change the situation. This approach is very different from current discussions of "Vietnamizing" the war, whether presented in the Nixon administration's context or that of a peace movement that concentrates solely on withdrawing American power instead of on ending the killing.

Similarly, the arms race is an obstacle to most of the world's population participation in the fruits of industrialization. A strategy of American initia-tive acts, even if unsuccessful, would bring pressure to bear on the powers which prefer the risks of an arms race to the risks of disarmament; for such powers are obstacles to the new nations' desire for rapid economic develop-ment. Turning to internal pressures, today's students are one example of an important group in most of the major powers that would work internally for a positive response to genuine world without war initiatives.

d. *When the initiative acts change an opponent's course of action by opening alternative means through which he may, without violence, pursue his goals.*

An initiatives policy offers hope of regaining a perspective on security and the pursuit of justice that can turn men from present dominant reliance on mass violence or national military power. For many, despite thermonuclear weapons, there now appears to be no alternative. A peace initiative policy would reject and seek to control violence, even as it accepted and opened channels for political conflict and its nonviolent resolution.

Initiative acts, properly undertaken, may not be immediately reciprocated in a given situation but may still be useful and important steps. They can aid in establishing the understandings and precedents necessary to contain new stages in the arms race or new threats of war. Since confusion over who is initiating a new stage, and who is merely responding to the other side, is the usual justification for each new stage, there is enormous value in acts which help identify and isolate those political forces committed to continuing the arms race.

AN INITIATIVES POLICY

There is nothing new in the idea of unilateral initiatives. The Soviet Union has for years jammed or stopped jamming the Voice of America as a way of signaling a change in Soviet attitude. As simple an act as inviting a foreign head of state to visit this country, as potentially significant an act as President Nixon's announcement regarding American cessation of research and stockpiling of bacteriological weapons or even the very limited steps taken recently to change U.S.–China trade relations are unilateral initiatives. President Kennedy's announcement, in his 1963 American University speech, of a unilateral American cessation of nuclear testing in the atmosphere was an important peace initiative that clearly aided in the successful achievement of agreement on the nuclear test ban treaty.

What would be new would be a *policy* of initiative action to end war. There was a period early in the '60's when attention for a time focused on the initiative idea. Premier Khrushchev called for a policy of "mutual example." The Carnegie Endowment's fiftieth anniversary project in 1961 sought to elicit suggestions of unilateral steps the United States could take to improve the prospects of peace. Other research agencies worked on lists of American initiative acts they deemed desirable and feasible.

But no policy was ever enunciated.

Doing so would involve a clear and comprehensive statement of goals essential to achieving a world without war. It would require a planned series of initiative acts — not isolated gestures, but a deliberate, graduated set of initiatives designed to move us toward each goal. Such a policy would include careful thought as to what must be done to create or exploit the conditions outlined above that would make reciprocation most likely.

With regard to disarmament, for example, in Antarctica and outer space, agreement on general and complete disarmament has been achieved. What

377

could be done to extend zonal disarmament to other areas? Could the United States designate a segment of this country—say New England—as a disarmed zone open to international inspection? How could that initiative engage the U.N. and other international agencies? What other acts by our government and private agencies could maximize internal and external pressure on the Soviet Union to reciprocate by naming a single disarmed area within the Soviet Union? How could these zones be extended? What would be the most likely countries in Africa willing to designate disarmed zones? What approaches should be made to governments there?

Since inspection is a key to the disarmament problem, at what point should the United States authorize "inspection by the people" of all U.S. disarmament initiatives? That is, specifically state the U.S. citizen's moral obligation to report any violation of disarmament initiatives (or any subsequent international agreements) to an international agency. What appeals to specific elites and age groups within the Soviet Union, what Russian traditions, what realities of domestic Soviet politics and what possibilities of pressure from world opinion give promise, if properly exploited, of a favorable response to this initiative? How can the facts of extensive governmental controls and ideological barriers to a sense of world community, within Soviet society, be overcome?

It is this kind of detailed thinking extended to each of the major goals considered above that would be necessary to construct an initiatives *policy*.

There have been two widely different approaches to a policy of American initiatives. One emphasizes the reduction of international tension and sees as the central problem creating an atmosphere of mutual trust in which agreements, previously thought impossible to achieve, may be reached. Just as an arms race is a form of unilateral but reciprocal tension-*increasing* activity, this approach recommends unilateral but reciprocated tension-*decreasing* activity. Another initiative approach views more soberly the reality of the conflict that produces the tension, and focuses on the problem of producing sufficient pressure to move recalcitrant national leaders to make the desired reciprocal response. A combination of reduction of threat *and* coercive pressures, both internal and external, to force reciprocation, is the approach recommended here.

All initiative approaches require a carefully thought out policy involving prior public announcement of the act and its intention and suggested possible reciprocal moves. The degree of risk involved in each step would have to be carefully calculated. What, for example, would we risk if we took seriously the proposal to make the DEW line (Distant Early Warning line) an international guarantor of warning against nuclear attack, a warrant that America seeks security from such an attack, not only for our nation, but for others, or, what would we risk if we tied reduction in our arms budget to problems of capital needs in the developing nations?

An initiatives policy would relate disarmament moves to acts strengthening growth toward world law. There have been, for example, proposals for American initiatives to internationalize control of the Panama Canal. Such an agreement could provide a model for international control of waterways and thus a step toward eliminating situations that have in the past led to war. Repealing the Connally Reservation (thus ending a situation in which the United States and not the International Court of Justice determines when the Court has jurisdiction in cases involving what the U.S. might regard as a domestic issue) is another example of a unilateral act in the world law area that properly undertaken could encourage reciprocation by other nations committed to growth toward world law. An unarmed World Peace Brigade for service on war-threatened borders, opening selected American editorial columns to Communist Chinese editors (and requesting reciprocation), U.N. chartering of international corporations: there is no shortage of specific ideas of how initiatives by our country could have a beneficial impact on economic and political relations, international law, and international organization and problems ranging from population and space research to economic development. We do not attempt here to list these, or to sort the sound from the unsound. Our purpose is to introduce the idea, not to spell out a full policy of American initiatives.

* * *

Such an American initiatives policy could provide the dynamic for at least the minimal goals of no further expansion of the arms race, a serious attempt to begin closing the gap between the very rich and very poor nations of the world, and temporary political settlements to defuse the three key explosive areas of S.E. Asia, the Middle East, and Germany. Such a policy, however, goes far beyond initial steps and temporary settlements. It recognizes that the awesome threats to man in the remainder of this century—nuclear war, hunger, population, the poisoning of our environment, the fragmenting new separatisms and development agonies of the new nations, are of such a magnitude that only international cooperation by presently opposed great powers and new world organization can resolve them.

Can we form the will which is the essential requisite for the pursuit of such a policy? Have we a President capable of such an initiative? Are we now a nation capable of responding to such leadership?

One need only examine the character of our present peace movement to see that we do not yet even have a citizens peace effort with such a perspective, let alone a government committed to it.

WHY?

One must number among the causes of war many of the readers of this book, for the essential problem is a failure of the public will and that failure is a consequence of individual inaction. Our failure of will is at root a matter of faith, but it also stems, for many, from the lack of acquaintance with a believable and sophisticated perspective on how to pursue the goal of ending war. There is no will to end war, in part because few encounter a coherent body of thought that gives rational sustenance to such a goal. Very different currents would move in American politics were there widely shared ideas of how to pursue the goal of a world order rooted in belief in the dignity and

379

worth of individual men and capable of processing conflict and change without organized violence. We have tried to state such a perspective, to demonstrate that there are understandings that can help in ending war. We believe individuals can help advance those understandings. If we are right, the individual, by his action or inaction, becomes a possible cause of war. For if it is true that you could act, and your action could be important if not decisive, it follows that your inaction is also a cause of war.

But are you convinced, as we are, that there *is* a body of thought worth acting on? The problems that might lead you to doubt, if not reject the *To End War* approach have been discussed, we hope, adequately. Many, nevertheless, may still regard work against war skeptically, in part because conviction comes from experience and experience relates to the facts—and the facts today are the facts of war, not peace.

Still, if you needed the experience of a world without war to believe it possible, you would not have picked up this book. Conceiving an end to war —as at one time conceiving an end to slavery—requires more than knowledge of past experience. What is needed is the faith that men can pursue high goals and that this pursuit is the best way to discover what it is possible for men to achieve. This book has been written for those who share that faith, and who, whatever the odds, cannot imagine being alive at this time in history without doing something specific and thoughtful to help achieve a world without war.

Note that Pickus and Woito consider the need to change "recalcitrant national leaders'" attitudes through bringing to bear on them both internal pressures, from public opinion and diverse political factions, and the external pressures of world opinion. Osgood tends to emphasize the role of initiatives in increasing mutual trust. What implicit model of causation for the arms race and for the present divisive international competition lies behind the "combination" view (emphasizing the need to *change* leaders as well as to encourage their trust), as distinct from Osgood's view? Consider again the discussion of the leaders' role in initiating large-scale conflict, in the last section of Chapter 3, and particularly the questions on pages 132–33. Does the Pickus-Woito approach suggest that at least points (ii) *and* (iii) must be addressed through "initiatives"?

Possible initiatives for the United States. What are some of the initiatives that might help us move towards a reduction of the problems posed by the present massive armaments? Consider the possible effects of the following:

a. The United States announces an end to all classified research.

b. The United States announces the abolition of all penalties for espionage.

c. The United States announces that a ten-million-dollar reward will be posted with a third party, for payment to any person who finds a substantial United States violation of any arms-limitation agreement.

d. The same as c., except the reward is payable to any person who finds a substantial violation of an arms-limitation agreement by *any* country.

e. The United States announces a "zero budget" for new warship construction (including submarines) in the next fiscal year.

f. The United States invites the Russians to select any ten United States scientists to visit Russia for three months.

g. The United States offers 25 million dollars to the United Nations to establish an international peace research institute, where nationals of all countries can work together on problems of world peace and disarmament.

h. The United States offers to finance a program by which 10,000 United States college students will be able to travel in Eastern Europe and Russia for three months at a time, in successive "waves," a total of 40,000 a year, and invites the Russians to set up a reciprocal program.

i. The United States announces that once every three months the Russians will be allowed to select any ten United States military officials and, using specified drugs or hypnotic techniques, ask them in the presence of a group of international representatives, "Are you planning to attack us?" and "Are you violating any treaties dealing with armaments?"

Some, like "e" and "i," are clearly far from being politically feasible within this country today. Others, like "f" and "g," could easily happen at almost any time. A small mobilization of public and professional group support might rapidly make them a reality. Can it fairly be said that *none* of these initiatives, even the most "extreme," poses a genuine threat to United States safety or security?

Other initiatives, of course, might be more concerned with internal mechanisms for decision-making than with substantive policy. Consider:

j. The United States creates a Cabinet-level "Department of Peace," giving it substantial funding and a mission to counterweigh the Pentagon in advising the President and in national planning.

k. The "Department of Peace" is given its own independent intelligence-acquisition and intelligence-evaluation resources.

l. The United States announces that the Pentagon has been ordered by the President to cease evaluating Russian and Chinese intentions and capabilities through "worst feasible case" analyses, and instead to support all evaluations with specific "hard" intelligence data. Would this initiative become more likely if some of the previous initiatives, such as a. through e. above, had previously been announced and been *reciprocated*?

Are *any* of these unilateral "initiatives" ones of unilateral *disarmament*? Is either Pickus or Osgood talking about initiatives of unilateral disarmament? What is the importance of the distinction? There might, in fact, be considerable danger in any really high measure of unilateral nuclear disarmament; in any case, it is not a political possibility. Assuming *complete,* unilateral United States disarmament, and role playing with real honesty, what do *you* predict the reactions in Moscow to be? Now assume total, unilateral *Soviet* disarmament. Role play the reactions in Washington, with an eye to such problems as Berlin, the Mideast, and Southeast Asia. In general, in delineating a *strategy* of initiatives, the initiatives can be arranged from hardest to easiest, from (a) initiatives that involve strategic risk; (b) initiatives that involve major economic cost; (c) initiatives that involve neither of the foregoing, but that *do* involve internal political risks; to (d) initiatives that involve none of the preceding. Thus, (d) would be the best category with which to begin.

Other kinds of initiatives. There are, of course, many possible initiatives that have some other, or broader, bearing than on the question of *armaments* — including some of those just described. Consider the possible effects of the following:

a. The United States offers 200 million dollars to the United Nations to help establish an international university, whose chief function will be to train an international civil service with a sense of international citizenship. The United States also offers money to establish a related senior secondary school for grades 10 through 12, and to place funds in trust which can be used for scholarships for successive "entering classes" of 100 U.S. 16-year-olds each year, to be selected by the United Nations Secretary General or his delegate.

b. The United States offers to help the United Nations obtain permanent financial support by chartering a "United Nations Bank" which will be allowed to operate as a regular profit-making commercial bank throughout the United States, and to take in deposits from private depositors totalling up to two billion dollars. The bank will be subject to normal banking regulations for depositors' protection, and federal deposit insurance will be in effect. Would *you* deposit your money in such a bank? (I would.) From a political point of view, would the "two billion dollars" limitation make the idea easier to sell?

c. The United States offers to recognize mainland China (in addition to concurring in its admission to the United Nations).

d. The United States offers mainland China a good price on five million tons of wheat.

e. The United States removes major categories of goods, including important industrial technologies, from the prohibitions against export to communist states. (In relation to this initiative, consider once again the discussion of trade relationships in Chapter 5.)

Are there also possibilities of initiatives of varying kinds which have their impetus with private decision-makers, rather than government? Consider:

a. The introduction within the scientific community of a "Hippocratic Oath" not to use one's knowledge for purposes of creating new weapons of destruction or for other socially abhorrent purposes.

b. An American oil company offering access to part of its Mideast oil to an Eastern European country, or to Russia.

c. A college community taking the initiative to finance a year of study by a student (one fluent in the language) in Russia.

Initiatives with China and Russia. What may be the role of initiatives with respect to China over the balance of this century, in terms of the basic problems of population and resources? China has a population around 750 million (20 percent of the world's total) but only a little more than the land area of the United States. Large parts of the land are arid or uncultivable, and only small areas are forested. Food production is concentrated on rice and wheat, with little area available for dairy farming, livestock, or industrial crops. The population is 80 to 85 percent rural. Railroad, road, and water transportation systems are minimal. Substantial deposits of high-grade coal and reasonably adequate oil and iron ore resources exist, but are not yet well developed. Per capita gross national product as of the mid-1960's was under $100 per person, approximately the same as that of India (about one thirty-fifth of the per capita GNP in the United States and one fifteenth of that in Russia during the same period). Population today is growing at a rate of about 20 million people a year. China, however, has nuclear and thermonuclear weapons and almost certainly possesses biological weapons. What measures might decrease the likelihood of China's initiating local or general conflicts in the next decades because of the direct or indirect effects of basic resource shortages? Consider the following possibilities:

a. Extensive food-import patterns grow up with the West.

b. Extensive technology-import patterns grow up with the West, especially to promote intensification of food production, new cereal strains, and desalinization of water.

c. Same as b., except with regard to birth-control technologies.

d. Same as b., except with regard to heavy industry, power production, or transportation technologies.

What might the *priorities* among the foregoing possibilities be? What if China can't afford to pay for these imports?

What impact might unilateral *Russian* initiatives be expected to have upon the United States leadership? Consider the fact that the last two Presidents to lead the United States into war (Truman and Johnson) faced mounting unpopularity that led them to choose not to run for another term of office. Consider President Nixon's Vietnam position: he is far from satisfying many people, true, but has he taken the position that the war should be intensified or "won"? What has happened to United States troop levels and casualties? Consider Mr. Nixon's statements on bringing "a generation of peace" to Americans. Consider the role of dissenting or critical political leaders vis-à-vis a President taking a warlike posture. Do the political pressures within the United States today tend to move a president chiefly toward war or chiefly toward peace? If the latter, consider again the opening question of this paragraph. Did the Russians probably increase or *decrease* their overall security through their 1968 invasion of Czechoslovakia? How would Czechoslovakia evolving towards a more open and independent society, without Russian interference, have changed United States public views of the nature of Russian Communism and of the Russian "threat"?

Community Action for Peace, Bearing on Initiatives and Other Paradigms

In addition to classroom use over the past three years, major portions of these materials were utilized in 1970–71 at a series of weekend retreats in which community leaders, clergymen, lawyers, psychologists, housewives, students, and teachers joined together in the Seattle, Portland, and Chicago areas to consider the prerequisites for creating a world without large-scale lethal conflict. Perhaps a second volume, developing out of those weekend experiences, will deal with some of the problems of grassroots community action to end large-scale lethal conflict. (*To End War,* from which an initiatives-strategy excerpt earlier in this chapter is taken, lists some available and highly useful material on this subject.) But certain salient points about the experience of the people at those retreats, and about the cumulative community-action experience that dozens of people brought to those retreats, demand at least this brief summary:

An effective commitment to ending war and other lethal conflict requires both an intellectual and an emotional engagement.

A useful emotional engagement is *not* one that seeks new enemies in our midst, or that simply shifts "worst feasible case" analysis of motives from the Russians and the Chinese to the Pentagon and the American Presidency.

To develop a really *useful* motivation and engagement, several features appear to be needed. *One* is to form an understanding and supportive community of persons with whom constructive work to end lethal conflict can be carried on over time, and who have built up a trust in each other's commitment and good judgment.

A *second* is, within that working community, to mutually recognize that no one in the peace field who wishes to be effective is likely to be a "Renaissance man." As in any other highly complex undertaking, there are varieties of emphasis and specialization.

A *third* is to understand the full weight and horror of the problems, and to work through and "talk out," consciously and fully, the sense of helplessness and frustration that is the very reasonable first response of a sensitive man or woman.

A *fourth* is to acquire a perspective on the effective approaches to the problems, within a framework of basic commitment to humane and democratic values (the excerpt on page 374 attempts to express such a framework).

A *fifth,* and last, is to formulate ways in which the community working for peace can actively bring to bear its collective contacts, expertise, and know-how *at the community level* to encourage a particular initiative or other action aimed at achieving the goals. The effort, for example, might be to get the local Grange to take a position favoring agricultural trade with mainland China, the local school to sponsor

385

a student exchange with Poland, the local churches to urge a stand-still ceasefire to end all the killing in Vietnam and not just "Viet-namize" it, the local Rotary to urge their Congressmen to support new foreign-aid priorities, or the local conference of Catholic bishops privately to urge the Pope to reverse his position on population-limitation through birth control. Some people within the community working together for peace might be leaders themselves in the relevant group or organization; some might have close friends who were such leaders; some might be able to articulate a coherent viewpoint on the particular issue for the leaders at a luncheon briefing, or for the membership at a meeting or church service. Some might use good contacts with the media to produce a story, for example, on a constructive round-table discussion of the question (focused not on "debate" or on "who is wrong," but on "what can we *do* to make things better"); others could contact the people for such "round tables"; others could participate in them (in the first example, a local Grange official, a local professor specializing in economics or Asian studies, an ex-foreign service officer, a student who had done a paper on the Canadian trade experience); others could make sure that the media reports were seen and understood by leaders and members in the relevant group or organization (in that example, preeminently, the local Grange). Especially when local peace work reached a point in size and continuity where full-time staff members were needed, some could raise funds so the work could go on; others could volunteer services as researchers, newspaper clippers, typists, hostesses for dinners bringing the people involved together, and many other essential functions.

All of these things are being done today, in various communities around the country. Thus far, there are only perhaps a couple of thousand people actively engaged in this kind of constructive peace work, in less than a score of cities. But these small numbers, through their dedication to constructive, non-violent, consensus-building, non-polarizing, broadly community-engaging work for peace, are already having an enormous impact for education and for initiative action. Constructive peace work today seems at about the same stage where the environmentalists were five years ago: the problem is known, a number of solutions are known, and there are a small but growing number of people beginning to apply this knowledge and to show others how to do so. A congressional enactment requiring Detroit to clean up its cars by 1975 was as "unimaginable" five years ago as a legislated end to classified research and espionage laws is today. But the cleanup law and many others today are the first important results of a vigorous campaign to save the environment. With dedicated work by thousands more people, we might have research and espionage legislation as well, in five years or less, as part of a strategy of initiatives to end large-scale lethal conflict.

There is one very important thing that those already constructively engaged for peace have consistently found. *Most* of the people who take initially antagonistic positions on peace issues ("Trade with the commies?" "Let's bomb the bastards," and so on) espouse those positions superficially, and largely as a convenient means of venting frustrations that arise out of entirely different, personal problems. A very high proportion of citizens will support a reasonable initiatives policy if it is explained to them so that they understand the grave need, the particular proposal, and the fact that a given step does not increase the "threat" but decreases it. It appears that most citizens' foreign-policy views are only skin-deep, and they will rapidly alter these views when they fully understand that the problem is one of *survival,* and that reasonable alternatives to present positions are available. If, however, one approaches them threateningly or disparagingly, then they will react against what they perceive as an attack on themselves, their status, their good faith, or their intelligence, by defending to the last gasp the superficial views that are the nominal subject of the attack. If one accuses a man, because of his views, of being a "rotten imperialist," he will defend those views with an enormous emotional investment, because he perceives (generally accurately) that it is *he* as a person that is being attacked, not his views. If, however, one points out a common context of values, in which the other person can see that these particular views on foreign policy are a threat to what he himself holds dear and to his own primary values, and that those views will not *achieve* the kind of world that he, too, wants for his children and grandchildren, then he is very likely to change those views. By the same token, *you* must not react to criticism as a personal attack, but must be the "peace therapist," conscious of the motivations at work. These observations reflect the widespread experience among those who are concerned with effectively working for the goal of peace, and not simply desirous of using "peace" as a convenient excuse for venting personal frustrations on a nearby scapegoat or whipping-boy. *Broad community consensus and meaningful community action on peace strategies can be obtained, if one is willing to work sensibly towards the creation of such consensus and such action.*

The hardest issues on which to change people's minds are, of course, the ones that are already full-blown crises, like the war in Vietnam. But if this book has accomplished a single thing, it should have been to persuade the reader that ending the Vietnam war, or ending any single current conflict or series of conflicts, still leaves large-scale war and revolution dreadfully probable over the coming years. Vietnam probably represents less than one percent of the threat that war currently poses to mankind. What we must end is the *method* of resolving disputes by lethal conflict. We must create *general, alternative modes* of processing conflict, of satisfying needs, of ending frustrations, of supplying status, *in lieu of* deadly conflict. We must change the atmosphere of international life, so that people can breathe again, as fully as we must change the air in our cities. We must make large-scale conflict, as a means of achieving *any* end, as unthinkable as large-scale slavery or large-scale piracy have become after persisting thousands of years as social institutions. Try to persuade a man that he should get rid of the car he is driving, and you may not have much luck. Urge him that his *next* car and all those thereafter should be diesel or four-cylinder and low-octane, and you may succeed. This is not to say that work on the Vietnam issue is irrelevant. It *is* to say that one should not be discouraged, nor judge the prospects for successful peace work by the results of tackling a single, immediate, emotion-laden issue. The goal of general peace is not only much broader, it is — paradoxically — at least in some ways much easier.

The Amelioration Paradigm

Land reform in Vietnam. In the manuscript on land reform (pages 174–180), I continue the discussion as follows:

It was actually President Thieu who first came around to a perception of the rather obvious point that land reform was essential if there was ever to be any hope of peasant support for the Saigon regime. In late 1968 he ended, with surprising effectiveness, the process by which landlords had returned to reassert their rights in newly secured villages. This move coincided, pragmatically, with the "accelerated pacification" campaign that began in the 1968–69 winter. In April 1969 he put into operation a country-wide freeze on all evictions, preparatory to more sweeping measures.

By far the most important land acquisition of the Diem land reforms had been 575,000 acres—about 10 percent of the country's cultivated land—acquired in 1958 by the French government from the former French landowners and presented as a gift to Diem for distribution to the peasants. But these were fine lands, and the temptation proved too great. Instead of distributing them, Diem allowed local officials to rent the bulk of them out and pocket the proceeds. The tenants remained tenants. By year-end 1967, only 11,000 acres had been distributed to some 2,700 families.

In mid-1969, Thieu decreed the accelerated *free* distribution of these and other government-owned lands, under drastically simplified administrative procedures. For 1969–71, the distribution—chiefly of the French lands—affected 500,000 acres, giving title to some 130,000 ex-tenant farmer families. Much of the rest of these lands presently lie abandoned or uncultivable, but all present signs indicate that all other lands capable of being distributed will be distributed in 1972.

The Land-to-the-Tiller bill, a companion measure to provide for distribution of privately owned lands, was introduced in July 1969 and passed in March 1970 after a desperate fight with the National Assembly, won by Thieu through persistent pressure. Curiously, some of those who spoke articulately (and in flawless English) of the need for "democracy" and "freedom" in the Saigon salons proved unwilling to cast their support with the landless peasants.* The *New York Times* editorially characterized the Land-to-the-Tiller measure as "probably the most ambitious and progressive non-Communist land reform of the Twentieth Century."

* * *

But the Land-to-the-Tiller program in South Vietnam is both more simplified and more sweeping than any of these previous programs, with the possible exception of the program (essentially "grab-your-own") in Bolivia. Thieu's measure affects *all* tenanted land—together with the government-lands distribution, it covers over 60 percent of all cultivated land in the country—and the recipient is normally the present tiller (so no administrator has to pick and choose). He gets what he presently tills (identifiable on aerial photos, so no surveyor has to be sent out, and no dikes have to be torn down and rebuilt around the paddies). And he gets it free (along with a moratorium on real estate taxes, so *no one* has any excuse to approach him for any payment under

---

*I recall one curious encounter when I returned to Vietnam in late 1969 with Mary Temple and others from Clark Kerr's National Committee for a Political Settlement in Vietnam. A meeting was arranged with some Vietnamese from a political group considered by most American observers to be on the ultra-liberal fringe. When we discussed land reform, we were perplexed to see that they supported cumbersome and basically unworkable measures of a kind Thieu—and even the United States Agency for International Development by then—had firmly rejected. Finally, one member mentioned that the leader of their group had been having some difficulty communicating with his daughter in Switzerland. Our casually offhand inquiry, as to what the economic background of this clearly prosperous leader might be, elicited the response that he owned a "large plantation" in the Mekong Delta. This, presumably, was divided and rented out to a few-score miserable tenant families, most of whom probably supported the Vietcong, while part of the landlord's income went to oppose Thieu by denouncing him as "repressive" to sympathetic American listeners.

any pretext). The landlords will be paid the fair value of the lands, in cash and bonds, by Saigon. The total cost (400 million dollars) equals about five days' cost of the war at 1968–69 levels, and the United States has indicated that it will pick up around one-third of the bill.

By late 1971, Land-to-the Tiller distribution had affected nearly 1,000,000 acres, and over 300,000 titles had been issued.

Of the 800,000 tenant-farmer families living in the countryside at the start of 1969 (comprising 5,000,000 people), over half had become owners of their own land by September 1, 1971, and it was expected as this was written that by the same date in 1972, nearly all of the 800,000 tenant-farmer families should be landowners.

Evidence of political results is accumulating. Peasants throughout the Delta are telling interviewers "this is the first time Saigon has kept its word to us." Title issuance has been accompanied by wild celebrations. Observers whose judgment I trust have reported to me that "Here at the moment the Vietcong are concentrating their fire in an unprecedented manner on the land-to-the tiller program." Moreover, the Saigon government has now made low-interest agricultural credit available, and in village-level elections the tenant farmers and ex-tenant farmers have supplanted the old gentry — now outnumbering the old landlord group three-to-one in village office-holding.

It is hoped that the threatened erosion of grass-roots support for the NLF will yet be translated into political movement at Paris. Cyrus Vance has been among those who have suggested that major land reform could supply bargaining leverage ultimately translatable into political settlement.

Meanwhile, although it is hard to measure the impact of other variables, especially against the background din of the tub-thumping by Pentagon press agents for the invasions of Cambodia and Laos, it seems likely that it is the land reform measures that have had the most significant relationship to the sharp decline of Vietcong recruitment (to far less than half its former level), and to the other signs of real grass-roots improvement in the political and military situation.

While the Vietnamese Presidential elections of October 1971 were clearly a "minus" for some urban monks and university students, the simultaneous changes in the countryside — amounting to a profound economic and social revolution — constitute a clear "plus" for the grass-roots population, and must be weighed in any final evaluation of the Thieu government.

Multilateral support for land-reform initiatives. The carrying out of such a program is, in effect, an *internal initiative* (see the further discussion of effects on pages 174–180). Ultimately, such initiatives, of varying degrees of cost, difficulty, and complexity, would appear essential to dealing with the problems that give rise to large-scale internal violence. For less developed countries, however, such initiatives may need supporting initiatives from other nations, resembling some of the international initiatives discussed in the previous section.

To support internal land reform programs, I have suggested that the developed nations offer to subsidize portions of the cost.*

What I suggested back in 1966 was that major resources be channeled, chiefly through a multilateral mechanism, to support land reforms in countries that wished to undertake them but were forestalled by the landlords' effective political opposition, arising out of fears of confiscation. Landlords who have much of their wealth tied up in land are unwilling to see substituted for it twenty-year Government-of-"X"-bonds, where "X" clearly does not have resources that lend confidence that the bonds will be paid off. On the other hand, my field interviews in Brazil, Colombia, the Philippines, and Vietnam, and discussions involving many other countries, have persuaded me of what common-sense would suggest: that if there is a really credible promise to pay the full equivalent of the land's value, many fewer landlords will be inclined to promote a *coup d'etat* over the program, and many will indeed see it as positively beneficial. Credible compensation becomes, in effect, a further variable that can take the place of highly centralized power in the government sponsoring the reform. Douglas MacArthur in Japan could *take* the land, but Eduardo Frei in Chile had to *pay* for it, or forego reform.

At least three extensive programs have thus far been based on the promise of full compensation to the landlords: those in Taiwan, Venezuela, and now Vietnam. But leaders in other countries who have appeared to be genuinely desirous of large-scale land reform—Indira Gandhi in India, Marcos in the Philippines, Frei in Chile—were substantially or wholly blocked, in their own legislatures or by fears of a *coup,* because they did not have the resources to carry out a large-scale full-compensation program. Frei met less than 20 percent of his goal in Chile, and after Allende was elected with strong peasant support, he appointed Jacques Chonchol (who had quit Frei's cabinet in disgust because of the slow pace of land reform) to his cabinet as land reform minister.

What I have suggested is that American aid in this area be used chiefly to support a guarantee, by a bilateral or preferably a multilateral agency, that the bonds issued to the landlords would be paid. Either by a direct guarantee of the bonds, or a guarantee of the adequacy of the sinking fund used to retire them, landlords would be given

---

*Note that the multilateral support program suggested is, in effect, an agreement by two or more nations to jointly undertake an initiative towards some other nation. It thus combines elements of both "agreement" and "initiative."

a "Federal Deposit Insurance Corporation" type of assurance that the bonds were safe. In countries where reasonable investment opportunities exist, they would also be strongly encouraged or required to put a substantial portion of this compensation into productive investments.

In countries where there is a little more elbow room for planning, and less immediate political competition than in Vietnam, the recipients of land would pay a substantial part of the land costs back into a sinking fund, which would then be used to retire the bonds. The relation of rents to land is normally such that this annual payment would be substantially less than the rents formerly paid, quite apart from the increase in production that usually occurs upon land distribution. But the multilateral guarantee agency would also subsidize some of the interest payments to ex-landlords, and occasionally some of the principal amount paid for the land, to assure that this immediate increase in income accrued to the beneficiaries in every case, by reducing the land payments. The guarantee agency would also help to set up an adequate sinking fund mechanism to collect the payments from the land recipients. (On a pilot test of a parallel operation for lending money to impoverished *campesinos,* the Pan American Development Foundation's repayment mechanisms have achieved a 97 percent repayment rate.) There would also be a support program to make agricultural credit available to both the new land recipients and previous smallholders. In recognition of the low "opportunity cost" of labor and the high "opportunity cost" of capital goods, such credit would aim to make available hand tools, small irrigation pumps, and other inputs suitable to a tract of a few acres, worked principally by hand, *not* heavy tractors and combines geared to some Midwestern fantasy of what a "real farm" should look like.

I have calculated that, for an expenditure equal roughly to one-sixth of our current foreign-assistance program, during each year of the next decade, we could support massive land-reform programs in a dozen of the neediest countries. This expenditure, some 500 million dollars a year, would be channeled to an "Agricultural Credit and Insurance Fund" administered by the World Bank or Inter-American Development Bank — *if* they were desirous of handling such a program sensibly and imaginatively — or to a new multilateral agency. This 500 million dollars would be matched by similar contributions from other nations, so that over a decade, 10 billion dollars would be available. Calculating that up to one-half the total cost of the average country's program would be supported by some form of subsidy or collateral assistance from the fund, while the other half would be paid for through sinking-fund repayments, the 10 billion dollars would be adequate to achieve land ownership for roughly 20 million families — about 100 million people — over the decade. This estimate is based on the per family costs of the full-compensation programs in Venezuela, Taiwan, and Vietnam, together with calculations for such a program in northeastern Brazil, and data on land values in a number of other countries.

This would constitute the largest program of planned democratic development ever carried out, and would make a substantial dent in the problem. Even so, the annual United States contribution and the scope of the program could be doubled, and quite possibly this would happen after the first few years, assuming the reforms showed themselves to be nearly as successful as the previous non-Marxist land reforms of this century.

Other initiatives for internal reform. What other general problems of the less developed world might be ripe for supportive strategies of this type by the developed nations?

What problems of the *developed* nations might yield to a strategy of internal ameliorFatOry reforms? Consider again Chapter 6. Which of the following reforms might bear on the discontents of the white radical extremists? The black radical extremists?

1. Legalize marijuana.

2. Give sensitivity training to police.

3. Reform criminal law and court and prison systems, transforming many offenses into minor infractions punished by a fine (for example, hitchhiking where it is illegal, female age-of-consent laws where age difference is not great, and so on). Where imprisonment is required, emphasize farm and campus-style facilities.

4. Improve housing, especially for blacks and the poor whites (including adequate privacy and open spaces).

5. Same for education.

6. Same for job training and opportunities.

7. Reform landlord-tenant, consumer-protection, and small-loan laws.

8. Raise income taxes in the higher brackets; end percentage depletion; raise gift and inheritance taxes to 99 percent on amounts in excess of 1 million dollars; lower military spending; with the resulting revenues, then devote at least another 30 billion dollars per year to needed reforms and improvements.

393

9. Establish "ombudsmen," extensive internal channels of community communications, other mechanisms to give individuals a voice in public affairs.

10. Clean up the environment.

11. End the draft.

12. End the Vietnam involvement.

13. Move towards more communal family structures (that is, more than one "mother" and "father" for each child).

14. Limit population growth.

15. Establish day-care centers; create more meaningful and varied roles in society for women.

16. Carry out elaborate emotional testing of children, with supportive psychiatric services for "violence-prone" children.

17. Expand methadone maintenance program for heroin addicts.

There may be a number of varying perceptions on the relative priority of these various ameliorative initiatives. What would you think of grouping the initiatives roughly "high," "medium," and "low," as follows, for dealing with the problems posed by black radicals and white radicals, respectively:

	BLACK RADICALS	WHITE RADICALS
"High" group:	2, 4, 5, 6, 8, 9, 10, 14, 15, 16, 17	2, 3, 8, 9, 10, 12, 13, 14, 15, 16
"Medium" group:	3, 7, 11, 12, 13	1, 7, 11
"Low" group:	1	4, 5, 6, 17

Actually, there has been quite marked progress on a few of these over the past two to three years. Which ones?

Should there be other major items on the list of needed ameliorative reforms?

The Utopian Paradigm

Technocratic utopia. R. Buckminster Fuller, in *Utopia or Oblivion*,[5] quotes physicist John Platt of the University of Chicago as observing, "The world is now too dangerous for anything but Utopia." Fuller sees it as a central fact that Utopia *is* attainable, not for a minority (which he sees as self-defeating and not really "Utopian") but for *all:*

. . . for the first time in the history of man, it was in evidence that there could be enough of the fundamental metabolic and mechanical energy sustenance for everybody to survive at high standards of living—and furthermore, there could be enough of everything to take care of the increasing population while also always improving the comprehensive standards of living. . . .

He adds:

The primacy of political ideologies is obsolete because they were all developed on the basis of the exclusive survival only of your party or my party— simply because there was not enough for both. . . .

He finds, he later notes:

. . . nothing illogical in the concept that when there is enough to go around men will not even think of fighting. . . .

Thus, he believes, the central problem is "doing-more-with-less"— applying the vast capabilities of modern technology to the creation of adequate resources, so that all mankind can live, as he puts it, "at a higher standard of living than all yesterday's kings."

Although some have criticized Fuller as a "technological optimist," a large part of his predictions as to our future capabilities seem on solid ground. Certainly, enormous breakthroughs are in sight or already in existence. The most knowledgeable experts predict that technology will be capable of such things as the following in the next few decades: harness the virtually inexhaustible power-source of the sun, or of hydrogen through controlled fusion reaction; multiply several-fold the productivity of agricultural land, and open extensive new food resources in the oceans; desalinate sea water economically; automate and increase dramatically the production of comfortable modular housing units; and expand communications, computer effectiveness and the processing of knowledge by an enormous factor. Thus, through new technologies we are likely to have the capacity to supply enormously expanded quantities of food, water, shelter, and energy, and to accumulate and process ever more rapidly the knowledge of how to do these things still better. The full use and dissemination of these technological breakthroughs, Fuller believes, can come with "political unblocking," in which politics performs a future "secondary" function "of polite supervision." As an example, Fuller sees an integrated United States–Russian–Chinese power grid that will allow the optimum use of power resources for industrialization of China and for increased production in the other two countries.

Commenting on current political organization, in *Operating Manual for Spaceship Earth*,[6] Fuller observes:

. . . before the invention and use of cables and wireless 99.9 percent of humanity thought only in the terms of their own local terrain. Despite our recently developed communications intimacy and popular awareness of total Earth we, too, in 1969 are as yet politically organized entirely in the terms of exclusive and utterly obsolete sovereign separateness.

This "sovereign" — meaning top-weapons enforced — "national" claim upon humans born in various lands leads to ever more severely specialized servitude and highly personalized identity classification. As a consequence of the slavish "categoryitis" the scientifically illogical, and as we shall see, often meaningless questions "Where do you live?" "What are you?" "What religion?" "What race?" "What nationality?" are all thought of today as logical questions. By the twenty-first century it either will have become evident to humanity that these questions are absurd and anti-evolutionary or men will no longer be living on Earth.

Fuller's vision of the future may be thought of as "technocratic utopia," in which the primary goal is achieving fullest utilization of the best technology for the satisfaction of man's wants. There is little doubt, from what we have seen previously, that increased food, water, housing, and power can significantly reduce the frustrations that lead to certain kinds of lethal conflict. But does Fuller's utopian vision include everything that is needed for the effective, long-term elimination of large-scale lethal conflict? Is his conception of the problem cast too much in terms of material satisfaction, and too little in terms of other kinds of needs? Is he too optimistic when he says that there is "nothing illogical in the concept that when there is enough to go around men will not even think of fighting?" Even if this might have been true in paleolithic times, it is too narrow a conception of the causes of conflict in the twentieth century. The three and a half billion people on the earth today, organized into nation-states, inbred with ideologies, and led by those who are currently selected to lead them, have a whole range of "invented" reasons for lethal conflict, many of which appear to have little or nothing to do with whether there is "enough to go around." Or are we simply being too narrow by defining "enough" in *material* terms? "Enough" could also be interpreted

396

to mean enough status, enough roles, enough love, enough psychological satisfactions. Furthermore, it could mean "enough" material and non-material satisfactions *relative to* the satisfactions possessed by other groups in the society. (Remembering the role of "relative deprivation," does Fuller seem too absolute in his assessment of "needs"?) But even giving Fuller's ideas such a broad interpretation, can his technology, no matter how sophisticated, by itself provide the solutions? Moreover, most experts would not strongly disagree with Fuller's view that it might be possible to maintain a high standard of living for "the increasing population." Recent research, such as the M.I.T.-assisted computer study, *The Limits to Growth,* suggests that the combination of natural-resource exhaustion and pollution in a world economy oriented towards continued growth of material production, *plus* continued population growth, is not supportable by the planet much beyond the year 2020. Even on optimistic assessments of technological improvements as the century wore on, a collapse of the industrial base would be inevitable, as demands for both food and raw materials outstripped available supplies. (And, of course, major wars might break out between societies intent on monopolizing the remaining resources.) *Limits* strongly makes the point that world population must at least be stabilized—some planners call for a long-term *decrease*—and that the goal of continually increased production of material goods must be discarded. Instead, emphasis must be on fewer, longer-lasting goods, with maximum recycling of resources, and a shift in popular preferences for "growth" or accumulation away from material goods and towards service, such as education and recreation.

But, even if some enlightened combination (M.I.T. + Fuller) of technological improvement, population stabilization, and pollution-control and resource-conservation measures does appear capable of eliminating a significant number of the reasons underlying lethal conflict, it clearly does not appear capable of eliminating all such reasons. It does not seem adequate, for example, to meet the problems exemplified by the warrior in the primitive society going on a raid to prove his status and "manhood"; by the white radical who favors revolutionary violence, coming from a comfortable middle-class home in which his parents ignored his emotional needs; or by the national leader self-selected for an enormous drive to power and status? If Fuller's technocratic utopia is not, of itself, sufficient to deal with these problems, what additional elements might be needed for a fully matured "utopian" solution?

397

Changing the leaders. There are a variety of ways in which knowledge in the fields of psychology and sociology can be applied to the development of a long-term "utopian" solution. Consider the following additional excerpts from Jerome Frank's *Sanity & Survival:*[7]

Leaders' personalities, of course, are as varied as those of everybody else, but their achievement of power (inherited power is becoming increasingly rare) implies possession of certain personal qualities—charisma, for example, the mysterious personal magnetism that inspires loyalty and submission but defies adequate psychological analysis, possibly because it resides in the leader-follower interplay rather than wholly in the leader.

In practically all modern societies leadership positions can be gained only through a person's own persistent efforts, implying a strong drive for power in those who reach the top. The gaining of power need not be an end in itself—power can be used for any number of purposes, from the most selfish to the most altruistic. Since all human behavior has complex motives, not all necessarily fully conscious, there is no reason to think that the striving for leadership is an exception. But since power is in limited supply, it seems safe to surmise that all important leaders must have a certain degree of ruthlessness. To inspire confidence in others, moreover, they must have considerable self-confidence, at least at a superficial level.*

Leaders must have won more conflicts than they lost on the way up, or they would not have reached the top (there are always, of course, such rare exceptions as Abraham Lincoln), hence, whatever the initial basis for self-confidence, faith in their own powers and judgment would certainly have been reinforced. They must have been able simultaneously to shield their self-esteem from the effects of the failures and defeats that are the lot of any rising leader no matter how skilled; hence, they would be expected to possess well-developed techniques for maintaining their public and private images as resolute and successful, which would also be necessary to hold their followers' allegiance in periods of adversity. Thus, national leaders would be expected to be adept at denying errors, explaining them away, or shifting blame to others. In short, they would be expected to dwell on their successes and minimize their failures to buttress their optimism about their ability to prevail in any conflict.

That leaders have generally been victorious in their domestic contests suggests that they have more than average courage, energy, and determination. Since all political conflicts involve competitive risk-taking, they probably have a high tolerance for uncertainty and a greater than average capacity to persevere in an apparently lost cause. Because of the conspiratorial aspect of politics, successful leaders must also be adept at sensing and forestalling or counteracting plots, so their suspicions of others' motives must be easily

---

*The apparent self-assurance of some national leaders seems to be an overcompensation for self-doubts. Maintained at the cost of considerable personal strain, great pressure may cause their façade to crack, leading to erratic behavior or even a mental breakdown—notable examples are Wilhelm II and James Forrestal. And it is perhaps worth noting that neither had to fight his way up through the ranks in which process their weaknesses might have been exposed.

398

aroused, while at the same time they are probably skilled at dissembling when necessary. Leaders would be expected to be men of action rather than contemplation, more concerned with the short-term than the remote consequences of their decisions, since the path to power requires endless decisions about immediate practical issues. Although national leaders are skilled at expressing high ideals, it is safe to suspect a large underlying streak of hard-headed realism and practical shrewdness. Most are probably expert manipulators of their countries' political and bureaucratic processes.

Ruthlessness, overweening self-confidence, energy, and suspiciousness as typified by a Trujillo or a Sukarno would be expected to be more prominent in leaders whose countries do not have firmly established and well-defined legitimized paths to power, and whose populations are illiterate, impoverished, and embittered. As genocidal weapons spread, such leaders will pose an increasing danger because some will inevitably get into their control.

*   *   *

. . . . Many political leaders show mild manic and paranoid traits which occasionally approach the pathological — Churchill, for example, whose energy was often stupendous, had frequent periods of lethargy and depression that he called "black dog"; Stalin's suspiciousness reached pathological proportions in his last years.

People with manic or paranoid tendencies are quick to anger, especially when opposed, but it is not clear to what extent this may affect their attitudes and behavior toward opponents, although the effect may well be greater than appears. A man can appear cool and collected while his anger is gently prodding him toward choosing harsher tactics and words, and is reducing his ability to listen to his adversary's view point or his willingness to entertain alternatives that might contribute to the latter's welfare.

I have suggested that in order to get and keep power, leaders must be concerned with maintaining their image and be willing to take risks. An interesting relationship between these two qualities was revealed by an elaborate psychological study whose subjects, hundreds of male and female undergraduates, were given a variety of tests that required risk-taking — games of chance, opportunities to bet on their skills, and the number of clues they required before hazarding a guess on the outcome of a situation. When their behavior was checked against a large number of personality variables as determined by other tests, the pertinent finding was the emergence of a relationship between anxiety, defensiveness (defined as concerned with maintaining one's image), and risk-taking. Among those who were high in both qualities and had a risk-taking bent, "to change decisions in the face of failure is to acknowledge that a risk-taking course is something less than wise. One must therefore pursue risk-taking all the more irrevocably." Male subjects of this type expressed more satisfaction with their bets, when betting on their own skills, the less they won; failure caused them to increase rather than reduce their risk-taking. Conservative, anxious, and defensive subjects used failure to justify their continuing all the more rigidly in a conservative path, while those with little anxiety or defensiveness took more rational risks, expressed satisfaction or dissatisfaction appropriate to the outcome, and modified their risk-taking on the basis of the previous trial's outcome.

While most national leaders probably do not become unduly anxious or defensive in crisis situations, the disquieting implication of this study is that the exceptional ones who do have "test-anxiety" (although they may be adept at concealing it) would be apt to cling to an erroneous decision and to react to its bad consequences by becoming more reckless. The qualities which enable a person to gain power are not identical with those which enable him to exercise it wisely. The hallmark of a good leader is that he can make decisions that serve his group's best interests, even when the group opposes him. Some personal attributes that facilitate rise to leadership roles — love of adulation, personal ambition, a low suspicion threshold — may impair his judgment by leading him to reject valid criticisms or be overly swayed by the desire to be popular; they can be disastrous in times of crisis.

How can one solve the pervasive problem that "The qualities which enable a person to gain power are not identical with those which enable him to exercise it wisely"? Consider the possible effectiveness of the following long-term approaches, alone or in combination:

The psychological testing of potential leaders as a precondition to assuming leadership positions, suggested many years ago by Harold Lasswell. However, note the importance of deciding *what* was being tested for, and the question of the adequacy of present psychiatric knowledge to obtain reliable test results. Also, might cheating be possible? If so, would we have to be willing to accept "Peace Probe"-type intrusive testing, using such tools as drugs and hypnosis? Might there be potentially dangerous asymmetries in the attitudes of leaders of different nations if only one or a few nations, or other centers of power, employed such selective testing? Are there other problems?

The provision of sophisticated psychiatric counselling to leaders personally, and as an integral part of the apparatus of governmental decision making. Does such use of psychiatry require, however, that we know considerably more about the human mind than we do today?

The mandatory location of leaders and their families in exposed positions, where they would be likely to be among the first to die in case of large-scale lethal conflict.

The development of *non-violent techniques* for the processing of conflict that emphasize the leader's *personal* participation — with relish, energy, and enthusiasm — in bringing about the result. This might range from frequent use of the existing "hot line" (which might also be up-graded from a Telex link-up to a direct voice, or even voice-plus-video, link) to regularly scheduled summit meetings. It might

400

include conferences aimed at improving man's long-term prospects, as well as those dealing with immediate crisis situations — starting, perhaps, with subjects on which there was likely to be great mutual concern and little antagonism, such as the environmental problems.

Mandatory "sabbaticals" in which a large proportion of top decision-makers took six months every three or four years to join with counterparts from other nations at an international university or "think tank" in an extension of the conferences just described.

Uniform international standards by which top leaders who left power were given insignia of high status and substantial material benefits, *unless* they were found by an international tribunal to have been substantially responsible for an initiation or intensification of lethal conflict while they held office. For example, there might be a large United Nations-granted pension for such former leaders and United Nations-bestowed title of "peace laureates" (linked, of course, to "world citizenship"), entitling them to numerous continuing signs of respect and honor after leaving office (21-gun salutes, an honorific title such as "Laureate Nixon, Citizen of the World," a portrait and bust by the most distinguished of contemporary artists and sculptors for an "International Hall of Peace," and perhaps certain hereditary honors carrying down as far as grandchildren or even great-grand-children). Interestingly, the 1971 Nobel Peace Prize went to Chancellor Willy Brandt of West Germany, in recognition of his efforts to achieve détente with the Soviets.

Certain similar honors for opposition party leaders who were found to have worked strongly against the initiation or intensification of lethal conflict, or who actively cooperated with leaders in power who were seeking peaceful solutions.

Can you think of additional approaches to the "utopian" goal of producing leaders who will be *consistently more strongly motivated to avoid lethal conflict than to engage in it?*

Reducing general causes of lethal conflict.   There are other kinds of psychological problems, as well, which may contribute to various kinds of lethal conflict. How would you view the following long-term approaches, some already mentioned, to a "utopian" state of *zero lethal conflict:*

Encourage new kinds of family structure in which there are multiple "mothers" and "fathers," so that emotional indifference by just *one* pair of "parents" does not create frustrated and enraged children.

Psychological testing for violence-proneness in children, with therapeutic follow-up. This, perhaps, would require considerably less development in psychiatric knowledge than the kind of testing of potential leaders discussed previously.

Intensified training for psychological awareness in schools, and efforts to deal by preventative counselling and therapy with those facets of parental personality that may lead to violence-prone children.

Creation of multiple effective roles for women in the society, possibly linked to job-sharing and child-sharing.

Intensified research on the features of our existence that may give rise to strong proclivities to personal violence — for example, degrees of overcrowding, extent of exposure to violence through the visual media, particular child-rearing techniques — with consequent corrective action.

Introduction at all levels of programs — psychotherapy, encounter groups, school training — aimed at re-establishment of full human contact and the re-creation of a sense of human community.

The above discussion balances the technologically and environmentally oriented viewpoints by suggesting, in effect, that in a "utopian" society "every man a psychiatrist" will be at least as necessary as "every man a technician" or "every man an environmentalist." While we cannot fully conceive of the knowledge and sensitivities that will be needed, we are saying that the "technician-scientist-engineer," the "environmentalist-urban planner," and the "psychiatrist" are the closest contemporary analogs to the roles that would have to predominate in a world society that might hold out real hope for human survival over the long term — to 3000, and beyond.

The Peaceful Society

I should like to add one brief afterword on what I mean by "peace." In a sense, this is a strange place to offer such a discussion. But many mental perceptions are so habitual, it seemed to me essential to wait until the reader had finished the preceding chapter (and the book) before venturing a fuller definition of "peace."

If the reader looks back upon Quincy Wright's chart of "battles" (page 31), he will observe a period of time, around 1720–60, when

402

there was an apparent slackening of such large-scale lethal encounters. Arnold Toynbee (page 189) later suggests that this was the period when the West was between a series of religious wars and a coming series of nation-state wars. Was this a period of "peace"? My answer is that it was *not*. It was, at best, a period of "non-war" — a statistical freak, an aberration, a period of waiting, when events still wholly *non*understood and *un*controlled were leading mankind on to further horrors.

I think it is extremely useful to distinguish *three* states, not just *two*. They are the state of being at war (or, generally, engaged in some form of lethal conflict), the state of non-war, and the state of *peace*. The state of "non-war" is the mere absence of lethal conflict, a curiosity non-duplicable by deliberate human effort. It is passive. It is a period of waiting for the storm.

The state of peace, by contrast, is a state in which events are understood and actively dealt with. It is a state that recognizes that conflict will always be with us, and that it must be *processed* actively, enthusiastically, understandingly — and *non-violently*, if it is not to be processed violently. Look back over the suggestions of the past chapter. Do they reduce to the idea that peace will be with us if we are just cheerful and non-participating? Not at all. They require an application, an imagination, a drive, a genius, an up-and-doing that is fully as engaging of energy and enthusiasm, that indeed sets a program ten times as challenging and complex, as any war ever fought. *This* is the program of "peace" for mankind and its leaders, or at least it is a beginning glimmering of what such a program must be. We need not seek new ways of mobilizing human energies by the "conquest" of outer space (although I have no objection to it). The *conquest of peace* is a program of activity and engagement sufficient to mobilize every kind of human energy for generations to come.

FOOTNOTES, CHAPTER 8

[1] Jerome D. Frank, *Sanity & Survival* (Toronto: Random House of Canada, 1967), pp. 215–24.

[2] Herbert F. York, *Life*, Vol. 69, No. 24 (December, 1970), p. 41.

[3] Charles E. Osgood, *Perspectives in Foreign Policy* (Palo Alto: Pacific Books, Publishers, 1966), pp. 25–34.

[4] Robert Pickus and Robert Woito, *To End War* (World Without War Council, Berkeley, 1970), pp. 183–91.

[5] R. Buckminster Fuller, *Utopia or Oblivion: The Prospects for Humanity* (New York: Bantam Books, 1969), pp. 123–4, 151.

[6] R. Buckminster Fuller, *Operating Manual for Spaceship Earth* (Southern Illinois University Press, 1969), pp. 19–20.

[7] Frank, *Sanity & Survival*, pp. 166–69.

Acknowledgments

Associated Press Newsfeatures.

Berelson, Bernard and Gary Steiner: from *Human Behavior: An Inventory of Scientific Findings.* © 1964 by Harcourt Brace Jovanovich, Inc. Reprinted by permission of Harcourt Brace Jovanovich, Inc.

Bloomfield, Lincoln: from *Disarmament and Arms Control,* p. 17. Foreign Policy Association, New York, 1968. Reprinted by permission of Foreign Policy Association, Inc.

Buresh, Bernice: "Ghettos Rising High." Copyright Newsweek, Inc., September 7, 1970. Reprinted by permission of Newsweek, Inc.

Charlton, Linda: "Views Attributed to Miss Dohrn Indicate a Shift from Violence," December 25, 1970. © 1970 by The New York Times Company. Reprinted by permission of The New York Times Company.

Cockroft, Sir John: "The Perils of Nuclear Proliferation," in Nigel Calder, ed., *Unless Peace Comes: A Scientific Forecast of New Weapons.* Copyright © 1968 by Nigel Calder. All Rights Reserved. Reprinted by permission of The Viking Press, Inc., and International Literary Management.

Coser, Lewis: from "Violence and the Social Structure," *Science and Psychoanalysis,* VI, pp. 30–42. Grune and Stratton, Inc., New York, 1963. Reprinted by permission of Grune and Stratton, Inc.

Davidson, J. W.: from *New Cambridge Modern History,* Vol. XII. Reprinted by permission of Cambridge University Press.

Denenberg, Victor and M. H. Zarrow: "Rat Pax," *Psychology Today,* May 1970, Vol. 1, No. 12, p. 67. Reprinted by permission of the publisher.

Fleming, Karl: " 'We'll Blow Up the World,' " October 12, 1970. Copyright Newsweek, Inc., October 12, 1970. Reprinted by permission of Newsweek, Inc.

Freud, Sigmund: the material on p. 145 is from "Totem and Taboo," in Dr. A. A. Brill, trans. and ed., *The Basic Writings of Sigmund Freud.* Copyright 1938 by Random House, Inc., copyright renewed 1965 by Gioia Bernheim and Edmund R. Brill. Reprinted by permission.

Freud, Sigmund: "Why War?" in Ernest Jones, M.D., ed., *The Collected Papers of Sigmund Freud,* Vol. 5. Basic Books, Inc., Publishers, New York, 1959. Reprinted by permission of Basic Books, Inc., Publishers.

Frank, Jerome: from *Sanity and Survival,* pp. 215–224, 166–169. Copyright © 1967 by Jerome P. Frank. Reprinted by permission of Random House, Inc., and Barrie & Jenkins, Ltd.

Mead, Margaret: "Warfare Is Only an Invention — Not a Biological Necessity," *Asia*, XL, 1940, pp. 402–405. Reprinted by permission of the author.

Milgram, Stanley: from "Some Conditions of Obedience and Disobedience to Authority," *Human Relations*, Vol. 18, No. 1. Reprinted by permission of Plenum Publishing Corporation.

Montagu, Ashley: from *The Human Revolution*, pp. 95–96, 149–156. Copyright © 1965 by Ashley Montagu. Reprinted by permission of The World Publishing Company.

Morris, Desmond: from *The Human Zoo*. Copyright © 1969 by Desmond Morris. Reprinted by permission of McGraw-Hill Book Company and Jonathan Cape Ltd.

Noel-Baker, Philip: "We Have Been Here Before," in Nigel Calder, ed., *Unless Peace Comes: A Scientific Forecast of New Weapons*. Copyright © 1968 by Nigel Calder. All Rights Reserved. Reprinted by permission of The Viking Press, Inc., and International Literary Management.

Osgood, Charles: from *Perspective in Foreign Policy*, Second Edition, pp. 25–34. Pacific Book Publishers, Palo Alto, 1966. Reprinted by permission.

Pickus, Robert and Worto, Robert: from *To End War*, pp. 183–191. World Without War Council, Berkeley, 1970. Reprinted by permission.

Prosterman, Roy: "Analysis: A Dialog on Deterrence." This is the first publication of this selection. All Rights Reserved. Permission to reprint must be obtained from the publisher and author.

Prosterman, Roy: "Peace Probe." This is the first publication of this selection. All Rights Reserved. Permission to reprint must be obtained from the publisher and author.

Prosterman, Roy: "An Imaginary *Playboy* Interview with a 'Weatherman.'" This is the first publication of this selection. All Rights Reserved. Permission to reprint must be obtained from the publisher and the author.

Richardson, Lewis: from Quincy Wright and C. C. Lienan, ed., *Statistics of Deadly Quarrels*, pp. 4, 4–7, 128–129, 131–132, 153, 156, and 161. Boxwood Press, Pittsburgh, 1960. Reprinted by permission of Boxwood Press.

Rubin, Trudy: "Young Radicals Finding Violence a Dead End," *The Christian Science Monitor*, January 14, 1971, p. 1 (Eastern edition). Reprinted by permission of *The Christian Science Monitor*.

Russett, Bruce et al.: "Deaths from Domestic Group Violence," *World Handbook of Political and Social Indicators*. Yale University Press, New York, 1964. Reprinted by permission of Yale University Press.

Storr, Anthony: from *Human Aggression*, pp. 41–46, 91–99. Copyright © 1968 by Anthony Storr. Reprinted by permission of Atheneum Publishers and Penguin Books, Ltd.

Bibliographical Notes

Innumerable volumes in addition to those cited in the footnotes could be mentioned here, but the following represent the most useful and readily available works in the field. Most contain extensive bibliographies.

Ardrey, Robert. *The Territorial Imperative; A Personal Inquiry into the Animal Origins of Property and Nations*. London: Atheneum, 1966.

Berkowitz, Leonard. *Aggression; A Social Psychological Analysis*. New York: McGraw-Hill, 1962.

Boulding, Kenneth. *Conflict and Defense*. New York: Harper and Row, 1962.

Bradbury, William C. *Mass Behavior in Battle and Captivity*, edited by Samuel M. Meyers and Albert D. Biderman. Chicago: University of Chicago Press, 1968.

Buchan, Alastair. *War in Modern Society, An Introduction*. New York: Harper and Row, 1968.

Converse, Elizabeth. "The War of All Against All: A Review of The Journal of Conflict Resolution 1957–1968," *The Journal of Conflict Resolution*, 12 (December 1968).

Coser, Lewis. *The Functions of Social Conflict*. Glencoe, Illinois: Free Press, 1957.

Daniels, David N., Marshall F. Gilula, and Frank M. Ochberg (eds.). *Violence and the Struggle for Existence*. Boston: Little, Brown and Company, 1970.

Ehrlich, Paul, and Anne H. Ehrlich. *Population, Resources, Environment*. San Francisco: W. H. Freeman, 1970.

Fisher, Roger. *International Conflict for Beginners*. New York: Harper and Row, 1969.

Fried, Morton, Marvin Harris, and Robert Murphy (eds.). *War: The Anthropology of Armed Conflict and Aggression*. Garden City: Natural History Press, 1967.

Hendin, Herbert. *Black Suicide*. New York: Harper and Row, 1971.

Huntington, Samuel P. *Political Order In Changing Societies*. New Haven: Yale University Press, 1968.

Kahn, Herman. *On Thermonuclear War*. Princeton, N.J.: Princeton University Press, 1960.

Kissinger, Henry A. *Problems of National Strategy*. New York: Praeger, 1968.

Lapp, Ralph E. *Arms Beyond Doubt; The Tyranny of Weapons Technology*. New York: Cowles Book Co., 1970.

Lemberg Center for the Study of Violence. *Riot Data Review*. Waltham, Mass.: Brandeis University Press.

Noel-Baker, Philip. *The Arms Race*. New York: Oceana, 1958.

Pickus, Robert, and Robert Woito. *To End War: An Introduction*. New York: Harper and Row, 1970.

Purdom, Tom. *Reduction in Arms*. Berkeley: Berkeley Publishing Corporation, 1971.

Rathjens, George W. *The Future of the Strategic Arms Race*. Carnegie Endowment for International Peace, 1969.

Rummel, Rudolph J. "Dimensions of Conflict Behavior within and between Nations," *General Systems*. Yearbook of the Society for the Advancement of General Systems Theory. Ann Arbor, Michigan: 1963.

Singer, J. David (ed.). *Human Behavior and International Politics*. Chicago: Rand McNally, 1965.

Textor, Robert B. *A Cross-Cultural Summary*. New Haven: H.R.A.F. Press, 1967.

Index

[Note: Unless otherwise indicated, all index items should be understood as referring to the connection between the particular entry and aggressive behavior.]

416

417

Russett, Bruce M., 14–16
Russia, 203–4, 276–77, 279, 291–99, 301–4, 308, 332, 347–49, 361–65, 371, 384
Ruwala Bodawin, 146–47

SALT, 301–2, 363
Sane Society, 10
Sanity and Survival, 352–58, 397–99
Sansom, Robert, 174
Schlesinger, Arthur, 301
seabed, draft treaty, 362
Seale, Bobby, 265–66
seals, 53–55
Semang, 162
Serbia, 204
Sex and Temperament in Three Primitive Societies, 153–59
Shirer, William L., 207
shrew, 55
SLBM, 292
smallpox, 327
sociological views of aggression, 168–69
Some Conditions of Obedience and Disobedience to Authority, 85–101
Sorokin, P., 31, 35
South Africa, 331–32
Soviet Union (see Russia)
Spain, 42
sport of kings, 189
spy satellites, 302, 364–65
Stalin, Joseph, 398
Stati Belligerens, 305–6
Statistics of Deadly Quarrels, 34–41
status model of aggression, 124
Steiner, Gary A., 75–77
Stern, Fritz, 231
Storr, Anthony, 68–74; 122–23
stress model of aggression, 123
strontium-90, 284
student radicalism (see domestic group violence)
Students for a Democratic Society, 220–34
A Study of History, 188–90

422